PRECARIOUS VICTORY

PRECARIOUS VICTORY

The 2002 German Federal Election
and Its Aftermath

Edited by

David P. Conradt
Gerald R. Kleinfeld
Christian Søe

Berghahn Books
NEW YORK • OXFORD

Published in 2005 by
Berghahn Books

www.berghahnbooks.com

© 2005 David P. Conradt, Gerald R. Kleinfeld, Christian Søe

All rights reserved.
Except for the quotation of short passages
for the purposes of criticism and review, no part of this book
may be reproduced in any form or by any means, electronic or
mechanical, including photocopying, recording, or any information
storage and retrieval system now known or to be invented,
without written permission of the publisher.

Library of Congress Cataloging-in-Publication Data

Precarious victory : the 2002 German federal election and its aftermath / editors, David P. Conradt, Gerald R. Kleinfeld, Christian Søe.
  p. cm.
Includes bibliographical references and index.
  ISBN 1-57181-864-2 (alk. paper) — ISBN 1-57181-865-0 (pbk. : alk. paper)
  1. Elections—Germany. 2. Germany. Bundestag—Elections, 2002. 3. Germany—Politics and government—1990– 4. Germany—Foreign relations—1990–. I. Conradt, David P. II. Kleinfeld, Gerald R., 1936– III. Søe, Christian.

JN3971.A95P74 2004
324.943'0882—dc22

2004047673

British Library Cataloguing in Publication Data

A catalogue record for this book is available from
the British Library.

Printed in the United States on acid-free paper

Contents

List of Illustrations	vii
Acknowledgments	ix
Introduction *by David P. Conradt, Gerald R. Kleinfeld, and Christian Søe*	x
1. The 2002 Campaign and Election: An Overview *David P. Conradt*	1
2. Who Won and Why *Dieter Roth*	25
3. Gerhard Schröder and the Unlikely Victory of the German Social Democrats *William E. Paterson and James Sloam*	37
4. Hold the Champagne: Edmund Stoiber's CDU/CSU and Bundestagswahl 2002 *Clay Clemens*	58
5. Saving Schröder: The Greens in 2002 *E. Gene Frankland*	83
6. A False Dawn for Germany's Liberals: The Rise and Fall of *Project 18* *Christian Søe*	108
7. The PDS Implodes *Gerald R. Kleinfeld*	135
8. Ladies' Choice: Returning the Schröder Government to Power in 2002 *Mary N. Hampton*	153
9. Dogs That Did Not Bark: German Exceptionalism Reconsidered *David F. Patton*	170

10. The Poisoned Relationship: Germany, the United States, and the Election of 2002   185
   Stephen F. Szabo

11. German Policymaking and the Reform Gridlock   205
    Helga A. Welsh

12. Can Gerhard Schröder Do It? Prospects for Fundamental Reform of the German Economy and a Return to High Employment   220
    Irwin Collier

Appendix   256

Notes on Contributors   262

Index   265

Illustrations

Tables

1.1 State (Landtag) Elections: 1999 to 2002	7
1.2 The Schröder Economic Record	15
1.3 Party Support by Occupation in West Germany, 2002	19
1.4 Party Support by Occupation in East Germany, 2002	19
1.5 Party Support by Religion, 2002	20
2.1 Chancellor Candidates: Personality	34
2.2 Chancellor Candidates: Policy Competence	34
7.1 PDS Support in the Eastern States, 1998 and 2002	149
12.1 International Comparison of Shares of Marginal Value-Added by Labor for Taxes, Social Insurance Contributions, and Increase in Worker Income	230
12.2 Pension Reform Scenarios à la Rürup	237
A.1 Bundestag Elections since 1949	256
A.2 Distribution of Bundestag Seats since 1949	258
A.3 East-West Differences in the Bundestag Elections, 1990–2002	260
A.4 The Bundestag Election of 2002 in the Western and Eastern Länder	261

Figures

1.1 SPD vs. CDU/CSU, 1999–2002	6
1.2 Expected Winner: Government or Opposition?	16
1.3 Preferred Chancellor: Schröder vs. Stoiber	17
1.4 Ballot Splitting, 2002	22
2.1 Best for New Jobs? Schröder vs. Stoiber, 2002	28
2.2 Public Opinion and the Iraq War	33
8.1 Female Vote for CDU/CSU-FDP vs. SPD-Green, 1990–2002	155
8.2 Female Party Vote by Age, 2002	155
12.1 Unemployment in Germany	222
12.2 Real GDP Growth in the EU-15, Japan, and United States	223

12.3	Junior and Senior Citizen Ratios	224
12.4	Social Insurance Rates in Germany	225
12.5	Hourly Labor Costs in Manufacturing	228
12.6	Aggregate Hours in Manufacturing	228
12.7	Beveridge Curve in Germany	232
12.8	Fiscal and Monetary Policy Changes, 2000–2002	245
12.9	Very Short-Term Interest Rates: The Fed vs. the ECB	247
12.10	Fiscal Indicators of the Growth and Stability Pact	249

Acknowledgments

Like its predecessors, this new volume in our German election studies has benefited from the help of many people. The individual chapter authors have enriched the study by bringing their professional expertise to the project. Reinhard Schwarzer of the Federal Press and Information Office arranged for several of us to participate in a study tour of the 2002 election. We are grateful to him and to Goethe-Institut Inter Nationes, who organized that research opportunity. The support of the German consulates in Atlanta and Los Angeles was also important. We are grateful to the many German colleagues who shared their political insights with us both before and after the election. The German Information Office in New York has shown interest in and support of our undertaking. As always, Dieter Roth was generous in making available important data and analysis, including the Blitzumfrage and exit polls of the Forschungsgruppe Wahlen in Mannheim. Wolfgang Gibowski again helped us gain access to important discussion partners. Wolfgang-Uwe Friedrich provided several of us with an opportunity to stay abreast of German political developments through the annual summer meetings of the Deutsch-Amerikanischer Arbeitskreis. The preparation of the manuscripts was facilitated by the fine work of Bernice Bailes and Scott Adams. As publisher, Marion Berghahn has been strongly supportive of this study from beginning to end.

Introduction

On 22 September 2002, German voters went to the polls for the fifteenth time in the history of the Federal Republic and the fourth time since the 1990 unification of the once-divided country. In 1998 these voters for the first time removed an entire coalition government and for most of the 2002 campaign it appeared that the Schröder government would make history again as the first government ever voted out of office after only one term. But a powerful last-minute swing to the governing parties, due in large part to a series of unique unpredictable events, including the most serious crisis in German-American relations since the founding of the Federal Republic, gave the ruling SPD-Green coalition a narrow victory. In this book we examine this 2002 election and its aftermath.

As we emphasized in our two previous volumes—*Germany's New Politics* and *Power Shift in Germany*—which analyzed the federal elections of 1994 and 1998, the electoral landscape of unified Germany bears little resemblance to the stable and predictable patterns of the "old" Federal Republic. The classic cleavages of class and religion continue their slow but steady decline, and generational and regional influences become more significant. Issues, candidates, the media, and unpredictable events produce short-term oscillations from election to election, which can be decisive. In 2002, for example, a foreign policy issue, the Iraq war, a natural disaster, the floods in the eastern region, and a media event, the first ever one-on-one television debates between the chancellor and his challenger, impacted enough undecided voters to give the incumbent coalition a razor thin victory.

This electoral volatility is largely a result of the steady decline in voter identification with the political parties. The undecided, floating segment of voters continues to grow in Germany as elsewhere in Western Europe. In western German states the proportion of the electorate with either a weak attachment to the political parties or none at all has grown from 40 percent in 1972 to 67 percent at the time of the 2002 election. In the eastern states, where data, of course are available only since 1991, the corresponding level is stable at about 70 percent. Unification added millions of new voters, who lacked any history of identification with the parties and hence

---

Notes for this section are located on page xv.

accelerated electoral volatility. Thus, by 2002 at least two out of every three voters had either a weak attachment to one of the political parties, or none at all.[1] This is a critical contextual factor which helps explain how discreet, unpredictable campaign events can be decisive.

While much of this volume follows the format of our previous books, we have added a chapter on the crisis in German-American relations that developed during the campaign and two new chapters, which examine the major policy problems that were not really addressed in 2002. Indeed, the outcome in 2002 reflected the deadlock and immobilism that has characterized German politics for most of the post-unification period.

This book, like the two previous volumes, examines the political developments that led up to the respective Bundestag election. Taken together they provide a record of German politics since unification. We begin with a brief overview of the campaign and election. Then Dieter Roth, Germany's leading pollster and election analyst, draws on a wealth of public opinion and voting data to develop the thesis that in 2002 the personal component of the vote provided the critical margin of victory for the government. The 2002 election continues a two-decade trend during which the personal factor has slowly increased. Although almost two-thirds of German voters still consider the parties more important than the chancellor candidates, about 30 percent rank personality above party. The personality factor in 2002 provided the government with its very small margin of victory. "Enough voters," he finds, "supported the SPD and the Greens because of these two personalities [Schröder and Fischer] to overcome the voters negative opinions of their policies and parties." Roth dismisses the "accident" theory of the election, the ideal that unforeseen events such as the flood and the Iraq war, distorted the voters' will. In its response to these events the "CDU/CSU was unable to fulfill the genuine need of voters to be reassured when they were confronted with problems that were other than economic."

The Parties

While voters' attachment to the parties continues to weaken, they remain the major actors at any election. Even in the personalized, quasi-presidential atmosphere of the 2002 campaign, over 60 percent of the voters stated that the parties are more important than the chancellor candidates.[2] In 2002 the two major parties finished in a dead heat and neither was satisfied with the results. In the case of the Social Democrats, the analysis of William Paterson and James Sloam contends that the SPD's victory in 2002 was "built on sand." The popularity of Chancellor Schröder and the impact of unique events were the critical factors in the narrow victory, not any substantial policy success or convincing vision for Germany's future. Despite their decisive victory in 1998, the Social Democrats were deeply divided between the modernizing chancellor and his traditional, but powerful finance minister. It was only after his departure and the CDU/CSU finance scandal that the SPD was able to stabilize itself and put together a string of modest policy successes. The sharp economic downturn in 2001 and 2002 together with the recovery of the Christian Democrats (CDU/CSU) put the Social Democrats once again on the defensive. Only the reliance on Schröder kept the party in power. Paterson and Sloam conclude that this approach will "not work the next time around."

Viewed from the perspective of the 1999–2000 finance scandals, the Christian Democrats (CDU/CSU) dead heat with the Social Democrats was a remarkable achievement. The scandal, which brought down the Union's apparent 2002 chancellor candidate, Wolfgang Schäuble, was in the view of some analysts, life-threatening for the party. But as Clay Clemens demonstrates the Union, not only recovered quickly, but also appeared headed for a stunning victory, which would have brought the first Bavarian in the history of the Federal Republic into the chancellery. But Stoiber failed to counter Schröder's "personalized, presidential style campaign." Instead the Union's efforts were "bland and one-dimensional" (the economy). The voters were offered "Stoiber light," that is, without the sharp, confrontational tone that characterized his numerous victorious campaigns in Bavaria. Nonetheless, just months after the 2002 poll, the Union, once again, held a commanding lead over Schröder's Social Democrats. The party's search for a winning formula continues.

Gene Frankland's study of the Greens, based in large part on in-depth interviews with the party's voters, members and leadership, demonstrates clearly that the party, once the erratic enfant terrible of German politics, has become an established component of the party system. In 2002 the Greens saved the Schröder government with an emphasis on leadership and policy innovation. Their "Greatest Hits" included issues such as consumer protection, the reform of food and drug laws as well as the classic Green issues of the environment and minority rights.

Christian Søe's analysis of the Free Democrats (FDP) argues that they seriously misread the political situation of 2002 as one that favored their advance to major party status. With the ambitious "Strategy 18," the FDP emphasized its political autonomy and even named its own chancellor candidate. Weakened by a leadership rift and tainted by charges of populist appeals to voters, the FDP improved its standing only marginally. It remains a small and vulnerable opposition party, struggling for survival and influence and hampered by a paucity of organizational resources.

The clear loser of the election was the Party of Democratic Socialism (PDS), which failed to secure the 5 percent minimum needed to participate in the proportional distribution of seats. The PDS was also unable to win three district victories, which would have waived the 5 percent rule. It ended up with only two seats. In his examination of the former communists, Gerald Kleinfeld challenges the conventional wisdom that the PDS defeat was the result of the loss of its lone media star, Gregor Gysi, the Iraq war issue or the floods in the East. He argues that the decline of the party was well underway long before the election and was the result of PDS participation in state governments in Berlin and Mecklenburg-West Pomerania as well as the party's aging and declining membership. By assuming political power, the PDS was now held responsible for at least some of the myriad economic problems in the eastern states. It was no longer a "pure" protest party.

In 2002, as in 1998, Germany's female voters played a major role in the campaign strategies of the parties and the final outcome. Mary Hampton's analysis emphasizes that the opposition Christian Democrats knew that they had to improve their performance among women if they were to oust the government. Stoiber had a particularly difficult time among the "career-aged" female vote, that is, those between ages 25 and 49. His selection of a young single mother from the East to his shadow cabinet or "competence team" was an attempt to reach out to a voter segment that had been the property of the SPD and especially the Greens. Stoiber's wife was also a feature of his campaign, another first for the CDU/CSU. The Union did increase its support among women by about 1.5 percent, but this was far below its 5.5 percent gain among men. Female voters remained essentially loyal to the SPD-Green coalition. Indeed, Hampton shows, female voters responded more strongly to the chancellor's anti-war message than males. Viewed from the perspective of gender alone, women in 2002 saved the coalition. Among males the SPD in 2002 lost 11 percent of its 1998 support; the drop in female support, however, was only one percent. The Greens' concentration on the "empowerment of the modern woman" paid large dividends for the party as it received almost ten percent of the female vote.

In his contribution David Patton adds a comparative dimension to our analysis of the 2002 election. The survival of the SPD-Green government was the exception in European politics. By mid-2000, 10 of the 15 European Union member states were governed by conservatives. Since 1998 center-left governments, similar to the SPD-Green alignment in Germany, had been removed from office in France, Italy, the Netherlands, Denmark, and Portugal. In his attempt to solve the puzzle, Patton focuses on the absence of any significant populist, protest party on either the right or left in German politics. In spite of Germany's large foreign population, sluggish economy and high unemployment, right-wing populism was not a factor in the election. Patton emphasizes the leadership factor as critical difference in Germany. No German protest party has ever had an attractive leader. The major parties, however, both had leaders who effectively limited any flanking maneuvers on their right (Stoiber) or left (Schröder). Stoiber's well-known hard line on immigration and Schröder's anti-American position deprived protest movements of their favorite issues.

Policy Issues

The final section of the book presents three chapters that explore the major policy issues, which were either part of the campaign or have dominated its aftermath. In 2002 foreign policy and specifically the U.S.-German conflict over the Iraq war played an important role in the campaign. This was the first time since 1972, when the Brandt-Scheel government tried to turn the election into a plebiscite on *Ostpolitik*, that foreign policy was so prominent in a campaign. The sharp rift in German-American relations, the most severe in the postwar period, could be one of the most important legacies of this election.

Steven Szabo presents an in-depth analysis of the "Poisoned Relationship" between Berlin and Washington and its impact on the campaign and election. Drawing on his extensive knowledge of both the American and German foreign policy process, Szabo's work demonstrates that the 2002 dispute reflected a divergence on social and political values, which will also influence future German-American relations. Of particular importance is his analysis of the cultural and stylistic differences between the White House and the chancellory in 2002 and the personality contrasts between President Bush and Chancellor Schröder.

At this election, reform gridlock (*Reformstau*) was the 600-pound gorilla in the corner. During the campaign the critical domestic policy problems facing the Federal Republic were not really addressed by any of the political parties or the major candidates. The calcified character of the Federal Republic's institutions, the myriad assortment of veto players at all levels of government and the consensus at all cost approach to policy have produced an unprecedented reform gridlock. The most obvious manifestation of the blockage is Germany's miniscule economic growth, chronic unemployment and soaring public debt. Neither the government nor the opposition offered the electorate any clear alternatives to dealing with these problems.

Following the election, however, the *Reformstau* could not be avoided. In their contributions, Helga Welsh and Irwin Collier focus on the policy problems that did not go away after 22 September 2002. Welsh introduces us to the broad contours of the problem and puts it into a comparative context. Other countries, including several in Europe such as the Netherlands, Sweden and Denmark, have faced similar problems and have been able to make meaningful changes in their social, economic and fiscal polices. Why not Germany? In her analysis, she focuses on four major factors: (1) a large number of veto players due in large part to the decentralized and fragmented character of political institutions; (2) staggered elections at the national, state and local level that foster permanent electoral campaigns making it difficult for the national government to develop long-term reform projects with high start-up costs; (3) a judicialization of politics that inflates the role of the Federal Constitutional Court; and (4) a strong legacy of corporatism that has created a dense network of path dependent processes with corresponding disincentives for change.

Irwin Collier's study of the comprehensive reform package proposed by the Schröder government after the 2002 election provides an ideal follow-up to Welsh's presentation of the general *Reformstau* issue. Collier's work is the most comprehensive and up-to-date study of the *Agenda 2010*—the government's term for major changes in labor market, social, economic and fiscal policies—currently available in the scholarly literature. Collier begins by dissecting the three core problems facing the economy: high unemployment, sluggish growth, and tax and social insurance programs that stifle job creation and growth. On all three counts, he argues, "Schröder's Germany, much like Kohl's Germany before it, is in very serious trouble … and there is a growing sense that the day of reckoning is nigh." The core of his contribution is a rigorous analysis of the proposals in the Agenda. Overall, from his perspective as an economist, he considers many of the reform measures as a significant step in the right direction. But *Agenda 2010*, he cautions, may be "too slow, too little, too late."

— David P. Conradt, Gerald R. Kleinfeld, and Christian Søe

Notes

1. Forschungsgruppe Wahlen data cited in Russell J. Dalton, "Voter Choice and Electoral Politics," in *Developments in German Politics 3*, ed. Stephen Padgett et al. (New York and London: Palgrave MacMillan, 2003), p. 72.
2. Forschungsgruppe Wahlen, Survey No. 1339, August 2002.

Chapter 1

THE 2002 CAMPAIGN AND ELECTION
An Overview

David P. Conradt

In 1998 German voters elected the first Social Democratic-Green government in the Federal Republic's history. It was a decisive victory with both the Christian Democrats and the Free Democrats, the ultimate survivor party, forced into opposition. The clarity of the SPD-Green victory was not matched, however, by its policy plans. Indeed, voters in 1998 wanted a new chancellor and not necessarily any major policy changes. The SPD and to a lesser extent the Greens played to this dominant voter sentiment. Schröder's "new center" was deliberately vague and gave the voters no hint about the magnitude of the country's fundamental problems.

Four years later this government presented itself to the electorate for re-election with a mixed record of achievement. It had delivered on issues such as liberalizing citizenship laws, adopting a timetable for the removal of nuclear power from the energy system, lowering taxes for individuals and businesses and adjusting the pension system to the demographic realities of lower birth rates and longer life expectancy. But it had failed badly to achieve its own goal of reducing unemployment. Indeed all-major economic indicators were negative by the time the campaign began. The government appeared headed to a certain defeat. The post-unification German electorate, however, had become far less predictable than in the stable and prosperous past.

The forecasts of increasing electoral volatility, which have been a constant in electoral research for about the last 20 years, are apparently being validated.[1] The demographic moorings of class and religion continue to weaken. Ticket splitting, another indicator of volatility, has increased from about 5 percent in the early 1960s to 22 percent in 2002.[2] The millions of new voters in the East have added further volatility. Issues, personalities, media image, and campaign event have become more important predictors of

---

Notes for this chapter begin on page 23.

voter choice. These are by no means uniquely a German phenomena. They can be found in all established democracies.[3]

This chapter will first examine the major political developments since the 1998 election. The role of state elections in national politics, including their influence on party strategy and candidate selection, are also essential for understanding the context of the national electoral struggle. Thirdly, the campaign strategy and tactics of the parties and candidates will be discussed. We conclude with a brief analysis of the results.

Electoral Mechanics

The German electoral struggle takes place within the context of one of the world's most complex voting systems.[4] As in past elections, it also played role in the strategy of the parties and candidates in 2002. It is usually termed a "mixed" system, since the voter elects a district candidate by a plurality with his or her first ballot, and votes for a party with the second ballot. Half of the parliamentary seats are determined by the district vote (first ballot), and the remaining half by the party vote (second ballot). However, the second ballot percentage usually determines a party's final parliamentary representation since the first ballot district victories are subtracted from the total due a party based on the second ballot percentage.

In essence, then, this is a proportional system with three important exceptions to "pure" proportionality: (1) to participate in the proportional payout a party usually must secure at least 5 percent of the second ballot vote; (2) this 5 percent requirement, however, is waived if the party secures at least three district seats (i.e., direct election of three candidates by a plurality in at least three of the 299 districts); if it succeeds, it can then also participate in the proportional distribution regardless of its second ballot percentage; (3) if a party wins more district seats than it is entitled to under its second ballot percentage, it is allowed to keep these excess seats (*Überhangmandate*) and the parliament is simply enlarged by the number of these excess seats.[5]

For the 2002 election the number of districts was reduced from 328 to 299 thus lowering the total size of the Bundestag from 656 to 598 (before *Überhangmandate*). A reduction of this magnitude coupled with the requirement to adjust the districts for population changes resulted in a total redistricting. Since there has been a net out-migration from East to West since unification, the eastern regions lost proportionately more districts than the West. The eleven western states lost 15 seats and the five eastern Länder have 13 fewer districts; Berlin lost the final seat. The proportion of eastern seats declined from 20 percent to 18 percent. This probably hurt the chances of the PDS in East Berlin. In two of the four direct seats it won in 1998 (Berlin Mitte and Friedrichshain/Kreuzberg/Prenzlauer Berg-Ost) West Berlin voters were added in 2002.

The redistricting for this election probably played a role in the sharp reduction of excess mandates from 16 in 1998 to only five in 2002 (four for the SPD and one for the CDU). Most of the excess mandates in 1994 and 1998 came from the eastern regions where a combination of small districts and three-cornered races (due to the PDS) created conditions ideal for a large party to win where it ordinarily would not.[6]

The Inter-election Period: 1998–2002

For both government and opposition the inter-election period was characterized by a series of roller coaster-like ups and downs. The sweeping SPD-Green victory in September 1998 was followed by one of the worst starts of any government in the Federal Republic's history. Only the second Erhard government (1965–1966) got off to a comparably inauspicious beginning. The innovative campaign strategy of the SPD's Kampa team in 1998 was not matched by a corresponding plan for governing. Serious personal and ideological differences within and between the governing parties, which had been suppressed in the common task of defeating the Kohl government, surfaced soon after the new government began its work.

The major, but by no means only intra-governmental conflict was between the newly minted Chancellor Schröder and Oskar Lafontaine, who as SPD leader had done more than anyone except Schröder himself to defeat the Kohl coalition. Lafontaine could mobilize the SPD's blue-collar core and many Greens, the very groups who were suspicious of Schröder and his "new center" modernizing. Schröder, in turn, could appeal to the center of the electorate that had given Kohl and the Christian Democrats four straight victories.

But soon after the election, serious differences between the SPD's leadership duo became evident. Lafontaine wanted Germany to lean against the prevailing neo-liberal winds. Globalization with its unrestricted capital and labor markets was "casino capitalism" that would ultimately destroy the German model of a structured, i.e., heavily regulated, social market economy. Ignoring the negative if not incredulous responses from Washington and London, Lafontaine pressed on. His finance ministry assumed control over international economic policy from the Economic Ministry, whose designated head left the government even before he could be sworn in.

Lafontaine's plan to cut personal income and corporate taxes also made little legislative headway. Business interests argued that the plan did not go far enough to reduce their costs, especially the *Nebenkosten,* the elaborate pension and health care contributions which amount to about 50 percent of core wage costs. A new ecology (*Ökosteuer*) tax, a longtime Green proposal, would compensate the treasury for the revenue lost by the tax cuts. Another key proposal of Lafontaine and the Greens was the closing and dismantling of all nuclear power plants within the first legislative period with little compensation to the energy industry.

These problems can be traced back to the 1998 campaign. Chancellor candidate Schröder gave little content to his "new center" electoral appeal. He and the Social Democrats encouraged the belief among voters that they could have "painless reform." The Red-Green government did not have a mandate from the voters to make the hard decisions necessary to reduce unemployment and make the economy more competitive. Of course, they did not ask the voters for such a mandate.

When the government finally introduced its new citizenship law, one of the few points of consensus in the coalition, it gave the CDU/CSU its first major post-election opportunity. In February 1999 in Hesse the CDU appeared headed toward a defeat. The SPD-Green government of Minister-President Eichel was relatively popular and held a comfortable lead. The Schröder government's draft citizenship law, which allowed for dual citizenship, mobilized the CDU into a populist petition movement. Suddenly the campaign turned around. While the SPD slightly increased its vote, the Greens slipped badly, the CDU made big gains and the FDP with 5.1 percent, to its great surprise, just managed to stay in the Wiesbaden Landtag. The Eichel government was defeated and more importantly the national coalition had lost its Bundesrat majority. The citizenship law in its original form was dead.

Shortly after the Hesse election the simmering conflict between Schröder and Lafontaine came to a head when, in March of that year, Lafontaine—following an emotional cabinet meeting at which Schröder stressed that the government must stop antagonizing business interests—resigned as finance minister and party chairman.

At this March 10 cabinet meeting Schröder called on the government to reflect on the reasons for their election victory: "We appealed for the support of the new center and we actually received it. But some members of this cabinet now believe that we can govern this country against *die Wirtschaft* (business). This is not true." He then went on to mention the plans of the Family Ministry to introduce paid "sabbaticals" (*Erziehungsurlaub*). This, he said, is a sore point for business and "totally unacceptable." Later in the meeting Schröder reacted to remarks by the environment minister about new summer smog speed limits by observing that SPD-Green transportation policies always seem to be controversial. The chancellor turned next to the confusion surrounding the tax reform package and its impact on energy prices and business costs. "It can't go on like this," he reportedly said. His target for this remark was clearly Finance Minister Lafontaine, whose ministry supplied the data for the proposed legislation.[7]

Following Lafontaine's departure the government's policy and electoral problems continued. A revised citizenship law was past in May with the help of the FDP contingent in the Rhineland-Palatinate government, but little else was accomplished. The SPD suffered heavy losses at a series of state elections beginning in September and the Greens continued their losing streak in state elections. Schröder's Red-Green coalition was sinking fast. His last stand would be in June 2000 at the election in North Rhine-Westphalia, by far the country's largest state and a stronghold of the Social Democrats. A loss in this state would make Schröder's position untenable. If the Christian Democrats held a two-thirds majority in the Federal Council, it would have been able to block Schröder's entire program. The governing coalition would have resigned followed by either new elections or a Grand Coalition with the CDU.

Kohlgate: A Reprieve for the Government?

With its back to the wall, the government received an unexpected break in the form of the CDU finance scandal, which broke into the headlines in November 1999. Kohl at a tense press conference in Berlin admitted that he indeed had kept secret bank accounts outside of regular party channels to reward favored CDU regional organizations and leaders. A few weeks later, Angela Merkel, the then CDU general secretary, called for Kohl to reveal the names of the donors to his secret fund. Merkel attempted to limit the damage.

In mid-January 2000, following further revelations of illegal donations and secret slush funds, Kohl resigned as honorary chairman of the Christian Democrats. He refused to make the names of the anonymous donors to his secret funds public. Several weeks later prosecutors revealed that during Kohl's administration more than $70 million was illegally paid in kickbacks to middlemen on the sale of tanks, an oil refinery, and a chain of East German service stations. In February the CDU was hit with the biggest fine ($21 million) for breaking campaign finance laws in the nation's history. Some political observers feared that the scandal could have threatened the party's survival and created a vacuum that would have been filled by an extreme right-wing movement.

The scandal then spread to Kohl's successor as CDU leader, Wolfgang Schäuble, who admitted that he had also received campaign contributions from the same German-Canadian arms dealer under investigation in the Kohl case. Schäuble resigned under heavy pressure from CDU members of parliament. Significantly, the Bavarians managed to avoid the scandal and later in the year Stoiber began to emerge as a possible chancellor candidate.

As figure 1.1 shows, as the scandal unfolded, support for the CDU/CSU rapidly declined. More importantly, the SPD stopped the string of losses at state elections (table 1.1). At one point Schröder was even not planning to campaign in Schleswig-Holstein, where the government of Heidi Simonis was expected to lose to a resurgent CDU under the leadership of Volker Rühe. Kohlgate saved Simonis and dashed any chancellor candidate hopes Rühe might have entertained.

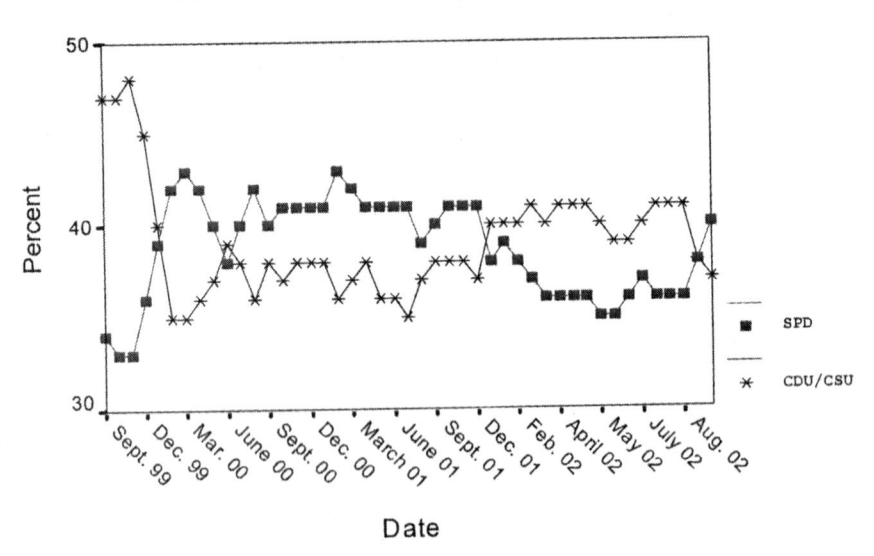

FIGURE 1.1 SPD vs. CDU/CSU, 1999–2002 (vote intention)

The lift for the government provided by the finance scandal was followed in 2000 by a strong economic performance, which was projected to continue into 2001. In spite of high energy prices, the economy in 2000 grew at a real rate of about 3 percent, the best performance since the 1990 unification. The weak Euro and strong demand from the recovering Asian markets boosted exports by 13 percent, as compared to only a 5 percent gain in 1999. Unemployment dropped to 9.1 percent while inflation climbed to 2 percent largely due to oil prices.

In July 2000 the government was able to make the first installment on its promise to make Germany more competitive in the global economic arena. A comprehensive package of tax cuts for individuals and business coupled with major reductions in social programs, above all pensions, cleared the parliament. The high point of the year for the Schröder government came in July when he skillfully guided a major tax reform package through both houses of parliament. Under the new law, the most significant since World War II, the top corporate tax rate was scheduled to drop from about 52 percent to 39 percent by 2005. Individual rates were also to be cut from a current high of 51 percent to 42 percent, while the bottom rate was scheduled to drop from 24 percent to 15 percent.[8]

The CDU/CSU Comeback

The selection of Angela Merkel as party leader was an attempt to break cleanly from the Kohl Era and to stop the hemorrhaging from the finance scandal. This was only partially successful. The Union declined at both

TABLE 1.1 State (Landtag) Elections: 1999 to 2002—Party Percentage of the Popular Vote
(percentage gains or losses since last Landtag election in parentheses)

Land	Percent Voting	CDU[1]/CSU	SPD	FDP	Greens All.'90/Gr.	PDS	REP[2]	Other Parties
Hesse, 7/2/1999	66.4 (+0.1)	43.4 (+4.2)	39.4 (+1.4)	5.1 (-2.3)	7.2 (-4.0)	—	2.7 (+0.7)	2.2 (-0.1)
Bremen, 6/6/1999	60.2 (-8.5)	37.1 (+4.5)	42.6 (+9.2)	2.5 (-0.9)	9.0 (-4.1)	2.9 (+0.5)	—	6.0[3] (-8.9)
Brandenburg, 5/9/1999	54.4 (-1.9)	26.5 (+7.8)	39.3 (-14.8)	1.9 (-0.3)	1.9 (-1.0)	23.3 (+4.6)	—	7.0[4] (+4.8)
The Saar, 5/9/1999	68.7 (-14.8)	45.5 (+6.9)	44.4 (-5.0)	2.6 (+0.5)	3.2 (-2.3)	0.8 +0.8	1.3 (-0.1)	2.2 (-0.9)
Thuringia, 12/9/1999	59.9 (-14.9)	51.0 (+8.4)	18.5 (-11.1)	1.1 (-2.1)	1.9 (-2.6)	21.3 (+4.8)	0.8 (-0.5)	5.3[5] (+3.0)
Saxony, 19/9/1999	61.1 (+2.7)	56.9 (-1.2)	10.7 (-5.9)	1.1 (-0.6)	2.6 (-1.5)	22.2 (+5.7)	1.5 (+0.2)	5.0[6] (+3.4)
Berlin, 10/10/1999	65.5 (-3.1)	40.8 (+3.4)	22.4 (-1.2)	2.2 (-0.3)	9.9 (-3.3)	17.7 (+3.1)	2.7 0.0	4.3 (-1.7)
Schleswig-Holstein, 27/2/2000	69.5 (-2.3)	35.2 (-2.0)	43.1 (+3.3)	7.6 (+1.9)	6.2 (-1.9)	1.4 (-0.5)	— (-3.6)	6.5[7] (+0.3)
North Rhine-Westphalia, 14/5/2000	56.7 (-7.3)	37.0 (-0.7)	42.8 (-3.2)	9.8 (+5.8)	7.1 (-2.9)	1.1 (+1.1)	1.1 (+0.3)	1.1 (-0.4)
Baden-Württemberg, 25/3/2001	62.6 (-5.0)	44.8 (+3.5)	33.3 (+8.2)	8.1 (-1.5)	7.7 (-4.4)	—	4.4 (-4.7)	1.7 (-1.1)

(Continued on next page)

TABLE 1.1 State (Landtag) Elections: 1999 to 2002—Party Percentage of the Popular Vote
(percentage gains or losses since last Landtag election in parentheses)

Land	Percent Voting	CDU[1]/ CSU	SPD	FDP	Greens All.'90/Gr.	PDS	REP[2]	Other Parties
Rhineland-Palatinate, 25/3/2001	62.1 (-8.7)	35.3 (-3.4)	44.7 (+4.9)	7.8 (-1.1)	5.2 (-1.7)	— —	2.4 (-1.1)	4.5 (+2.3)
Hamburg, 23/9/2001	71.0 (+2.3)	26.2 (-4.5)	36.5 (+0.3)	5.1 (+1.6)	8.6 (-5.4)	0.4 (-0.3)	0.1 (-1.7)	23.2³ (+10.0)
Berlin, 21/10/2001	68.1 (+2.6)	23.8 (-17.0)	29.7 (+7.3)	9.9 (+7.7)	9.1 (-0.8)	22.6 (+4.9)	1.4 —	3.6 (-0.7)
Saxony-Anhalt, 21/4/2002	56.5 (-15.0)	37.3 (+15.3)	20.0 (-15.9)	13.3 (+9.1)	2.0 (-1.2)	20.4 (+0.8)	— —	7.1 (-8.1)
Mecklenburg-West Pomerania, 22/9/2002	70.6 (-8.8)	31.4 (+1.2)	40.6 (+6.3)	4.7 (+3.1)	2.6 (-0.1)	16.4 (-8.0)	0.3 (-0.2)	4.0 (-2.3)

[1] CSU in Bavaria
[2] The far right-wing Republikaner Party
[3] Includes 3 percent for the far right-wing DVU (German People's Union), and 2.4 percent for the voter initiative AFB (Work for Bremen and Bremerhaven), which in 1995 had won 10.7 percent.
[4] Includes 5.3 percent for the DVU.
[5] Includes 3.1 percent for the DVU.
[6] Includes 6.3 percent for the DVU, and 1.9 percent for the SSW (Danish minority party).
[7] Includes 2.8 percent for the DVU, and 5.6 percent for the populist Statt-Partei (Instead Party).
[8] Includes 19.4 percent for the populist Schill Party.

state elections in 2000, but came back in March 2001 with a solid win in Baden-Württemberg. In the remaining 2001 state elections, however, the party suffered substantial losses including a record 17 point decline at the October 2001 Berlin election. By mid-2001 the sentiment was growing among CDU/CSU leaders such as Roland Koch in Hesse and Peter Müller in the Saar that the party might have a chance in 2002, but not with Merkel as the chancellor candidate.

After the defeat at the October Berlin election, Merkel's fate was sealed. She came under heavy pressure from both the CDU and CSU to support Stoiber. Leading the draft Stoiber movement was a former health minister in the Kohl government and CSU stalwart, Horst Seehofer. Dubbing his followers the Mut und Zuversicht (Courage and Confidence) group Seehofer argued that given the two core themes of the 2002 campaign, the economy and security, there could be only one candidate, Stoiber, who had a substantial track record in both areas.

Stoiber's interest in the chancellor candidacy increased as the economy continued to decline. A key inflection point occurred in late 2001 when it became clear that the chancellor's promise to reduce unemployment to 3.5 million by the September 2002 election could not be met. The higher than expected unemployment numbers announced in December 2001 produced a jump in CDU/CSU support. The balance tipped in favor of the CDU in early January 2002 following Stoiber's nomination as the CDU/CSU's chancellor candidate. In December the government still held a lead in most polls and the proportion favoring no change in government was at 36 percent in comparison to 31 percent who wanted a new government. By January, 39 percent favored a new government and only 32 percent supported no change, a twelve-point swing.[9]

The weaker economy gave the Union new hope. Merkel in her two-year tenure as party leader was unable to unite the party or develop any convincing electoral strategy to defeat Schröder. Stoiber, on the other hand, was the unquestioned leader of the Bavarian CSU. The Courage and Confidence ("M and Z") group also assured Angela Merkel that she would remain as CDU leader after the 2002 election, if she endorsed Stoiber. In the fall of 2001 few expected Stoiber to win, but it was hoped that he would keep CDU/CSU losses at a minimum. A Merkel candidacy it was feared would cause many CDU voters to switch to the FDP thus enabling an SPD-FDP coalition.

By October 2001 CDU/CSU voters preferred Stoiber to Merkel by almost a 3 to 1 margin and by over 2 to 1 among all voters. But neither candidate was able to come close to the popularity enjoyed by Schröder. The chancellor's margin over Stoiber was less but still substantial (56 to 37). Over 52 percent of all voters expected the government to be returned in 2002, only 26 percent felt that the opposition would win.[10]

Facing a defeat in her own party, which would probably have meant the end of her national political career, Merkel seized the initiative and arranged a meeting with Stoiber at his home outside Munich. During their working breakfast, she dropped her own candidacy thereby making Stoiber the 2002 chancellor candidate. She then returned to the CDU conference in Magdeburg and announced that after conferring with Stoiber she had decided that it would be in the best interests of the party if she withdrew her candidacy in his favor.

Had she not acted, the CDU executive was about to announce the party's support for Stoiber over its own leader, Ms. Merkel. In that event, her position as CDU national chairman would have become untenable. By withdrawing before her own party's vote, she retained her position in the CDU and her political future. In the event of a Stoiber victory, she could have claimed much of the credit, given the critical importance of a unified campaign for the Bavarian. In the event of his defeat, she could quietly have said, "I told you so," and, like Helmut Kohl following the 1980 Strauß loss, renew her candidacy for 2006.

Stoiber, of course, understood her tactic. It was, however, also in his interests that the candidate question be settled with as little intra-party conflict as possible. A formal vote in the CDU's presidium or parliamentary caucus, would have divided the party on the eve of the campaign, a sure recipe for electoral disaster in a political culture where voters want their parties to be united. Merkel thus turned a certain defeat into a "tactical victory."[11]

Campaign Strategies

SPD: Auf den Kanzler kommt es an

The Social Democrats' campaign began and ended with Chancellor Schröder. With few electorally effective policy successes, a poor economy and an opposition that refused to come out and polarize, the SPD had little left except Schröder.

In one of his few mistakes during the 1998 campaign Schröder confidently predicted that unemployment would be brought down to at least 3.5 percent by the end of his first term and if it was not his government "did not deserve to be re-elected." By June 2002 the jobless rate was over 4 million and actually rose in the summer months for the first time in nine years.

In 2000 the economy grew by a respectable 3 percent and unemployment dropped to 9.1 percent. Most economists at year's end predicted a similar growth rate for 2001 and a further dip in unemployment. But a sluggish world economy in the wake of the American downturn in late 2000 soon made these forecasts hopelessly optimistic. Instead of a predicted real growth rate of 2.7 percent in 2001, it was a paltry 0.6. By early 2002 it was clear that Schröder would not meet his goal of reducing unemployment to 3.5 million by the 2002 election.

Apart from the economy and the government's record, the most serious problem for the SPD campaign has been its misjudgment of Stoiber. At the outset, the Kampa 02 (the SPD campaign staff) has assumed that the Bavarian, consistent with his earlier record and like his mentor, would project a *kantig*, confrontational image that would enable Schröder to label him as a hard-right polarizer, a typical Bavarian politician not suited for national political responsibility. Stoiber and his campaign team confounded the SPD strategists by studiously avoiding a *Lagerwahlkampf* style thus depriving the SPD of any opportunity to link him with his confrontational past. Stoiber emphasized his moderate, business-like approach to policy problems. At times, it has seemed that he was not even campaigning.[12] Like Schröder in 1998, he avoided specific policy proposals preferring the tried and true generalities about "change," a "new dynamic," and "generational contract."

Another major blow to the SPD campaign took place in April 2002 at the state election in Saxony-Anhalt. The SPD minority government saw its support drop from 36 percent to only 20 percent. The CDU and the FDP increased their combined percentage from 26 percent to 51 percent. Even for the East these were unusually large swings. The election coupled with the continued poor economic numbers had a chilling effect on the chancellor's inner circle. Defeat even in Kampa 02 was seen as not only possible but increasingly probable.

The Saxony-Anhalt loss underscored a fundamental problem for the SPD in the eastern states. Since unification, electoral support for the Social Democrats in the East has lagged well behind the party's western level. While they are the undisputed major party on the center-left of the political spectrum in the old Federal Republic, they had to share this space in the East with the PDS, the Party of Democratic Socialism, the successor to the ruling Communist Party of the German Democratic Republic. At the time of unification many observers expected the old, discredited communists to quickly disappear as a significant political force. The great bulk of the communist support would then go to the Social Democrats, the only real democratic alternative on the left. Thus far this has not happened. The PDS between 1990 and 2002 was able to consistently draw the support of between 20 to 25 percent of eastern voters at regional elections.

This put the Social Democrats in a dilemma. Should the SPD continue to oppose the PDS as the party of the Communist dictatorship with its Berlin Wall and "Shoot to Kill" order, or should it try at least in the short-run to cooperate with the PDS in selected eastern states? Thus far to the consternation of the national SPD and especially Chancellor Schröder the eastern SPD has chosen the former course. It is now in coalition governments with the former communists in Berlin and Mecklenburg.[13]

The CDU/CSU: Stoiber and His Springer Guru

Stoiber first attracted national attention when he managed the unsuccessful 1980 campaign of his mentor, Franz Josef Strauß. The Strauß candidacy marked the first and until Stoiber's nomination, the only time that the Christian Democrats turned to its Bavarian sister party for their top candidate.

Stoiber's initial political success was due above all to his unconditional loyalty to Strauß, the undisputed political boss of Bavaria until his death in 1988, and his command of administrative and legal detail. By training and temperament Stoiber is a man of the state administration. He tends to seek the solution of political problems through proper administrative definition and execution. He is hardly a supporter of the minimalist or *schlanker Staat*. Bavaria's economic success has not come about through unfettered free market policies, but rather by strong state initiative and direction. The state has systematically pursued its own version of industrial policy. Key potential growth sectors were identified and supported through state funds and tax policies. There is more than a modicum of what some Germans call Prussian values in the Bavarian's leadership style. In this sense he is far different than the freewheeling Strauß who had little interest in devouring *Akten*.

Planning the campaign was not an easy task for the Union. The year 2001 marked the first time since 1983 that the CDU was competing in a national election as an opposition party and the first time since 1980 with a chancellor candidate from Bavaria. Surrounded by either Bavarian provincials, who had never run a close, competitive, much less national campaign, or the survivors of the Kohl-era CDU (Merz, Merkel, Meyer, Rühe), Stoiber had to look outside the party for campaign leadership. Shortly after his selection he made an unusual, but critical personnel decision. He selected Michael Spreng as his chief media and campaign coordinator. Spreng, former editor of *Bild am Sonntag*, was not a member of the CDU and had no experience in political campaigns. Obviously, Stoiber believed that neither the CDU nor the CSU could provide the advice in needing in running a national campaign.

Spreng's appointment raised some eyebrows in the CDU above all those of Helmut Kohl and his supporters. While Spreng's conservative credentials were in order, he was nonetheless a one-time friend of Chancellor Schröder and a harsh critic of Kohl during the 1998 campaign and the CDU finance scandal. In June 2000 in an editorial he even called for Kohl's resignation from the parliament. Spreng was not a member of any party and thus lacks what Germans call the proper "stable smell" (*Stallgeruch*). To this Spreng responded that while he does not have a stable smell, he knows how stables smell. Party veterans were also suspicious that Spreng and his eight-person team could wander off the reservation. The Spreng group was tightly integrated into a variety of campaign organizations.[14]

Spreng produced the Bavarian's main slogan—"A Serious Man for Serious Times." Stoiber was portrayed as exceptionally knowledgeable, competent and objective in contrast to the telegenic, media-savvy, but content-free Schröder. Stoiber's careful avoidance of his confrontational past also enabled his campaign to minimize the conflicts between the CDU and CSU, a major failing of the 1980 Strauß effort. The CDU north of the Main showed little enthusiasm for the Strauß style. Indeed some in the Union, including Helmut Kohl, encouraged and ultimately profited from the intra-Union conflict. The Strauß defeat enabled Kohl to regain the leadership of the Union and ultimately the chancellorship.

Stoiber and his campaign team took more than one page from the Kampa's 1998 playbook. They focused almost exclusively on Schröder and his government's "failures" and "broken promises." Their own plans for dealing with the country's problems were kept just as vague as Schröder's *Neue Mitte* of 1998.

FDP: Outside the Box

Following the 1998 defeat the FDP found itself in a unique position: for the first time in its history it had to share the opposition stage with a major party. During its previous (brief) opposition period, the 1966–1969 Grand Coalition, it was the sole opposition party.[15] Thus, after 1998 it had the difficult task of competing with the CDU/CSU for the attention of the media and the public. This is the key to understanding the party's sometimes bizarre behavior during the inter-election period. Whether it was a parachute jump on a Spanish beach, the 18 percent vote target, the chancellor candidacy of its leader, or its flirtation with the taboo of anti-Israeli statements and the radical right, the FDP certainly got attention. For the party's leadership, negative publicity was better than none at all. No party has embraced the new media more than the FDP. Internet campaigning, a "virtual" seventeenth state organization, fund-raising dinners (Westerwelle's birthday!), telemarketing and media events such as tax free gasoline sales were standard fare for the *Spaß* party.

Following the 1998 vote the FDP decline continued. In state elections and polls the party hovered around the 5 percent mark. But in late 1999, like the Schröder government, it became a beneficiary of the CDU finance scandal. Union voters displeased with the scandal, but unable to vote SPD, found the FDP a convenient halfway house. After losing six of seven state elections between February and October 1999, the FDP saw its support increase at the two state elections held in 2000.

For most of the campaign the FDP's new look appeared to be successful. In late 1999 the party was below the 5 percent mark and trailed the Greens, who were also in decline. By June 2002 the FDP was projected to receive 10 percent of the vote. This was far from the 18 percent "goal" of the Westerwelle team, but any double-digit total for the FDP would have been a victory.

In the campaign's final days the FDP quietly abandoned its *Project 18*. The revised election goal was now to top the Green vote by at least 2 percent.

In this last phase, however, the FDP made two critical errors: it failed to state clearly its coalition partner and the allegedly anti-Semitic statements of one of its key regional leaders brought the party unneeded controversy.

The Greens: Beyond Environmentalism

In 1998 the Greens finally entered the promised land (at least for the Realos) of national political responsibility. But this achievement cost the party dearly at in state elections. After 1998 the Greens lost support at 14 straight state elections as much of its core electorate abandoned the party. Many Green activists felt betrayed by the party's support for military action in Kosovo and Serbia. They also questioned the nuclear power agreement as being too generous to the energy industry. The Greens were especially weak in the East where their *Bündnis 90* allies, have long since found a home in other parties or have pursued other outlets, such as environmental groups, to promote their issue concerns.[16]

In government the Greens expanded into other policy areas. In addition to the foreign policy successes of Foreign Minister Joschka Fischer, the Greens since 2000 have led the agriculture ministry, which was renamed in the wake of the mad cow disease scandal, the Ministry for Consumer Protection, Agriculture and Nutrition. Renate Künast, the first non-farmer and woman to head the ministry in the history of the Federal Republic, became one of the more popular political figures. Civil liberties and the rights of minorities such as children, gays and foreign residents became prominent Green issues.

Like the SPD, the hopes of the Greens rested largely with the party's leader, Foreign Minister Joschka Fischer, the country's most popular political leader. While campaigning for the Greens, he made it clear that he wanted above all to remain as foreign minister. The Green campaign focused almost exclusively on their popular leader. Without Fischer the Greens would probably not clear the 5 percent hurdle and would not return to parliament. The party's campaign was closely coordinated with that of the Social Democrats. On September 15, one week before the election, both parties held an unprecedented joint rally at the Brandenburg Gate in Berlin with Fischer and Schröder as the featured speakers.

PDS: Life after Gysi?

In the inter-election period, the PDS continued to thrive as the tribune for the East. In early 2002 the party took a major stride toward the political mainstream when it entered into a coalition with the SPD in Berlin, the first time that the former communists had come to power in a "Western" Land. The party's 2002 campaign was focused on three themes: (1) "social justice," which meant a rejection of any cutbacks in the welfare state and a massive public works spending programs to reduce unemployment;[17]

(2) its special expertise and competence to deal with problems in the eastern states; and (3) its uncompromising opposition to any German military involvement in Afghanistan or Iraq.

The PDS campaign was rattled by the August resignation of Gregor Gysi, the party's most visible leader, over his use of frequent flyer miles. In the final phase of the campaign the party had planned to showcase Gysi and the Red-Red Berlin government. The party's "6 Prozent plus X" goal quickly faded as it sought to re-enter the parliament via the three-direct mandate route.

After Gysi's resignation the party suffered two additional campaign setbacks, which made even the three-mandate goal difficult to achieve. Schröder's Iraq position played well in the East and deprived the PDS of its strong position in the "peace" issue space. The August floods in the East and Schröder's strong response impressed many eastern voters and furthered damaged the PDS image as the best advocate of eastern interests.

Issues and Voters

The number one issue in the campaign was the economy and specifically unemployment. In table 1.2 we present the major economic measures for the Schröder years. The government had only one good year, 2000 when growth reached its highest level since unification. The prior year was not bad with 1.8 percent growth, but unemployment remained at over 4 million and the deficit, already high in the Kohl years, was over 30 billion Euros. The strong performance of the economy in 2000 was expected to continue through at least 2001, but a downturn in the world economy and the September 11 terrorist attack ended the short-lived recovery. By 2002

TABLE 1.2 The Schröder Economic Record

Indicator	1999	2000	2001	2002
Gross domestic product (%)	1.8	2.9	0.8	0.2
Unemployment	4.1 million	3.9 million	3.9 million	4.1 million
Percent unemployed	9.7	9.1	9.0	9.5
Inflation (%)	0.6	1.4	2.0	1.4
Budget deficits/ surplus (euro billions)	-30.6	+26.8	-58.9	-74.3

Source: Deutsches Institut für Wirtschaft, Berlin. 1999; Statistisches Bundesamt, Wiesbaden, 2000–2001; Deutsche Bundesbank, Frankfurt, 2002.

unemployment was again over 4 million and economic growth a miniscule 0.2 percent. The 2002 deficit estimates were far too optimistic. By July 2002, it was apparent that higher than expected unemployment and reduced tax revenues will bring the projected deficit to at least 60 billion euros. The 2001 deficit of 59 billion euros amounted to 2.8 percent of GDP, perilously close to the 3.0 percent limit.[18]

The slowdown in 2001, which worsened following the September 11 terrorist attacks, had little immediate impact on the government's re-election prospects. In part because the CDU/CSU had no candidate. As figure 1.2 shows, as late as December 2001 almost 55 percent of the electorate expected the government to be re-elected and only about 20 percent thought that the Union could return to power. In early 2002, however, a key inflection point was reached following the selection of Stoiber as the Union's candidate. The poor economy could now be linked to a credible alternative, i.e., the Stoiber candidacy. By late March the electorate was equally divided. Between April and June the balance tipped in favor of the opposition. The Saxon-Anhalt debacle and the high unemployment number in June yielded a further advantage to the opposition, which was increased throughout the summer. Continued high unemployment the Babcock bankruptcy, the dismissal of Telekom chief Sommers, and the departure of

FIGURE 1.2 Expected Winner: Government or Opposition?

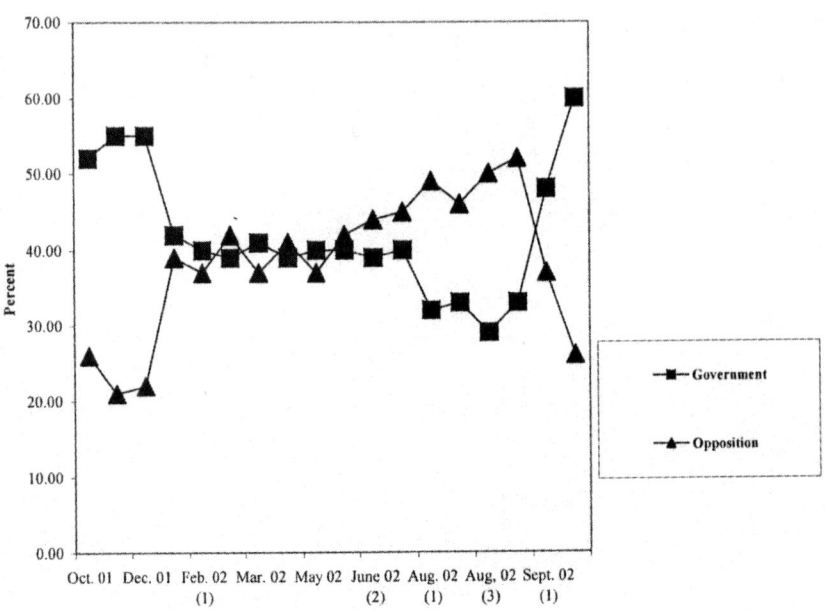

Defense Minister Scharping were all additional events that had a negative effect on the government's prospects. In about nine months, the opposition's election prospects went from about 20 percent to almost 50 percent. With less than six weeks before the election, less than one voter in three expected the Schröder government to be re-elected.

But in mid-August the rains came in the East and the chancellor's antiwar position finally mobilized the SPD core and attracted much of the undecided segment of the electorate. The Iraq position tapped the latent pacifism of many Germans and the anti-Americanism of some elements of the SPD and Green Left. It also struck a positive chord among East Germans who had no personal experiences with American support for Germany during the Cold War and weaker attachments to NATO and other institutions of German and American cooperation. Within about two weeks the CDU/CSU lead has disappeared and with about ten days before the election most voters expected the government to survive.

Candidates

But even before the August turnaround the one bright spot for the SPD throughout the campaign had been Schröder's constant lead over Stoiber in the "preferred chancellor" question (figure 1.3). The basis of Schröder's advantage over Stoiber was his great "credibility," "winning style," (*Siegertyp*) and general "likableness." When chancellor preference was linked to the economy and job creation, Stoiber was the winner even in

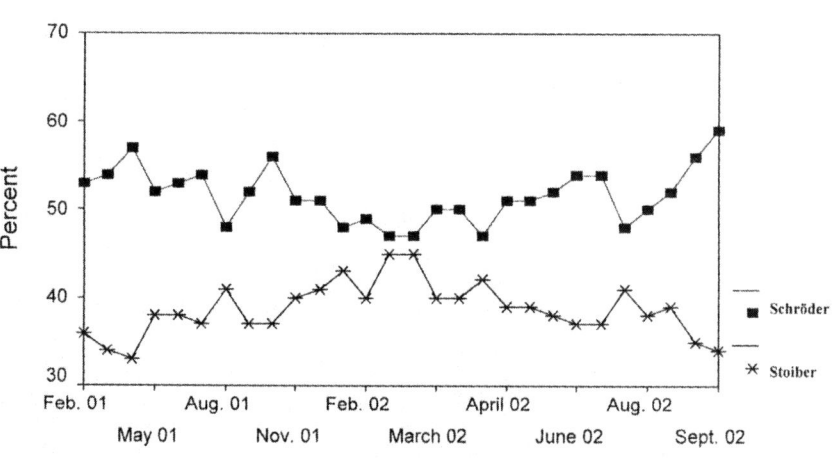

FIGURE 1.3 Preferred Chancellor: Schröder vs. Stoiber

polls conducted during the last days of the campaign. Germans voters wanted Schröder to remain as chancellor even though their support for his party and most of his policies remained well below that of the opposition throughout the campaign. Voters were less satisfied with the work of the government than they were with the opposition. In the important economic competency area the CDU/CSU overtook the SPD in early 2002 and by late July held a solid 18-point point advantage, which they maintained throughout the campaign. But Stoiber and the CDU/CSU's high competency ratings were not enough.

The Results

The two major parties finished in a virtual dead heat. Each received 38.5 percent of the party vote and after almost 48 million votes were counted only about 6000 votes separated the SPD from the CDU/CSU. In the hectic final days of the campaign the Christian Democrats stopped the hemorrhaging caused by Iraq, the floods and the debates and pulled even with the Social Democrats.[19] But while the SPD was in danger of falling short at the finish line, the Greens were gaining support in the final days and came to the government's rescue.

Voting Behavior: Class and Religion

In 2002 in the West the influence of the classic cleavages of class and religion on voting choice continued to decline. Among blue-collar workers the Social Democrats lost 8 percent, more than twice their national average while the Christian Democrats gained about 9 percent (table 1.3). In 1998 the SPD had a 23-point lead over the CDU/CSU among blue-collar workers; in 2002 this dropped to only 7 percent. Among blue collar workers with trade union ties support for the Social Democrats dropped even more, from 67 percent to 56 percent. The Christian Democrats gained 10 points among this group.

The weakened relationship between class and voting is even clearer among two non-manual groups: civil servants and the self-employed (*Selbstständige*, professionals, small business owners). In terms of values and beliefs these are two of the most conservative segments of the electorate and historically they have been the core of the CDU/CSU and FDP electorate. Yet, in 2002 the Greens almost tripled their vote among the self-employed in the West. Among civil servants, Green support reached a record 16 percent in 2002. Note the critical importance of these new Green supporters for the survival of the government.

In the East the influence of class on voting behavior has been much weaker than in the West. This pattern did not change in 2002. Indeed, the East is a topsy-turvy world for election analysts. Here, blue collar and white-collar voters support the SPD at the same level (table 1.4). Among white-collar voters the SPD has a 16-point advantage over the CDU in the East as compared to only a 4 point lead in the West. The eastern CDU gets more votes from white-collar voters than it does from those in blue-collar occupations. Among eastern small businessmen and free professionals the former communists (PDS) receive more support than either the Greens or the FDP. Among civil servants over 60 percent support either the Social Democrats or the PDS.

In the West, the influence of religion was less dramatic than in previous elections. Most trends held steady in 2002. Three-fourths of Catholics, for example, with a strong attachment to the church as measured by church attendance continued to support the CDU/CSU, but the size of this group relative to the total population continues to decline. Almost 60 percent of

TABLE 1.3 Party Support by Occupation in West Germany, 2002 (results 2002 and differences to 1998)

	SPD	CDU/CSU	Greens	FDP	PDS
Total	38.2	40.8	9.4	7.6	1.2
	-4.1	3.8	2.1	0.6	0.0
Occupation					
Blue-collar workers	45 -8	40 +9	5 +1	7 +3	1 0
White-collar workers	41 -3	37 +4	11 +2	8 0	1 0
Civil servants	32 -5	43 +2	16 +5	6 0	1 0
Self-employed	21 -1	52 +7	11 +7	13 -3	1 0
Farmers	13 +3	76 0	3 +1	5 -4	1 0

Source: Forschungsgruppe Wahlen, *Wahltagbefragung* (exit polls).

TABLE 1.4 Party Support by Occupation in East Germany, 2002 (results 2002 and differences to 1998)

	SPD	CDU/CSU	Greens	FDP	PDS
Total	39.8	28.2	4.8	6.4	16.8
	4.7	0.9	0.7	3.1	-4.8
Occupation					
Blue-collar workers	41 +2	30 +4	3 +1	7 +4	15 -3
White-collar workers	41 +7	25 +2	6 0	6 +2	19 -8
Civil servants	37 +3	25 -8	4 -2	5 +2	24 +4
Self-employed	22 +2	44 +7	8 +3	10 +1	13 -7
Farmers	36 -1	40 -1	2 -1	7 -1	13 +4

Source: Forschungsgruppe Wahlen, *Wahltagbefragung* (exit polls).

Germany's Catholics supported the CDU/CSU or FDP while the SPD and Greens garnered over 50 percent of the Protestant and "no religion" groups (table 1.5). These latter two segments now comprise about two-thirds of the electorate. Most easterners, 60 percent, have no religious affiliation as compared to 17 percent in the West. The small minority of eastern Catholics, about 5 percent, contribute little to the CDU's national vote. Among voters with no religious affiliation both major parties made gains in 2002.

TABLE 1.5 Party Support by Religion, 2002 (results 2002 and differences to 1998)

		SPD	CDU/CSU	Greens	FDP	PDS
	Total	38.5	38.5	8.6	7.4	4.0
		-2.4	3.3	1.9	1.2	-1.1
Religion*						
Catholic		30 -6	52 +6	8 +2	7 +1	1 0
Protestant		44 -2	36 +3	8 +1	8 0	2 0
No religion		40 -1	25 +4	11 +2	8 +4	11 -5

*Proportion of sample: Catholic, 34 percent; Protestant, 40 percent; no religion, 26 percent.
Source: Forschungsgruppe Wahlen, *Wahltagbefragung* (exit polls).

Iraq and the Floods

Surveys conducted in the final days of the campaign indicated that the Iraq issue and the floods probably provided the coalition with its tiny victory margin. As Dieter Roth points out in chapter 2, about 94 percent either opposed the Iraq invasion or wanted it dealt with by the United Nations. More importantly, among independent voters, those with no partisan attachment, and a critical swing group, almost 60 percent stated that the Schröder government could do a better job of representing Germany's interest with the United States on the Iraq question.[20] Within the coalition, the Greens in the West were the prime beneficiary of the war issue in the final days of the campaign. Among opponents to the Iraq invasion over 20 percent intended to vote Green, more than double the party's western vote total.

In the East the pivotal importance of the Iraq issue for independent voters was even stronger since they make up about half of the electorate as compared to about 25 percent in the West. Among independents in the East who opposed the war 53 percent supported the Social Democrats and only 19 percent backed the CDU.[21] The PDS, with the best anti-war credentials of any party, was not rewarded for its strong opposition to both the deployment of German troops in Afghanistan and the Iraq war. It received the support of only 10 percent of eastern independent voters opposed to the war.

As Patterson and Sloam demonstrate in chapter 4 the quick response of Schröder to the floods and specifically his relief program resonated well with voters throughout the country. About two-thirds of voters agreed that the government had done enough to meet the needs of flood victims. As in the case of Iraq the floods helped the coalition among independent or swing voters. In the West, 57 percent of independents who approved of the handling of the flood issue intended to vote for the SPD as compared to only about 30 percent for the CDU/CSU. Among eastern independents who rated the government positively on this issue, 56 percent stated shortly before the election that they intended to support the SPD and only 25 percent opted for the CDU/CSU.

Conclusion: A Precarious and Hollow Victory?

While the government survived, there were little grounds for celebration. The fundamental structural problems that the Schröder coalition did little to resolve between 1998 and 2000 remained. Within weeks after the vote the government released new economic figures that were even worse than the poor growth, employment and debt numbers that were used in the campaign. The CDU/CSU and FDP charged that Schröder and his finance minister had deliberately concealed this bad news until after the election. A parliamentary investigation committee, dubbed by journalists, the "Lies Committee," even held inconclusive hearings on this "shocking" development.

By the end of 2002 the worsened economic and budgetary situation forced the government to raise taxes, cut social programs and borrow more money. As expected, the budget exceeded the 3 percent limit set by the European Monetary System's "Growth and Stability" Pact. By mid-2003, the September 2002 dead heat had turned into a 15 to 18 percent lead for the Christian Democrats. Chancellor Schröder's status also declined, but unlike the SPD he has thus far avoided the public opinion basement. In September 2003, for example, he trailed his 2002 challenger by only one point.

Losses in state elections in 2003 gave the CDU/CSU and FDP a commanding majority in the Federal Council (Bundesrat), which has a veto power over about 60 percent of all legislation including almost all of the key proposals for fundamental changes in the health care, social security, labor market, and tax systems. Thus, Germany now has divided government and is ruled by a de facto "Grand Coalition." Little or no major legislation can be passed without the support of the parliamentary opposition, which in turn holds a majority in the Federal Council.

In March 2003 Chancellor Schröder unveiled his "Agenda 2010," which was touted as the most comprehensive domestic reform program in the Republic's history. This reform package, which is examined by Irwin Collier in chapter 12, was passed in revised form in December 2003 only through the support of the Christian Democrats. The political futures of both the government and the opposition as well as their leaders are now connected to this policy mix of lower taxes, less spending for social programs, less rigid labor markets and more individual initiative.

Appendix: Ballot Splitting in 2002

The two-ballot electoral system enables voters to easily divide their vote. It has become so commonplace that the media under public service announcements instructs new voters on the procedure. In 2002 ticket splitting set a new record at almost 22 percent. As figure 1.4 shows, splitting is most common between Green and Free Democratic second ballot voters. In 2002 about 60 percent of the Green second ballot vote came from first-ballot Social Democratic supporters who were attempting to maximize the combined SPD-Green parliamentary seat total.[22] Only 33 percent gave both their second and first ballot vote to the Greens. For the FDP, the party that first made the splitting tactic a major feature of German elections, only 33 percent of second ballot voters supported their traditional partner, the Christian Democrats with their first ballot. Overall, about 52 percent of second ballot FDP voters went elsewhere. Thus, the Greens have replaced the FDP as the party with the most tactical voters. This unusually low level of FDP-CDU splitting was probably the result of the

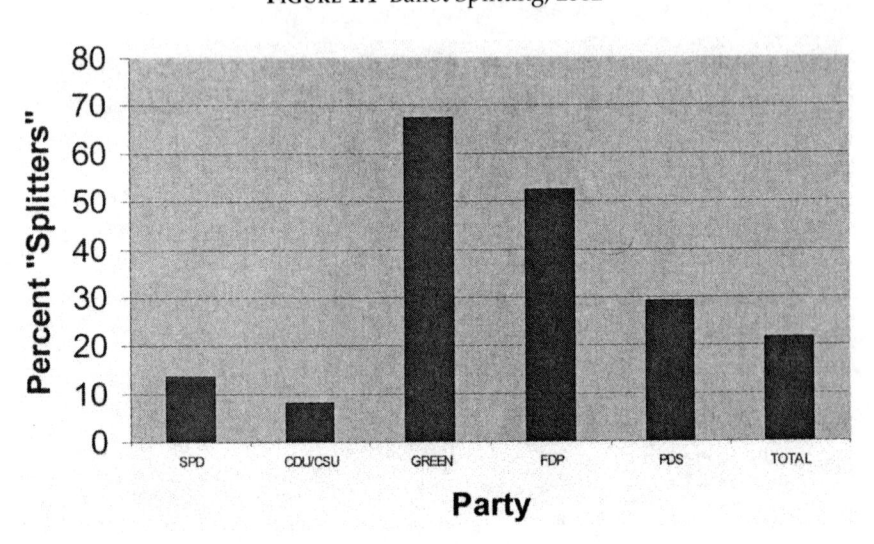

FIGURE 1.4 Ballot Splitting, 2002

Note: Percent second-bill voters who supported a different party with their first ballot.
Source: Federal Statistical Office Sample.

party's "independence" strategy, which is examined in Christian Søe's contribution to this volume (chapter 6). Simply put, unlike earlier elections, the Free Democrats did not clearly state their coalition preference. They sent no clear message to Christian Democrats that a second ballot FDP vote would enable a CDU/CSU-FDP government. This decision might have cost the opposition the election.

Notes

The Forschungsgruppe Wahlen, Mannheim, provided all survey data used in this report. As always, I am grateful to Dieter Roth for his generous support. Mr. Scott Adams provided additional research assistance.

1. Christopher J. Anderson and Carsten Zelle, eds., *Stability and Change in German Elections* (Westport, CT: Praeger Publishers, 1998); David P. Conradt and Russell Dalton, "The West German Electorate and the Party System: Continuity and Change in the 1980s," *Review of Politics* 50, no. 1 (1998): 3–29; Wolfgang Hartenstein, "Fünf Jahrzehnte Wahlen in der Bundesrepublik: Stabilität und Wandel," *Aus Politik und Zeitgeschichte* (24 May 2002).
2. For 2002 Federal Statistical Office, "Wahl zum 15. Deutschen Bundestag am 22. September 2002. Ergebnisse aus der Repräsentativen Wahlstatistik," Berlin, 22 January 2003.
3. Harold L. Wilensky, *Rich Democracies* (Berkeley: University of California Press, 2002).
4. This system has been the subject of much scholarly analysis. See, for example, Thomas Gschwend et al., "Split Ticket Patterns in Mixed Member-Member Proportional Election Systems: Estimates and Analyses of Their Spatial Variations at the German Federal Election, 1998," *British Journal of Political Science* 33, no. 1 (January 2003): 109–128; Eckard Jesse, "Split-Voting in the Federal Republic of Germany: An Analysis of the Federal Elections from 1953 to 1987," *Electoral Studies* 7 (1988): 109–124; Beate Hoecker, "The German Electoral System: A Barrier to Women?" in *Electoral Systems in Comparative Perspective*, ed. Wilma Rule and Joseph F. Zimmermann (Westport, CT: Greenwood Press, 1994), pp. 65–77; Hans-Dieter Klingemann and Bernhard Weasels, "The Political Consequences of Germany's Mixed-Member System: Personalization at the Grass Roots?" in *Mixed-Member Electoral Systems: The Best of Both Worlds?* ed. Matthew S. Shugart and Martin P. Wattenberg (New York: Oxford University Press, 2001), pp. 279–296; Susan E. Scarrow, "Germany: The Mixed-Member System as a Political Compromise," in Shugart and Wattenberg, *Mixed Member Electoral Systems*, pp. 55–69.
5. Until unification, *Überhangmandate* were relatively rare. The highest number at any federal election between 1949 and 1987 was five in 1961. At the four elections between 1965 and 1976 there were no excess mandates.
6. David P. Conradt, "The Campaign and Election: An Overview" in *Germany's New Politics*, ed. Conradt et al. (Providence and Oxford: Berghahn Press, 1995), pp. 1–4.
7. This account of the 10 March 1999 meeting is drawn from reports in *Der Spiegel, Die Zeit*, and the *Süddeutsche Zeitung*. For Lafontaine's version, see his *Das Herz schlägt links* (Düsseldorf: Econ Verlag, 1999).
8. In December 2003, the last phase of this tax plan was moved up from 2005 to 2004 as part of the government's "Agenda 2010" program. See chapter 12 for a thorough analysis of this program.
9. Renate Köcher, "Die Wechselstimmung wächst," *Frankfurter Allgemeine Zeitung*, 12 June 2002, p. 5.

10. Forschungsgruppe Wahlen, *Politbarometer*, October 2002.
11. Karl Feldmayer, "Kehrtwende zum taktischen Erfolg," *Frankfurter Allgemeine Zeitung*, 14 January 2002, p. 3.
12. Matthias Geis, "Der laute Leisetreter," *Die Zeit*, no. 28 (July 2002).
13. Until 2002, in the state of Saxony-Anhalt the Social Democrats governed with only a plurality of the parliamentary seats and were "tolerated" by the PDS. That is, while it was not in the government, the PDS still supported the SPD when needed. Thus, this was a de facto SPD-PDS coalition. It ended when the CDU and FDP won an absolute majority of the seats at the 2002 state election.
14. Susanne Höll, "Ein Pfadfinder im Gestrüpp der Harmonie," *Süddeutsche Zeitung*, 25 February 2002.
15. During the 1957-1961 parliament, the party split and some members did join the Adenauer government.
16. Doris Kowitz, "Auf keinen grünen Zweig gekommen," *Süddeutsche Zeitung*, 7 August 2002.
17. As one Green leader quipped during the campaign, "The PDS domestic program equals the SPD + the Greens + 15 percent."
18. These final numbers for 2002 were even worse than the government's estimates. The deficit ballooned to over 74 billion euros or 3.5 percent of GDP.
19. Tracking poll data kindly provided to the author by Wolfgang Gibowski.
20. Forschungsgruppe Wahlen, *Blitzumfrage*, 16–20 September 2002.
21. *Blitzumfrage*. See also Robert Rohrschneider and Dieter Fuchs, "It Used To Be the Economy: Issues and Party Support in the 2002 Election," *German Politics and Society* 21, no. 1 (Spring 2003): 76–95, for additional analysis of the *Blitzumfrage* data.
22. These figures are drawn from the representative sample of ballots analyzed by the Federal Statistical Office. For the first time since 1990, the Office was authorized to once again include gender and age questions on sample ballots. For a report and an analysis of the official sample, including data on the voting behavior of different gender and age groups, see Tim C. Werner, "Wählerverhalten bei der Bundestagswahl 2002 nach Geschlecht und Alter. Ergebnisse der Repräsentativen Wahlstatistik," *Wirtschaft und Statistik*, no. 3 (2003): 171–188.

Chapter 2

WHO WON AND WHY

Dieter Roth

This was a close election. The governing parties, SPD and Green, won 306 seats, only four more than an absolute majority, but eleven seats more that the combined CDU/CSU and FDP total. The two remaining PDS deputies are hardly relevant. The result means that the chancellor has to maintain close contact and good relations with the SPD's parliamentary party (*Fraktion*) in order to pass major legislation. The CDU/CSU majority in the Bundesrat, which followed the state elections in February 2003, is an additional obstacle to any reform programs. This does not necessarily mean that the Schröder government must be weak. There is an additional factor in the policymaking equation, namely, public opinion, which can be mobilized to support the government's reform program.

By the final weeks of the campaign, if not earlier, it was clear that the election would be very tight. In spite of the relatively exact measurement of political preferences, which is possible through representative surveys, there were still the usual misrepresentations of such data by the media and also in party by the strategists of the opposition during the course of the campaign. Since each party sought to mobilize its respective clientele at very different time points and with varying degrees of success, the opinion data, although properly collected, did not give any really clear indication of what results to expect in September. The CDU/CSU, for example, mobilized its core electorate very early in the campaign, in fact shortly after the nomination of Edmund Stoiber in early 2002. But there is a risk in mobilizing the core so early: it has to be sustained so that it can be used as a means to attract the less attached or unattached voters to the party's electorate. The Social Democrats, on the other hand, for a long time had great difficulties in mobilizing their core electorate. This was due to a number of factors: intra-party factional disputes, their finance in North Rhine-Westphalia, the CDU/CSU success with the economy issue and the unexpectedly moderate approach of Edmund Stoiber. The CDU/CSU strategists

---

Notes for this chapter are located on page 36.

had transformed Stoiber into a centrist, which made it difficult for the SPD to remind voters of his hard-right past.

It was not until the SPD's election party conference in early August that the party activists' enthusiasm and will to win became apparent. The actual break through for the SPD came in the "hot phase" of the campaign through events, which offered the chancellor and the government the opportunity to demonstrate decisive leadership ability. This then had the effect of bringing the undecided voters into the government camp.

Party Strategies

In 2002 campaign strategists for all the parties should have learned something from the 1994 and 1998 elections. In these years a mid-campaign lead in the polls for the opposition parties was not enough for a clear victory on election day. The basic disposition of German voters to support the incumbent government, that is, not to change, will in the final stage of the campaign reduce or eliminate whatever secure lead the opposition once enjoyed. In 1998 the large, early lead of the SPD led opposition dropped dramatically in the last two months of the campaign. After a CSU victory in Bavarian, just two weeks before the 1998 national election, the CDU/CSU under Helmut Kohl believed that it had a real chance to pull out a last-minute victory just as it had in 1994. In 1998, however, in contrast to 2002, there was a stronger disposition to change. While this weakened in the final phase of the campaign, it remained dominant. This pervasive feeling that the government was finished could not be found in 2002 as it was in 1998. The support levels of the government and opposition parties in 2002 were similar to those in 1994. In both cases the government pulled even with the opposition about a month before the election. With three weeks left in the campaign the government then took a narrow lead, which it held. These "last-minute swings" are made possible by the one-third of the electorate who have either a moderate or a weak attachment to the political parties.

These non-attached voters, whose ranks have grown over the past two decades, are most likely, of course, to make their decision late in the campaign. Thus, predictions made several months before the election on the basis of surveys are not very accurate. In 2002 this pattern was intensified by the strategy of the parties to personalize the campaigns as seen above all by the new campaign instrument of the Schröder-Stoiber television duel.

Red-Green in Power: 1998–2002

The parties never win federal elections only on election day. All elections have a history and in 2002 this was fast changing. Popular evaluations of the government and opposition throughout the four-year legislative period were more volatile than usual. After 1998 voters had great expectations for the new Schröder government. But less than a year later the government's approval ratings plummeted. Schröder's own support level dropped from 54 percent on election day 1998 to only 23 percent ten months later.[1] This led to losses in state elections throughout 1999. This post-election drop in support is not unusual and was reported after the 2002 election. In addition between 1998 and 202 there were two events which led to substantial shifts in the electorate's judgment of the parties: the 1999–2000 CDU finance scandal and the September 11 terrorist attacks in the United States. These extraordinary events changed our conventional wisdom about the pattern of support between elections for government and opposition.

They did not change, however, the electorate's ranking of domestic problems. After the 1998 elections the main problems were unemployment and the fundamental reform of the tax, pensions, and health care systems. A stronger economy in 2000 was indeed producing more jobs, but the media and many voters were impatient and no quick fix was in sight. The mood was pessimistic. The government continued to lose state elections and the CDU/CSU went up in the polls. (Nonetheless, after 1998 it took one year for the government to hit bottom in the polls as compared to only three months after the 2002 vote.)

The 1999–2000 CDU finance scandal changed the political landscape overnight. It impacted not only Helmut Kohl's status as an esteemed former chancellor, but also brought down the entire CDU. The new chairperson of the party, Angela Merkel, needed several months to reverse the downward trend. In addition, the Union made several tactical mistakes in parliamentary votes on the government's pension reform, which did not help the party's standing in the polls. The Union could not cut into the SPD lead. Without any noteworthy accomplishments of its own, the Schröder government was able to remain ahead of the CDU/CSU. It was not until the middle of 2001 that the tide began to turn in favor of the Union. But then came September 11, which changed the opinion climate once again in favor of the government.

The advantage for the SPD and even more for the chancellor lasted until the end of 2001. Then the public turned once again to the country's major unsolved problem: the poor economy and the resultant steady rise in unemployment. It appeared that the time had come for the opposition and its candidate, Edmund Stoiber. He was considered above all a successful economic problem solver. The CDU saw an opportunity to defeat the government with a campaign focused on the economy. After the much-described "Wolfratshausen Breakfast" at Stoiber's home Angela Merkel withdrew her candidacy, but thereby gained new respect within the party.

With the selection of Stoiber as chancellor candidate in January 2002, the CDU/CSU campaign began. In its first phase the party emphasized its unity and harmony. All campaign plans were to be made by mutual agreement of the two sister parties, CDU and CSU. Unemployment, a negative for the CDU/CSU in 1998, how became its major issue against the Schröder government. Under the SPD and Greens, the CDU/CSU charged, Germany had become the caboose on the European train. As figure 2.1 shows, the CDU/CSU and Stoiber retained their advantage over the government in the area of job creation throughout the campaign.

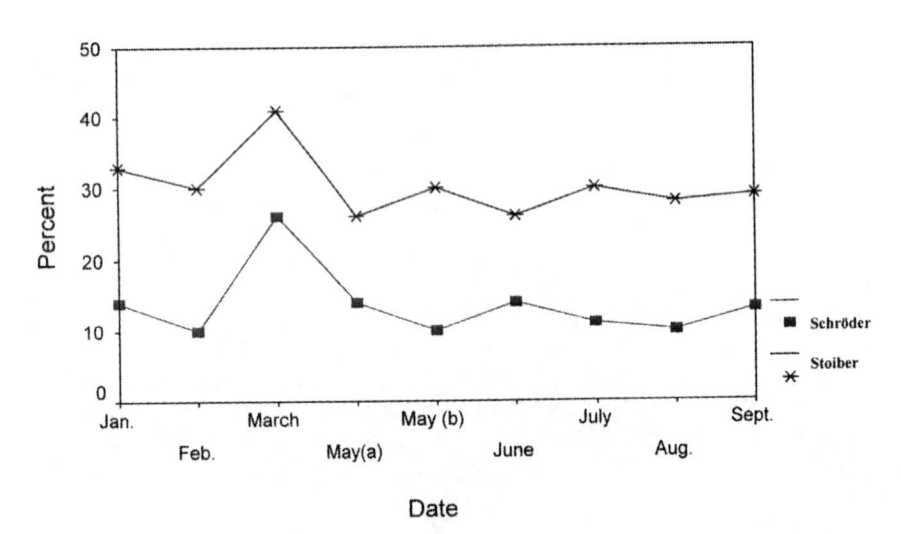

FIGURE 2.1 Best for New Jobs? Schröder vs. Stoiber, 2002

Stoiber at the outset had a positive image in the polls, but in the course of the campaign his new moderate "soft" style caused him to lose ground to Schröder in areas such as "credibility," "decisiveness," and "will to win." But the SPD was unable to portray him as a hard right conservative. Stoiber surprised SPD strategists with an entirely different campaign style. He had, critics charged, "chewed chalk" and been "rinsed soft" by his handlers. But his popularity never approached that of Schröder, and he had major problems in the eastern states, to an extent in the North, and among women. But his popularity deficit vis-à-vis Schröder was more than compensated for by the CDU/CSU's substantial lead over the SPD. Thus, in spite of problems with Stoiber, CDU/CSU strategists for a long time were confident.

This changed dramatically in mid-August with the floods in the East. The floods were a great opportunity for the government and caused the CDU/CSU campaign to lose its rhythm. Stoiber's response to the questions brought forth by the flood were never clear to the voters and his proposed solutions, in contrast to those of the government, never had majority support. The Union's arguments that tax cuts would stimulate economic growth were, in view of Germany's high debt, problematic even before the floods. The costs of the floods left little room for any tax cuts and damaged the Union and Stoiber's credibility in economic questions. Similarly, when the Iraq question emerged as a campaign issue in the final weeks of the campaign the Union could not offer any convincing alternative to the government. The power to act was ceded completely to the government, the opposition appeared speechless and helpless in the final phase of the campaign.

The Small Parties

The flood and Iraq put the small parties in the shadow of the CDU/CSU and SPD. Yet during the 1998–2002 parliament they also had their successes and failures.

The FDP

Opposition after 1998 was a difficult role for the FDP. It had a hard time developing its own profile since it had been content to live off the problems of the CDU/CSU, specifically the finance scandal. But what could a conservative voter do, but vote for the FDP unless he or she wanted to leave the conservative camp entirely? Thus, as long as the finance scandal gripped the Union, gains for the FDP in state elections were almost automatic. In the May 2000 election in North Rhine-Westphalia their performance surprised even the party leadership in that state headed by Jürgen W. Möllemann. But the FDP did not understand the reason for its success (i.e., a weak CDU). Instead, the party believed that it was on the right road to a double-digit result in 2002. Following the state election, they developed the bold concept "18" (i.e., 18 percent of the vote, for the whole country). If successful, the FDP would have become the third major party and the party system would have changed fundamentally. The party's continued strong performance at the April 2002 state election in Saxony-Anhalt (13 percent), led it to greatly over-estimate its national potential. The party did not realize that the reasons for its success were related to the particular problems of the two large parties in this state and could not be generalized to other eastern states, much less the entire country.

After these state elections the FDP came to the conclusion that it could abandon its traditional strategy to campaign as the coalition partner of the CDU/CSU. Instead, the party believed that it did not have to commit itself to the Union before the election. This decision flew in the face of poll results, which clearly found that most of its core electorate wanted the FDP as the CDU/CSU's governing party.

In addition to this erroneous strategy, the party had to deal with a leadership crisis when Jürgen W. Möllemann, the chairman of the largest state organization, made a series of statements critical of Israel and at least one prominent member of Germany's Jewish community. During the campaign most FDP leaders only half-heartedly distanced themselves from Möllemann out of concern that it would hurt the FDP in his state, North Rhine-Westphalia. A few days before the election Möllemann repeated his statements about Israel and German Jews in a pamphlet sent to voters in the state. Following the election, the party leadership as a reason for its poor performance frequently mentioned this Möllemann incident.

The Greens

In state elections between 1998 and 2002 the Greens had mainly losses to report. One reason for this poor performance at the state level was the disappointment of many Green voters that their "born opposition party" had now become part of the ruling establishment in Berlin. This was difficult for many "old" Greens to accept. (The 1998–2002 Green losses in state elections, however, must be seen in the light of pre-1998 Green victories when it took advantage of a divided SPD.)

Although the Greens and SPD cooperated famously during the 2002 campaign and the subsequent coalition negotiations, they had had their share of conflicts following the 1998 victory. First, they disagreed early on about the extent and timing of closing Germany's nuclear power plants. Second, there were disagreements over the ecology or energy tax. Third, there was sharp disagreement in November 2001 over the deployment of German troops to Afghanistan that resulted in several Greens voting against the government. On these occasions Green leader and Foreign Minister Joschka Fischer had to convince the party to ultimately support the Social Democrats.

Ecological modernization and the support for renewable energy sources were less controversial, because these issues had substantial public support. In several social-economic policy areas such as labor market, welfare and unemployment reform the Greens were closer to the Christian Democrats than the Social Democrats.

Party of Democratic Socialism (PDS)

For much of the campaign it appeared that the PDS would play a key role in determining which parties would govern. No one really wanted the PDS as a partner, but if the party had returned to the parliament in full proportional strength, it was expected that neither Red (SPD)-Green, nor Black (CDU)-Yellow (FDP) would have a majority. As a regional party they could miss the 5 percent minimum, but still have a good chance to participate in the proportional pay out, if they won three districts. Thus, the PDS remained a noticeable political factor at least during the campaign. The party lost its most prominent media star, Gregor Gysi, who resigned as the chairman of the parliamentary party and later as Berlin's Senator for the Economy. The role of "peace party" was also lost to the PDS after Chancellor Schröder positioned himself at the head of the movement against the Iraq war. Finally, its role as the tribune of the East was diminished when the floods put Schröder and the national government in the spotlight. Thus, by the end of the campaign the party had no political purpose.

Campaign Issues

As in 1998 the dominant campaign theme was unemployment. Contrary to Chancellor Schröder's promise unemployment increased during his tenure to well over four million: "If we cannot significantly reduce the unemployment level, then we neither deserve to be re-elected, nor will we be re-elected." That was his position in 1998. In addition to unemployment, the general economic situation in 2002 was judged more negatively than in 1998. Indeed, the public's estimates of the economy were at the lowest level since unification. These were ideal conditions for the Christian Democrats, who traditionally have been considered more competent to solve economic problems, to win the election. Why did they fail?

Since early 2001 economic conditions steadily worsened. After September 11 it was clear to all participants that the government's optimistic economic goals would not be met. The Union's chances to remove the government with a campaign focused on the economy appeared excellent. This assumed, however, that no new issue such as war, terrorism or some other catastrophe emerged to deflect voter concerns from the economy.

In early 2002 the Union's advantage over the SPD in economic questions, including unemployment, was over 10 percent. But about 40 percent of the electorate believed that neither party could solve the country's economic problems. This situation was not new, but it showed how dangerous it could be for the Union to limit the campaign to a single issue.

The final election result made it clear that it is not enough to concentrate on one issue area, even if it is the economy, to win an election. And even in these areas the Union's lead became quite small in the final phase of the campaign. In the 1980s through the election of 1994 economic competence was the decisive factor especially for the CDU/CSU. But since 1994 a plurality of voters no longer considers any single major party competent to solve the country's economic problems and only 18 percent see any solution in the short term. Thus, if the relative economic advantage of the union is small and a large number of voters do not think either party is competent, then other issues, although perceived as less important, will play a role in the final vote.

In examining these other campaign issues we find that the evaluation of the parties by the voters was quite different than in the economic issue area. Only in the law-and-order area did the CDU/CSU have a substantial lead over the SPD. In the education issue space it held a very narrow advantage over the government. But in all other areas the SPD in pre-election polls actually held a slight advantage. In comparison to the 1998 competence ratings the SPD retained its higher rating over the CDU in the crime area and dipped slightly on the "security of pensions" question. In 2002 as in 1998 the SPD lagged behind the Union in the voters' judgment of which party could best deal with the growing state debt. None of the two large parties could approach the Greens in the environmental protection space. Indeed, the proportion of voters judging the Greens to be the most competent rose from 38 percent in 1998 to 53 percent in 2002. Finally, when asked which party could best deal with the future, the government in 2002 retained the advantage that it had in 1998. To be sure, it was a small lead but so was its election victory.

Family issues were a strong positive for the Social Democrats. They held a 13-point advantage (43 to 30) over the Christian Democrats throughout the campaign; among young women the lead more than doubled (48 percent to 22 percent). Among no age group did the Union have a larger deficit as in the family area even though the party prided itself on its newly developed family program and its attractive leadership.

The floods and the Iraq question, both unanticipated events, brought important changes in the electoral prospects of the parties. Without question, the chancellor had more opportunity to profit from these developments than his opposition. The government can appeal to those impacted by these events and mobilize them for the election. The government's proposal to pay for flood damages by postponing the next stage of the scheduled tax cut was supported by a majority of the population for the remainder of the campaign. Only a minority endorsed the CDU's vague counter-proposals. Overall, the flood accelerated the opinion swing to the governing parties.

The Iraq war issue also negatively impacted the government. Although generally domestic issues decide German elections, as in other democracies, national security questions can intensify ongoing trends. Security and foreign policy issues offer the government an opportunity to demonstrate decisiveness and a capacity to act. Gerhard Schröder with his first statement opposing any German participation in the Iraq war could count on the support of an overwhelming majority of voters. At the beginning of August 2002, over 80 percent of registered voters were against any German participation. When the question was modified to make German military participation conditional upon a United Nations mandate, there was still a clear majority against military involvement (figure 2.2).

The Iraq issue had three positive effects on the SPD campaign. First, it took the campaign debate away from economic issues. Secondly, Iraq had a mobilizing effect on SPD activists. Third, it gave women, especially those over 60 who had in 1998 contributed greatly to the SPD victory, a rational basis for remaining with the party.

FIGURE 2.2 Public Opinion and the Iraq War

"Should Germany Participate in a War against Iraq?"

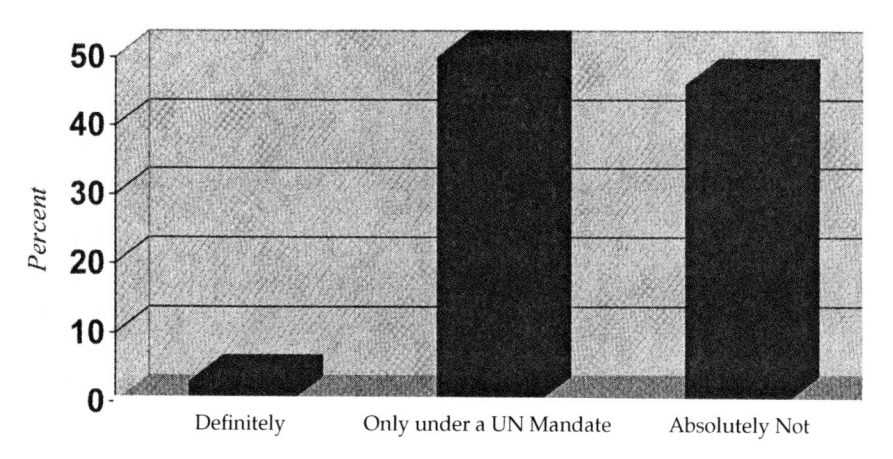

Source: Forschungsgruppe Wahlen, September 2002.

Overall the political themes of the final campaign weeks and their treatment by the chancellor and the government led to an improvement in the SPD's position and strengthened the already present aversion to change. Given the floods and the Iraq issue, it did not require much additional campaigning to win over the late deciders and the undecided for the government.

Candidate Influence

The presentation of all these campaign themes takes place via the candidates, especially those at the top. They have the task of articulation and at least for the government this fell upon the chancellor and the foreign minister. Gerhard Schröder held a clear and widening lead over Stoiber throughout the campaign. The Greens' Joschka Fischer was the country's most popular political figure. Their popularity was the government's major resource throughout the campaign. After the SPD was clearly committed to another coalition with the Greens even joint appearances by the chancellor and foreign minister were possible. But there were problems with this new joint campaign strategy. The attempt by the Greens to encourage SPD voters to split their ballots did not weaken the coalition, but it did hold down the SPD vote total. Our data show that about 30 percent of the second ballot Green vote came from firm SPD supporters. This is the highest proportion of tactical voters we have ever found. They attempted to maximize the impact of their vote. They sought a specific coalition, namely, Red-Green, and they also wanted to prevent another possible coalition, SPD and FDP.

In the direct competition between the chancellor and the Union's candidate many observers, especially in the SPD camp, saw a personalization or Americanization of the campaign. This reached its high point in the oft-cited statement of the chancellor: "me or him." The media was pleased to encourage this personalization. The CDU/CSU had no choice. They had to play this game. At first, it did not seem to damage the Union's campaign because Edmund Stoiber had the same strong backing of this followers that Gerhard Schröder enjoyed among SPD and Green loyalists. But this support from Union voters did not last. In the final weeks of the campaign 11 percent of CDU/CSU voters wanted Schröder as chancellor, 82 percent Stoiber and 7 percent were undecided. Among SPD voters, 98 percent supported Schröder as did 96 percent of Green voters. This type of loyalty can hardly be topped. In the area of personal and political leadership qualities, Schröder also held the advantage (table 2.1).

TABLE 2.1 Chancellor Candidates: Personality

	Schröder	Stoiber	No difference/don't know
Who is …?			
more credible	40%	20%	40%
more sympathetic	63%	17%	20%
more of a winner *(Siegertyp)*	61%	13%	26%

Source: Forschungsgruppe Wahlen, pre-election survey, September 2002.

Only when asked about the ability to create jobs and to solve economic problems did voters prefer Stoiber to the incumbent, and these numbers did not change over the course of the campaign (table 2.2). The large proportion of voters who did not see any difference between the candidates limited Stoiber's lead in economic questions.

TABLE 2.2 Chancellor Candidates: Policy Competence

	Schröder	Stoiber	No difference/don't know
Who can best …?			
solve economic problems	24%	33%	43%
create new jobs	18%	33%	48%
solve future problems	34%	26%	39%
secure German interests	52%	21%	27%
lead the government	42%	22%	36%

Source: Forschungsgruppe Wahlen, pre-election survey, September 2002.

By the end of the campaign, Schröder held a 58 percent to 34 percent advantage over Stoiber. In the East it was even larger, 65 percent to 27 percent. Even in the South, Stoiber's home region, Schröder held a 13 percent lead (52 percent to 39 percent). Among males, the chancellor's lead was 21 percent and among females, 27 percent. With these numbers and the strong campaign emphasis on the chancellor, one must ask why the SPD only achieved a dead heat with the CDU/CSU. Did Stoiber's modest advantage in the economic area compensate for all his other disadvantages, or are the personalities of the candidates not as important as the media and parties believe?

The existing political science research has found that over the last twenty years the personal component of the vote has increased slightly.[2] But this increase has been due largely to the growing number of voters with little or no attachment to the parties. Among voters firmly tied to a party, there has been no significant change. The personality factor is simply not as important as the media or party strategists have speculated.

The measurement of individual variables determining the party vote is difficult and requires a multi-variate analysis with a large number of cases. The responses to the straight-forward question—"What is actually for you more important: the parties who will form the government after the election, or the person who will be chancellor?"—do not contradict the long-term findings of political science. Sixty-four percent of registered voters state that the parties are more important, 27 percent consider the chancellor more important and 8 percent are undecided or did not respond. That still means that Gerhard Schröder and to a lesser extent Joschka Fischer, by virtue of their personal appeal, prevented a defeat for policies attributed for the most part to the parties they led. Enough voters supported the SPD and the Greens because of these two personalities to overcome the negative opinions of their polices and parties.

Conclusion

After the election a number of observers, largely from the losing camp, discussed the possibility that the result was an accident. Ms. Köcher, for example, from the Institut für Demoskopie Allensbach, questioned whether the election result still represented the will of the people, since throughout almost the entire campaign period most voters supported the opposition parties.

One does not do justice to the sovereign in a democracy, the voters, when the election result is treated like a net roller in a tennis match; a bad break that leads to the loss of the game. In this election the will of the people was also evident. The governing parties were return with a margin of almost 600,000 votes. This was not an accidental decision by the voters. On the contrary the vote is a relatively complex decision process, which is determined by social-structural preconditions, the dependency of the individual on his or her environment, fundamental interests, judgments about the past actions of the parties, and also events, which can strengthen or upset these basic orientations.

Without a doubt there were events in this campaign, which were unforeseen, but what separates a good campaign strategy from a bad one is whether the campaign can respond to the unexpected. With the flood issue and the Iraq question the CDU/CSU and its chancellor candidate had either no response or a confusing one. By concentrating on a single issue, unemployment, it found itself trapped when the campaign themes changed dramatically in the final weeks. The CDU/CSU was unable to fulfill the genuine needs of voters to be reassured when they were confronted with problems that were other than economic.

The Union did not take into account an important lesson from past campaigns: the essentially pro-governmental or statist core position of many voters, especially those who were not attached to any party and who decided late in the campaign. This means, as we have seen in almost all governments before 1998, that in the final phase of the campaign the incumbent parties always have a good chance to improve their support levels because it is for many simply more difficult to change than it is to stick with what one knows. Elections take place on an exact, predetermined date, and that is when the only voter decision that counts takes place.

Notes

1. William Drozdiak, "Schröder's Party Faces Tough Fight in Election," *Washington Post*, 3 September 1999, p. A19.
2. See Frank Brettschneider, *Spitzenkandidaten und Wahlerfolg* (Opladen: Westdeutscher Verlag, 2002). See also Christopher J. Anderson and Frank Brettschneider, "The Likable Winner versus the Competent Loser: Candidate Images and the German Election of 2002," *German Politics and Society* 21, no. 1 (Spring 2003): 95–121.

Chapter 3

GERHARD SCHRÖDER AND THE UNLIKELY VICTORY OF THE GERMAN SOCIAL DEMOCRATS

William E. Paterson and James Sloam

Introduction

On 27 September 1998, the sixteen-year premiership of Helmut Kohl was over. The German Social Democrats (SPD) and Green Party had together gained a majority in the Bundestag that became the new government. This was a landmark election in Germany for a number of other reasons. It was the first and—as yet—only complete change of government (both senior and junior coalition partners) since the inception of the Federal Republic. The SPD had overtaken its main rivals, the Christian Democratic CDU/CSU, in terms of the share of the vote for only the second time in its history. These were the first elections, furthermore, for the new Bundestag in the Berlin Republic.[1]

The central issue for the SPD was the reduction of unemployment, and the SPD chancellor candidate, Gerhard Schröder, declared that an SPD government should be judged upon whether it brought the number of unemployed down from above the 4 million mark to under 3.5 million. The SPD had profiled itself on a program of "Work, Innovation and Justice," illustrating the wish to be seen as a modern party of the center (innovation) while continuing to focus on core Social Democratic issues (work and social justice): "innovation" rather than "social dismantling" was the answer to economic success.[2] This two-pronged approach was epitomized by the party leadership headed by the charismatic, pro-business candidate, Schröder (*der Genosse der Bosse*), and the SPD chairman, Oskar Lafontaine, who was much more in touch with the party's grassroots support. These positions were associated with coalition preferences. Schröder was thought to favor a coalition with the Christian Democrats or the Free Democrats, but Lafontaine preferred an alliance with the Greens. The SPD

Notes for this chapter begin on page 55.

in this way aimed to achieve gains among the *Neue Mitte* (new center) of society, while maintaining its standing among rank-and-file supporters. A well-grounded electoral strategy was allied to an advanced system of electoral communications. The new *Kampa* electoral machine offered the party modern media and news management techniques—imported from the Democrats in the United States and New Labour in Britain—far in advance of their opponents.

Four years later the Social Democrats emerged with the narrowest of victories—barely six thousand votes more than their Christian Democrats rivals and a five-seat majority for the Red-Green coalition in the Bundestag. Yet this in itself was a remarkable turnaround from even a month prior to the 2002 poll. Within this context, the chapter will explain the unlikely victory of the German Social Democrats and their revival from such a poor starting point. It will begin by looking at the successes and failures of the SPD as a party of government after the 1998 elections, identifying an initial period of confusion and poor performance (1998–1999), a stage of stabilization and recovery (1999–2001), and a phase characterized by stagnation and major economic downturn (2001–2002). The chapter will continue by looking at the election campaign itself, examining the failure of the party to make any inroads into the Christian Democrat lead at the early stage of campaigning, and the eventual rise of the SPD through the popularity of the chancellor and party chairman, Gerhard Schröder, coupled to fortuitous circumstances that highlighted his leadership qualities. Finally, the results of the 2002 election will be assessed along with the implications for the SPD and the future challenges faced by the party. We will conclude by arguing that the narrow victory of the German Social Democrats was achieved through the combination Gerhard Schröder, good fortune and the failure of the opposition to present the electorate with a more plausible alternative, but that the very nature of the electoral success will result in serious difficulties for the SPD as it governs in its second term.

The SPD in Government

The seeds of the conflict that manifested itself during the first year in office, after October 1998, were already laid during the election campaign. The contrast between the business-friendly Schröder and the more traditional Social Democrat, Lafontaine, while an advantage in terms of electoral strategy, proved increasingly unmanageable once images were interpreted into concrete policy in the reality of government. While Schröder became chancellor of the first Red-Green government, Lafontaine took over the Finance Ministry with extra powers for coordinating European policy. It was the finance minister who appeared to make the running in the first few months, setting out the government's financial policy and pushing for greater economic and social policy coordination at the EU-level. In his uncompromising pursuit of policies that may have been acceptable within the SPD or the Greens, Lafontaine nevertheless alienated too many external actors (e.g., the business world, the media, and the governments of other states). One example was his emphasis on a demand-side EU employment policy, which angered both the business community at home and European partners with more liberal market economies such as the United Kingdom. Without the support of the chancellor, Lafontaine's approach was even more likely to be frustrated, and this ultimately led to his resignation in March 1999 after less than five months in office. This was not before public support for the SPD and the Red-Green government had plummeted in the opinion polls, as illustrated by the loss of the states of Hess and the Saar in 1999.[3]

After the exit of Lafontaine, it looked as if the *Neue Mitte* course backed by the chancellor would take root in the party and the government. Taking up the position of party chairman alongside the chancellorship, Schröder aimed to promote "reformist" policies, which—he reasoned—would command wider support in the country, winning over the political center-ground. Under the influence of Bodo Hombach, minister of state in the chancellor's office, Schröder tried to present himself as a proponent of a more free market style of social democracy similar to Tony Blair's Labour Party. Emphasis was placed on budgetary stability, but also on a welfare state that would act as a "trampoline" rather than a "safety net."[4] This attempt to reorient the party was pursued through the publication of the Blair-Schröder paper, which—amongst other things—stated that "public expenditure as a proportion of national income had more or less reached the limits of acceptability."[5] Although the paper created barely a ripple of excitement in the United Kingdom, it was seen as a radical change in policy direction for the SPD. Whereas the British Labour Party had been able to effect radical policy change in the 1990s, it was very different for the German Social Democrats where the SPD leadership enjoyed little autonomy within the party's federal organizational structure and was not the inheritor of a post-Thatcher, deregulated state. Schröder had underestimated the power of traditionalists in the party and the SPD's traditional allies in the trade unions to resist this reformist agenda.

The paper was published, furthermore, only a matter of days before the elections to the European Parliament, and was thus blamed (rightly or wrongly) for the poor performance of the SPD in those elections. The party scored 32 percent, down only one and one-half percentage points from the previous elections in 1994, but the relative success of the CDU/CSU—up ten points to 48 percent—exaggerated this effect. At this stage, the new finance minister, Hans Eichel, launched an ambitious "savings package" to cut government spending, which aimed to reduce the public deficit to zero by 2006 in marked contrast to the first budget of his predecessor. Rather than a "leftist savings policy" that aimed to make cuts in "non-social democratic" policy areas such as defense, Eichel proposed cuts across the aboard, which would mean some trimming down of the welfare state. The apparent advance of the *Neue Mitte* group of reformers ignited a furious internal debate over the future direction of the party. Major figures on the Left and center-left of the party at the national and Länder levels insisted that any savings package had to go hand in hand with a fairer distribution of wealth in society, and advocated the reintroduction of a "wealth tax" and an increase in inheritance tax. The 'Sommerstreit' (summer quarrel) in the SPD in 1999 contributed to a further slide in the polls. This state of affairs could not continue and Gerhard Schröder resolved to find a compromise solution for the party. This involved both bringing in the major Left-wing figures to government (e.g., Reinhard Klimmt—a close associate of Lafontaine and his successor in the Saarland—as transport minister) and embarking on a programmatic review, which would consider the various policy alternatives. In terms of the party organization Franz Müntefering was appointed to the new post of general secretary. An experienced politician, with an intimate knowledge of the SPD, he would serve to provide better internal cohesion and a more effective link between party and government.

It was made clear that any reforms that would take place would be a compromise between the preferences of the employers and the trade unions in Germany. This compromise was confirmed at the Berlin party conference in December 1999. The Left of the party achieved small gains such as the extension of co-decision in the workplace to companies of fewer than 50 workers, but any expansion of state spending was out of the question given the budgetary constraints of government (any concessions in this area took the form of a more moderate slimming down of the German state). The party tried to please big business with its tax reforms in 2000, reducing the top rate of income tax, corporation tax and abolishing capital gains tax on the sale of cross-shareholdings in German companies.[6] At the same time, the Red-Green government sought to put barriers in the way of hostile takeovers of German firms in the light of the Vodafone takeover of German communications giant Mannesmann in 2000.[7] The major problems faced by the party in its first year in office were largely a result of the fact that its two leaders, Lafontaine and Schröder, were operating within different networks. Schröder, the professional politician and chancellor candidate, was in step with the preferences of the median voter, while Lafontaine (the party chairman) was influenced much more by the party. Schröder nevertheless showed greater flexibility by adjusting his political position to take greater account of the SPD and its core supporters, thereby stabilizing the party after a short period of turmoil. The search for a consensus was epitomized by the Bündnis für Arbeit (Alliance for Jobs), a forum for employers, trade unions, and the government that was supposed to be the centerpiece of Red-Green policy. In an attempt to build a consensus on issues ranging from the labor market to pensions reform, the idea was to agree on wage moderation from the unions in return for job creation from the employers, in an attempt to build a consensus on issues ranging from the labor market to pensions reform. Unfortunately, the entrenched positions of the social partners precluded any major breakthrough in any of these areas.

The stabilization of the SPD and the Red-Green government was accompanied by a perceived improvement in performance. First, the chancellor's reputation as a *Macher* (fixer) was enhanced by a string of political successes. In November 1999, he personally stepped in to organize a financial rescue package for the ailing construction giant, Holzmann. In European and foreign policy, Schröder established a good reputation and high profile in international affairs in the context of the European Union (under the German Presidency of the Council) and in relations with other center-left leaders (e.g., Tony Blair and Bill Clinton). Second, the government succeeded in pushing through changes beyond the realm of economic policy. This included a landmark "citizenship law" in 1999 that finally recognized Germany as a land of immigration and eased the process of naturalization for long-term foreign residents. The government also took German troops into combat situations for the first time since World War II in the context of the war against Kosovo—a remarkable transition for the pacifist Greens and an SPD that had been violently divided on this issue only seven years previously. The economic reforms that were achieved were far less ambitious in their scope. Here, the stabilization and recovery of the SPD and the Red-Green government was achieved at the price of a less radical reform agenda. This was true in the areas of the welfare state and labor market policy, where reform was watered down by institutional compromises that led to outcomes marked by "incremental change" along the lines of Katzenstein's model of semi-sovereignty.[8] This was illustrated by the new pensions agreement, which encouraged citizens to invest in private or semiprivate pensions schemes, but would not—in the end—make this compulsory. Third, the achievements of this period were accompanied by a marked improvement in the country's economic prospects. Economic growth had increased, unemployment had moved below the psychologically important four million mark in 1999 and business confidence had increased significantly. The positive performance of the SPD-led government, in addition, came at time when the opposition Christian Democrats were engulfed by an illegal funding crisis that enveloped former Chancellor Helmut Kohl and his natural successor, Wolfgang Schäuble. The scandal, for a time at least, robbed the CDU of any credibility. These factors all contributed to the success of the SPD in keeping hold of Schleswig-Holstein and the party's heartland of North Rhine-Westphalia in 2000.

The popularity of the party and Chancellor Schröder remained high through 2000 and most of 2001, but support began to wane by late 2001. In part, this was due to the rehabilitation of the Christian Democrats, but it had much more to do with the slowing down of the German and world economy. The SPD, in addition, was rocked by a series of funding scandals itself. While they did not extend to the heart of the federal party machinery as they had with the CDU, instances of illicit fund-raising in the SPD led to the prosecution of party officials in Cologne in the spring of 2002.

In the wake of the global slowdown in 2001 and 2002, the weak levels of economic growth had a strong impact on Germany's export-oriented economy and the economic situation deteriorated. Unemployment was now rising and economic growth was decreasing. This hurt the credibility of the party in terms of its economic competence, and it soon became clear that the government would not be able to fulfill Schröder's promise of bringing unemployment under 3.5 million by the end of the term. The good reputation of Finance Minister Eichel was, furthermore, affected by his inability to achieve his targets for reducing the budgetary deficit, given the poor levels of tax receipts that accompanied weak growth. Within this context, the *ruhige Hand* (steady hand) with which the government wished to steer the economy seemed helpless and the party in government appeared to have no real ideas to meet these problems. Although the Christian Democrats offered no radical reforms of their own to rectify this situation, they naturally profited from the worsening economic climate.

The Election Campaign

All these indicators did not bode well for the SPD in the elections set for 22 September 2002, and—despite the struggle for the leadership of the Christian Democrat electoral challenge—the party trailed its main rivals by a worrying five percentage points by the spring.[9] Political commentators agreed that the "desolate economic situation and the worries connected with it, most motivates voters."[10] According to Emnid surveys, the number of people expecting "an improvement in the economic situation within six months" had fallen from only 20 percent in the spring of 2002 to a paltry 13 percent, which was bad news just five weeks before the elections.[11] The early phase of the election campaign was marked by the launch of the party manifesto at its Berlin conference at the start of June. The program, however, offered a package of ideas almost identical to the 1998 program in the key areas of the economic growth and employment. The party could only praise the JUMP program that had "created 400,000 jobs" and training places for young people and the Job-AQTIV-law (2000) that marked a sustainable "qualifications offensive" in the context of 1.2 million open places and the linkage of people to jobs through the Bundesanstalt für Arbeit.[12] These policies had little credibility given the fact that unemployment had just risen back above the four million mark, well above the target Schröder had set in the 1998 campaign. Low growth had, furthermore, increased public debt, putting Eichel's savings plan in jeopardy as the national deficit edged worryingly close the limit set by the EMU stability criteria.

The big new idea in the "program for government" was the transposition of the German economic model onto the international plane, where the party would ensure that "the German idea and tradition of the social market economy and the welfare state continued" in the European Union.[13] The first main section of the program was devoted to "Germany's role in Europe and the World" (SPD, 2002, pp. 12–18), giving unparalleled prominence to European policy (within the framework of economic globalization) in an election document. The novel approach of the SPD, in prioritizing the EU as the means to achieve their key domestic goals, nevertheless, totally failed to catch on in the media or the electorate. This one innovative message in the manifesto was drowned out by the continuing bad news from the economy. The humiliation of the government, as it narrowly escaped a "blue letter" from the European Union Commission for exceeding the 3 percent deficit threshold, moreover made it hard for the SPD to profile itself on European Union policy. To add to this, the party suffered more scandals that further chipped away at its support. In July 2002, the SPD faced allegations over the use of air miles by its MPs, while the party in government lost Defense Minister Scharping (whose position had been very weak for some time) after inappropriately close relations with a public relations firm were revealed. In desperation, leading members of the party—including General Secretary Müntefering—turned on the press for victimizing the party, but this only backfired as editors even from "friendly" papers united in their criticism of this stance.

As the SPD entered the final, intensive period of campaigning in August, therefore, the CDU/CSU maintained a convincing five-point lead, and almost all analysts and journalists expected a Christian Democrat victory.[14] What made matters worse for the Social Democrats were the low poll ratings of the Green Party and the relatively high scores of the Free Democrats (the likely coalition partners of the Christian Democrats). At this time a CDU/CSU-FDP coalition enjoyed 50 percent in the polls compared to only 42 percent for the Red-Green coalition.[15] The intensive part of the campaign saw the party place less emphasis on an election program that had appeared ineffectual and more on a targeted electoral strategy. The SPD focused on two main groups. First were the voters of eastern Germany. The SPD knew that around 70 percent of floating voters were located in the East, where political identification was significantly lower than in the West. The party could point to the "solidarity pact" agreed to by the Red-Green government, which secured a further 156 billion euros for the regeneration of the eastern states between 2005 and 2019. Schröder therefore devoted a significant chunk of campaign time to trips to the East, including the opening of a 1.5 billion euros microchip factory in Frankfurt (Oder) and a 130 million euros Porsche assembly plant in Leipzig. The second part of the strategy was to bring SPD core voters out to vote and so protect the party's strongholds in the north of Germany—particularly in the most populous state of North Rhine-Westphalia. A key element in this strategy was to concentrate on labor market reform (see below). These tactics were aided by the image of the Christian Democrat chancellor candidate, Edmund Stoiber, who "had fought against the state equalization system,"[16] and whose reputation for liberal economics brought the unions (strongly associated with the party's core support) out strongly in favor of the SPD and the "re-election of Gerhard Schröder."[17]

The SPD attempted to recapture the initiative by focusing on labor market policy. For this purpose, the party latched on to the reform proposals of the government commission led by Peter Hartz, a former director of Volkswagen and close associate of the chancellor. Just a few weeks before the elections, parts of the report were leaked to the media in July and the proposals were embraced by the party on their eventual publication in August. The reforms aimed to cut unemployment levels drastically, something the Red-Green government had conspicuously failed to do when judged by its own targets. A key recommendation made by the commission was for a restructured, more efficient Federal Labor Office that would assume the duties of an "employment agency" rather than simply paying out benefits and providing a quicker link between job seekers and job vacancies. The initial idea had been to create a consensus on labor market reform through this report, but the overtly partisan use of the commission meant that the Christian Democrats, despite sympathetic noises at first, attacked the proposals, as did the business federations. The party furthermore bowed to its traditional allies in the trade unions by watering down the severity of penalties for unemployed people who refused offers of employment.[18] Although the reforms proposed by the commission provided a new raft of proposals in a key policy area just a few weeks before the elections, there is no evidence that the adoption of these ideas gave the electorate any greater confidence in the competence of the party in this field. The proposals made by the commission were of a technical nature, so that the success of the program had to be taken on trust by the electorate, which—given the dissatisfaction with the party's record in government—was not forthcoming. According to Allensbach polls recorded in *Die Welt*: "Only 24 percent expect that the application of this concept will lead to a clear reduction of unemployment in the long-term. Sixty percent do not believe it."[19] The focus on the central Social Democratic issue of unemployment may nevertheless have helped to bring out core supporters for the party. The adoption of many of the report's recommendations also enabled the chancellor to enter the fight with some new ideas to resolve the current malaise and he was judged by the public to have won on labor market reform in subsequent television debates.

In the context of the worsening economic climate, the SPD, however, still wanted to draw the spotlight away from domestic economic issues. After September 11, security issues had become more prominent. While

Chancellor Schröder had pledged to stand shoulder to shoulder with the United States and had been prepared to participate in the "War against Terrorism" in Afghanistan, Germany still retained much of its "civilian power" tradition built up after World War II. The SPD had undergone fierce internal battles over German troops' participation even in United Nations peacekeeping operations in the early 1990s. By 2002, however, the situation had changed drastically. The SPD-led government participated in NATO operations in Kosovo without the sanction of the United Nations or OSCE and committed itself to controversial peacekeeping duties in Macedonia and Afghanistan. This reflected a qualitative change in SPD policy. The 2002 program for government explained that "the return to civil war and genocide in Southeast Europe, right outside our front door, and the terrible events of 11 September 2001 in the U.S. have made us confront our own security policy tasks in the international community. We have taken responsibility in the framework of our powers and helped politically and diplomatically, humanitarianly and also through the deployment of the Bundeswehr."[20] The change in policy was justified in the terms of "an active peace policy.... One may not withdraw from responsibility when genocide or the escalation of violent conflict loom."[21] This multilateral commitment was reflected by German backing for the intervention in Afghanistan where Schröder in November 2001 made the support of the parliamentary party a confidence issue rather than relying upon the CDU/CSU opposition. Those who thought that a rubicon had been crossed had nevertheless underestimated the chancellor's ability to sacrifice strategy to tactics. With what seemed like an impending U.S.-led war in Iraq at the start of August, the chancellor took the unprecedented step of turning to security policy in the midst of an election campaign. Schröder warned against intervention in Iraq and in a speech in Hanover stated unambiguously that German troops would not take part in what he called an "adventure" or contribute financially as the country had done in the Gulf War of the early 1990s even with the backing of a United Nations mandate.[22]

In the past, Germany had always taken particular care not to depart dramatically from the line of its American allies or from the position taken by the United Nations. Thus, this was a major departure for German diplomacy. There can be little doubt, however, that political opportunism was involved, given the timing and high profile style of the pronouncements. In terms of the electorate, only 4 percent supported participation in a possible war with Iraq without United Nations backing, while the figures for participation with a United Nations mandate were more evenly split—45 percent for, 50 percent against.[23] According to an Emnid poll, 80 percent of Germans "do not want a strike against Saddam Hussein."[24] The unequivocal position of the chancellor was designed not only to draw support for his position and attention to his own person in a time of international insecurity, but also as a test for the opposition Christian Democrats. With the strong support for the Atlantic alliance within the CDU/CSU, it was harder for them to offer such a clear-cut position. The leading Atlanticists in the SPD had stepped down, so the opposition to Schröder's position in the upper echelons of the party was very weak.[25] This stand was of great appeal to many of the party's core voters, and also to the voters of the Party of Democratic Socialism in eastern Germany and the Greens. While criticizing what he described as the chancellor's populism and "anti-Americanism," Stoiber could only state that a Christian Democrat government "would support United Nations-led action in Iraq, but was *unlikely* [authors' italics] to supply troops."[26] He therefore seemed indecisive and weak in comparison to the chancellor, who scored especially well on this issue in the television debates with his rival.

In the framework of their position on Iraq, the SPD introduced the idea of a "German Way" independent of the United Nations that sought an "active peace policy." The concept, thus used in reference to foreign policy (indicating a different German approach) nevertheless resonated badly with regard to Germany's past, and was swiftly altered to refer only to the defense of the German socioeconomic model in the context of globalization. Schröder argued: "We want to continue the [economic] renewal of our land, and at the same time make sure that social justice does not fall by the wayside."[27] This was intended to form a central part of the SPD profile in the final weeks of campaigning as part of the attempt to mobilize the party's core supporters. This concept was similar to the idea of trying to promote the German economic model at an international level as advocated by the party program. Rather than concentrating on EU-level and international solutions, however, which had failed to capture the public imagination, the emphasis was shifted to an attack on business leaders who were acting as "the fifth column of the opposition" and taking United States-style pay increases instead of "providing for training places."[28]

The personalization of the campaign around the two chancellor candidates was seen as extremely advantageous to the SPD, because of the continuing popularity of Gerhard Schröder, which far outstripped that of his party and of Edmund Stoiber—50 percent preferred Schröder as chancellor to just 38 percent for Stoiber.[29] While the popularity of the party leaders was not everything—according to polls two-thirds of Germans still thought that the party is more important—the personality of the leader was particularly important to eastern voters according to party analyst Jürgen Bittberger, and Schröder enjoyed more than twice the support of Stoiber in eastern Germany.[30] Despite the personal lead of the chancellor, the Christian Democrats retained their 5 percent lead then moved into the end-phase of the campaign strongly supported by the Free Democrats. The SPD meanwhile began to play more visibly to its main strength, and the chancellor played an increasingly central role in rallies, official functions, advertising literature, and party political broadcasts. These tactics were further aided by the personalization of the campaign by the German media, assisted by the first-ever televised debates between the two main candidates in the history of the Federal Republic—two so-called television duels. Schröder implicitly revealed the SPD strategy: "The task we have is carry over the trust that is placed in the individual to the party, which in the end must be voted for."[31] Particularly in the television format, Schröder was shown to be far more popular. In the second television duel, 49 percent judged Schröder to have "performed better" with only 26 percent seeing Stoiber as the winner, 61 percent saw Schröder as the more "likable" compared to only 19 percent for Stoiber, and 54 percent thought Schröder was "fairer" with a mere 9 percent for Stoiber.[32]

Circumstances certainly offered the chancellor the opportunity to build on his own position and that of his government. The worst floods in a century swept through central and Eastern Europe in mid-August. In Germany, the most damaged areas were in Saxony and other eastern Länder. Schröder emerged with huge credit for his personal response, showing gravity and decisiveness in the face of natural disaster. The chancellor visited the affected sites in eastern Germany, and extra funds were quickly made available for dealing with the consequences of the flood damage. The leaders of the opposition, Stoiber and CDU chairwoman, Angela Merkel, found it hard to find a role for themselves during the crisis, and could only respond to the agenda laid down by the chancellor (e.g., the postponement of tax cuts to pay for the damage). As with the Iraq question, Schröder tried to offer stability in a time of insecurity. While the floods did not improve the ratings of the SPD directly, their leader's handling of the crisis saw his ratings increase (according to Emnid) by 10 percent to 55 percent and Stoiber's fall by 2 percent to 34 percent.[33] The strength of the chancellor in the country appeared to be filtering through to the party for the first time late August, when the polls started to show a narrowing of the Christian Democrat lead so that the major parties were running neck and neck by early September.

The attention devoted to the chancellor and the government at this time and the erosion of the opposition lead in the polls placed enormous pressure on the CDU/CSU and FDP to edge their way back into the spotlight. For the Union, this meant bringing the subject of immigration into the electoral race. Stoiber, flanked by his nominated interior minister, Günther Beckstein, took the line that "Germany cannot handle any more immigrants" and that the government should concentrate on tackling unemployment instead.[34] This position was underlined in television and newspaper interviews given by Stoiber. Beckstein went further, to state that the government's "new law allowing controlled immigration threatens Germany's national identity and would open the way to a multicultural society.... We want to reduce the influx of migrants from outside the European Union to a socially bearable level."[35] The SPD had long expected such words on this issue, however, and SPD interior minister, Otto Schily, could point to the extreme nature of these views by emphasizing that they went against the findings of the Christian Democrat head of the recent immigration commission, Rita Süssmuth, as well as the churches, employers' groups and unions, thus neutralizing this issue for the political centerground.[36] He muted the issue yet further through the offer to compromise on more moderate demands such as laying down the limits to immigration in the preamble of the law. If immigration made an impact, therefore, it was only in mobilizing core supporters on both sides.

With such a close battle between the two large parties, the results of the smaller parties were key. The FDP was rocked by the actions of their maverick deputy chairman, Jürgen Möllemann, who had become embroiled in a row with Germany's Central Jewish Council over his criticism of Israeli policy in the Middle East that labeled Israeli Prime Minister Ariel Sharon a "warmonger" in the summer. FDP honorary chairman, Otto Lambsdorff, complained that there was "no doubt" that Möllemann's attacks on Israel had "damaged the party."[37] The FDP's slide from 9 percent at the start of the campaign to only 7.4 percent in the final standings was crucial given the meagre majority won by the Red-Green coalition. Parallel to the reduction in the FDP score was the increase in support for the Greens. Bolstered by the attention given to environmental issues after the floods, and by the personality of the foreign minister, Joschka Fischer (consistently the most popular politician in Germany), their ratings moved up from 6 percent at the beginning of August to an unexpected 8.4 percent in the election itself to enable the narrowest of majorities for the government. Another critical factor for the SPD was the poor performance of the Party of Democratic Socialism (PDS), the communist successor party, in its home in the East. The resignation of the party's most popular and charismatic leader, Gregor Gysi, from his post as finance senator for the Berlin state government, impacted heavily on the party, leaving its largely left-wing and pacifist voters vulnerable to the advances of the SPD. The problems in the PDS complemented the SPD's eastern strategy as well as the particularly high ratings in the East for Gerhard Schröder—especially after the floods—and his policy on Iraq.

The Outcome

The SPD had entered the final phase of the 2002 campaign with a mountain to climb. The party trailed the CDU/CSU by five points, and the Red-Green coalition trailed a potential Christian Democrat-FDP alliance by eight points. Many deemed this lead to be unassailable given the state of the German economy. While the proportion of Germans that were optimistic and pessimistic about the economy at the time of the 1998 elections was about fifty-fifty, the proportion of pessimists to optimists by the time of the 2002 poll was a staggering fifty to five.[38] The Social Democrats were behind in the key issues of concern to the electorate, reflecting big changes in the judgment of party competence. In 1998, the SPD led the Christian

Democrats on the issue of "creating new jobs" by 42 points to 24, yet support on this issue had turned in favor of the CDU/CSU—29 to 38—by 2002.[39] The Union also enjoyed a five-point lead on the question of the parties' general competence to run the economy.

The SPD's adoption of the Hartz proposals had seen no marked increase in its support, and voters remained skeptical about the success of these measures and of the party's ability to achieve successful labor market reform (see above). The element of good fortune for the party's electoral chances came with the floods in August. In an assessment of the elections, it cannot be ignored that support for the SPD and the chancellor grew in the eastern Länder after this disaster. According to Elisabeth Noelle-Neumann of the Allensbach Institute, the SPD could count on around 26 percent of second votes in the East up until the end of August, but the following three weeks (the aftermath of the floods) saw its support rise by almost 10 percent.[40] The floods were, however, only partially responsible for the turnaround. They helped to reinforce the party's end-strategy, continued through the Iraq issue and the personalization of the campaign with the help of the television duels, to divert attention away from the economic situation in the country and place chancellor Schröder in the limelight. Despite the floods, the candidate duels and the Iraq debate, the dominant concerns remained the state of the economy, unemployment and taxation—all points on which the Union was stronger (see above).[41] Even the well-oiled *Kampa* machine could not claw back the opposition's lead on these issues. This is why the further personalization of the elections in the final stage of the campaign was so important. The polls clearly showed that German voters preferred Gerhard Schröder to Edmund Stoiber as chancellor, so the focus on the chancellor during the floods and the Iraq question as well as in the televised head-to-heads, enhanced the importance of this dimension in the elections. As a consequence of Schröder's superior performance, the gap between the popularity of the two leaders rose from 12 percent to 25 percent between early August and election day, and pollsters agreed that "the large lead of the office holder in the chancellor question (58 percent, Schröder, 34 percent, Stoiber) prevented worse losses for the SPD."[42] Manfred Güllner, head of the polling organization Forsa, emphasized that "many people want Schröder, but not necessarily the SPD. With the Union it is the other way round."[43] Given the narrowness of the eventual winning margin, there can be little doubt that this was a crucial factor in deciding the outcome of the election.

One of the prominent features of the election results was the regional division of the vote between the two main parties. While the SPD lost 2.4 percent overall, they lost 4 percent in the West but gained 4.6 percent in the smaller population of eastern Germany. The CDU/CSU gains of 3.3 percent, on the other hand, related to an increase of 3.8 percent in the West and only 1 percent in the new Länder. The story was even more differentiated than this, however, as the CSU part of the Christian Democrat alliance moved up eleven points in Bavaria (and over two points to 9 percent nationwide), accounting for over 90 percent of CDU/CSU gains.[44] One of the reasons for the Christian Democrats strong showing in the South was, of course, the much closer identification with the minister-president of Bavaria, Edmund Stoiber. Conversely, one of the main reasons for the CDU/CSU inability to win the elections overall, was the CDU's failure to make significant inroads in the North and the East where only one percentage point was gained. These results were echoed by the relative appeal of the two main chancellor candidates in the regions: Schröder enjoyed a 20-point advantage in the West by the time of the elections (56 percent to 36 percent for Stoiber), but a massive 31 point lead in the East (68 percent to 27 percent).[45] Thanks to the implosion of the PDS, the support for Schröder could be more easily translated into real gains at the polls in the new Länder. The SPD had therefore succeeded in its strategy of targeting voters in the North and the East. Despite the ability of the SPD to protect its levels of support on a regional basis, some interesting shifts were observable in votes by social class between 1998 and 2002. While the party lost 5 percent among workers in general, it lost 7 percent in its traditional clientele of unionized manual workers, but actually gained 3 percent of white-collar union members.[46] The strengthening of the party amongst white-collar workers continued the trend from 1998 and may have been a result of the prominence of New Left views in this group—attracted by the chancellor's position on Iraq and frightened by the conservative views of Stoiber on issues such as immigration.

If the Social Democrats suffered only small losses in their political heartlands these could, furthermore, be put down in some part to the use of tactical voting in the elections. The German system allows voters to support both a local candidate and a party. The seats allocated in the Bundestag are taken from the direct mandates topped up from the party list to receive a number proportional to the vote for the party. Due to a nuance of the voting procedure, however, split-ticket voting for a candidate of one party and a second vote for a different party, can make a vote go slightly further. Tactical voting for a Red-Green ticket was rife in the 2002 elections, when an estimated 30 percent of Green voters "identified with the SPD"—more than ever before. Many Social Democrat supporters had therefore used their second vote to support the Greens as a potential coalition partner. The two parties in question actively encouraged this tendency—Gerhard Schröder and Joschka Fischer took the unprecedented step of appearing together at the same pre-election rally at the Brandenburg Gate just a week before the elections. The effectiveness of this coalition strategy was illustrated by the fact that the first vote for the Greens was only 5.6 percent, about three points less than the second vote. This discrepancy was not only the outcome of tactical voting by SPD supporters, but also by Green voters who supported Social Democratic candidates in their first vote. In fact, some Green candidates took the unusual step of encouraging their voters to support SPD candidates where they themselves had no chance of winning. According to Noelle-Neumann, the FDP's refusal to state its preference of coalition partner, on the other hand, hindered any campaign for second votes.[47]

The Red-Green victory was not just about the success of a Red-Green electoral strategy. It was also bound to the failure of the opposition to capitalize on the favorable (for them) economic climate, to convince the electorate that they could solve the country's economic problems. This was in spite of the coup of persuading the successful and well-respected businessman, Lothar Späth, to become the Christian Democrats' nominated minister for economics. While people had slightly more faith in the competence of the CDU/CSU with regard to the key economic issues (as illustrated above), they were pessimistic that either party could solve the country's problems. Added to this was the insecurity created by the floods and the potential conflict in the Middle East. The thing that tipped the scales in favor of the SPD was the far greater belief in Chancellor Schröder than in Edmund Stoiber to navigate the country through this period of insecurity and economic downturn. Another factor that must be brought into the equation is that of the electoral cycle—the fact that closer to the elections the electorate tends to focus less exclusively on the down-points of the government and more on the alternatives that are presented by the opposition. In this vain, the Allensbach pollsters have argued that the answer to the unexpected victory of the SPD "perhaps lies in the unusual situation, that the month-long CDU/CSU lead rested less on the belief that the CDU/CSU will solve the country's problems better than the SPD, than on unhappiness with the policies of the government."[48]

The wafer-thin SPD victory in 2002 inevitably led the party to question how it could improve its performance in government. It is clear that the SPD would not survive an election against stronger opposition in a similar economic climate, and that Schröder will not be able to save the party again if his promises of "renewal" are not met. So, what conclusions have the SPD drawn from the 2002 elections? The party's *Kampa* unit was blamed for presenting the electorate with a party that "lacked substance" yet it was difficult to sing the praises of a party that had clearly not performed well in its self-professed priority areas—creating economic renewal and radically reducing unemployment. In a paper published by a "young" group of SPD members of the Bundestag just after the elections the following case was argued: "We must be clear that the election victory in 2002 was less about broad enthusiasm about the last four years' work of the Red-Green government, and more about the recipes and cultural definition of our opponents.... The SPD fought for the opportunity for further renewal of our country, for modern and pragmatic goals and organizational reconstruction of the party. We want to utilize this opportunity decisively over the coming four years."[49] In an effort to turn around poor economic performance—low growth and high unemployment—the party leadership has sought to set forward a centrist, *Neue Mitte* agenda in three main ways encapsulated in the "Agenda 2010" concept revealed shortly after the elections. The first, set out by Finance Minister Eichel, has been to continue on the path of budgetary consolidation and decreases in direct taxation. The second and more controversial area concerns the implementation of the proposals of the Hartz Commission under the minister for the new Department of Economics and Labor, Wolfgang Clement. Clement, the former SPD minister-president of the party stronghold in North Rhine-Westphalia (Germany's most populous state) was specially appointed to oversee radical labor market reforms. Finally, the government set up a Commission on pensions and healthcare under Professor Bert Rürup, to devise an ambitious agenda to tackle the looming demographic crisis and the spiraling costs of medical care.

The Red-Green coalition will need strict discipline, however, if it is to enforce this broad range of reforms with a minimum of concessions, given its tiny majority in the Bundestag. While the SPD parliamentary group can count on a strong majority in favor of the reforms, it must win over almost all its members to succeed. The situation is more difficult than this, however, as the government will have to make compromises with the opposition parties for reforms to pass through regional chamber, the Bundesrat. The idea of the commissions is to build up a consensus over policy issues, but the SPD must also fight the battle for public opinion if they want to see these reforms implemented. While there was public support for the budgetary course (62 percent in October), the crucial area of labor market reform will need to be addressed given the skepticism with regard to the Hartz proposals—in November only 26 percent though that they would have 'an effective contribution to the reduction of unemployment.'"[50] The portents in the months following the election did not look particularly good, with the strong support for a "wealth tax" from the SPD regional premiers that would offset the long-term aims of the party leadership for tax reductions. The re-elected government nevertheless showed a willingness to move toward a system of tax incentives and (limited) welfare penalties and the chancellor himself has spoken of the need to link opportunity with responsibility, and the swift passage of legislation (as early as January 2003) illustrated a strong sense of purpose.[51] Significant health and social security reforms, which hit at the core of the German *Sozialstaat*, will be more difficult to achieve. With this in mind, the government faces the challenging task of securing agreement for the far-reaching recommendations of the Rürup Commission (e.g., a gradual raising of the official retirement age, the introduction of a "sustainability factor" into pensions increases.

Even with the fading of the elections, the Iraq issue remained a problem area for the government. In the last week of the campaign, Herta Däubler-Gmelin had taken German-United States relations to a postwar low when she compared President Bush to Adolf Hitler in seeking to use foreign policy to divert attention away from domestic difficulties. Däubler-Gmelin was sacked as justice minister, but the episode demonstrated the deep cultural gulf between a government dominated by "68ers" and an American administration dominated by Christian Right ideologies.[52] These differences have intensified. In the run-up to the invasion of Iraq, the federal government aligned itself with France and Russia in impeding the efforts of the United States and Britain to achieve diplomatic support at the United Nations. The cultural gulf between the values of the Schröder government and the Bush administration has exacerbated the wide differences in policy. Already difficult relations were further soured by a series of incautious remarks made by the chancellor during the Lower Saxony state elections, and the normalization of relations seems unlikely before a change of administration in Germany or the United States.

Rising without Trace

The first four years of the Red-Green government was a mixed bag of limited success blighted by major failure in core social democratic policy areas. While the party scored significant victories in the passing of its new citizenship law and the reordering of the taxation system, it was unable to make any major breakthroughs in the central areas of labor market policy, pensions and healthcare. Despite the chancellor's reputation as a *fixer*, he was unable to find a solution to the impasse over economic reform. The obvious parallel is with Helmut Schmidt. Schröder and Schmidt both succeeded visionary chancellors who had neglected domestic reform issues, but Schmidt was—given his economics background and incisive intellect—in a far stronger position to identify and steer through reform priorities. Schröder, by contrast, has been reliant on the borrowed authority of expert reports and commissions.

Similar to the Kohl governments, Schröder found it impossible to push a radical reform agenda past the many veto-players in German society such as big business, the trade unions and even his own party. Any achievements that were made could therefore not be translated into improvements in economic performance, which was consistently deteriorating after 2001. While much of this could be attributed to the slowdown in global trade, the government seemed incapable of providing any concrete ideas for improving the situation in the way that Helmut Schmidt was able to manage so successfully in the equally difficult post-oil shock era of the 1970s. This explained the failure of the SPD to make any real inroads into the CDU/CSU lead during the early months of the election campaign. The situation was made worse by the scandals that followed the party through into the summer of 2002. Events nevertheless conspired to give the chancellor the opportunity to drag his party back into contention for the elections. The floods and the Iraq issue gave Schröder vehicles with which to profile himself in the country to the detriment of his rival, Stoiber.

The need to utilize the continuing popularity of Gerhard Schröder led the SPD to pursue an almost presidential style of campaigning, personalized around the chancellor and party chairman, whose image was the used almost alone in the party in posters, party political broadcasts and television interviews. The state of the German economy and the opportunities presented by the Iraq question also enable an emphasis on foreign policy issues. The chancellor's clear "No" to German participation in the conflict departed from the previous cross-party consensus but correctly anticipated the public mood. These factors were enough to convince the electorate that, given the lack of ideas coming from the CDU/CSU and their lack of sympathy for the Union candidate, the Red-Green government could offer more stability amid insecurity. The emphasis placed on Schröder and on foreign policy nevertheless merely papered over the failure of SPD policy on key domestic economic issues. The worsening economic climate and the lack of a genuine government reform program was the main reason why the Hartz Commission was originally set up. It was also designed to break through the logjam of competing societal interests and establish a consensus on labor market reform, but lost much of its value in this respect, as it was used by the SPD as a partisan campaigning tool.

The chances for a political revival therefore rest on the success of the Agenda 2010 reforms. Although a number of the Hartz proposals were implemented soon after the elections—key changes came with the relaxation of job protection in small enterprises, the introduction of an element of "conditionality" in the payment of unemployment benefits, and the planned mediation of vacancies through "job centers"—significant concessions were made to the unions with the softening of penalties for those not accepting employment. Minister Clement will have to have the support not only of the chancellor, but will have to convince powerful domestic (e.g., trade unions and opposition parties in the Bundesrat) and internal party veto players if further changes are to be achieved. Despite the fact that the barriers to reform seemed less intimidating with the weakening of the key IG Metall union after the debacle of a failed strike in June 2003, real doubts remain about the degree to which the new reforms will reduce unemployment. A second key issue after the election has been the tax burden. The situation was inflamed by the tax cuts that were postponed after the floods, while it has become clear that further increases in social insurance will have to be made. The tax cuts were nevertheless brought forward again soon after the elections, as part of the Agenda 2010 package, to help stimulate economic growth. This was to be paid for by a reduction in government subsidies. Boxed in by the EMU stability criteria, Finance Minister Eichel has continued on his path to a balanced budget. The ability of the government to reduce taxation will be very much contingent upon economic growth and its ability to push through social reforms. The recommendations of the Rürup Commission have included increasing the retirement age from 65 to 67 and the introduction of a "sustainability factor" (decreasing pension levels as a proportion of average earnings)—challenging reforms for a Social Democrat-led government. For these measures to succeed the party and the chancellor must have the determination and political skill to face down severe pressure from the trade unions in particular if the SPD is to do more than merely survive until 2006. It is possible that, as after 1998, the SPD will stage a recovery after a shaky start, but with the unfavorable economic climate this does not look likely.

The SPD's post-election prospects look bleak, and the party has recognized that it needs to start winning on economic policies and economic performance because the heavy reliance on Schröder will not work next time around. The unlikely victory of the Social Democrats appears to have been built on sand, as the once impregnable popularity of the chancellor plunged disastrously after the elections when voters came to focus on domestic economic issues once more. The SPD will nevertheless continue to rely on Schröder, who has already indicated that he intends to run in 2006 (despite earlier statements to the contrary). This is testimony to the chancellor's undimmed ambition and the absence of alternatives. He is the last of the *Enkel* (grandchildren), a group of 68ers (Engholm, Hauff, Lafontaine and Schröder) identified and nurtured by Willy Brandt as future leaders of the SPD. The failure of the party to develop a plausible leadership cadre beyond the 68ers is damaging but predictable.[53] Brandt was in the unusual position of being party chairman though not chancellor. Chancellors or those who aspire to the position have little incentive in identifying their successors. The policy weaknesses of the SPD have begun to be addressed, but there is little to suggest that the crucial long-term issue of future leadership is attracting comparable attention.

Notes

1. Much of the research undertaken for this article was conducted as part of a project funded by the Leverhulme Trust on "Policy Transfer and Programmatic Change in East Central Europe" and carried out at the Institute for German Studies, University of Birmingham (http://www.igs.bham.ac.uk/research/PolicyTransfer.htm). Other publications by the authors for the project include James Sloam, "Responsibility for Europe: The EU Policy of the German Social Democrats," *German Politics* 12, no. 1 (2003); William E. Paterson and James Sloam, "Failing Successfully: European Social Democracy in the 21st Century," in *When Parties Prosper*, ed. Kay Lawson and Peter Merkl (forthcoming, 2004), as well as forthcoming edited volumes with Daniel Hough and Marcin Zaborowski—*Social Democracy in East Central Europe* (2004) and *Learning from the West: Policy Transfer and Programmatic Change in the Communist Successor Parties of East Central Europe* (2005).
2. SPD, *Wahlprogramme*, 1998, p. 6, http://www.spd.de.
3. These defeats were precipitated as much by the huge losses for the Greens as by those of the SPD.
4. Bodo Hombach, *The Politics of the New Center* (Oxford: Blackwell, 2000), p. xxxix.

5. Tony Blair and Gerhard Schröder, *Europe: The Third Way/Die Neue Mitte*, June 1999, http://www.labour.org.uk.
6. The abolition of the capital gains tax challenged a key pillar of the German economic system, as any subsequent decrease in this cross-institutional investment would mark a major shift for the German "stakeholder society" toward an economic system that placed far greater stress on "equity value."
7. The stance taken by German MEPs caused the last-minute defeat of the European Union take-over directive in the European Parliament.
8. Peter Katzenstein, *Policy and Politics in West Germany: The Growth of a Semi-Sovereign State* (Philadelphia: Temple University Press, 1987).
9. Forschungsgruppe Wahlen, *Politbarometer*, May 2002.
10. *Die Welt*, 21 August 2002.
11. Ibid.
12. *Erneuerung und Zusammenhalt, 2002;* SPD, *Wahlprogramme*, 2002, p. 25, http://www.spd.de.
13. SPD, *Wahlprogramme*, 2002, pp. 9, 14.
14. Forschungsgruppe Wahlen, *Politbarometer*, 9 August 2002.
15. Ibid.
16. *Der Spiegel*, 6 August 2002.
17. Klaus Zwickel, *Berliner Zeitung*, 6 September 2002.
18. Unemployment benefit would still be available at up to 67 percent of the unemployed person's previous salary for twelve months, and then 57 percent for a limited period.
19. *Die Welt*, 21 August 2002.
20. SPD, *Wahlprogramme*, 2002, p. 18, http://www.spd.de.
21. Ibid., p. 12.
22. Gerhard Schröder, *Neujahrsansprache 2002/2003 von Bundeskanzler Gerhard Schröder*, 2002, http://www.bundesregierung.de.
23. Forschungsgruppe Wahlen, *Politbarometer*, 13 September 2002.
24. *Die Welt*, 12 September 2002.
25. Foreign policy expert Han-Ulrich Klose was the only figure of note to criticize the chancellor's views.
26. *Financial Times*, 13 September 2002.
27. *Der Spiegel*, 5 August 2002.
28. Gerhard Schröder, interview *Der Spiegel*, 5 August 2002.
29. Forschungsgruppe Wahlen, *Politbarometer*, 9 August 2002.
30. *Der Spiegel*, 8 August 2002.
31. *Die Welt*, 13 August 2002.
32. *Der Spiegel*, 9 September 2002.
33. *Die Welt*, 21 August 2002.
34. Ibid., 13 September 2002.
35. *Financial Times*, 15 September 2002.
36. Der *Spiegel*, 16 September 2002; *Financial Times*, 16 September 2002.
37. *Der Spiegel*, 18 September 2002.
38. Forschungsgruppe Wahlen, *Politbarometer*, 13 September 2002.
39. Ibid., 16 August 2002.
40. *Frankfurter Allgemeine Zeitung*, 25 September 2002, p. 12
41. Dr. Renate Köcher, *Frankfurter Allgemeine Zeitung*, 19 September 2002, p. 5.
42. Forschungsgruppe Wahlen, *Politbarometer*, 8 August 2002 to October 2002, weekly surveys.
43. *Der Spiegel*, 6 September 2002.
44. Economist Intelligence Unit, October 2002, p. 15.
45. Forschungsgruppe Wahlen, *Politbarometer*, October 2002.
46. Ibid.
47. *Frankfurter Allgemeine Zeitung*, 25 September 2002, p. 12.
48. Ibid.

49. Heinz Bartels et al., "Heute für Reformen Kämpfen: Was die gewonnene Bundestagswahl für die nächste sozialdemokratische Generation bedeutet," *Berliner Republik*, September 2002, http://www.b-republik.de.
50. Forschungsgruppe Wahlen, *Politbarometer*, November 2002.
51. Gerhard Schröder, Neujahrsansprache 2002/2003 von Bundeskanzler Gerhard Schröder, 2002, http://www.bundesregierung.de. Wolfgang Clement, "Erstes und Zweites Gesetz für moderne Dienstleistungen am Arbeitsmarkt," November 2002, speech to the Bundesrat in Berlin, http://www.bmwi.de.
52. W. E. Paterson, "Has the Left a Future? A Comparative View of the British Labour Party and the German Social Democratic Party," in *Disillusioned with Party Politics: Party Government in the Past and Present Discussion*, ed. Adolf M. Birke and Magnus Brechtken (London: Saur, 1995), pp. 93–99.
53. The loss of power in the chancellor's home state of Lower Saxony in February 2003, in addition, marked defeat for one of the few promising candidates from the younger generation, Sigmar Gabriel.

Chapter 4

HOLD THE CHAMPAGNE
Edmund Stoiber's CDU/CSU and Bundestagswahl 2002

Clay Clemens

Around eight o'clock on 22 September 2002—election night—Edmund Stoiber greeted cheering supporters at CDU headquarters in Berlin, "The CDU/CSU, the great party of the center, is back.... I won't open champagne yet, but soon." The bottle never got uncorked. Though none could dispute Stoiber's first claim about his Union having made a comeback—indeed, more than one since losing power in 1998—optimism that he might help it regain power after just one term in opposition proved premature. Despite running what seemed a textbook campaign and leading in most polls throughout 2002, the CDU/CSU—with 38.5 percent—was narrowly bested by Chancellor Gerhard Schröder's Social Democrats, who—along with their Green allies—would retain power.

Reactions varied, depending on the point of comparison. From a historical perspective, this was the second worst Union and CDU showing since 1949. From the vantage point of its *worst* result since then—1998—things seemed a bit better, as the party gained 3.3 percent. And viewed from the depths of a crisis in early 2000, when some observers were predicting a complete implosion, 38.5 percent was a miracle. Yet for those basing their assessment on the prospects as 2002 began—when the Union had rallied, overtaken its rival and held a lead—the actual outcome was, again, a bitter disappointment.

A Wild Ride: The CDU/CSU in Opposition, 1998–2000

According to Konrad Adenauer's famous maxim, a new campaign begins as soon as the last one ends—and plainly the Union's 2002 effort started amid its 1998 debacle. After sixteen years in government under Helmut Kohl, the party had offered little new, including no cure for unemployment,

---

Notes for this chapter begin on page 81.

and many voters flocked to Schröder's centrist "new middle." The CDU was wiped out in eastern Germany and even lost longtime western bastions.[1] Yet some Union leaders saw hope for renewal, as their party could now finally shake itself free from Kohl's long hegemony. Though Wolfgang Schäuble was undisputed heir as CDU chair and joint Union caucus chief, the party could now also find younger, more energetic leaders and begin developing a clearer programmatic profile. Selection of Angela Merkel as general secretary seemed a first step: she would be the first woman and first eastern German to serve in that high an office in either major party. Other Union strategists shared this optimism, albeit for different reasons: whether the CDU/CSU renewed itself or not, they simply counted on regaining power by pounding away at the new Red-Green coalition's internal frictions and failures.

Events quickly seemed to vindicate this more cynical cheer. One of Schröder's first major initiatives, dual citizenship for German-born foreign residents, aroused fierce controversy. Roland Koch's CDU in Hesse mounted a petition drive against the plan, which helped it to mobilize voters and thus win a January 1999 Land election.[2] That gave the Union a blocking minority in the Bundesrat. The party then benefited from further Red-Green frictions sparked by SPD chair Oskar Lafontaine's rivalry with Schröder. By mid-year the Union was soaring to new heights in surveys and second-level elections. Despite sensing that they might be rivals for the title of chancellor candidate in the 2002 federal election, Schäuble established an effective working relationship with CSU chair and Bavarian Minister-President Edmund Stoiber: the sister parties presented a strong common front.

Yet plainly these triumphs masked lingering vulnerabilities. As the heir to several strands of center-right thought and interests, the Union had always presented a broad, if vague programmatic image. During Kohl's long tenure, moreover, it had largely been reduced to accepting compromises crafted in his coalition's inner circles. So long as the party was facing what it could depict as a plainly left-wing opposition, such pragmatism's costs could be contained. But how would it deal with Schröder's bid for the center? Merkel launched discussion of the Union's programmatic image, but soon faced fire from conservatives, including in the CSU. And the party's rapid electoral revival in 1999 seemingly further reduced the incentive to continue pursuing such a renewal.

Then disaster struck. Kohl had been settling—albeit grudgingly—into the role of retired senior statesman, emerging mainly to receive laurels for past success, such as on the tenth anniversary of the Berlin Wall opening. But that same week a small news item about his former party treasurer's legal problems presaged revelations that the longtime chair had himself long taken unreported donations and stashed them in a slush fund to reward loyal allies. Pressed by Merkel, Schäuble began distancing the CDU from Kohl, who retaliated by mobilizing loyalists against and even implicating his protégé, which prompted him to quit. Hesse's recently victorious Koch also faced charges in a related scandal.

It seemed the CDU had rallied from its worst defeat ever only to now suffer its worst scandal and crisis ever. As revelations flowed, fierce infighting raged between Kohl loyalists and critics. Members defected and Land leaders distanced themselves from the federal party. For a quarter century it had been held together mainly by Kohl's grip, but now seemed totally devoid of centripetal forces—personal or programmatic. Some analysts predicted that the CDU might collapse, like its Italian sister party a decade earlier, with a radical right-wing rival like Austria's Jörg Haider filling the vacuum.

Instead, propelled by its rapid descent, the roller coaster surged upward. Benefiting from her advocacy of a clean break, Merkel emerged as the CDU's untainted new hope. At impromptu regional conferences to rally the troops, members greeted her with long ovations and cheers of "Angie." Overnight, a party long accustomed to male leaders who rose through the organization now found itself counting on a modest, unassuming, fairly inexperienced young women propelled by media spectacle. In Essen in April 2000, CDU delegates confirmed her selection as chair: buoyed by her image for honesty, she came in with an array of new faces and pledges to accelerate renewal. In the Bundestag, another young media star, Friedrich Merz—only in his second full term—took over Schäuble's post as caucus chief. By late spring, party poll ratings had stabilized and were creeping back upwards.

Yet the coaster still faced some tight curves. Merkel struggled to fend off challenges from Kohl loyalists, party conservatives and even in some cases Merz. She proved unable to preserve a common Union front in dealing with Schröder's summer 2000 tax reform plan; the chancellor lured key CDU minister-presidents into supporting it. Discord also prevailed over how to revive growth—through fiscal stimulus or restraint. Even as unemployment—after a brief dip—began to rise again, Schröder's own ratings remained high, boosting his otherwise shaky Red-Green government. The Union had to restore an image of unity and competence if it was going to exploit his poor economic record, but that would also require rallying behind a leader who could at least threaten a popular incumbent chancellor.

To be sure, the first months of Merkel's chairmanship *did* banish scandal from the headlines and voters' minds—partly through her own image, although ironically also because of attention focused on her woes.[3] Her CDU had *not* crumbled. Yet as 2001 began, Merkel was pressed on all fronts. Conservatives accused her of being too liberal on social policy. They and others faulted her for not adopting a sharper, more confrontational tone with the coalition.[4] Nor did she seem able to preserve a common front on key policies, such as pension reform. She was now backing away from her own effort to promote programmatic renewal, having realized that her heterogeneous party was disinclined to debate let alone agree on general principles. Instead she was restricting her role to analyzing and moderating.[5]

There were also growing charges of amateurishness and incompetence, leveled more often at her newly named CDU general secretary, Laurenz Meyer, but with the chair herself as a secondary target. When party headquarters put out a "wanted poster" with a mock mug shot of Schröder to attack his pension reform plan, top Union officials—including those in Länder facing elections—openly complained that they had not been consulted, and criticized it sharply. They charged that Merkel and Meyer lacked talented assistants at headquarters (while admitting that the problem lay partly in scarce funds). In this case and others, Merz openly distanced himself from Merkel. Communication between the party and parliamentary leadership was at best loose, at worse contentious. The chair also seemed unable to control leaders of various Land branches. Yet again, fear of internal fissures mounted.

While some mainly younger CDU officials from northern or eastern Germany, and many women, generally defended Merkel, they did not constitute a cohesive, sizable or even reliable base. Nor did her home region: Mecklenburg-Vorpommern's CDU was the party's weakest regional branch. She thus seemed to depend ever more heavily on a small, discrete, but closed coterie of mainly female advisors (giving rise to talk of her "girls camp"), but they lacked deep or extensive party networks. Merkel tried to expand her own base by relying on tactics perfected by Kohl: telephone calls—including reputedly even on Sundays—to gauge the party's mood, and breakfast invitations to friends or foes.[6]

Her woes notwithstanding, there was little threat to Merkel as chair: after decades under Kohl, the CDU was unused to regicide, and it had only been a year since Schäuble's traumatic fall. Moreover, few potential rivals really wanted to take over the divided, financially crippled party at this point, and some who did enjoyed only thin support. In any case, the real question was not Merkel remaining party chair but her aspirations to be 2002 Union chancellor candidate. Her first title gave her a presumptive claim to the second, and here too she benefited to some degree from the problems of potential rivals. Merz briefly tried to present himself as a candidate in early 2001, but few were yet impressed by his leadership of the caucus, and critics charged him with often impulsively polarizing opinion to little effect. Emerging from his own scandal in Hesse, Koch once again enjoyed growing respect in the CDU, especially after his party's triumph in March 2001 local elections. But most voters still distrusted him (only 35 percent wished a larger political role for him) and he was deferring any plans for national office until after 2002 and re-election in Hesse.[7] Schäuble too was mounting a comeback, but also still bore the burden of scandal and, in any case, spurned calls to resume a national role.

Averting a Family Feud: The *K-Frage*, 2001

Outside CDU ranks, however, loomed a formidable and immediate rival for the title of 2002 Union chancellor candidate. Stoiber enjoyed an image of diligence, experience, authenticity, seriousness, and, above all, competence—particularly on economic policy—that made for a growing contrast with Merkel. Bavaria's minister-president had shielded his CSU from the damage of Kohl's scandal and had done what he could to prevent his northern sister party's total implosion, earning himself even more respect among Christian Democrats. Unless Stoiber took himself out of contention, his mere availability as a candidate posed yet another challenge to Merkel's leadership.

Yet he would not commit to run, a caution based on experience. As a young official in 1980, Stoiber had managed the campaign of then-party chief Franz Josef Strauß, the first and last Bavarian chosen as joint Union chancellor candidate. It had failed disastrously, in part because CDU officials scornful of the brilliant if bombastic, beer-guzzling right-wing CSU minister-president had all but abandoned him. Two decades later it still remained unclear if they would back a candidate from "south of the Main [river]." To be sure, a less stereotypical Bavarian than Strauß, Stoiber seemed comparatively ascetic, austere, and dry. One wag noted that his reputed arrogance might even appeal to haughty northern Germans. Above all, he had CDU admirers because of his competent stewardship of a prosperous Land. Yet Stoiber had also made a national reputation in the 1990s as a right-wing populist, sharply critical of Kohl's enthusiasm for European Union integration, large federal subsidies to the eastern Länder, and an influx of foreigners into Germany. CDU conservatives loved him for that all the more. On the other hand, it added to doubts that liberals, moderates, and easterners would really rally to him. Stoiber thus wanted clear evidence of national backing for his candidacy before making a bid.

He also wanted to see something else. In retrospect, it was clear that in 1980 the CDU had agreed to have a CSU man atop their joint ticket only because many considered an election against popular SPD incumbent Helmut Schmidt lost from the start. Thus, Stoiber would also hold off until trends seemed to hold out good odds of ousting Schröder's Red-Green coalition. In the meantime, he stressed, there was no need to name a Union candidate until early 2002.

That timetable raised another issue. The Union had never devised an accepted mechanism for formally selecting its joint nominee. For years, the larger CDU had sought a dominant say in any such process, while the smaller CSU insisted on parity—with any choice being made in the joint Bundestag caucus, where it in effect wielded a veto. With Kohl as an incumbent chancellor since 1982, this problem had been moot for two decades. Now it could again prove contentious.

Then there was the coalition question. Right after 1998, one of the Union's main problems was its apparent lack of a partner: the FDP had just barely made the 5 percent threshold and, out of power for the first time in decades, was struggling to survive. But it had rallied, thanks partly to voter defections from the CDU amid Kohl's finance scandal. Still, while some in the FDP endorsed reviving a center-right alliance, others like its dynamic young chair Guido Westerwelle worried about committing too soon to a troubled Union; his rival and deputy Jürgen Möllemann, even urged a deal with the SPD. Though ultimately the Liberals still seemed likely to join the Union, they were thus maintaining an ostentatious independence. Would the conservative Stoiber or a novice such as Merkel be better suited to woo them?

As 2001 began, the CDU chair seemed to have weaker cards. Merkel's ratings and those of her party were in a tailspin. Merely two-thirds of CDU supporters and only half of all voters still approved of her leadership: support remained firm only in the East and among older Germans. Worse, 59 percent voiced no confidence in the CDU's competence to solve key problems.[8] Blame fell on its apparent disunity. Land leaders facing tough re-election bids in March, such as Baden-Württemberg's Erwin Teufel, openly criticized their national leaders, as did the CSU. Key business, senior citizen, farm and church groups—longtime allies—all voiced uneasiness, as did those Liberals inclined toward a center-right alliance.[9] Ironically, the weaker Merkel's CDU appeared, the less likely *Stoiber* seemed to make a run, given his reluctance to take the helm of a floundering ship. But the Land election in March gave her a boost. The CDU lost ground in Rhineland-Palatinate, but not much, and even gained a bit in Baden-Württemberg, salvaging an alliance with the FDP. Union poll ratings nationwide picked up slightly. But if anything, it only complicated the *Kanzlerfrage*: her CDU's showing stabilized Merkel, while also feeding talk of Stoiber making a bid as the Union was now recovering. In any case, neither was ready to disavow interest in the chancellery. In April, they even agreed to resolve the nomination between themselves as party chairs in early 2002. This discrete if not fully democratic plan drew criticism from CDU caucus members, who warned against "privatizing" so vital a decision, and still left open the question of what would happen if, even then, both still wanted the nomination.

As if she needed more headaches that spring, Merkel drew fire for failing to forge a common Union position on coalition plans for pension reform, as Schröder lured some CDU minister-presidents into backing him in the Bundesrat. Then her management of party headquarters came into question when the cash-short party accepted a donation from the very former treasurer whose secret handling of contributions had triggered the finance scandal two years earlier. Merkel and her general secretary, Meyer, faced criticism for needlessly exposing the CDU to fresh accusations. Both her party's ratings and her own slipped yet again: by May, 37 percent of voters thought Stoiber the Union's best candidate, compared to just 23 percent for Merkel. Although the minister-president himself continued to insist that a decision not be made yet, some CSU officials such as former Health Minister Horst Seehofer publicly urged that the Union embrace Stoiber, "the only one that is taken at all seriously as a rival to Schröder." Dismissing notions that some Germans might resist voting for a Bavarian, he added: "We've had popes and emperors." Despite some urging from backers and even critics to insist that CSU officials stop undercutting her authority, Merkel remained cautious about forcing a showdown.[10]

Instead, the CDU chair put out a statement of her basic policy principles just before a mid-year "small" party conference. Supporters embraced it, but those on the right charged that her appeal to the center omitted conservative principles (even the word conservative). Though of the same view, CSU officials quietly allowed CDU allies to make their case for them. And then in mid-June, Berlin's city government—a CDU-led Grand Coalition with the SPD—collapsed amid bankruptcy and scandal. Mayor Eberhard Diepgen resigned and the party needed a new candidate to stand in early elections. While the Berlin CDU wanted a local figure, many federal-level CDU officials felt that the race's national impact required bringing in a more prominent politician. Merkel at first agreed, and sounded out Schäuble. But a vengeful Kohl emerged from exile to publicly rally Berlin's CDU around its young Senate caucus chief. Merkel hedged, and Schäuble took his name out of contention. Angry CDU officials blasted her for abandoning him. Yet again she seemed unable to control her own party.

Merkel planned to spend that summer in a nationwide speaking tour focused on employment, and party officials began drafting a programmatic statement on the "new social market economics." But both traditional CDU trade unionists and Union conservatives—including in the CSU—each for different reasons, warned that this longstanding philosophy did not need "reinventing." Once again the party's right wing complained of being shunted aside, and even talked of somehow getting Koch as a candidate. Merkel then made Union support for plans to deploy peacekeepers in Macedonia conditional upon more military spending, only to be undercut by Schäuble, ex-Defense Minister Volker Rühe, and top caucus defense experts, who accused her of intruding on their turf.

Survey data showed that Union voters had greater confidence in Stoiber generally and on key traits, including—by a two to one margin—economic competence. Likewise polls depicted him as the Union's only real hope against Schröder: he did twice as well as Merkel, albeit still trailing considerably. Surprisingly, he even enjoyed more confidence among easterners.[11] Yet still the Bavarian delayed. Though some CSU Bundestag members were prodding him to run (ever more fearful of losing their seats if Merkel topped the ticket), others shared his concern that CDU discord— on face value, more *her* problem—would make it hard to mount a successful campaign. CSU Landtag deputies worried that a wounded Stoiber would be less able to preserve their majority there in Bavaria's election, set for 2003. Moreover, his wife talked openly of her own resistance to him running. Thus, Bavaria's minister-president continued refusing to announce his candidacy, insisting he was content to remain in Munich. Still, his sharply populist speeches attacking government policy—including on immigration—galvanized the Union faithful, even in northern Germany, more than Merkel's more nuanced pronouncements.

Politics, including the Union's informal "primary," were overshadowed by the events of 11 September 2001. Opposition leaders fell in behind the government in pledging full solidarity with a shattered America. Moreover, Germany's stance at first burnished Schröder and Fischer's credentials as statesman. But the Union could sense limits to SPD and Green support for U.S. military action against terrorism or tough internal security measures, positions more closely associated with the CDU/CSU. Some began to hint that this crisis might break up the government and make a Union-SPD grand coalition necessary.

Yet even September 11 did not alter the German political calendar. In Hamburg city elections later that month, voters turned out the long-governing SPD and its Green ally, which the Union could declare as the onset of a national trend. But the liberal CDU mayoral candidate did poorly, and could govern only with help from a local right-wing, law-and-order party under Ronald Barnabas Schill that garnered almost 20 percent. Merkel insisted that this group benefited from conditions unique to Hamburg and would not begin spreading nationwide at her party's expense. A more confident Stoiber noted that his CSU's hard-line law-and-order stance made a "Schill-party" in conservative Bavaria superfluous and would stem any emergence of such a phenomenon nationally. Indeed, his party began to press its larger sister to take a tougher stance on crime, and even to help block Federal Interior Minister Otto Schily's proposed new immigration rules as too lax. At the CSU's mid-October conference in Nuremberg, Merkel did a poor job as guest speaker, while Stoiber's combative oration galvanized delegates. They threw their man an elaborate sixtieth birthday celebration, depicted him as the only serious rival for Schröder, and some even urged nominating him now rather than waiting.

Just when—and in part because—the CSU appeared triumphant, Merkel seemed to rally, partly by implying that Stoiber supporters were running roughshod over her larger CDU's interests. Even her critics felt they had to defend their party against what seemed to be mounting Bavarian arrogance. When, as expected, Berlin's CDU fell from over 40 percent to below 24 percent in late October city elections, losing thousands of votes to the FDP, dismayed Union leaders did not fault Merkel further, blaming the disaster instead on local problems.[12] Koch's Hesse CDU and the even larger North Rhine-Westphalian branch rallied behind her and rejected calls to advance the date for selecting a candidate. To avert a rift, Stoiber publicly cautioned his CSU to show more solidarity with its sister party.

Yet he still had more momentum. In early November, Schröder had to force Green and SPD critics in line behind his support for military action in Afghanistan by making it an issue of confidence. An early change of coalitions or new elections suddenly seemed possible and, in such a case, Stoiber appeared the most likely Union choice to head a new government. As it was, Schröder clung on, but seemed weaker than ever, making a Union win in 2002 appear more plausible—one of Stoiber's tacit preconditions for running. Moreover, the CDU/CSU caucus had Merz speak in this no-confidence debate, further sign that Merkel enjoyed little support there. Schröder's troubles also increasingly persuaded CSU Land politicians that their chief could in fact lead the Union to victory, allaying concern about a failed campaign backfiring against them in Bavaria. With more now openly urging him to run, Stoiber seemed to begin sensing that further ambiguity about his intentions could slow the bandwagon. Thus, he began to openly express his readiness to run, albeit without pushing for a rapid decision.

A real test would come at the CDU's early December conference in Dresden, where both chairs would speak. In a faintly absurd effort to gauge their support, journalists promised to measure who received longer applause. After an unusually feisty speech by Merkel, delegates clapped boisterously for six minutes and thirty-three seconds. Yet many interpreted this more as a sign of party solidarity with its chief than as a preference for her as candidate (for similar reasons, Meyer—despite criticism—won a huge vote of confirmation as general secretary). The next day, Stoiber got an equally warm reception and applause that lasted almost as long: at six minutes and eighteen seconds, the CDU conference chairman began to gavel proceedings along, as diehard fans of the Bavarian guest booed and kept on clapping. Both thus left Dresden stronger—Merkel because it seemed to bolster her grip as chair and credibility as chancellor candidate (especially among northerners, easterners, and trade unionists); Stoiber because it showed his popularity among CDU members—particularly in Baden-Württemberg, Hesse, Rhineland-Palatinate, and Westphalia (if not the industrial Rhineland).

Indeed, the Union as a whole emerged stronger. In addition to endorsing a joint platform, both leaders had given feisty, yet friendly, speeches. Meyer's stage management had amplified the effect: showing close-ups of delegates on a huge screen behind the podium sparked louder, competitive clapping, which came across on television. So to did the simple decorations—a bold red CDU logo on one side and a national flag on the other. Despite an open competition, the event bespoke unity and patriotism—a contrast to sharp SPD divisions. Indeed, the Stoiber versus Merkel *K-Frage* was becoming a media feeding frenzy, generating a positive dynamic for the Union.[13]

Yet it remained unclear how to pick a winner and who it would be, sewing doubt and rumor. Were Stoiber and Merkel to meet in January as planned without agreeing, there would have to be a caucus vote, with Stoiber likely to win. But that was a worst-case scenario, producing divisiveness and an unhappy loser. Another idea was for Koch and Lower Saxony CDU chief Christian Wulff to sound out opinion in their party as the basis for a recommendation to its executive committee: should they not back Merkel, it would be a sign for her to give in. But nothing ever came of that plan.

Just after New Year 2002 the race heated up. Until now both party chairs had voiced interest in being chancellor without declaring themselves candidates. But Merkel now did so, claiming to be provoked by Stoiber's reminder that, in worst case, the caucus would decide. Not to be outdone, he promptly followed suit. His CSU endorsed him in the winter cold of its Alpine retreat, Bad Kreuth—site of a famous 1976 vote to break up the Union. The very split that most dreaded now seemed possible. Merkel responded by quickly mobilizing her strongest supporters: CDU branches in North Rhine-Westphalia and the East, as well as the labor wing, openly endorsed her candidacy. But this tactic backfired. Warning of a costly power struggle, other CDU leaders such as Koch and Wulff, hitherto publicly neutral, complained that she could not overcome support for Stoiber in the CDU, or in polls. Regional party leaders held long telephone calls with Merkel cautioning against a divisive, futile battle. Even some supporters cautioned that she might put her position as party chair at risk.

Merkel thus ended the drama on her own. Just before a scheduled 11 January meeting of the CDU executive committee in Magdeburg—where rumor now even had it that a challenge to her as chair might take place—she telephoned Stoiber and invited herself to breakfast at his home in the Alpine foothills south of Munich. There she agreed to bow out and fully back his candidacy, reputedly in exchange for his future support. That same afternoon, Merkel flew north to Magdeburg, surprising fellow CDU leaders with news that she had given in and, indeed, that Stoiber would arrive to accept their nomination the next day. Just like that, the Union's *K-Frage* had its answer.

It's the Economy, Stupid: Stoiber's Campaign, Spring 2002

Stoiber quickly faced key decisions on organization, personnel and strategy that would define his entire race. Having given up the top post to their ally, CDU leaders quickly made known that they would not surrender control of the campaign: even conservatives such as Koch felt obliged to caution against CSU predominance, and insisted that the election could not be managed from Bavaria, nor by dual headquarters—one in Berlin, one in Munich. They wanted the CSU chief and his advisors tied into a joint arrangement. Stoiber agreed, ever mindful of frictions that had hurt Strauß's 1980 bid. Somewhat to the surprise of his sister party, he greeted the idea of a joint Berlin-based campaign team. Still wary, CDU leaders nixed the idea of giving him guest privileges in their presidium and were reluctant to let his staffers work at their headquarters itself, worried that the latter would still interfere. But a separate campaign headquarters like the SPD's legendary 1998 *Kampa* was impractical, given that fines imposed for Kohl's party finance infractions had depleted the treasury. Ultimately, it was agreed to run their joint enterprise from the modernistic CDU *Zentrale* near Potsdamer Platz.

Key decisions would be reached by a high-level group dubbed "Team 40+"—a reference to the goal of achieving beyond 40 percent of the vote (some grumbled that it could instead be mistakenly read as the age bracket of most Union voters). This staff would have rough parity, if slightly greater CDU representation: Stoiber and Merkel as party chairs; their two general-secretaries, Meyer and his CSU counterpart Thomas Goppel, who would confer in person several times weekly; Bundestag caucus chief Merz and his Bavarian deputy, Michael Glos; former Health Minister Seehofer from the CSU; two CDU Land leaders, North Rhine-Westphalia's Jürgen Rüttgers and Lower Saxony's Wulff; and finally Schäuble, who was assigned a special role—drafting the Union's action plan for policy initiatives during its first one hundred days in office. Under "Team 40+," the campaign also set up a special advisory group for operational issues made up of Stoiber and Merkel confidantes.[14] To be sure, the CSU chief would also have an informal campaign team in Munich, but it was more his personal staff than that of his party. The campaign would indeed be a joint venture. As Meyer observed, "There will not be the least opportunity to endanger [intra-Union] unity, even partially," and Stoiber's chief of staff confirmed, "No one in the CSU wants to suppress the CDU's identity."[15]

Both parties had a special stake in a final personnel issue: Stoiber's choice of campaign manager. Some Bavarian allies envisioned one of their own, while other early rumors centered on a top official in Koch's Hesse CDU. But the CSU chief picked Michael Spreng, editor of the right-wing tabloid *Bild am Sonntag*—a journalist and media expert, not even a party member, and also known to have once advised no less a personage than Gerhard Schröder. Spreng would bring in eight more staffers, all Union members, and rely on two public relations firms already under contract: McCann-Erickson for the CDU and Serviceplan for the CSU.[16] He would craft television ads, brochures, and posters—all under the eye of Meyer and Goppel—but also advise Stoiber on themes and issues.

One final set of organizational-personnel decisions had to do with Stoiber's selection of a shadow cabinet, labeled his "competence team." He would name top CDU and CSU leaders (again slightly more of the former), hoping to capitalize on their image for greater proficiency in key policy areas. But rather than announce them all at once and too early, he would wait and make an appointment each week in order to generate some suspense—and ideally media attention.

These organizational and personnel decisions—including the label given Stoiber's team of policy advisors—also reflected an overall strategy. Rather than a totally personalized or polarizing campaign, the Union would stress its collective competence and moderation on key policy issues. To be sure, Stoiber himself already enjoyed some popularity among voters, but it had little to with his at best dry, humorless persona, which could not match Schröder's charisma and media presence. Where poll respondents *did* give the Bavarian high marks, it was for more effective management and greater expertise in five key policy areas—labor markets, finance, economics, internal security and education.[17] Trumpeting this reputation could help offset the chancellor's own unassailable popularity ratings. Above all, the campaign would thus stress economic issues, namely, Schröder's unmet pledge to drive unemployment below four million nationwide, failure to accelerate rebuilding of eastern Germany, and violation of fiscal criteria in the European Union stability pact: these latter two themes would ideally help offset reminders that Stoiber had in the 1990s criticized subsidies for the new Länder and plans for the euro. Focusing on the economy had another advantage: voters credited him with competence partly due to his stewardship of prosperous Bavaria, so hyping its blend of tradition with high tech modernity (*Lederhosen und laptops*) could further offset qualms about a conservative southern leader.

To avoid risks of a one-theme campaign, there would be pledges to ensure social equity, where his Land also had a good record. Other themes would include education and family policy. But Stoiber would not stress his hitherto strong support for crucifixes in classrooms or opposition to gay marriage, crowd-pleasing stances in Bavaria. He would even publicly pledge not to reverse Red-Green government legal recognition of the latter. Instead his campaign would call for higher educational standards (again citing his Land's record) and new federal aid payments for those raising children. One tactic that would both enhance Stoiber's personal image and display his commitment to strong families would be frequent appearances on the podium and in posters by his wife Karin, as well as his daughters—relatively rare in German campaigns. Moreover, of course, any reminder of his own 34-year-long marriage would draw an implicit contrast with the chancellor's multiple divorces.

Finally, though Stoiber would not ignore the hot-button issue of immigration, neither would he place it front and center, nor trumpet a hard line. Campaign advisors worried about rhetoric that could alienate CDU liberals and give Schröder's campaign a chance to depict him as a provincial Bavarian right-wing nativist. Attacks on government policy would thus be measured and often tactical, designed mainly to show that law and order-minded Interior Minister Schily lacked broad Red-Green support.

Stoiber would thus stress competence above concepts or conflict, aiming to woo undecided northerners, easterners, women and young voters, including in the CDU and FDP. Aides talked of "expanding his image to the center without losing his conservative profile," adding "If [the SPD] can't trap Stoiber in the right-corner, we'll clean up Schröder's 'new middle.'"[18]

Early polls seemed to hold out promise. Thanks partly to publicity sparked by his race with Merkel, Stoiber had pulled almost even with the chancellor, while his Union—rising from 38 percent support in December 2001 to 44 percent in January 2002—now for the first time led its SPD rival, which fell to 39 percent. While 90 percent of respondents felt that he had his party's full support, only 71 percent said that about Schröder. Stoiber rated higher for competence (84 percent to 75 percent) and ability to achieve his goals (88 percent to 76 percent). Voters also placed him closer to the political center—albeit to the right of his Union, while they saw the chancellor as more moderate than his own SPD.[19]

An added bonus of Stoiber's candidacy became apparent almost immediately. With him atop the ticket, there seemed less chance that hard-line conservative voters would drift away to Schill's new law and order party, dampening its prospects of further success beyond Hamburg. Stoiber confidently dismissed any concern about, or notion of a deal with, this right-wing splinter group.

Stoiber made his first television appearances as a candidate in late January on the popular Sabine Christiansen interview show and ZDF's "What now?" Though on the first he appeared antsy, avoided eye contact, and issued a flood of detail in monotone, on the other he seemed more in command. And on both he avoided controversy, conceding that his administration would be unable to completely rollback Red-Green initiatives on tax reform, phasing out nuclear power, or gay marriage, explaining "A government can not totally reverse all that another government has done."[20]

Stoiber's team officially kicked off his campaign with a well-staged event in Frankfurt's convention center in early February: over 4,000 supporters attended and another 15,000 requests for tickets had to be turned down. All CDU leaders praised his speech for demonstrating great self-confidence and rallying their members to take on the government. None seemed more supportive than Merkel, whose quick embrace off her former rival was surprising even CSU skeptics. A few days later Stoiber opened his eastern front (*Offensive Out*), visiting factories in Brandenburg, the new Land with Germany's worst joblessness, to highlight Schröder's failure on unemployment.

But nothing better reflected Stoiber's strategy than his speech at the annual CSU Ash Wednesday rally in Passau. Strauß—decked out in traditional Bavarian *tract*—had always roused the nearly ten thousand beer-guzzling faithful by ripping into the left for some three hours, with no topic off-limits. Stoiber's two-hour speech did attack Schröder ("For him it's not about substance, for him its all about power"), his cabinet, and their failures on unemployment—but it downplayed hot-button topics such as immigration and family values. Moreover, he wore a suit rather than Alpine garb, and aides further tried to modernize the event with flashy lighting effects.

Still, as spring approached, the initial buzz surrounding Stoiber's nomination was fading. Although he had been picked in large part for having the stature necessary to match a "presidential" incumbent, he still compared unfavorably with Schröder in the media and their periodic parliamentary debates. Pundits pointed out that his policies also now seemed unclear or contradictory. Would he abolish the Green's ecological energy tax, or merely not raise it? Would he rescind or revise the phase-out of nuclear power? Did he agree with colleagues who urged accelerating tax cuts, or fellow Land leaders who worried about losing revenue? Would he liberalize the labor market and cut welfare—and if so, how? Would he trim federal spending, and if so, what of his hard-won subsidies for Bavaria? Would he block the new immigration law despite claiming that it would not play a "central role" in his campaign?[21] Stoiber's apparent lack of clarity or even conviction also soon led other Union leaders to start offering their own interpretations of his intentions, and contradictory forecasts of a CDU/CSU-led government's agenda. To complicate matters, newly released figures for 2001 showed that Bavaria's own economy had slowed: it now ranked only sixth among the sixteen Länder. The huge Munich-based Kirsch media conglomerate, beneficiary of subsidies from his government, faced collapse. Such developments put his main asset—an image for economic competence—at risk.

Partly as a result, by April Stoiber had slid back to ten points behind his SPD rival in surveys and ranked only seventh among leaders whom respondents wished to see play a major role in public life, behind Schröder, Fischer—and even Merkel.[22] And yet, due largely to perceptions of its greater economic competence, his Union was still gaining ground on the SPD, even in the new Länder, and led it by 5 percent nationwide. Thanks as well to the Greens' slide in most polls and the FDP's support of around 8 to 10 percent, voters increasingly seemed to favor a center-right majority.

Germany's last Land-level contest before September seemed to confirm such a trend. Though both sides had been careful to stress the unique conditions in Saxony-Anhalt—a region poor even by eastern standards—the outcome there in late April was stunning. Only one voter in five backed the SPD while a once-moribund CDU soared to 37 percent and the FDP tripled its support, garnering a record 13 percent. A center-right Land government took office. Stoiber called it a boost to his own campaign. For his part, Schröder declared that the SPD campaign would now be even more heavily "personalized" to exploit his own popularity. Making a virtue of necessity, Stoiber did just the opposite. Rather than trying to sustain his waning appeal, he would instead focus more heavily than ever on teamwork.

In early May, the Union unveiled a 70-page joint election manifesto. It pledged to ease tax and pension payment burdens on lower income workers; remove some employee protections that hindered hiring; cut starting and top income tax rate levels more quickly than envisioned by the government; cancel plans for another stage of the ecological energy levy; trim some company taxes, if not on capital gains; reduce the share of pension costs covered by workers and employers as an incentive to hiring; and lower rates and basic benefits for health care by making coverage in more areas optional. To be sure, pundits derided the manifesto's lack of a clear timetable for implementing steps such its "3 times 40" pledge—to bring the federal share of FDP, top tax rates and pension contributions all under 40 percent. Others wondered how these would impact a federal budget already deeply in deficit. Business leaders noted the lack of an overall guiding vision for opening up Germany's market economy. SPD and Green spokesmen derided the manifesto as lacking in social compassion.[23] Nonetheless, the Union program at least filled in some substantive gaps, and underscored the government's own inaction.

Likewise, the first appointees to Stoiber's competence team drew praise. Former Baden-Württemberg Minister-President Lothar Späth, a one-time CDU rising star and manager of a huge privatized firm in the former GDR, was greeted for his lively intellect and originality; he confirmed his reputation as a maverick by quickly distancing himself from the manifesto's tax reform pledge. Popular, moderate Baden-Württemberg Education Minister Annette Schavan won plaudits. The veteran Schäuble would cover foreign policy; former CSU Health Minister Seehofer, health issues; and Merz, finances and taxes, his area of expertise. Bavaria's tough, popular interior minister, Günther Beckstein, had a lock on the portfolio for internal security, including law enforcement and immigration.

Though hardly new faces, these appointees bespoke the competence Stoiber prized, and compared well with Schröder's cabinet which—Fischer and Schily aside—had few stars. While the team's first members were weighted heavily toward the south and west (as a party chair and Stoiber's equal in protocol terms, Merkel opted out), Stoiber would partly fill that gap with Katherina Reiche, a young Thuringian, slated to deal with issues affecting women and families. Few foresaw her selection, or the failure to name an environmental spokesman, as real problems.

In mid-June, the CDU invited Stoiber to its election year conference in Frankfurt, an event well orchestrated by Merkel and Meyer to highlight the manifesto, his competence team and unity. All major party leaders rallied the one thousand delegates behind their CSU ally. With the finance scandal now history, even Kohl gave a major speech, conjuring up the halcyon days of German unification. Stoiber's rousing final address stressed economic issues and education, citing a newly released European Union study that ranked Bavarian students among Europe's best schooled. Delegates gave him and wife Karin rapturous applause. He followed that up with a speech on basic values in Berlin, arguing that obsession with consensus was sapping German political culture of vital energy needed to face the implications of an aging population, slipping educational standards and slumping competitiveness.

When It Rains, It Pours: Stoiber's Campaign, Summer 2002

By June, Stoiber and the Union thus seemed to have found their second wind. Not since January had the campaign appeared so on message: though he still trailed Schröder, surveys continued showing a solid Union lead over its SPD rival: his goal of topping 40 percent seemed easily within reach. Moreover, the Liberals were still at 10 percent (even after Möllemann's effort to win right-wing voters by encouraging anti-Israeli sentiments backfired by evoking charges of anti-Semitism). Although the FDP still avoided an advance coalition deal with Stoiber, the math favored a center-right majority.

Such an edge made it easier to survive some "summer theater." First, Reiche proved a controversial choice for the competence team. Encouraged by Merkel, Stoiber had appointed this young, unwed mother from the East in order to neutralize SPD charges that the Union had an outdated image of the family. But veteran female Bundestag specialists on women's issues resented being passed over for a 28-year-old. Conservatives—echoed by top Catholic clergy—protested that an unwed mother could not speak for a Christian party. Stoiber did not drop Reiche, but narrowed her portfolio to issues affecting women and youth, not families—a concession to the right that earned SPD derision.

A second spat broke out over the campaign's core economic theme. To boost his own flagging image on job creation policy, Schröder had sought proposals for labor market reforms from a commission headed by Volkswagen executive Peter Hartz. As the report's contents began leaking out in late June, Späth quickly greeted its ideas as "revolutionary," while Stoiber was more critical, even labeling some provisions lacking in social compassion. They quickly healed this public rift, but it again cracked the Union's vaunted unity and claims to economic competence, helping Schröder—who embraced the Hartz report gratefully—look a bit more reform-minded.[24]

Both CDU/CSU and FDP poll ratings briefly sagged just enough in June to dampen confidence. But this rough patch seemed to pass quickly. Early July brought grimmer than expected unemployment figures, bad news for the chancellor; new feuding within his government; and revelations about payments from a public relations firm that triggered the resignation of Defense Minister Rudolf Scharping. As Germans headed on vacation, their preference for Schröder over Stoiber narrowed to just seven points in some late month polls.[25]

Stoiber thus sought to remain on message, carrying out a planned summer campaign tour. It started in eastern Germany, with Merkel at his side. Eager to exploit anger there at Schröder's jobs record, and overcome his own image as an *Ossi*-hater, the candidate proposed millions in new public investment. Delays and hecklers dogged him, but the reception was cordial. Then came another swing through traditionally hostile north Germany, and the last of several brief trips to burnish his foreign policy credentials: having visited Moscow, Madrid, Paris, Washington, and London, in early August he flew to Kosovo, reviewed German peacekeeping troops, and was even met by the commander of Russian forces there—which optimistic aides read as proof that the world reckoned with a new chancellor.

Yet two details of his Balkans visit foreshadowed a shift in momentum. Rather than inquire about the Kosovo mission, reporters began pressing him for comment on Schröder's sudden, yet already widely publicized, effort to distance himself from American calls for possible military action against Saddam Hussein's Iraq. Stoiber criticized the chancellor's pledge to take Germany down its own path of noninvolvement regardless of what allies or even the UN Security Council decided on eliminating Baghdad's weapons of mass destruction. He promised instead to seek a joint European response. Yet he remained vague when asked if a Union-led government would back, let alone take part in, armed action: under investment in the Bundeswehr made new overseas missions unfeasible, he said, but quickly added: "I've said nothing about Iraq. The topic is not on the agenda."[26] Stoiber was plainly eager to portray himself as a reliable ally, yet wary of committing himself given rapidly mounting public opposition to what most Germans saw as a risky, unnecessary U.S. war.

But trouble came in pairs. Journalists on his Kosovo visit noted that heavy rains had dampened mounds of dust long plaguing German soldiers there. But such weather patterns were wreaking serious damage back home, in Bavaria and especially eastern Germany, where the Elbe river and its tributaries began to flood. By mid-August, large parts of Saxony-Anhalt and Saxony were under water, including Dresden, where the famous city center had only just been restored. Continual television coverage of the catastrophe soon included pictures of ministers, led by Schröder, visiting victims and pledging aid. The Greens argued that this unstable weather vindicated their call to combat global climate change.

Stoiber continued with his campaign schedule and even a planned vacation on the island of Sylt. Pollsters doubted that Schröder's publicized flood visits would make a big difference, and Allensbach's figures reflected no change in party preference.[27] Yet the chancellor's own ratings among easterners did rise sharply, and his lead over his Union rival nationwide soon stood at 55 percent to 36 percent.[28] In mid-month, with the floods Germany's number one story, Stoiber finally interrupted his holiday, but had already lost vital time in this public relations battle. Critics also noted that his competence team did not even have an environmental policy expert. Then the chancellor trapped him with a proposal to finance federal reconstruction aid for the damaged regions without worsening Germany's deficit (already too deep for European Union standards) by delaying implementation of the next stages of his 2001 tax reduction. By putting his major success on the table, he showed both solidarity with the East and fiscal discipline. Tactically, by making an offer hard to refuse, he boxed in his rival, since Bundesrat—and thus CDU/CSU—approval would be needed for delaying the tax cuts. Union leaders responded in confusion. Some rejected the idea; others said it was worth discussing. Stoiber and Merz called the proposal as it stood unacceptable because, since the cut in corporate rates had already taken effect, business would be exempt from paying its share. Schröder quickly offered to raise rates on big firms as part of a compromise. Stoiber then shifted ground, refusing to block the plan, but calling it bad for the economy, and promising to offer alternative funding for flood reconstruction after the election.

At this key moment in late August came an event that both campaigns had been working toward for several months—the first of two nationwide televised debates. Few worried about Stoiber holding his own on policy, but style was another question, as he could come across as either shrill or—by overcorrecting—monotonous. As it was, the CSU chief feistily charged his often too-smug rival with breaking promises to German voters on tax, labor market and immigration policy. Most instant polls gave the challenger a narrow victory, as his performance had bested expectations.

Yet one group of voters was still unimpressed—easterners. A Leipzig survey indicated that most there had found Schröder more persuasive. Still hoping to counter his negative image in the new Länder, Stoiber made his first visit east since the floods. As usual, left-wing militants tried to disrupt his speech in Leipzig's market square, though their tactics and slogans against the Bundeswehr—which had been sandbagging dikes—backfired. Stoiber praised Schröder's efforts on behalf of flood victims, while reminding listeners that the government had failed them for four years on unemployment.[29]

The candidate also counted on his basic message to help offset the Iraq issue. With polls now showing huge support for Schröder's anti-war stance, especially among easterners, SPD and Green leaders called on Stoiber to unequivocally oppose military action and disavow Union colleagues who actually urged him to back U.S. policy. In reply, he condemned Schröder's bluntness for isolating Berlin, but also began openly distancing himself from Washington as well: there was a consensus in Germany, he insisted, against risky solo action lacking a UN mandate. But above all, the candidate tried refocusing attention on jobs. On 31 August, he and Merkel issued a legislative program for their first days in office that would subordinate everything to fighting unemployment; it included accelerated tax cuts to spur growth. SPD leaders claimed that, given his pledge to fund flood reconstruction and other programs, he could do this only by slashing social programs or deepening Germany's deficit.

As the campaign entered its last three weeks, Union support slid below 40 percent in all major polls, including Allensbach's. Seeing odds of a center-right majority slip too, Liberals grew even warier about committing to the CDU/CSU: Westerwelle cited the option of an SPD-FDP alliance and Möllemann stressed his preference for it. Some angry Union leaders hinted that Stoiber should no longer rule out a Grand Coalition, though few took that threat seriously. The only real hope of reassuring the FDP lay in renewed Union momentum. Yet his frustrated campaign staff seemed at a loss about how to counter Schröder's media dominance, especially on Iraq. Stoiber was making few headlines, and his competence team seemed all but invisible. While some Union leaders argued that the only way to grab attention would be an attack on immigration, Stoiber's focus remained on citing bleak jobless figures, albeit with sharper attacks on the chancellor for lying about economic growth.

His last chance to make these charges stick came with the second televised debate on 9 September. In a sharper confrontation than their first, Stoiber stuck to his theme, a bit too doggedly: he turned to unemployment from the start, even when queried on other topics. Worse, this time, a more serious chancellor better blunted such attacks, citing Bavaria's own rising joblessness. When Stoiber tried putting Schröder on the defensive over Iraq with charges of having damaged German-American relations, his rival turned the tables, pressing him as to whether a Union-led government would support U.S. action—"Ja oder nein?" While insisting that only pressure would get Saddam to disarm, the CSU chief avoided a direct answer. Schröder also capitalized on a minor gaffe: when Stoiber, speaking too rapidly, referred to a bill regulating "36-Mark jobs" (instead of "360 Mark jobs"), his SPD rival cut in to correct him, flustering the CSU policy wonk.

CDU/CSU strategists tried putting the best spin on this performance. But just as Spreng was explaining why his candidate was the winner on points, instant survey graphics began appearing on a giant screen behind him in the press center: in each, a red bar rose higher, indicating that more respondents found the chancellor persuasive. Most journalistic analyses came to the same conclusion. Polls early the following week showed the SPD and CDU/CSU dead even at best, and for the first time in months some even pointed to the possibility of a renewed Red-Green majority. At an executive committee meeting in Berlin, some uneasy CDU leaders such as Koch urged their side to go on the offensive, even implying need for a new strategy that would attack Schröder's government across a wider range of issues. Union leaders and Stoiber's campaign team at CDU headquarters in Berlin retorted that, with just ten days left, such a major shift would lack credibility, but did promise to hit harder on unemployment. Attention-grabbing stickers would be slapped on Union posters throughout eastern Germany highlighting the most recent jobless figures. As a member of the team put it, "If there are a hundred good reasons to vote for the Union, take the best one and say it one hundred times."[30]

To be sure, Stoiber's strategists also continued to accuse Schröder of hyping war fears for domestic political gain, alienating allies with his isolationist course—and lying to voters: once re-elected, they claimed, he would have to bring Germany in line with Washington. Still, despite urging from some CDU foreign policy experts to heat up the rhetoric even further, Stoiber—mindful of polls—remained wary of appearing to back U.S. policy, and warned Washington against going it alone. Moreover, partly in order to counter the war anxiety that was working in Schröder's favor, above all in eastern Germany, the campaign did also finally take a somewhat harder line on immigration, albeit cautiously: it linked this issue—"theme number 1b"—to unemployment. On 15 September Beckstein issued a seven point plan, pledging to revise the government's plan for expanded immigration, arguing that there must first be greater effort to integrate foreigners already in Germany, and a provision that newcomers be let in only if there were jobs for them. Although the Union carefully couched this issue in a largely economic context, SPD leaders accused it of hyping anti-foreigner sentiment out of desperation. Some pollsters calculated that this CDU/CSU stance could tap into public concern about immigration's economic impact, but others warned that government policy had defused this issue, and raising it now just looked like panic. In either case, Union focus on foreign policy and immigration faded slightly even before election day. Iraq's pledge to let in UN inspectors offered hope of defusing war anxiety and reducing the issue's salience, commensurately reducing the campaign's new focus on foreigners. In his last major pre-election press conference on 17 September, Stoiber did not mention immigration at all.

With just hours to go, Union strategists thus hoped that events would defuse the war issue and refocus voter attention on economic concerns. Allensbach even suddenly indicated a very narrow Union lead again, but other surveys showed a dead heat. Much would thus depend on how smaller parties fared. If, as polls had suggested for months, the FDP finished ahead of the Greens, a center-right government was still likely. Stoiber thus publicly proposed such a coalition, with a top post for Westerwelle, but not Möllemann, who had just clashed with leaders of Germany's Jewish community. But clinging to their independence, and uncertain which way to jump, even now the Liberals would not commit—despite warnings that they might lose voters who wanted a center-right alliance.

Stoiber held his final rallies in the Ruhr and on Friday evening, 20 September, addressed some 7,000 ardent supporters at Berlin's Max Schmelling Hall. Trading places, thus underscoring unity within their Union until the end, Merkel rallied 3,000 CSU voters at Munich's Marienplatz. Steady rain dampened spirits, but—as she rose to speak—the sun burst out. Would it prove an omen or a fluke?

Celebration and Recrimination: Assessing the Union Campaign

Very early projections on election night showed Union gains over 1998, and an edge over the SPD. Even before these figures had stabilized or possible coalition majorities could be safely calculated, Stoiber and Merkel greeted cheering supporters in the atrium of CDU headquarters in Berlin. "One thing is clear," the candidate proclaimed with a broad smile, "we have won the election." But as returns trickled in, this lead narrowed and then disappeared altogether. Both major parties ended up with 38.5 percent, though Schröder's SPD eked out a narrow victory thanks to a slim six thousand vote margin. Due to an anomaly in German election law, it clung on as the largest Bundestag caucus by garnering 251 seats to the Union's 248. Moreover, contrary to expectations, the FDP barely exceeded its 1998 vote and won just 47 seats, while Fischer's Greens did better than forecast with 55 seats. Germans who stayed up late finally learned that they had retained their incumbent chancellor and his coalition. Retracting claims of victory, a stoic Stoiber conceded defeat—and forecast that this narrow Red-Green majority of just five Bundestag seats would not last a complete legislative term.

The Union's showing was 3.3 percent better than in 1998, but short of most final poll forecasts. Stoiber had proven a favorite son: in Bavaria, his CSU gained one million votes more than in 1998, winning 60 percent there and all but one directly elected Bundestag seat. Technically, that made it Germany's third largest party after the SPD and CDU (though, of course, the joint Union caucus would continue), eclipsing the Liberals and Greens. Silver linings were harder to find outside Bavaria: there the CDU won only 29 percent, picking up just 100,000 votes. It finished second in every eastern Land except its bastion Saxony, and even there got just 33.6 percent to the SPD's 33.3 percent. Only 39 of 248 CDU Bundestag members would now be from the region. Most Union gains were "floating" voters won back from the SPD, mainly in southern and western Germany (losses that Schröder partly offset by winning away former PDS supporters in the East). The Union did best among men, especially above the age of sixty, as well as suburban and rural voters, although relative to 1998, it made slight gains among workers and even union members. It did poorly among women, above all, those under thirty.[31]

While some leaders accentuated the positive in this outcome, others demanded a frank postmortem. Had the party's strategy really put it in a strong position throughout 2002—just over 40 percent—only to be tripped up by unforeseeable late events and a last-minute voter switch to the SPD?[32] Or had the campaign operated on flawed premises from the outset, leaving it highly vulnerable?

According to one view, the CDU/CSU did as well as could be expected, not merely given its near-death experience of 1999–2000, but given the selection of Stoiber. With a CSU man at the helm, there was one necessary (if not, as it turned out, sufficient) precondition for success: absolute unity between the sister parties. From this perspective, Stoiber's team learned the right lessons from 1980: had he emphasized populist issues such as immigration, major elements of the CDU would have abandoned him, offering the coalition and media chances to exploit intra-Union differences. By instead rallying them all around a central theme—the economy—he achieved unprecedented unity. It did not deliver a knockout blow due mainly to unforeseeable events such as the floods—as well as the FDP's refusal to make a coalition pledge, and its late stage collapse, which cost the center-right a majority.

A more critical view suggested that, while Stoiber was right to focus on the economy rather than polarizing social issues, his team played it *too* cautiously: all they did was to assail the chancellor's failure to cut joblessness rather than presenting a clear alternative. Thus, when Schröder embraced the Hartz Plan for labor market reforms, Union leaders appeared at a loss to respond.

A far more critical verdict (mainly among Bavarians) castigated the campaign as bland and one-dimensional because of undue deference to Merkel's CDU and reliance on outsiders such as Spreng. Such critics complained of counting too much on the economy: had Schröder really *cut* unemployment, they asked, would the Union have called for his re-election? Avoiding themes that had worked so well for their candidate's own CSU, including immigration, and gimmicks such as appointing someone as liberal as Reiche to the competence team, all cost Stoiber: while loyal conservatives plainly did not defect, in this view a sharper national campaign could also have won over some of the roughly 2 percent who backed small radical right-wing parties, and even centrist swing voters, as Koch had done in Hesse in 1999.

An altogether different criticism of the Union campaign suggested that the party simply lacked someone who could counter Schröder's flagrantly personalized, presidential-style campaign. Although two-thirds of German poll respondents continued to insist that party mattered more than candidates, the chancellor's popularity plainly helped stem what might have been even larger SPD losses. He bested Stoiber on measurements of credibility (40 percent to 20 percent), effectiveness (41 percent to 24 percent), and personability (63 percent to 17 percent).[33] Surveys gave no reason to suspect that Merkel or anyone else could have done better.

Plainly, such differences, however hard Union leaders sought to downplay them, would also be reflected in deliberations over post-election strategy and personnel. Despite doubts about the campaign's effectiveness, Stoiber's reputation emerged intact. Especially given the CSU's huge gains, he was undisputed in both of his longstanding posts as party chair and minister-president. Under his leadership, the party faced Bavaria's fall 2003 Land election campaign with confidence, though knowing that this would be his last term intensified backroom maneuvering over a successor. The CSU chief's national role was more uncertain. No one was in a rush to take the title of chancellor candidate from him, and most expected that he would be the Union's designated chief of government were Schröder's fragile coalition indeed to collapse prematurely. Nor were any others inclined to deny him a second bid in the election of 2006, but most considered that by then age alone would dissuade him from running.

Modest CDU gains and her own conspicuous solidarity with Stoiber bolstered Merkel. Whereas a year before her failed bid for the chancellor candidacy even seemed to put her position as party chair at risk, she was now secure. Moreover, with Stoiber's support, she ousted Merz as caucus chief right after the election, and appeared stronger than ever. Yet qualms persisted, as did potential rivals. A bitter Merz remained in the CDU leadership. Moreover, Koch seemed certain to challenge her for the 2006 chancellor candidacy and maybe even as chair, especially after leading his party to a smashing re-election victory in Hesse's February 2003 Land elections. His success with sharper, more confrontational tactics enjoyed broad support in the CDU and Stoiber's CSU as well.

As for strategy, defenders of the 2002 campaign rejected all talk about a need for major change. At most Merkel and others stressed a need to focus more on winning urban voters, among whom Union support was plainly eroding, and easterners in particular. Other, more impatient, especially younger leaders urged the party to make a pitch for disenchanted easterners, including defectors from the struggling PDS, and to finally develop a credible profile on environmental issues. Not surprisingly, conservatives disagreed: to them, Stoiber's success throughout Bavaria indicated the wisdom of stressing traditional party principles and implementing them effectively, rather than catering to minorities. As one CSU leader put it, "Germans outside of Bavaria just can't be that much different."[34]

Similarly, as in 1998, some younger, more liberal national and regional CDU leaders now urged expanding cooperation with the Greens, including Land level coalitions: they saw real areas of agreement with the ecological party—on genetic engineering and Europe, for example—and wanted to avoid further dependence on the fickle FDP. But Merkel downplayed such an option; Koch resisted it—arguing at most for limited cooperation on legislation—and Stoiber's CSU as always gave a firm no.

This debate reflected a broader stasis. Victory would have meant working to support a Stoiber-led government, making any Union leadership or strategy questions moot for four years. Defeat, by contrast, revived the internal stalemate that had prevailed before 2002's election: no one figure in the CDU/CSU had a clear mandate to lead, and each could be blocked by others, while no particular strategy commanded a clear consensus, and anything new or controversial seemed likely to be vetoed. That meant the Union would in all probability once again rely mainly on the Red-Green coalition's own problems to create opportunities and help define its agenda.

And, indeed, within weeks after his narrow victory, Schröder's government was paralyzed by uncertainty over tackling economic reform, while Land election outcomes gave the Union leverage to block almost all major domestic legislation in the Bundesrat. The luck that had deserted Stoiber's campaign in 2002 now seemed to be belatedly catching up with his CDU/CSU. How long that good fortune would last and how well the Union would exploit it remained to be seen. But a party that had briefly glimpsed its own demise and then suffered the narrowest of defeats—both in little more than two years—would by now have presumably learned to take nothing in politics for granted.

Notes

The author wishes to thank Professor Karl-Rudolf Korte for his analysis of the 2002 election and Professor Wolfgang Uwe-Friedrich, whose sponsorship of the German-American Traveling Workshop made possible a number of interviews that helped in the writing of this chapter.

1. Clay Clemens, "The Last Hurrah: Helmut Kohl's CDU/CSU and the 1998 Election," in *Power Shift in Germany: The 1998 Election and the End of the Kohl Era*, ed. David P. Conradt, Gerald R. Kleinfeld, and Christian Søe (Berghahn: New York, 2000), pp. 38–58.
2. Alice Holmes Cooper, "Party-Sponsored Protest and the Movement Society: The CDU/CSU Mobilises against Citizenship Law Reform," *German Politics* 11, no. 2 (August 2002): 88–104.
3. No one questioned her modesty; indeed, to help recruit an inexpensive public relations consultant for the cash-strapped party's upcoming campaign, she allowed headquarters to publish an advertisement with a distinctly unflattering photograph of herself with the slogan "Make more out of your type."
4. Even party youth leaders in the Young Union—normally her allies—faulted her for failing to exploit a series of press reports connecting Green leaders to violent radicals in the 1960s.
5. Konrad Adam, *Die Welt*, 27 January 2001.
6. Those usually mentioned in this connection included her office director Beate Baumann, CDU press spokesperson Eva Christiansen, Baden-Württemberg Minister of Culture Annette Schavan, and young Union chief Hildegard Müller. *Die Welt*, 9 April 2001.
7. A Dimap survey, cited in *Die Welt*, 3 February 2001.
8. Ibid.
9. *Die Welt*, 18 February 2001.
10. *Focus*, 18 June 2001, pp. 50–52.
11. Emnid data, cited in *Die Welt*, 9 July 2001.
12. Voters blamed the CDU's previous leadership for the capital's near-bankruptcy and its candidate, young Frank Steffel, ran an ineffective gaffe-prone campaign, even clumsily praising Munich—in Stoiber's Bavaria—as Germany's best run city. His attacks on their new PDS-backed SPD government as a harbinger of things to come at the federal level did not have much effect.
13. Some compared it to Schröder's 1998 "primary" against Lafontaine, which had helped the SPD.
14. Merkel's representatives included CDU business manager Willi Hausmann and Young Union chief Müller, as well as the party chief from Mecklenburg-Vorpommern, Eckhard Rehberg, and Bundestag caucus business manager Peter Repnik. Its three CSU members

were Goppel's deputy Michael Hoehenberger, Stoiber's chief of staff Erwin Huber, and Bundestag caucus business manager Peter Ramsauer.
15. Erwin Huber, cited in *Die Welt*, 13 January 2002 and 15 January 2002.
16. As one commentator noted, Spreng and these two firms lent yet another transatlantic touch to an already Americanized campaign, with its "headquarters" or "war room" ready to "fight" by showing a capacity for "flexible response" and "first strike." *Die Welt*, 18 January 2002.
17. Emnid survey data, cited in *Die Welt*, 13 January 2002.
18. CDU presidium members, cited in *Die Welt*, 14 January 2002.
19. ZDF Politbarometer data, cited in *Die Welt*, 14 January 2002; Emnid survey, cited in *Die Welt*, 16 January 2002.
20. Cited in *Die Welt*, 27 January 2002.
21. *Economist*, 9 March 2002.
22. *Die Welt*, 18 April 2002; *Economist*, 27 April 2002.
23. *Die Welt*, 7 May 2002.
24. A third gaffe was solely of Stoiber's making. In justifying his decision not to answer Schröder's speech on the economy in parliament, he offhandedly remarked: "People overrate the Bundestag." For a longtime regional leader who rarely spoke in that chamber, it was perhaps a natural response, but SPD foes quickly tried to depict his comments as a sign of contempt for the legislature.
25. Politbarometer data, cited in *Die Welt*, 27 July 2002.
26. Cited in *Die Welt*, 9 August 2002.
27. For Allensbach data during this time, see the compilation of surveys located at *Wahlen, Wahlrecht und ahlsysteme*, http://www.wahlrecht.de/umfragen.
28. Politbarometer data, cited on Phoenix Online, *Ereignisse*, 25 August 2002.
29. *Die Welt*, 28 August 2002.
30. Cited in *Die Welt*, 11 September 2002.
31. Statistisches Bundesamt, Pressegespräch, "Wahl zum 15. Deutschen Bundestag: Ergebnisse aus der Represäntatives Wahlstatistik," 22 January 2003, http://www.destatis.de.
32. The Allensbach Institute's survey director even suggested that suddenly pessimistic poll data by rival organizations had demoralized many CDU/CSU voters in later summer. Others charged that Allensbach's own rosy figures, even after the floods, encouraged Union complacency.
33. Forschungsgruppe Wahlen data.
34. Thomas Goppel, cited in *Die Welt*, 10 January 2003.

Chapter 5

SAVING SCHRÖDER
The Greens in 2002

E. Gene Frankland

With the final wave of polls projecting their support at 7–8 percent, the Greens[1] capped their Bundestag campaign on 20 September with a rally headlining Joschka Fischer in Berlin's Tempodrom. There six months earlier the party had replaced its 22-year-old radical *Bundesprogramm* with a new reformist *Grundsatzprogramm* outlining its agenda through 2020. With only two days left, top leaders as well as grassroots members exuded confidence that the Greens would be returned to the Bundestag with more representation, but one could detect nervousness about whether the majority with the Social Democrats (SPD) would re-emerge. On 22 September, initial media projections of 9–9.4 percent for the Greens were greeted euphorically by supporters. However, the evening turned out to be a long and anxious one as the Greens' percentage slipped and the SPD's electoral share fell short of 39 percent. Not until after midnight were analysts sure that there would be a Red-Green majority in the new Bundestag. The editorial cartoon in *Der Tagesspiegel* (23 September 2002, p. 10) depicted a sweating Joschka Fischer carrying a rumpled Gerhard Schröder over the finish line with Schröder remarking: "I knew that we could do it!" At the morning-after press conference, Fischer stated that the Greens had achieved their three goals: (1) returning to the Bundestag as its third strongest party; (2) winning more than 8 percent of the votes; and (3) contributing to a Red-Green majority that would continue Germany's ecological and social renewal. The polling group, Infratest dimap, concluded in its election report: "The Greens are the only clear winner of the election. In percentage and politics they have won."[2]

The Greens' success on 22 September contrasted with their discouragement in February 2002 after Forschungsgruppe Wahlen put their national support at 4 percent (the first time since 1990 that they had fallen under the 5 percent threshold for representation).[3] In recent years, many journalists

---

Notes for this chapter begin on page 105.

had portrayed the Greens as struggling with an "identity crisis" that could push them over the edge in the 2002 Bundestag election. For example, Peter Finn observed, "From once radical roots the party is losing its way in the mire of the middle ground."[4] Germany's leading academic specialist on the Greens, Joachim Raschke saw the roots of the crisis in their organizational lack of a "strategic center" and predicted that they would fade away in 2002 or a couple of years later.[5] In Forschungsgruppe Wahlen's next survey, the Greens' support returned to the 5–6 percent level, where (except for February 2000) it had been hovering since 1999. In April 2002, the Greens suffered their nineteenth straight electoral setback since March 1998: they won 2 percent of the votes (-1.3 compared to 1998) in Saxony-Anhalt.

How does one explain the Greens' 8.6 percent—their best ever in a Bundestag election—on 22 September? In the morning-after press conference, co-chair Claudia Roth attributed success to an "extraordinarily professionalized and united party" that mobilized the *Basis* with its reform program. Tilman Gerwien, an editor of *Stern*, and many others chose to credit Fischer's "One-Man-Show" in the final weeks with saving the Red-Green project.[6] Downplaying the Fischer factor, Raschke stressed the optimal conditions for the Greens: the catastrophic floods in southeastern Germany (which lent credibility to ecological concerns), the Bush administration's Iraq policy (which raised war anxieties), the Stoiber candidacy (which activated Red-Green voters), and Gregor Gysi's withdrawal from the PDS leadership (which eroded that party's appeal).[7] Dieter Roth concluded that events in the final weeks allowed the SPD and the Greens, and in particular their top candidates Schröder and Fischer, to demonstrate thematic competence to undecided voters while the opposition was failing to provide a credible alternative.[8] Richard Stöss and Gero Neugebauer concluded that the Greens made no strategic errors during the campaign while the SPD, CDU/CSU, FDP, and PDS blundered to varying degrees.[9] There was no "accidental" Red-Green majority on 22 September, rather the Greens and the SPD won because they had made fewer combined errors than the opposition.[10] The contrast between the Greens' for-the-textbooks 2002 campaign and their nearly botched 1998 campaign[11] of tactical errors, factional quarrels, and uncoordinated leadership could hardly be more vivid. Despite conventional wisdom about the party's decline and possible extinction, the Greens were overcoming radical opposition reflexes and becoming a more professional-electoral party with a reformist identity *within* the system of media-democracy.

The thesis of this chapter is that this painful learning process made possible the Greens' victory in the 2002 Bundestag election. When the flood catastrophe struck and war clouds loomed over Iraq, the Greens were prepared in leadership, organization, and program to seize the electoral opportunity. Whereas the first Red-Green government arrived in 1998 as a mathematical surprise, the second was sought by both parties and ratified, albeit narrowly, by the electorate. Within a couple of months, ominous economic statistics had undermined the SPD in the polls; however, the Greens' support remained at the 8–9 percent level. Subsequent months have made clear the obstacles confronting a Red-Green "structural majority."[12]

We begin by reviewing the Greens' experiences during 1998–2001. The pre-campaign phase (January–May 2002) during which they decided their electoral strategy, nominated candidates, and approved programs is then described. The next section outlines the course of the Greens' campaign during the following four months. Then the election results on 22 September and the subsequent Red-Green negotiations and Green party conferences are discussed. The conclusion considers some implications of recent developments.

The Greens during 1998–2001

During the October 1998 coalition negotiations, the Greens made many concessions to the SPD, but the final agreement retained enough Green fingerprints to be endorsed by an overwhelming majority at the party's Bonn conference. For the first time in German history there would be Green federal cabinet ministers. A Red-Green government, bringing together a large, top-down party of modernizers and traditionalists that had been out of power nationally for sixteen years and a small, bottom-up party of *Realos* (realists) and *Linken* (leftists) that had not shared power nationally was likely to get off to a rough start. Getting underway was complicated by the intra-SPD struggle over economic policy between Chancellor Schröder and Finance Minister (and party chair) Oskar Lafontaine until his resignation in February 1999. While Green Foreign Minister Joschka Fischer was reassuring NATO allies of the continuity of German foreign policy and Green Health Minister Andrea Fischer was trying to contain medical costs without compromising health quality, Green Environment Minister Jürgen Trittin was taking a confrontational approach to exiting nuclear power that clashed with Schröder's consensual one; the latter soon postponed the new atomic law. Environmentalists were also upset by the feebleness of the coalition's ecological tax reform (which began on 1 April 1999). In face of critical media assessments of the government's first 100 days, the Greens' leaders played up the beginnings of reform in ecological taxes and nuclear energy, and the new citizenship law passed by the Bundestag.

The Hesse CDU waged a populist campaign urging voters to send a message against the new citizenship law (which would have permitted dual passports for ethnic minorities) by voting out the Red-Green government in Wiesbaden. A last-minute swing produced a CDU-FDP majority in the Landtag election in February 1999. The Hesse Greens saw their electoral share drop to 7.2 percent (-4.0), their lowest since 1983! Also compared to their 1998 Bundestag results in Hesse, the Greens lost votes, which hardly suggested grassroots enthusiasm about the federal party's ecological and social initiatives. The outcome changed the balance of power in the Bundesrat, which later passed a watered down version of the citizenship law only because of FDP votes.

NATO's air war against Serbia posed a more immediate threat to the Red-Green government than did the dispute over nuclear power. With diplomacy stymied, Foreign Minister Fischer, *Realos*, and *Regierungslinken* (governmental leftists) supported air strikes to halt violence against Kosovo's Albanians. However, anti-war opposition grew from the grassroots, forcing in May 1999 an extraordinary Green party conference in Bielefeld. A compromise motion calling for a bombing pause (which did not undermine Fischer) was backed by a majority of delegates. As a result of the perceived betrayal of a core principle (nonviolence), the Hamburg Greens' parliamentary group suffered a split (though it did not jeopardize the city-state's Red-Green majority), a few local parties suspended their campaigning in the European Parliament election, and a couple of hundred leftists and anti-war activists resigned from the party. The federal coalition had survived because most delegates recognized that the war would go on without the Greens and that the party could better influence peacemaking from within government.

In June 1999, the Green Party suffered major setbacks in the Bremen election (winning 9.0 percent, -4.1) and the European Parliament election (winning 6.4 percent, -3.7). Green spokespersons seemed relieved that losses had not been worse in view of recent negative news coverage. When autumn arrived, many Green supporters were still turned off. In September, the Saarland Greens won 3.2 percent (-2.3) and lost their Landtag group, the *first* time that this had ever happened in a western state. In the eastern states of Brandenburg, Thuringia, and Saxony, the Greens were reduced to fringe party status by polling 1.9 percent (-1.0), 1.9 percent (-2.6), and 2.6 percent (-1.5) in their respective elections. In October, the Greens lost more ground, winning only 9.9 percent (-3.3) in their Berlin stronghold.

The year 2000 provided grounds for guarded optimism. Schleswig-Holstein Greens won 6.2 percent (-1.9) of the votes in February. Tactical SPD voters shored up the Greens so that the Red-Green government in Kiel would survive.[13] In the May 2000 North Rhine-Westphalia elections, the Greens won 7.1 percent (-2.9). Although SPD Minister-President Wolfgang Clement had often clashed with the Greens, and the FDP was eager to return to government, Clement chose to renew the coalition with the Greens—after certain responsibilities were shifted away from their environment minister. Despite the vocal opposition of a number of local parties, the new coalition agreement was approved by the NRW Greens' party conference. At the federal level, the Greens and the SPD quarreled over Bundeswehr reform and arms exports to Turkey. However, the second stage of ecological tax reform was begun, and the government and the electrical power industry reached a consensus on closing nuclear power plants after an operating life of thirty-two years. The Greens favored a shorter time period than Schröder, but compromised and called it a victory (a view not shared by environmental groups that saw loopholes in the fine print). Fischer maintained his place in the polls at or near the top in popularity among German politicians. Wolfgang Rüdig observed, "By late 2000, the internal decision-making processes within the government had been stabilized...Most key elements of the Coalition Agreement had been dealt with one way or another."[14]

In January 2001, the crisis caused by the BSE (mad cow disease) led to the resignations of Green Health Minister Andrea Fischer and the SPD's agriculture minister. Schröder appointed the Greens' Renate Künast as head of a realigned Ministry of Consumer Protection, Food, and Agriculture and the SPD's Ulla Schmidt as head of the Health Ministry. The cabinet reshuffle was greeted by the Greens as an unexpected opportunity to advance their reform agenda on consumer and environmental protection. For the next four months, Künast was to rank third in popularity among top politicians.

In the March 2001 election, Baden-Württemberg Greens suffered a bitter setback by winning only 7.7 percent of the votes (-4.4). The ongoing national controversy over the Green-led Environment Ministry's program to transport nuclear wastes to the Gorleben storage site dampened grassroots support, but polls also indicated that economic policy (where the Greens tend not to be seen as competent) overshadowed all others in the southwestern state.[15] Fortunately for the party, losses were less in Rhineland-Palatinate, where the Greens won 5.2 percent (-1.7); otherwise, they would have lost their Landtag group.

In June 2001, Berlin's grand coalition collapsed. The SPD and the Greens formed an interim minority government (tolerated by the PDS) to govern the city-state until early elections. Hamburg's September election turned out to be a disaster for the Green-Alternative List, which won 8.5 percent of the votes (-5.4). Hamburg's Red-Green government was replaced by a coalition formed by the CDU, the FDP, and the law-and-order Schill-Partei. In October, the Berlin Greens won 9.1 percent of the votes, 0.8 less than in 1999. There was no majority of seats for the SPD and the Greens. After exploring a possible SPD-FDP-Greens coalition and rejecting it due to policy gaps with the FDP, the Greens went back into opposition. The Berlin SPD then negotiated a Red-Red coalition with the PDS.

In the aftermath of the September 11 terrorist attacks in New York and Washington, D.C., Schröder expressed, "Germany's unreserved solidarity with the United States."[16] When the United States' request for German troops for its war on terrorism came, Schröder feared a repeat of the August embarrassment of having to rely on opposition votes (because several Green and SPD Bundestag members had balked) to get approval for the participation of German troops in NATO's Macedonian peacekeeping mission. Fischer backed the chancellor's plan to deploy up to 3,900 troops in

Afghanistan and elsewhere, which would be the first combat deployment of German forces outside of Europe since World War II. To settle the matter, Schröder tied the policy vote to a vote of confidence in his government. He prevailed with 336 votes (two votes to spare) in the Bundestag. Four of the eight anti-war Greens had decided to vote with the chancellor, rather than bring down the government.

At the Greens' Rostock conference in November 2001, this issue was the subject of lively debate. Fischer implied that he would resign as foreign minister if his party failed to support German military participation in the war on terrorism. The outcome was a surprise endorsement with more than three-fourths of the delegates voting in favor of the cabinet's plan. Hans-Christian Ströbele, the leading Green leftist who had voted "no" in the Bundestag, urged the anti-war minority to stay in the party in order to continue the struggle. In the conference's aftermath, the press reported a stream of membership resignations, but a tidal wave never materialized.

In late 1998, the party had 51,812 members; three years later there were around 44,000, about 15 percent less.[17] (During the same period, the SPD's membership had declined 7.4 percent.)[18] The Greens lost members as well as voters because they were no longer able to tap anti-incumbent (and anti-establishment) protest as they had done as an opposition party. Many supporters' expectations for change were unrealistically high, given the imbalance of power between the coalition's junior and senior partners. While in three years a sizable number of leftist, pacifist, and anti-nuclear activists had left the party because of its perceived betrayal of core principles, others had become more pragmatic and stayed. For example, Angelika Beer, a leading anti-militarist, supported Fischer's stance favoring German military interventions in Kosovo and Afghanistan. Furthermore, new members partially offset the loss of old members. The consensus among Greens interviewed in 2001 by the author was that about 20 percent of the party's members had joined since 1998. Christiane Schlötzer reported that in some western states over half of party members had joined since 1992.[19] The general view of interviewees agreed with hers that the new members tend to be more interested in concrete changes and less in theoretical debates, and more positive toward government, which helps to explain the strong majority in Rostock for the leadership's motion—in effect, to stay in power.

The Greens entered the federal government in autumn 1998 with a decentralized weak party organization, a dual leadership, and a set of rules that sought to prevent the concentration of power. At the October 1998 Bonn conference, the most contentious issue was whether the Green ministers should give up their Bundestag seats in compliance with the party's stance favoring separation of powers. The issue was postponed due to Fischer's resistance. At the Leipzig conference in December, two-thirds of the delegates agreed to the creation a federal party council (Parteirat) with thirty members, no more than half of whom could hold parliamentary and/or ministerial seats at the state or federal level. Its mission would be to coordinate party activities inside and outside of government; however, the party's council of states (Länderrat) would remain the highest body between federal conferences. Fischer advocated doing away with the rules separating parliamentary mandate and party office and requiring co-speakers (under a quota system guaranteeing that at least one of the two speakers is a woman). Although there was no vote at the March 1999 Erfurt conference, the majority's mood was adverse to Fischer's views.[20]

In March 2000, structural reform was on the agenda of the Karlsruhe conference. The federal executive board (Bundesvorstand) had crafted a compromise that would allow half of its members to be ministers and/or parliamentarians. Leftists seized upon the national scandal stemming from unreported party funds during Helmut Kohl's long tenure as chancellor and CDU chair as evidence of the Greens' prescience in separating parliamentary/ministerial seat and party office. The motion fell short of the necessary two-thirds majority to change the party charter (Satzung). But other organizational changes did pass; most notably, the Parteirat was downsized and given responsibilities resembling those of the presidiums of the major parties. Indicative of the importance of the revamped Parteirat was the candidacy of Fischer for a seat; never before had he run for a federal party office. Lastly, the delegates at Karlsruhe approved what had been rejected sixteen months earlier, upgrading the party "speakers" to "chairs."

The separation rule's survival appeared to block Fischer's "dream team" for the party co-chairs: Fritz Kuhn and Renate Künast, who were the leaders of parliamentary groups in Baden-Württemberg and Berlin, respectively. Before the Karlsruhe conference, Gunda Röstel, who held the *Realo* co-speakership, had announced (under pressure) that she would not run again, but her leftist counterpart Antje Radcke stayed in the running. Kuhn and Künast decided to continue their candidacies and, if elected, to resign their parliamentary mandates. At the June 2000 Münster conference, Radcke, a critic of the Red-Green atomic consensus with the power industry, withdrew after the conference approved it. Kuhn and Künast were elected, winning 74 and 83 percent of the delegates' votes, respectively. *Realo* Kuhn has long emphasized the party's need to professionalize, to reach out to moderate voters, and to think more strategically. Künast, who began on the Left, has a leadership style that is pragmatic and charismatic. As pledged, they worked together as an integrated team. After Künast became a federal minister, Claudia Roth was elected at the March 2001 Stuttgart conference as her successor with 91 percent of the votes. Under the rules, Roth had to give up her Bundestag seat. Her warm gushing approach to politics complemented well Kuhn's cool calculating approach. Under their leadership, the media presentation of the Greens greatly improved.

The Pre-campaign

On 10 January 2002, Kuhn stated his party's primary goal: winning a higher percentage of the votes than in 1998 so that the Red-Green coalition could continue reforms with even more force.[21] Only a few days before, the SPD and the Greens had jointly run a newspaper ad portraying Schröder and Fischer as a team under the slogan "Responsibility and Trust." However, during the spring, SPD leaders would remind the public that they had alternatives if there was no Red-Green majority on 22 September. Since the SPD rejected any federal coalition with or tolerated by the PDS, its other options were: SPD-FDP, SPD-CDU/CSU, and SPD-FDP-Greens (though the Greens rejected governing with the FDP). The Greens, who also ruled out a coalition with the CDU/CSU, had only the Red-Green option—or opposition. Although there had been grassroots Greens during the controversies of 1998–2001 who had advocated a return to the opposition so that the party could rediscover its principles, there were no leading Greens making such an argument in early 2002. The only dissent over the party's strategy came from a couple of left-wing Bundestag Greens, who were open to cooperation with the PDS as a last resort.

The party was united behind a strategy for a *Richtungswahlkampf*.[22] In other words, one must vote for the Greens because only they would push the SPD forward in the renewal of Germany. The emergence of the conservative Edmund Stoiber as the CDU/CSU chancellor candidate on 11 January was greeted within the party as good news for the Greens' strategy. With the more moderate Merkel as the candidate, the campaign would not have been as clear-cut. The Bundestag Greens' co-chair Rezzo Schlauch declared: "With Stoiber, all reforms that the Greens have started will either be stopped or turned back."[23] For example, Stoiber's pronouncements that he would stop the exit from nuclear power and roll back ecological taxes would help to mobilize the Greens' supporters.

In contrast to the major parties, the Greens' political culture from the early days has been characterized by a distrust of strong personalities. But over the last decade, Green activists have developed more acceptance of the role of *Promis* (prominent figures) in simplifying policy complexities and providing emotional handles for voters. Yet the alternative party identity (as manifested in co-leadership) and factionalism remained strong enough in the 1998 Bundestag campaign to deter any official designation of a top Green candidate. This did not stop journalists from singling out the media-genic Joschka Fischer as "the" Green. *Stern*'s January 2001 photo exposé of the violent side of Fischer's radicalism in the 1970s did not damage his popularity. Gunter Hofmann, editor of *Die Zeit*, observed: "Germans are proud that they have a foreign minister who had a relatively 'colorful' biography."[24] In January 2002, Fischer was the most popular politician in the polls. Nevertheless, there were party insiders who favored a dynamic duo of Fischer and Künast to lead the Greens' campaign (and they might have prevailed if Angela Merkel had been the CDU/CSU's choice for chancellor). The Parteirat officially named Fischer as the Greens' top candidate for the Bundestag campaign. Yet he would be the head of a campaign team (*Spitzenteam*) that included six others: two Green federal ministers (Trittin and Künast), the federal party co-chairs (Roth and Kuhn), and the Bundestag Greens' co-chairs (Schlauch and Kerstin Müller). Journalist Knut Pries observed: "Team Fischer ... marks the final normalization of the Greens: first they were [a] parties alternative, then [an] alternative party, and now they are a party with a couple of alternatives."[25]

The Greens had supported the changes that downsized the 2002 Bundestag (see chapter 1 for a discussion of these changes). As a result, if the Greens were to win the same share of the votes as in 1998, they would qualify for 15 fewer seats. This (plus the fact that Roth, Kuhn, and Künast were seeking Bundestag seats) produced a scramble for promising list positions in a number of state parties. Most notably, in Baden-Württemberg, Oswald Metzger, one of the Bundestag Greens' leading neo-liberals, found himself without support for a promising list position and withdrew, and in Berlin, Hans-Christian Ströbele, the hero of the anti-war Left, lost out in the struggle for a promising list place to Werner Schulz, a leading figure in the 1989–1990 East German citizens movement. (Ströbele then sought a Bundestag seat running as a Berlin district candidate.) Although policy differences between *Realos* and the Left have lessened in recent years, factional identity and party loyalty still count when it comes to personnel decisions. Of the eight pacifist/leftist Greens who did not favor the position of the parliamentary *Fraktion* regarding Afghanistan, only one was to receive a promising list place.[26]

In February 1999, the Parteirat saw the need to develop a new *Grundsatzprogramm*. It would serve as a compass for Greens as a reformist party and replace the 1980 *Bundesprogramm*, which had been formulated by delegates whose majority were fundamentally opposed to the system. As a first step, the federal party in November 1999 held a strategy congress in Kassel where participants discussed the essential goals of Green politics. In February 2000 the Bundesvorstand appointed a Grundsatzprogrammkommission, chaired by federal party manager Reinhard Bütikofer. Following extensive intra-party dialogue and 12 meetings of the commission, its members approved the first draft unanimously in July 2001. Beginning in August, the draft became a focus of critical discussion at a series of regional conferences. However, the September 11 terrorist attacks and the U.S.-led war on terrorism delayed the revised draft, which was to have been acted upon at the November 2001 Rostock conference. This draft became the agenda of the Berlin conference (16–17 March). That there were over 1,200 motions to amend (roughly a third were accepted) indicated that party members took seriously envisaging policies through 2020. Following well-attended debates and some 50 votes on provisions, the 171-page program was overwhelmingly approved by the delegates.[27]

Although few voters were likely to read it, the completion of the multiyear process of identity redefinition facilitated the party's coming together for the Bundestag campaign.

The program's preamble starts with an emphasis on human dignity and ends with 12 specific key projects for the future. The Greens describe themselves as a party of the ecological and social market economy with leftist, value conservative, and *Rechtsstaat*-liberal roots. Today's Greens are seen as sharing four core values: ecology, self-determination, justice, and democracy. Only ecology remains from the four pillars set forth in the party's *Bundesprogramm*, and it is given *more* emphasis than in 1980. Second tier principles are nonviolence and human rights—in equal balance. The Greens omit the founders' pillar of *Basisdemokratie* in favor of "enlivened" democracy. They seek to be positively engaged as a reformist force within the parliamentary system in meeting the great challenges of the twenty-first century, such as globalization, demographic change, and biotechnology.

The provisions of the *Grundsatzprogramm* that emerged from the Berlin conference are aligned with the pragmatic views of the Bundesvorstand. Hard left positions typically garnered only 10 percent support. However, the leftist minority was able to sway enough delegates to score symbolic victories within the realist framework for Green policies. The new program in carefully crafted language departs from the *Bundesprogramm*'s pillar of nonviolence by allowing for the possible use of military force when legitimated by international law. But in a bow to the Left, delegates supported a constitutional reform requiring a two-thirds majority in the Bundestag for any foreign deployment of the Bundeswehr. Although anti-capitalist language is gone, the Left prevailed in asserting that the pursuit of ecological sustainability might require limits on economic liberty. The Left also succeeded in getting a majority to recognize the concerns of anti-globalization activists about social injustice. The program incorporates the demands of environmentalists for major policy changes; for example, the party's goal is to have 30 percent of German energy needs met by renewable energies by 2020.

The harmonious flow of the conference was threatened at a late stage by a grassroots proposal to strike a sentence from the final draft that accepted the basing of U.S. forces in Europe. Fischer sprang up to evoke memories of the "failure of Magdeburg" where four years earlier the party's conference had included within its electoral program a plan to raise the cost of gasoline (over a decade) to DM 5 per liter.[28] This generated scare headlines overshadowing everything else in the program and putting the Greens on the defensive for months; hammered by partisan foes the Greens saw their poll numbers plummet. If the majority stood against the leadership on this motion relating to U.S. relations, tabloid headlines on 18 March were likely to be: "The Greens vote 'Amis go home.'" Kuhn warned that the fruits of two years of programmatic work would be destroyed. Ultimately, Trittin crafted a compromise that coupled acceptance of U.S. engagement with recognition of the need for steps toward demilitarization. After the program's approval by 90 percent of the delegates, top candidate Fischer spoke and declared that the Greens' goal would be winning 8 percent plus. Most press reports saw a united party emerging from the Berlin conference with a chance to win back part of its frustrated clientele. In the following polls, the Greens' support went up one percentage point.

The last chance for the Greens to end their four-year long series of electoral setbacks before the Bundestag election would be in Saxony-Anhalt. The eastern state's Greens aspired to be returned by the voters to the Landtag on 21 April. However, the party faced formidable circumstances. Saxony-Anhalt's unemployment rate stood at 20.8 percent, the highest of any German state. Its voters appeared eager for a change of government; at 2–3 percent in the polls, the Greens were seen as irrelevant to the power equation. Despite the engagement of national Greens in the state campaign, Saxony-Anhalt Greens won only 2 percent of the votes (-1.3 since 1998) finishing fifth in a low turnout election. Forschungsgruppe Wahlen's analysis discounted the results as a "test election" for the Bundestag.[29] Undine Kurth, the top candidate of the Saxony-Anhalt Greens, found encouragement in polls projecting 4–5 percent support in East Germany for the Greens in the Bundestag election.[30]

On 4–5 May, the Greens met in Wiesbaden to adopt their electoral program, which concentrated on the next legislative period. The Greens' support for the first time since 1998 were relatively solid compared to the SPD's. The latter had sagged to 32 percent in an Infratest dimap poll while the Greens' support held at 7 percent; the CDU/CSU and FDP together enjoyed a majority (52 percent).[31] Accordingly, despite often-uneasy relations with the SPD, the Greens' speakers went easy on the criticism of their only available coalition partner. Also Greens fired no broadsides at each other! Of the 550 motions introduced, for the first time in memory no one challenged the agenda set forth by the Bundesvorstand. Contentiousness about foreign policies was absent compared to recent conferences. Motions mostly focused on social, economic, and interior policies. Party leaders worked hard to accommodate dissenters' concerns before the sessions; as a result, there were fewer than ten floor votes and time allotments for debate went unused. The two major issues that remained were ecological taxes and arms shipments to Israel. Evoking memories of Magdeburg 1998, the leadership prevailed: concrete numbers were left out of the provision favoring ecological taxes. The motion calling for an arms embargo to protest the militant actions of Prime Minister Sharon's government against Palestinians was opposed as "counterproductive" by Foreign Minister Fischer. Eventually compromise wording defused the issue. Ströbele directed his rhetoric skills against the opposing parties. Journalists observed that prominent Greens who spoke (regardless of how well) received standing ovations—"show time." just like in the major parties. Out of over 700 delegates, only three votes were cast against the final draft of the electoral program. In closing remarks, Fischer complimented the delegates: "You were really great."[32]

At the outset of the electoral program, the Greens declare that they are "the party of ecological modernization, social and economic renewal, and societal democratization."[33] The preamble lists their major accomplishments as a governing party and then outlines eight points at the core of their next legislative agenda: promotion of renewable energies, safe and healthy food, improvement of the lives of children, creation of jobs, integration of immigrants, equal powers for women, pursuit of just globalization, and strengthening of European democracy. Ecology is not only the theme of the first chapter, but also spills over into the second. Fischer's special emphasis on the problems of families with children is reflected in the second chapter, for example, in plans to make having children and a career more compatible. Within the third chapter there is a major section calling for more power and opportunities for women. The final chapter, on foreign and security policy, sets forth the aim of ending military conscription and reforming the Bundeswehr, but this four-year goal is presented without ideological packaging. Overall, the electoral program does tend to steer away from "neo-liberal" perspectives. Its primary objectives are to mobilize Green core voters and to appeal young voters and tactical SPD voters who favor ecological, social and democratic renewal.

Emerging from Wiesbaden with a remarkable unity, the Greens were further encouraged by the outcome of the run-off mayoral election in Freiburg. Dieter Salomon, the parliamentary leader of the Baden-Württemberg Greens, won 64.4 percent of the votes cast on 5 May and became the first Green mayor of a large (200,000+) German city.

The Campaign

A modern campaign requires managers as well as candidates and programs. In summer 2001 the Bundesvorstand picked Rudi Hoogvliet, a veteran parliamentary staff member of the Baden-Württemberg Greens, as its 2002 campaign manager. From the outset he stressed *Botschaftsdisziplin* (sticking to the message) so that, in contrast to the 1998 campaign, the party would maintain a sharp profile.[34] His management team included 10 staff specialists, which with interns meant that about 20 people were working full time on the campaign. They had three major tasks: providing a hot line phone service for candidates, planning tours and events, and handling communications. (KAMPA/02, the SPD campaign central, employed around one hundred full-time workers.) Strategic-political decision-making was the job of the Bundesvorstand. In January 2002, it hired the Hamburg-based public relations/advertising agency Zum Goldenen Hirschen to provide the marketing expertise. The youthful, award-winning agency promised a "spirited, humorous, and novel" campaign.[35] Its first poster showed the sullen faces of Angela Merkel, Edmund Stoiber, Guido Westerwelle, and Gregor Gysi under the heading, "Election campaign 2002: we are looking forward to you!" The agency worked on a daily basis with the management team and had a representative at the weekly joint meetings of the *Spitzenteam* (three federal ministers, two party co-chairs, and two parliamentary group co-chairs), the parliamentary manager, party and parliamentary press secretaries, and the party treasurer.

The Greens started out with about as much state money for the campaign as in 1998 (2.5 million euros). However, they succeeded in raising about 1 million euros more in donations from banks, industries, and individuals. (In their respective campaigns, the SPD planned to spend 25.3 million euros and the CDU/CSU, 25.1 million.)[36] The party, which once had qualms about information technology, fully embraced it in the 2002 campaign. Voters could click on its tag campaign Web site (http://www.gruenwirkt.de) and its top candidate's Web site (http://www.joschka.de), both with state of the art features. Campaign managers made heavy use of the Internet to distribute timely information to the local parties.

In April, the Bundesvorstand chose as its Bundestag campaign motto, "Grün wirkt" (Green works). As evidence, the party cited its "greatest hits": phasing out nuclear plants, promoting renewable energy, launching ecological taxes, initiating pension reform, passing a new citizenship law, and recognizing same-sex partnerships. The motto was to adorn the party's Web sites, posters, brochures, badges, and assorted paraphernalia. Hoogvliet urged local parties to recycle their old posters in favor of the new crisp, professional look with its colorful images and sharp slogans against a signature "Grün wirkt" backdrop. Zum Golden Hirschen produced two catalogs from which local parties could select campaign materials. September was to see a proliferation of "the second vote is the Joschka vote" posters and also stickers to update earlier posters. In the Berlin district of Friedrichshain-Kreuzberg-Prenzlauer Berg-Ost, Ströbele ran with his own posters and brochures; otherwise, candidates utilized the new template.

The Bundesvorstand planned a campaign with four overlapping phases. First, there would be the preparatory phase: getting the organization ready, adopting the programs, and motivating the membership (January–May). A second phase would follow focusing on the Greens' major themes (May–June). For example, posters addressed solar energy, multiculturalism, women's equality, healthy food, and right-wing extremism. The third phase would link issues with members of the *Spitzenteam* (June–August). Hoogvliet announced a schedule of theme weeks beginning in June with climate protection and ending in August with the quality of life for children.[37] To draw attention to the person-issue connection, Zum Golden Hirschen produced a series of humorous posters, such as Renate Künast waitressing and Rezzo Schlauch knitting. The fourth, "hot" campaign phase would begin in August. The second tier of the *Spitzenteam* would be blitzing the countryside in mini-buses. Fischer's tour (with a big bus) would be an integral part of the party's campaign, rather than independent as in 1998. The "hot" campaign would climax in the large cities with mass rallies starring Fischer and other members of the *Spitzenteam*.

The national polls in June indicated that the Greens' support was holding at 7–8 percent and the SPD was beginning to narrow its gap with the CDU/CSU. SPD General Secretary Franz Münterfering was speaking out for Red-Green and against other constellations. (The plurality of those polled by Forschungsgruppe Wahlen until late August 2002 favored a CDU/CSU-FDP coalition.) In the aftermath of the first "Möllemann affair," Schröder continued to distance himself from the FDP. However, with unemployment overshadowing all other problems, the press read midsummer polls as indicating little chance for a Red-Green victory and speculated about other color combinations. Kuhn reiterated his party's consensus that Red-Red-Green (SPD-PDS-Green) and Red-Yellow-Green (SPD-FDP-Green) alternatives were out of the question. Declaring that his goal was to govern with the Greens, Schröder in July ruled out a grand coalition. In the final month of campaigning, the chancellor, like the Greens, portrayed the campaign as a personalized *Richtungswahlkampf*: Schröder-Fischer or Stoiber-Westerwelle.

During the 1998 campaign, an informal "AG-7" committee brought together Left and *Realo* leaders to manage a series of self-inflicted crises. The Greens' *Streitkultur* lingered on to complicate the task of communicating their competence as a small governing party. In March 2002, cochair Roth reported that media analysis found that 70 percent of negative statements about the Greens in the press originated from themselves.[38] During the 2002 campaign, the party benefited from a "strategic center" and also a unity of purpose throughout the party. Not until late July were the Greens forced on the defensive, not because of any factional conflicts or campaigning missteps, rather because of the personal behavior of four parliamentary deputies, which the mass circulation *Bild Zeitung* sought to make into a "crisis."

Cem Özdemir, who had entered the Bundestag in 1994 as its first member born of Turkish guest workers and who had become the Greens' parliamentary interior policy spokesperson, admitted that he had taken a loan of 80,000 marks from the Hunzinger public relations agency.[39] This was the same agency from which recently fired SPD Defense Minister Rudolf Scharping had received $72,000 in royalties. Özdemir's loan (repayable with 5.5 percent interest when the bank rate was almost double) was an embarrassment to his party, which has long cultivated an anti-corruption image. After Özdemir donated the money saved by his low interest rate to a charity, Kuhn considered the matter closed since there was no shred of evidence of Hunzinger's influence on Özdemir. However, Ströbele and Winfried Hermann from the party's pacifist/leftist current called for a special meeting of the parliamentary group.[40] After it came to light that Özdemir had also used Lufthansa bonus miles from official flights for free private flights, he decided to leave the Bundestag.

Bild Zeitung's bonus miles exposé soon extended to additional past and present Bundestag members. Gregor Gysi, the former Bundestag member and current PDS Berlin economics minister, resigned and donated the monetary value of his private flights to a charity. Of the eight current members listed, four were Greens: Cem Özdemir, Ludger Volmer, Jürgen Trittin, and Rezzo Schlauch. With Volmer's and Trittin's cases not so clear cut, attention focused on Schlauch, who used bonus miles for a vacation flight (first class) to Thailand. While admitting his error of judgment, Schlauch saw no grounds for resignation after making restitution to a special Bundestag account. Despite angry e-mails from the grassroots and complaints from some members of the parliamentary group and two eastern state party chairs, the Parteirat stood behind Schlauch.[41] Fischer pointed out the lack of proportion in media coverage of "Bonusmeilen-Affäre": no laws had been broken and the monies involved were tiny compared to the recent CDU scandal over illegal campaign contributions. Green leaders attacked the *Bild Zeitung* for waging a "dirty campaign" to influence public opinion by holding back its information until later and then targeting Greens when many others had likewise sinned. Following the story's two-week run, the Greens' support went up in the polls.

Although national environmental groups have been critical of the compromises that the Greens have made as a governing party, the polls have shown that by a large margin the Greens have been viewed by the public as the most environmentally competent party. However, during the first 32 weeks of 2002, environmental protection was low on the list of public concerns. The catastrophic floods that struck Saxony and elsewhere in mid-August quickly changed the picture. The Greens were already well positioned on the issues. Environmental Minister Trittin had urged changes in river management, yet before the crisis no one had paid much attention. The Greens' spokespersons seized the opportunity to make the connection between flooding and climate change. Fischer observed that 16 laws relating to climate change had been passed with the Greens' support; all had been opposed by the FDP and 14 had been opposed by the CDU/CSU.[42] While "high-water" went up and down as a major concern in the late summer polls, "environmental protection" climbed from being mentioned by 2 percent of those polled in early August to 11 percent in early September.[43] Media coverage of the UN World Summit on Sustainable Development in Johannesburg, South Africa (25 August–4 September), where Trittin was actively engaged, helped to keep public attention on the local-global nexus of environmental problems.

Thanks to the increasingly bellicose orientation taken by the Bush administration toward Iraq, foreign and security policy joined environmental policy in the "hot" campaign as a distraction from the weak performance of the economy, which Stoiber's campaign team was counting on for victory. At their May 2002 Wiesbaden conference, the Greens had passed a resolution opposing military intervention in Iraq. While the party's stance on Iraq did not waver during the campaign, Fischer endeavored to make clear that it had nothing to do with anti-Americanism. Schröder's rhetoric opposing military action against Iraq became stronger the closer election day drew. When he spoke of a "special path" for German foreign policy, Fischer had to distance himself, given its negative historical connotations.

On 24 August, the Länderrat unanimously approved a "Vertrag für die Zukunft" (Contract for the Future), which condensed the 88-page electoral program down to 8 points. In brief, the Greens promised in a second Red-Green government: to strengthen climate protection, to guarantee healthy food, to create future-oriented jobs, to reform social welfare, to make the country more child friendly, to advance women's equality, to extend citizens' rights, and to work toward more just globalization. In the final weeks of the campaign, the focus narrowed even more to one point: "the second vote is the Joschka vote." Zum Golden Hirschen had designed a poster with a sympathetic looking Joschka under the heading "Außen Minister, inner grün" (Outside minister, inside green). Fischer starred (solo) in the Greens' television spot and movie theater spot. His 17,000-kilometer marathon bus tour drew crowds as if he were a rock star. Hoogvliet estimated that 135,000 people attended Fischer's election rallies.[44] This did not include the 20,000 who turned up for the unprecedented joint appearance of Schröder and Fischer on 15 September at the Brandenburg Gate. Following his performance at the Greens' final rally on 20 September in the Tempodrom, Fischer turned up on the Harald Schmidt Show, a popular late night television talk show. Although some Green activists were uncomfortable about the personalization of the "hot" campaign, even they would admit that it prevented the Greens from being squeezed out of the picture by the Schröder vs. Stoiber showdown amplified by Germany's first ever U.S.-presidential-style television debates.

The other noteworthy feature of the late campaign was that there were, in addition to top-level contacts between the SPD and the Greens, contacts at the lower levels of the party organizations. These were most significant in Berlin districts where the Green candidate did not have a chance, while the SPD candidate did, to come out ahead of the PDS. (A Red-Green majority would be impossible if the PDS managed to win three district seats, which would qualify it for its percentage of list seats even if it failed to win 5 percent of the list votes nationally.) Künast, the top candidate of the Berlin Greens, spoke explicitly at the Tempodrom rally: "You have two votes; vote red, vote green and in that order!" Furthermore, Greens warned that a vote for the PDS would be in effect a vote for Stoiber as chancellor. Ströbele's district candidacy in Berlin, on the other hand, drew open support from a group of SPD members (who were as a result later punished by their party). Though encouraged by mid-September polls projecting a Red-Green majority, the Greens took nothing for granted in the final week.

The Election Outcome and Its Aftermath

The Greens won 8.6 percent of the party vote (second ballot), a gain of 1.9 percent. It was their best outcome ever in a Bundestag election. (In the 1987 West German election, they had won 8.3 percent.) In 2002 they won 9.4 percent of list votes (+2.1) in western states plus West Berlin while winning 4.8 percent (+0.6) in eastern states plus East Berlin.[45] Their strongest performances were in Hamburg 16.2 percent (+5.4), Bremen 15.0 percent (+3.7), and Berlin 14.6 percent (+3.3); their weakest performances, Saxony-Anhalt 3.4 percent (+0.1), and Mecklenburg-West Pomerania 3.5 percent (+0.6). The Greens did even worse in the Mecklenburg-West Pomerania Landtag election also held on 22 September; they won only 2.6 percent of the votes. Their strongest district showing (first ballot) was 25.0 percent in Freiburg; their worse, 2.3 percent in Mansfelder Land, Saxony-Anhalt. The Greens gained ground in 285 districts across the country while losing ground in 14 districts (all eastern). Nine years after the merger of the (West) Greens and Bündnis 90, they were still shallowly rooted in eastern states.

Nationally, the Greens received 5.6 percent of the district vote (first ballot), a gain of 0.7 percent over 1998. Ströbele became the first Green to ever win a district seat by receiving 31.6 percent of the votes in Berlin-Friedrichshain-Kreuzberg-Prenzlauer Berg-Ost. While Ströbele's district candidacy benefited from the cross-over of SPD voters, the national pattern was the opposite: 65 percent of Green list voters crossed over for SPD district candidates while 13 percent of SPD district voters opted for the Green Party list. Looking at survey data about the party identity of the list voters, one discovers that 29 percent of Green voters were actually closer to the SPD. Thus, of the Greens' 8.6 percent, 2.5 came from SPD identifiers, who presumably preferred a Red-Green coalition. According to Infratest dimap, the Greens had a net gain of 500,000 votes from the SPD.[46] The *Richtungswahlkampf* strategy had paid off: the Greens ended up with 55 seats (their historic high) and the SPD with 251 seats—an absolute Red-Green majority of four seats.

The national demographic data indicated that the Greens' support had gone up in all age groups. They enjoyed the strongest support among those 18–29 (10 percent) and those 30–44 (11 percent). The Greens had more backing from women than men in all age groups, especially in the 18–29 and 30–44 age groups where 12 percent of women favored the party. Among occupational groups, their strongest support was from civil servants (14 percent) and lowest, from farmers (3 percent). The higher the educational level of respondents, the higher the support for the Greens. Only 4 percent of those with a basic education favored the Greens, compared to 18 percent of those with a university education. Regarding religion, the nonconfessional group was the most supportive of the Greens (11 percent). The more densely populated a district, the greater the support for the Greens, whether in the West or East. The East diverged from the West in only a few ways: there was no eastern gender difference in the Greens' support, the eastern self-employed were the Greens' most supportive occupational group, and confessionless easterners were not relatively more supportive of the Greens.

Fischer sought a revitalized leadership for the new Bundestagsfraktion that would professionally pursue the Red-Green reform agenda. Initially, Fischer had Kuhn in mind as parliamentary co-chair, but after second thoughts about the consequence of Kuhn's departure for the party leadership, Fischer backed Krista Sager, the *Reala* former federal party co-chair and former Hamburg senator.[47] With only five Bundestag Greens representing eastern states, Fischer also wanted an easterner in the new leadership to raise the Greens' profile there. Müller (elected in 1998 to represent the Left) signaled her desire to work in the foreign ministry. Schlauch wanted to stay on as co-chair, but was vulnerable because of the bonus miles affair and pre-existent complaints about his leadership style. He soon agreed to move into the economics super-ministry. Fischer supported 36-year-old Katrin Göring-Eckardt, a *Reala* from Thuringia, who was the Green parliamentary manager. Her 52-year-old opponent was Werner Schulz, a native of Saxony, whom Fischer had gone around in 1998 to back Schlauch as the (*Realo*) parliamentary co-chair. In the mid-October vote of the parliamentary group, Schulz lost again. Thus, the new Bundestagsfraktion (in which women outnumbered men 32 to 23) would have two female chairs, which was seen by insiders as countering any gender-specific appeal of CDU chair Angela Merkel. Volker Beck (*Regierungslinker*) was elected as the parliamentary manager. Interviewees in autumn 2002 agreed that only about five of the 55 Bundestag Greens were strongly identified with the party's pacifist-leftist current.

In view of the Greens' gains, Ströbele, Beck, and the Green federal women's council urged the party's negotiators to push for a fourth cabinet minister. However, the *Spitzenteam* early on had decided to seek enhanced policy responsibilities for the three current Green cabinet ministers. This they were able to accomplish in the negotiation rounds beginning on 1 October with the SPD, which also brought the Greens seven "junior" ministers (a gain of one). The parties clashed over foreign and security issues, but found quick consensus on reforming the job market and promoting new businesses. Although the Greens' goal of "sustainability" is embodied in the title of the coalition agreement, the parties diverged on specific issues, such as ecological taxes and coal industry subsidies. In the end, language would be found to bridge differences. The Green negotiators had learned from recent years that a coalition agreement is more a political understanding than a legal contract regarding policy development. Many Green activists shared little of the enthusiasm of the top Greens for the agreement signed with SPD leaders on 16 October. Generally, journalists found the agreement lacking in "bold, wide-ranging reforms."[48] Despite widespread anger in the party over Schröder's personal promise to the power industry to allow the Obrigheim nuclear plant to stay on line longer than the atomic consensus had foreseen, the coalition agreement was overwhelmingly approved by the Green delegates at the Bremen conference (18–19 October).

The party's grassroots chose to assert itself on the issue of separation of parliamentary seat and party office. Kuhn and Roth had forced the showdown by seeking to remain as party co-chairs after their election to the Bundestag, a situation incompatible with the Greens' charter (*Satzung*). The Bundesvorstand sought in the light of the excellent marks that the Kuhn-Roth leadership had earned in the campaign to abolish the separation rule. Then realizing that there would be no two-thirds majority for such a break given the lingering alternative identity of many Greens, it accepted a compromise allowing only two of the six party executives to hold parliamentary seats (though not be parliamentary group chairs, cabinet ministers, or European Union commissioners). After lively debate, the motion failed by twenty votes to win two-thirds majority support. Pro-grassroots democracy delegates joined Ströbele and his allies and individuals, such as Schulz, upset by top-down personnel decisions. The *Spitzenteam*, which had no Plan B, was visibly jolted by the outcome. Journalists saw the recently victorious party reverting to its old pattern of internal disunity. Kuhn and Roth decided to remain in office until the December 2002 Hanover conference at which a new party leadership would be elected.

A number of state organizations got behind an initiative to resolve this perennial intra-party issue with a membership referendum (*Urabstimmung*), which would take months to gear up for, and to grant Kuhn and Roth a special exemption from the separation rule in the meantime. However, the exemption failed by eight votes to receive the necessary *Satzung* changing two-thirds majority at the Hanover conference. Sixty-eight percent of the delegates did support a referendum on whether one-third of the Bundesvorstand could also hold parliamentary seats (though no other leadership offices). Reinhard Bütikofer, the outgoing federal party manager, who has had differences with Fischer, was elected co-chair with 90 percent of the votes while Angelika Beer, the former defense spokesperson of the Bundestag Greens, was elected as his female counterpart with 75 percent. Steffi Lemke, a former Bundestag Green from Saxony-Anhalt, was elected as Bütikofer's replacement. The three would serve on the Parteirat whose 13 other members were elected by the Hanover conference. Among the winners were nine Bundestag Greens: Kuhn and Roth, the two parliamentary co-chairs and the manager, the parliamentary environmental spokesperson, and the three federal cabinet ministers (interestingly, both Künast and Trittin had higher vote totals than Fischer). The four other members were state-level ministers, parliamentary or party leaders. That 12 of the 16 members of this important party body are also ministers and/or parliamentarians is indicative of the dominance of public office holders within the "alternative" Greens.

An additional step toward "normalization" was taken by the party membership in the referendum of 22 April–13 May 2002. Fifty-seven percent of the 43,391 members participated, which was more than in the Greens' only other national referendum in 1993 to ratify the merger of the Greens and Bündnis 90. An unexpected 67 percent of the voting members endorsed the loosening of the separation rule regarding parliamentary seats and party offices. The outcome was accepted by Ströbele who had positioned himself for a legal challenge of a narrow yes majority in a low turnout vote. *Promis* maintained a united front that there would be no direct consequences for the (non-parliamentarian) party co-chairs, Bütikofer and Beer, who had been elected to two year terms in December. Former co-chair Roth greeted the outcome as further proof of the "reform capacity" of the Greens.[49]

Implications

While public support for the SPD sank as economic statistics worsened, the Greens' support remained solid following September 2002. Events as well as their relative lack of clientelism, allowed the Greens to profile—as promised in their Bundestag campaign—as the coalition's "reform motor" for domestic policies. They were not hammered by divisive foreign crises such as those in 1999 and 2001. All wings of the party were united in opposition to the Bush administration's war against Iraq without allowing United Nations weapons inspectors the time to do their job. According to Infratest dimap's September 2003 survey, the Greens' share of the votes in a new Bundestag election would be higher (10 percent) while the SPD's would be much less (29 percent), and there would be a clear majority for the CDU/CSU (46 percent) and the FDP (6 percent).[50] In contrast to recent years, the weakness of the SPD, and not of the Greens, was clouding the future of Red-Green government.

In the early 2003 state elections, the Greens had seen their support increase.[51] In February, the Greens won 7.6 percent (+0.6 compared to 1998) of the votes in the Lower Saxony election and 10.6 percent (+2.9 compared to 1999) in the Hesse election. Yet due to losses by the SPD, no Red-Green government was possible in either state. In the May 2003 Bremen election, the Greens did well, winning 12.8 percent of the city-state's votes (+3.8 percent compared to 1999) while the SPD's support held up (42.3 percent, -0.2). However, SPD mayor Henning Scherf, who had steered his campaign away from federal themes, preferred to continue governing with the CDU (29.9 percent, -7.2).

During the first half of 2003, the Greens' membership grew by 2.3 percent (reaching 44, 900), which did not include 2,400 individuals availing themselves of "trial" membership. The percentages for the SPD, CDU, CSU, and FDP were -3.3, -0.4, +0.4, and -1.2, respectively.[52]

Although statistics are lacking, Roth and Künast have remarked about the resurgence of youthful activism as witnessed in the Greens' 2002 campaign. It seems reasonable to assume that the new members are even more pragmatic about questions of power and policy than those who joined during recent years.

In the post–September 2002 polls, Fischer has maintained the number one position as not only the most popular politician with the general public, but also with one's own party supporters. According to Forschungsgruppe Wahlen, in September 2003 his score was 1.9 (on a -5/+5 scale) with the public and 3.4 with party supporters, in contrast Schröder's were 0.3 and 2.7, respectively. During 2003, Fischer, who is in too small a party to hope to be chancellor, appeared to be positioning himself for a shot at becoming the European Union's first foreign minister. Such a career move would create turbulence within the ranks of the Greens since there is no obvious successor with foreign policy credentials (and charisma). Bütikofer made it clear under the coalition agreement that the Greens would not give up the post of foreign minister. Trittin, whose popularity with the general public has never been high, has the ambition if not the allies for the job; insiders reported that Fischer would prefer Künast. Fischer brought an end to speculations by stating in late August 2003 that he intended to remain German foreign minister beyond 2006.

Schröder, who announced his intention to stay the reform course as chancellor into the next legislative period, welcomed Fischer's decision with a (de facto) declaration of a Red-Green strategy for 2006. Already in June 2003 at the Greens' extraordinary Cottbus conference (which had been forced by the grassroots upon a reluctant leadership), 90 percent of the delegates had supported Schröder's Agenda 2010 to create jobs and to trim the welfare state—although dissidents wanted the better off to bear more of the burden of the reforms. While Schröder battled left-wing critics in his own party, the more united Greens enjoyed media attention for innovative proposals, such as a near universal *"Bürgerversicherung"* (common base insurance rate) to ensure the long-run survival of social programs. (See the contribution by Irwin Collier in this volume for an analysis of this proposal.) Schröder has charged some Greens with carrying out simultaneously opposition and government politics. Economics super-minister Clement, a potential successor to Schröder, has a long history of confrontations with the North Rhine-Westphalia Greens, and in 2003 has clashed with Trittin over energy policy. Clement would prefer to keep coalition options wide open. In short, the Greens realize their relationship with the SPD, despite Schröder's Red-Green remarks, will go up and down, with at times the Greens being attacked as a diversion from the SPD's internal problems. The Greens have an emerging cleavage between their "social democrats" and "neo-liberals," with the latter favoring more fundamental socioeconomic reforms and not wanting to be chained to the SPD.

In the aftermath of 22 September 2002, the press reported speculations by some prominent CDU members about a "Black-Green" coalition option at the state and federal levels. Kuhn dismissed it due to insufficient policy overlaps between the two parties. Another wave of speculations arose in early 2003 with the collapse of a CDU-FDP coalition in Cologne and its replacement by a CDU-Green coalition (approved by 79 percent of the local Greens). Although a dozen such local alliances were existent in North Rhine-Westphalia, Cologne's became Germany's first Black-Green government in a city of over one million residents. National and state Green leaders as well as CDU leader Merkel declared that Cologne was an interim local alliance and not a model for coalition politics elsewhere. However, a number of local and state CDU figures found the development more interesting. Discontent in Berlin with the SPD-PDS city-state government stirred speculations there about alternatives, including a CDU-Green coalition. However, a Forsa survey of Berliners reported in August that the Black-Green option was rejected by 57 percent of the general public and by almost 75 percent of Green supporters.[53] National polls during 2003 also found no noteworthy public support for a Black-Green coalition.

In conclusion, the Greens have developed as a professional-electoral party since 1998. The Parteirat has coordinated the message of Green ministers, party and parliamentary leaders. The 2002 campaign was well planned and managed, with the grassroots demonstrating solidarity behind its leadership team. The *Grundsatzprogramm* and *Wahlprogramm* succeeded in bringing together the party's factions. The Greens' political culture has changed not only to embrace professionalization, but also to allow an unprecedented personalization of the Bundestag campaign. The Greens under talented party co-chairs have become more media savvy since 2000. Nevertheless, compared to the major parties, they remain a "bottom-up" party in that resources remain more decentralized to state and local parties. The Bremen and Hanover conferences demonstrated that the federal leadership could not count on getting its way even in the afterglow of the party's biggest victory ever in a Bundestag election. The party's anti-elitist rule separating parliamentary seat and leadership office was loosened by the May 2003 membership referendum, but *not* abolished due to the participatory identity of many Greens. Despite media hyping of intra-party conflicts, pragmatism has become a way of life from the Right to the Left among its public office-holders. There are signs that the Greens are becoming a multigenerational party, with frictions likely to grow between the younger generations and the 68ers. During the 2002 campaign, Fischer was a tremendous asset for the party, but in 2003 while he was pondering a career shift to the EU, "No one said, Joschka, please stay, we can't do it alone."[54] After twenty-three years, the once radical Greens have become established as a reformist party within the system.

Notes

1. The official name of the party since the merger of West and East Greens in May 1993 has been Bündnis 90/Die Grünen. However, this chapter prefers the more commonly used, shortened name: the Greens (Die Grünen). In addition to the sources cited below, the author draws upon 27 personal interviews with Green politicians conducted in May–June 2001, September–November 2002, and April 2003. The author's field research during 2002 enjoyed the support of the Deutscher Akademischer Austauschdienst (DAAD).
2. Infratest dimap, *Wahlreport: Wahl zum 15. Deutschen Bundestag 22. September 2002*, p. 8.
3. Forschungsgruppe Wahlen, *Politbarometer Flash 02/2002* (KW 06), p. 1.
4. Peter Finn, "Germany's Greens Face an Identity Crisis," *The Guardian Weekly*, 28 February 2002, p. 37.
5. Joachim Raschke, *Die Zukunft der Grünen: So kann man nicht regieren* (Frankfurt am Main and New York: Campus Verlag, 2001), pp. 10, 23, 419.
6. Tilman Gerwien, "Joschkas Republik," *Stern*, no. 41 (2 October 2002): 28.
7. Remarks by Joachim Raschke at the Heinrich-Böll-Stiftung panel discussion, "6 Tage nach der Wahl," 28 September 2002, Berlin.
8. Dieter Roth, "Ablösung der Regierung vertagt: Eine Analyse der Bundestagswahl 2002," *Aus Politik und Zeitgeschichte*, no. 49–50 (8–15 December 2002), http://www.bundestag.de/cgi-bin/druck.pl?N=parlamen.
9. Richard Stöss and Gero Neugebauer, "Mit einem blauen Auge davon gekommen: Eine Analyse der Bundestagswahl 2002," *Arbeitshelfe aus dem Otto-Stammer-Zentrum*, no. 7 (November 2002).
10. Ibid., p. 108.
11. See E. Gene Frankland, "Bündnis 90/Die Grünen: From Opposition to Power," in *Power Shift in Germany: The 1998 Election and the End of the Kohl Era*, ed. David P. Conradt, Gerald R. Kleinfeld, and Christian Søe (New York and Oxford: Berghahn Books, 2000), pp. 80–97.
12. See Joachim Raschke, "Wo die Ziele unklar sind, gibt es auch keine Strategie," *Frankfurter Rundschau online*, http://www.fr-aktuell.de/ressorts/nachrichten_und_politik/dokumentation/?cnt=213959 (accessed 16 May 2003).
13. "Wahl in Schleswig-Holstein: Eine Analyse der Landtagswahl vom 27. Februar 2000," Berichte der Forschungsgruppe Wahlen, Mannheim no. 101 (1 March 2000): 54–55.
14. Wolfgang Rüdig, "Green Parties in National Governments: Germany," *Environmental Politics* 11, no. 1 (Spring 2002): 90.
15. "Wahl in Baden-Württemberg: Eine Analyse der Landtagswahl vom 25. März 2001," Berichte der Forschungsgruppe Wahlen, Mannheim no. 103 (28 March 2001): 61–63.
16. German Information Center (New York), *The Week in Germany*, 15 October 2001, p. 1.
17. Dietmar Strehl, the Greens' federal party treasurer, provided party membership data. Figures for 2001 are preliminary. (Membership data from understaffed state offices tend to be slow in being reported and verified.)
18. Calculated from data in Oskar Niedermayer, "Parteimitgliedschaften im Jahre 2001," *Zeitschrift für Parlamentsfragen*, Heft 2/2002, pp. 361–367. For the opposition parties there were also membership declines reported during 1998–2001: the CDU, CSU, and FDP lost 3.5 percent, 1.4 percent, and 5.7 percent, respectively. During 1998–2000, the PDS membership fell 11.8 percent.
19. Christiane Schlötzer, "Wandel durch Wanderung," *Süddeutsche Zeitung online*, http://www.sueddeutsche.de (accessed 7 January 2000).
20. German Information Center (New York), *The Week in Germany*, 12 March 1999, p. 2.
21. Nico Fried, "Klasur des Bundesvorstands: Die Grünen wollen 'deutlich zulegen,'" *Süddeutsche Zeitung online*, http://www.sueddeutsche.de/aktuell/sz/artikel111477.php (accessed 10 January 2002).
22. Reinhard Bütikofer, "Kämpfen, kämpfen, kämpfen," *Schrägstrich*, 4/5–2002, p. 11.

23. "Schlauch sieht Demontage Merkels," *Spiegel Online,* http://spiegel.de/politik/deutschland/0,1518,176676,00.htm (accessed 11 January 2002).
24. Cited in Lucian Kim, "Germans Debate Politician's Past," *The Christian Science Monitor,* 12 January 2001, p. 6.
25. Knut Pries, "Ganter vor," *Frankfurter Rundschau online,* http://www.fr-aktuell.de/fr/110/t110002.htm (accessed 22 January 2002).
26. Matthias Meisner and Hans Monath, "Einer für alle," *Der Tagesspiegel,* 4 May 2002.
27. *Die Zukunft ist grün: Grundsatzprogramm von Bündnis 90/Die Grünen,* Berlin, April 2000.
28. Kurt Kister, "Grundsatzprogramm für die nächsten 20 Jahre: Grüne schwören völliger Gewaltfreitheit ab," *Süddeutsche Zeitung online,* http://www.sueddeutsche.de/aktuell/sz/artikel133373.php (accessed 18 March 2002).
29. Forschungsgruppe Wahlen newsletter, "Wahl in Sachsen-Anhalt: 21. April 2002," 22 April 2002, p. 2.
30. Interview with Undine Kurth, "Gewählt wurde das vermeintlich sichere," *Schrägstrich,* 4/5–2002, p. 9.
31. "Schwarz-gelb im Stimmungshoch," *Spiegel Online,* http://www.spiegel.de/politik/deutschland/0,1518,194829,00.html (accessed 4 May 2002).
32. Quoted by Regine Zylka, "Ihr wart wirklich großartig," *Berliner Zeitung,* 6 May 2002.
33. *Grün wirkt: Unser Wahlprogramm 2002–2006,* Berlin, June 2002, p. 7
34. Interview with Rudi Hoogvliet, "Wir würden Deutschland auf den Kopf stellen ...," *Schrägstrich,* 11–12/2001, p. 8.
35. "Zum goldenen Hirschen," *Schrägstrich,* 01–02/2002, p. 17.
36. The figures for the Greens were reported to the author by members of the federal party office on 10 October 2002; those for the Social Democrats and Christian Democrats are from "Wahlkampf-Macher: Arena gegen Kampa," *Spiegel Online,* http://www.spiegel.de/politik/deutschland/0,1518,druck-180124,00.htm (accessed 1 February 2002).
37. Rudi Hoogvliet, "Grün wirkt!" *Schrägstrich* 5–6/2002, p. 7.
38. Interview with Claudia Roth, "Traumjob mit Albträumen," *Schrägstrich* 3/2002, p. 6.
39. "Özdemir erhielt Darlehen und PR-Honorar," *Spiegel Online,* http://www.spiegel.de/politik/deutschland/0,1518,206141,00.html (accessed 20 July 2002).
40. Vera Gaserow, " Wenn es um Geld geht, Sparkasse," *Frankfurter Rundschau online,* http://www.fr-aktuell.de/fr/101/t101005.htm (accessed 23 July 2002).
41. Vera Gaserow, "Die Beschwörung der Geschlossenheit," *Frankfurter Rundschau online,* http://www.fr-aktuell.de/fr/101/t101003.htm (accessed 6 August 2002).
42. "Die Bremswege sind lang," *Der Spiegel,* no. 34 (19 August 2002): 26–27.
43. Forschungsgruppe Wahlen, *Politbarometer Flash* 09/2002, p. 2
44. The statistics were reported in the Greens' election e-mail newsletter on 20 September 2002. See John Vincour's observations of Fischer on tour, "For Fischer, a Paler Shade of Green," *International Herald Tribune,* 13 September 2002, pp. 1, 5.
45. Unless otherwise indicated, this section relies on the statistics of "Bundestagswahl: Eine Analyse der Wahl vom 22. September 2002," Berichte der Forschungsgruppe Wahlen, Mannheim.
46. Also, the Greens had a net gain of 50,000 votes from the FDP. See Infratest dimap, *Wahlreport: Wahl zum 15. Deutschen Bundestag am 22. September 2002,* Berlin, October 2002, p. 40.
47. Matthias Geis, "Joschka gibt, Joschka nimmt," *Die Zeit,* no. 41 (2 October 2002): 4.
48. See, for example, "The Coalition Labours and Brings Forth Not Very Much," *The Economist,* 19 October 2002, p. 31.
49. Quoted by Lukas Wallraff, *die tageszeitung,* 24–25 May 2003, p. 1.
50. Cited in *Frankfurter Rundschau online,* http://www.fr-aktuell.de/_inc/_globals/print.php?client=fr&cnt=296050&r.dokumentation (accessed 6 September 2003).
51. This section relies on the election reports of Forschungsgruppe Wahlen: *Wahl in Niedersachsen: Ein Analyse der Landstagswahl vom 02. February 2003, Wahl in Hessen: Eine Analyse der Landtagswahl vom 02. Februar 2003,* and *Wahl in Bremen: Eine Analyse der Bürgerschaftswahl vom 25. Mai 2003.*

52. Statistics come from the Greens' Web site, http://www.gruene-partei.de/rsvgn/rs-dok/0,,40208-print,00.htm, and from "Der SPD laufen die Mitgleider davon," *Spiegel Online*, http://www.spiegel.de/politik/deutschland/0,1518,druck-261198,00.html (accessed 14 August 2002).
53. Jan Thomsen, "Berliner gegen schwarz-grünen Senat," *Berliner Zeitung*, http://www.berlinonline.de/.bin/print.php/berliner-zeitung/berlin/268071.html (accessed 13 August 2003).
54. An unnamed top Green quoted by Gerd Rosenkranz in *Spiegel Online*, http://www.spiegel.de/politik/deutschland/0,1518,druck-263696,00.html (accessed 30 August 2003).

Chapter 6

A False Dawn for Germany's Liberals
The Rise and Fall of *Project 18*

Christian Søe

In 2002 the Free Democrats competed for the first time in 33 years as an opposition party in a Bundestag election. Four years earlier, the small party had finally been displaced by the Greens as junior coalition party in the federal government. At the outset of the new campaign, it seemed possible for the FDP to recapture the position of balancer in the party system, and thus return to cabinet office. Instead, the Free Democrats proclaimed a goal that went far beyond such a restoration of the *status quo ante*. The FDP aimed at nothing less than a realignment of the established party system, with its own elevation to the rank of a major party.

Guido Westerwelle, the party's young and dynamic new chairman, tied this ambitious goal to a campaign that indulged heavily in orchestrated gags and studied unconventionality. When critics began referring to the "fun party," some Free Democrats found it necessary to explain that politics could be cheerful without becoming frivolous. Whether they always observed that fine distinction remains a matter of dispute, but a case can be made that, where it mattered most, Germany's self-proclaimed Liberals erred primarily on the side of earnestness. Their campaign's determinedly lighthearted delivery was secondary to the very serious main agenda, often referred to as *Project 18*.

Three Men and a Plan

The basic campaign plan bore the imprint of three men. Guido Westerwelle became a convert and enthusiastic sponsor, after adding an important emendation. In May 2001 he persuaded delegates at the annual party congress, who had just elected him party leader, to endorse his version of the strategic plan. That was a partial setback for Jürgen Möllemann, the newly elected

---

Notes for this chapter begin on page 132.

deputy leader of the FDP, who must count as the political godfather of the original project. After the retirement of the Genscher and Lambsdorff generation, this strong-willed political maverick was one of the small party's rare full-blooded politicians. He was certainly its most controversial one. Yet even his many critics in the party were impressed by Möllemann's chutzpah as leader of the state party in North Rhine-Westphalia, when he brought it from a political nowhere to a smashing Landtag victory in May 2000. The paternity rights for *Project 18* can be traced to a more obscure third man, Fritz Goergen, who had been Möllemann's strategy advisor in the successful Landtag campaign. A native of Austria, Goergen had been employed by the Liberals for some 25 years in high-level management positions and policy work, before establishing himself as an independent consultant. He was a seasoned campaign strategist, with a reputation for "hard ball" politics, tart political observations, and libertarian views.

The trio shared the conviction that the beleaguered FDP stood on the verge of a potential strategic breakthrough. Their teamwork had at least two basic flaws. The two politicians were rivals as well as allies. And both Möllemann and Goergen seem to have regarded Westerwelle as something of a political lightweight. They would later question his commitment to *Project 18* and distance themselves from his "fun campaign."[1]

The name of the basic campaign plan, which was also referred to as *Strategy 18*, came from the electoral objective it set for the FDP, namely, 18 percent of the vote on the crucial second ballot. This was a hyperbolic target for the small party. It amounted to twice its average result in all the Bundestag elections since 1949 and three times its most recent score (6.2 percent). Yet the plan prescribed an even loftier goal. Guided by their flamboyant leader and his determined deputy, the Liberals embarked on a high-flying quest to free the FDP from what both saw as its auxiliary position in the German party system. The aim was to bring the small party to a status of parity with the much larger *Volksparteien* of Christian Democrats and Social Democrats.

This is where it became important to Westerwelle that the FDP be presented as an autonomous and different kind of *Partei für das ganze Volk* (party of all the people). Möllemann showed fewer inhibitions about referring to the FDP as a *Volkspartei* in the making. He regarded it as essential that the FDP break with tradition and name its own "chancellor candidate," in order to demonstrate its claim to parity. In their determination to recast the established party constellation, both Free Democrats were in some ways reminiscent of British third party politicians who for years have dreamt of "breaking the mold" of their country's duopoly. Indeed, the first leader of the British Liberal Democrats had long referred to his party's preparations for a political realignment as "The Project."[2] It was a patient, long-term plan that reflected the particularities of the British political context, whereas Westerwelle and Möllemann's approach turned out to be far more immediate and histrionic in execution.

In retrospect, the intriguing question becomes how *Project 18* could have enjoyed even limited plausibility among seasoned politicians in the FDP. A good part of the answer must be drawn from the fact that the game plan took shape against a backdrop of Landtag elections in which the small party made a surprisingly vigorous comeback from the longest and most severe losing streak in its history. The unexpected turnabout in the fortunes of the beleaguered FDP left German Liberals exuberant, with many wanting to believe that their party's time had finally come. Westerwelle and Möllemann assured them that this was indeed the case.

In speeches and writings that mixed political orientation and exhortation, they portrayed Germany as undergoing an upheaval (*Umbruch*) during its transition from an industrial society toward an "information" or "knowledge" society. Traditional social structures and ties were loosening up, including those that had provided the Western part of Germany with so much electoral stability over the years. By now, voter behavior and the party system were already in flux, with one-half of the voters no longer close to any party and 30 percent willing to consider voting for the FDP. The best news was that the Free Democrats, with their liberal values of individualism and freedom, were particularly well suited to capitalize on this societal transition. The relative electoral success of their liberal sister parties in the Netherlands, Belgium, Denmark and Britain served as convenient evidence of what was possible in Germany as well.[3]

The FDP's attempted quantum leap was based on what turned out to be a fatal misinterpretation of the turnaround in the party's fortunes. German society is undoubtedly undergoing structural changes, and some of them may well present new electoral opportunities for a party like the FDP. But its impressive results in several Landtag elections could be explained in far more mundane terms. They coincided with a decline in support for the CDU after the media began to unravel details of a major scandal in connection with a secret political slush fund amassed by former Chancellor Kohl (CDU). As had happened on some past occasions, notably during the Berlin Crisis of 1961 when the FDP reached its all time high of 12.8 percent of the vote, many disaffected CDU-oriented voters had for a while transferred their support to the FDP.

The vision of a breakthrough for the FDP had a tonic effect in a party used to live in fear and trembling of its political mortality. Möllemann first introduced the scenario leading to "the new party landscape" of tomorrow in a galvanizing speech at the party congress in June 2000. The FDP would leave behind the position of "third force" as well as the subordinate status implied by its role as a majority maker and junior coalition party. Möllemann saw the *18* as an intermediate step on the way to an even larger size. The three old parties—SPD, CDU/CSU, and FDP—would all gravitate to the 30 percent zone, with the Greens and PDS left far behind, should they manage to survive. His rousing vision was populist, although he avoided that term, for he described the FDP as an integrative catch-all party that would attract politically homeless or disappointed voters as well as previous non-voters from across the political spectrum.[4]

For his part, Westerwelle was fond of a grand historical interpretation of the FDP advancing primarily on its own merits. He downgraded explanations of the FDP's electoral revival that emphasized voter reactions to the current political scandals of the big parties. These "affairs of others," as he called them, were merely "accompanying music" (*Begleitmusik*) in the structural transition to a new liberal era: "The party landscape is changing, not because of the affairs, but because society is changing."[5] Similar views were heard from Hans-Jürgen Beerfeltz, the party's federal manager and coordinator of its Bundestag campaign. He had argued for years that the FDP could enlarge its share of the vote significantly by dipping into what he considered to be a large and growing liberal potential in the electorate. Now he anticipated "a complete transformation of the party system in Germany."[6]

If *Project 18* had not been launched by Möllemann and promoted by Westerwelle, it is likely that the FDP would have adopted a far more conventional strategy and set of expectations. It had started out that way, when the party's campaign planners held their first meeting two years before the election. In his role as general secretary, Westerwelle reported to the party presidium that a consensus had been reached on two interrelated goals.[7] First, the FDP should seek to reach a double-digit result. That was an ambitious but not unrealistic goal that had been reached on four previous occasions (in 1949, 1961, 1980 and 1990). Second, the FDP should seek an electoral outcome in which no government, except for a grand coalition of CDU/CSU and SPD, could be built without including the FDP as coalition party. This traditional goal had been reached by the FDP in all ten elections between 1961 and 1994. The report added that the planners saw no reason "at this time" for a coalition commitment. It briefly acknowledged receipt of additional strategic materials, also from Möllemann, that the group planned to include in its later work.

In the months that followed, *Project 18* came to occupy the center of the stage before its formal endorsement in May 2001. The new strategy left room for much that was familiar in the FDP's campaign. Even the most active converts to the new vision had to operate within the existing German party system that they were seeking to transcend. As in past elections, the FDP devoted much energy to advance its relative position among the small parties in the Bundestag. Many of the FDP's electoral efforts, especially at the local level, followed a long established pattern, even when the gadgetry touted the *18*. Moreover, as in most political campaigns, the FDP had to respond to events that fell outside the script, such as the August floods along the river Elbe and Chancellor Schröder's surprise statements on Iraq. And no amount of "politainment" could cover up the self-inflicted wounds and signs of disarray in the leadership, when Möllemann's provocative campaign brought charges of "Haiderization" against the FDP in May of 2002 and later.

When the ballots were counted on 22 September 2002, the FDP had advanced from its low 1998 tally of 6.2 percent to 7.4 percent of the vote. It had significantly improved its position in the new eastern states and made notable advances among young voters and workers. From a conventional point of view, this outcome could have been rated as a modest but "solid" improvement over the results in 1994 and 1998. But it was a disaster from the point of view of the expectations associated with *Project 18*.

A Party on the Skids: The Electoral Disasters of 1999

Once the most successful small coalition party in Western Europe, the FDP has long been in a state of stagnation or decline, interrupted by occasional short-term revivals. In the early 1990s, it plunged into a prolonged crisis marked by huge membership losses, weak leadership, internal quarrels and dismal election results. The flailing party became increasingly dependent on and identified with its senior coalition partner. During the last half of the decade, the FDP survived in only four of the sixteen state legislatures (Landtage) and remained a junior partner in just two of the Land cabinets. Although it managed to hang on in the Bundestag, the slippage showed up there as well. The Greens overtook the FDP as "third force" in 1994. Four years later, they finally displaced the Liberals as majority-makers in a new governing coalition with the Social Democrats. Thus, the Bundestag election of 1998 ended the FDP's record stay of twenty-nine consecutive years in Germany's federal government, first with the SPD (1969–1982) and then with the CDU/CSU (1982–1998).

The Free Democrats had anticipated the power shift in 1998 and primarily concerned themselves with political survival that year. In 1995, the FDP had replaced Foreign Minister Klaus Kinkel as its party leader after only two years in office. Wolfgang Gerhardt, his amiable successor, proved equally unable to revive the party or stem its losing streak. In 1998, the FDP won only 6.2 percent of the vote in the Bundestag election, its second worst performance in history.

The new Bundestag that met after the 1998 election reflected the shifts in voter support, even as it maintained the basic constellation of two-big-plus-three-small parties that could be roughly arranged along a moderate Left-Right divide. As the big party on the right-of-center, the Christian Democrats had also recorded their second worst result in history, albeit with 35.1 percent or more than five times as many votes as the Free Democrats, their erstwhile junior partners. A similar ratio existed within the new left-of-center government coalition, where the SPD won 40.9 percent or six times more than its junior partner of Greens, who scored 6.7 percent. Further to the left and concentrated in the new eastern states, the PDS was able to meet the minimum requirement by winning 5.1 percent. In the 2002 election, the Free Democrats directly challenged this familiar constellation, with its routine coalition arrangements between a big chancellor party and a junior majority-maker as well as its less well defined tendency toward "Left" and "Right" blocs. The FDP's strategic reorientation only came about after the passage of another year of electoral catastrophes, 1999.

The FDP found it difficult to adjust to the opposition role after the long experience of co-governing. On occasion, the Free Democrats were still able to leave their imprint on the final version of a sensitive piece of legislation, as in the case of the compromises reached on double citizenship or same-sex partnerships. Such contributions were relatively rare, and they did not seem to improve the party's standing with the public any more than did its engagements in critical opposition.

The Free Democrats prided themselves on having a distinctive policy orientation that was relevant for the long overdue reform of the German economic and social system, the legendary *Modell Deutschland*. After becoming general secretary, Westerwelle had taken a key role in formulating a more distinctive programmatic profile for his party. The result was the 1997 Wiesbaden program in which the FDP reaffirmed its commitment to socioeconomic reforms that were more market-oriented than the approaches favored by the other parties in the Bundestag. Yet such a program, whatever its merits, was not necessarily a political asset in a country whose corporatist traditions and risk-averse culture emphasize the need to tame rather than release the energies of the market economy. Westerwelle and his party were often charged with being loudspeakers for "turbo-capitalist" and "neo-liberal" values that would undermine Germany's basic social contract and dismantle its time-honored welfare state. At the same time, the party could be accused of not always practicing what it preached. It was well known that the FDP would tenaciously defend regulations that protected the interests of its professional and business clienteles against the rough "winds of competition."

In another respect, the general secretary seemed to have second thoughts about the untrammeled market economy. Soon after the 1998 Bundestag election, he turned his party's attention to the alleged social deficit in the Wiesbaden program. As a practical politician, he probably recognized that the party's neo-liberal reputation could be a future stumbling block for potential supporters of the FDP as well as for potential coalition bids from the SPD. Unlike party leader Gerhardt, Westerwelle showed no ideological preference for a CDU coalition partner. Under the slogan "Liberaler ist sozialer" (More liberal means more social), the FDP devoted an important part of its annual congress in 1999 and again in 2000 to a discussion and eventual adoption of what Westerwelle considered to be responsible liberal answers to a variety of social problems.

The FDP derived no immediate benefits from these efforts to identify itself with what might be called compassionate neo-liberalism. Indeed, 1999 can be singled out as the *annus miserabilis* in the party's crisis-ridden history, if measured by its disastrous standings in public opinion polls and the intermittent state elections. Its national poll ratings hovered at about 5 percent, and frequently fell below that crucial mark. The FDP's electoral performance was much worse. In the 1999 election to the European Parliament, the small party hit its all-time low with only 3 percent of the national vote. In six of seven state elections that year, the results were even lower, ranging between 1 and 2.6 percent (in Saxony, Brandenburg, Thuringia, Berlin, Bremen and the Saar). Inevitably, these outcomes gave a new lease on life to the old joke that FDP really means "Fast Drei Prozent" (Almost 3 percent).

The earliest of the seven Landtag elections in 1999 had been held in February, in the state of Hesse. It was the only one where the FDP managed to pass the 5 percent hurdle. Even so, the party was saved by just a whisker, for its share of the vote plunged from 7.4 to 5.1 percent. Ironically, the vagaries of coalition arithmetic sweetened this particular setback, for the handful of Free Democrats in the Landtag unexpectedly found themselves as majority makers in a coalition with the CDU. The Christian Democrats had surged in Hesse, largely because of their role in mobilizing a petition drive against a planned federal law on double citizenship. The rare opportunity to join a state government clearly meant more to Hesse's FDP than any liberal misgivings about the new partner's willingness to play on popular fears of a tidal wave of immigrants receiving full citizenship rights. As a result, a new CDU-FDP coalition replaced the Red-Green Land government in Wiesbaden in a mirror image of the power shift that had taken place a few months earlier in federal politics.

A Party in Revival: The Electoral Triumphs between 2000 and 2002

Beginning in early 2000, the FDP started to surge ahead in its poll standings and Landtag election results. Soon the party membership began to rise for the first time since the year of unification, even as the other parties represented in the Bundestag reported continuing losses. The FDP alone was able to report a net growth for the years 2001 and 2002.[8] A large proportion of the new members were young people.

The U-turn came as a surprise, but it was not difficult to explain in conventional terms. It coincided with a barrage of media reports on the slush fund scandal, popularly known as "Kohlgate." The mounting publicity boosted the FDP poll standings even as the CDU ratings plummeted.[9] For a while, some CDU-oriented voters reacted to their own party's problems by shifting their support to the nearest alternative party, the FDP. A similar reaction, but on a more limited scale, appears to have taken place among some SPD-oriented voters in North Rhine-Westphalia, in response to a series of regional scandals involving Social Democrats in public office.[10] The FDP did not hesitate to capitalize on the situation by presenting itself as a "clean" alternative to the *Volksparteien*, almost two decades after its own involvement in the "Flick affair."

The sharp turnabout showed up most strikingly in the seven Landtag elections held between February 2000 and April 2002. The Free Democrats not only passed the 5 percent hurdle in every one of these seven states, their party increased its share of the vote in five of them. In several the advance was spectacular. By the end of this election series, the FDP had moved from representation in four of the 16 Landtage to nine, and from membership in three state coalition governments (including Hesse) to five.

The first contest took place in late February 2000 in Schleswig-Holstein, where Wolfgang Kubicki was the leading FDP candidate. In May, Jürgen Möllemann brought the FDP campaign in North Rhine-Westphalia to a conclusion. The two men were personal friends and coordinated some aspects of their Landtag campaigns. Both were open critics of Wolfgang Gerhardt's political style (too laid-back) and direction (too CDU-oriented). The election results in both states were stunning. Schleswig-Holstein has never been an easy territory for the FDP, but it was one of the four states where the Liberals had managed to retain a parliamentary foothold after the mid-1990s. Now they lunged ahead from 5.7 to 7.6 percent of the state's vote. This was the party's best Landtag result in the northern state in almost three decades and its second-best tally there in the entire history of the Federal Republic.

North Rhine-Westphalia, with more than one-fifth of Germany's population, was the most important political test facing the FDP. It was one of the twelve states where the FDP had been ousted in the most recent Landtag election. Möllemann followed a campaign plan, dubbed *Project 8*, which set the electoral goal of winning 8 percent of the vote. This numerical target was apparently chosen, because it amounted to a doubling of the party's result in the previous election (4 percent). Political observers, including many Free Democrats, regarded such a goal as absolutely unrealistic.[11]

The FDP's Landtag campaign gave a foretaste of how the later Bundestag campaign would be planned.[12] It was dominated by what appeared to be a very effective public relations effort, conceived largely by a small team of professional specialists that included the deliberately unconventional Fritz Goergen. The party's self-promotion was highly personalized, with a dynamic Möllemann appearing on posters and handbills, giving campaign talks, and descending in his blue-and-yellow parachute at political meetings. The slogans were catchy if not very substantive. One example was a large FDP poster message with the playful greeting "Guten Landtag!" Traffic congestion and public education were at the top of the agenda of items for which the FDP offered itself as a problem-solver. Its messages often poked fun at the Red-Green government's alleged failure to deliver. They demanded "more tempo" for North Rhine-Westphalia and tried to arouse interest through a tactic of limited provocation, the so-called daily breaking of rules or taboos. One planned poster that ran into a hailstorm of criticism for stepping over the line was promptly withdrawn. It depicted Hitler as well as a horror film character and cult leader with the message that "unless we quickly get more teachers, our children will seek out some on their own." The same message was used in posters showing skinheads and a drug addict taking a fix.

The election in North Rhine-Westphalia resulted in a second and even bigger triumph for the FDP. The party topped its own ambitious target by winning 9.8 percent of the vote, the best performance by the FDP in the state since 1954. As man of the hour, Möllemann seized the opportunity to propagate a similar campaign plan for the Bundestag election of 2002. At the annual party congress meeting at Nuremberg in June 2000, he gave a rousing talk on behalf of what he already called *Project 18*.[13] He repeated his basic argument in many political speeches during the following months. Boosted by the victory, Möllemann had gained an often-reluctant admiration and influence in the FDP. He used it to work for a change of both the party's national leader and its grand electoral strategy. Within a year, he had largely succeeded on both counts, but the chief beneficiary turned out to be Westerwelle.

Jürgen Möllemann was one of the party's most talented, ambitious and controversial politicians, who had established a reputation as a nonconformist risk taker. He had stumbled repeatedly during the three decades of his political career, but he always managed to rise again. His eyes had long been on the party leadership. He ran unsuccessfully against Gerhardt in 1995. Many Free Democrats remained deeply ambivalent about him, but Möllemann was a forceful politician who could not be ignored. As head of the largest state party, comprising fully one-fourth of the FDP's membership, Möllemann had his own power base. It had now been augmented by his new role as leader of the largest Landtag group of Free Democrats anywhere in Germany. When the national leadership seemed to elude him again, Möllemann began to promote Westerwelle for that position even as he insisted that the FDP should also nominate its own chancellor candidate. A complex political symbiosis developed between Möllemann and the general secretary, sixteen years his junior. Where Kinkel and Gerhardt had kept a distance from Möllemann, Westerwelle tried to maintain a cautious alliance. He was impressed by the ambitious and strong-willed politician, but also somewhat wary. After adopting a modified version of *Project 18*, Westerwelle eventually persuaded Goergen to join the federal campaign planners as a strategy consultant.

Möllemann had failed to reach one of his main political goals in his home state: to lead the Free Democrats into the Land government in place of the smaller parliamentary party of Greens. A coalition with Möllemann's larger FDP parliamentary group would have given Premier Wolfgang Clement (SPD) a somewhat broader and probably more stable base in the Landtag than the narrow and fissured parliamentary majority provided by the

SPD's alliance with the Greens. However, Clement would have to consider how such a reversal of coalitions in Germany's most populous state would affect the balance of power and governance at the national level. In the end, and after consultation with SPD leaders in Berlin, Clement decided to continue the Red-Green coalition.

Möllemann seemed surprised but did not give up the hope that premier Clement would eventually replace the Greens with the FDP. He had argued at least since the mid-1990s that the FDP should avoid identifying itself with a Left or Right direction or camp (*Lager*) in German politics. Instead, he favored a situational choice of coalitions with the SPD or the CDU as political circumstances permitted. In his eyes, Kinkel and Gerhardt had both identified the FDP far too closely with the conservative option. Möllemann did not belong to the "social-liberal" wing of his party that still had a distinctive voice in the Freiburg Circle. His interest in working with the Social Democrats was linked to his conviction that the SPD was more likely than the CDU to be Germany's strongest party for a while.

After a 10-month interlude, the series of state elections resumed in March 2001. It began with moderate electoral setbacks for the Liberals in the two southwestern states where they had the best starting position. The FDP leaders in these states, Walter Döring and Rainer Brüderle, belonged to the party's national leadership. They showed greater political self-confidence and less inclination to be impressed by Möllemann and his instant campaign solutions than some of their counterparts in states where the FDP had a much weaker base. As members of their respective state governments, the southwestern Liberals seemed to be constrained in their campaign efforts far less by complacency than by coalition considerations. It was a situation that was familiar to the federal FDP from its many years of co-governing in Bonn. In Baden-Württemberg, once regarded as a liberal stronghold, the FDP share of the vote dipped in 2001 from 9.6 to 8.1 percent. This was more than enough to continue as member of Premier Erwin Teufel's CDU-led coalition government. In the neighboring Rhineland-Palatinate, where there was a similar "adjustment" from 8.9 to 7.8 percent of the vote, the FDP also remained in a government coalition, here with the SPD under Premier Kurt Beck. Despite the reduction, it was the FDP's second highest result in this state since 1967.

The last three state elections in this series brought new advances, including two more triumphs for the FDP. In the fall of 2001, the Free Democrats returned to the assemblies in the city-states of Hamburg and Berlin, where they had been absent for several years. The Hamburg comeback was a shaky one, with the FDP winning 5.1 percent of the vote, up from 3.5 percent in 1997. The outcome was made more uncertain by the FDP's decision to join a CDU-led governing coalition that arithmetically required the inclusion of a right-wing populist protest party led by Roland Schill. It was remarkable that this upstart party, led by a judge with a reputation for a strict law-and-order outlook, could on its first try win almost one-fifth of the vote in this north German city—slightly more than the FDP's target for the Bundestag election! Berlin's early election in October 2001 gave the FDP another chance to come in from the cold. Here its tally rose dramatically from 2.2 percent in 1999 to 9.9 percent—a more than fourfold increase and its best result in the city since the early postwar elections of 1950 and 1954, when only West Berlin had voted. The election outcome city-states supported the general conclusion that the electorate had become more volatile.

The final test before the Bundestag election came in late April 2002 in Saxony-Anhalt, less than a month before that year's regular party congress. From the time of unification, the FDP had invested much political effort in this eastern home region of its elder statesman, Hans-Dietrich Genscher. In 1990, the voters of Saxony-Anhalt had given the FDP its highest results anywhere, in both the Bundestag election (19.7 percent) and the Landtag election (13.5 percent). In the next couple of years, the FDP's initial strength had collapsed throughout eastern Germany. In every one of the new states the FDP had failed to pass the 5 percent hurdle in the Bundestag and Landtag elections that followed. The high volatility of the eastern vote found a special expression in Saxony-Anhalt's 1998 Landtag election, where a well-financed campaign for the extreme right-wing German People's Union (DVU) mobilized almost 13 percent for a party that had no organization to speak of in the state. Four years later, discredited by self-inflicted wounds and without financial aid, the DVU did not compete.

In 2002 the disappearance of the DVU increased the likelihood of yet another electoral surprise in Saxony-Anhalt. The FDP continued to regard the state as its best opportunity to regain a foothold in the East. The party headquarters in Berlin, with important support from Möllemann's state party, conducted an expensive Landtag campaign there with a personalization focused on Cornelia Pieper. She had been picked as a distinctive eastern voice and promoted to the party presidium before Westerwelle chose her as general secretary in 2001. Pieper was widely pictured with sassy slogans and advertised as the state's next premier (*Ministerpräsidentin*). The outcome was another triumph for the FDP. By advancing from 4.2 percent to 13.3 percent, the party more than tripled its result of 1998. The Free Democrats were jubilant, tending to overlook the likelihood that the voters who had come so quickly could also depart in a hurry. Many saw the victory as a dress rehearsal for the Bundestag election.

Some Key Decisions: Düsseldorf, 2001, and Mannheim, 2002

A little over a year after the electoral breakthrough in North Rhine-Westphalia, but before the state elections in Hamburg, Berlin and Saxony-Anhalt, the regular party congress met at Düsseldorf in May 2001. In two key decisions, the delegates gave an enthusiastic endorsement of a man and a plan that promised the FDP an important new role in party and coalition politics. The Düsseldorf congress buzzed with excitement and optimism, but it was well orchestrated and—with two important exceptions to be discussed below—produced no great surprises or departures from the main script. The two central decisions amounted to official approval of arrangements made previously in the party's leadership circle.

It had been known since the beginning of 2001 that Wolfgang Gerhardt's days as party leader were numbered, despite his public insistence as late as December 2000 that he intended to run for another term in office. Möllemann and Kubicki had continued to accuse him of weak leadership and call for his replacement. Like Kinkel before him, Gerhardt reacted with a stoic forbearance and occasional shows of annoyance. He underestimated a growing willingness among other leading party members to back Westerwelle. They shared an interest in ending the FDP's authority crisis before the next round of elections, and many wanted to block Möllemann. No one appeared to doubt Westerwelle's political qualifications, at least not after he had come out of the wings to challenge Gerhardt in a private confrontation at the beginning of 2001. Gerhardt agreed to a proposed "tandem" settlement. He would remain leader of the parliamentary party in the Bundestag, while Westerwelle would replace him as party leader when his term ran out a few months later.

The transition went smoothly. Westerwelle was duly elected at the May congress, where he received support from close to 90 percent of the participating delegates (569 of 640 valid votes cast).[14] Möllemann, who had been encouraged by Westerwelle to be a candidate for the deputy leadership, was elected with 66 percent. That was not a high level of support, but it landed him between the two other deputy leaders, Rainer Brüderle (89 percent) and Walter Döring (51 percent). All three were considered to have been aspirants for the top post that now had gone to Westerwelle. Characteristically it was Möllemann alone who had taken active steps to remove Gerhardt. Döring was one of Möllemann's sharpest critics in the party, while Brüderle seems to have been rewarded for having stayed above the fray.

At 39 years of age, Westerwelle was the youngest person ever to head any of the mainstream parties in the Federal Republic. He had taken over a difficult post—one for which the revolving door would be an apt symbol. Each of his four immediate predecessors had presided over just one Bundestag election before resigning. But this new leader offered the small party something different. With his youth and drive, even with his reputation for flamboyant behavior and formulaic "sound bite" rhetoric, Westerwelle seemed to embody the FDP's hope for rejuvenation.

Despite his youth, Westerwelle could already look back on two decades of experience in party-related activities. In the early 1980s, he had been co-founder and then leader of the party's new youth organization, the Young Liberals (*Julis*). It continued to serve as a political base for him. As a member of the party's executive committee since 1988, he knew all the leading party members well—and they knew and generally respected him. Above all, he had been a very active general secretary for over six years.

In addition to their approval of the new leadership settlement, the delegates at Düsseldorf overwhelmingly endorsed the campaign plan that Möllemann had promoted ever since his victory in North Rhine-Westphalia. By now Westerwelle had embraced the plan and, with one exception, become its enthusiastic advocate. The element that had not been given his imprimatur was regarded by Möllemann as essential. Like several other leading Free Democrats, Westerwelle expressed reservations about having the FDP field its own chancellor candidate. He pointed to the obvious problem of credibility. Even with an 18 percent share of the vote, a coalition party would hardly get to name the head of government from its own ranks. Presumably, Westerwelle had another objection that he left unspoken. It was widely assumed that Möllemann intended to claim the role of chancellor candidate for himself in a kind of division of labor and power with the new party leader. Indeed, he had flirted with the idea in interviews and in a series of letters to several hundred leading Free Democrats.[15]

A future power struggle could be sensed when Möllemann strongly supported his state party's motion to include the chancellor candidacy in the new campaign strategy. Recognizing a challenge to his authority as party leader, Westerwelle responded in a speech that seemed to sway many of the delegates who had just cheered Möllemann. A 72 percent majority approved his recommendation that the FDP use the terms "leading candidate" (*Spitzenkandidat*) and "top team" (*Spitzenteam*) rather than "chancellor candidate."[16] Westerwelle also used the occasion to remind the delegates that he intended to be in charge as leader of the party. He underscored his claim to be in command by citing a jaunty couplet: "On every ship that steams or sails, there's one whose final word prevails!" To which he added: "And that's me!"[17]

Strategy 18 is a relatively short document.[18] It was followed by more detailed plans for its implementation, including one prepared for and approved by the party's executive committee on 18 February 2002.[19] The original contains the essentials, including a reference to the FDP's *Spitzenkandidat* (rather than *Kanzlerkandidat*). It presents a mini-version of what might be called Westerwelle's neo-Whig view of contemporary historical progress, including a new formulation of the familiar conclusion that the FDP has a historic opportunity to become "a party of all the people" who ask what they can do for their community and country instead of calling on the state to do it.

The final section includes four points that together constitute the most important departure from the party's traditional election strategy:

- The strategic goal is clear: The FDP must be so strong that no government can be built without it—except for a pact of stagnation between the SPD and the CDU/CSU. The goal is 18 percent.
- As a party of all the people, the FDP fights for support from people in all demographic groups. It is not a party for a certain occupational group, an age category, or an income class. It turns to everyone who wants more freedom and responsibility and less tutelage by the state.
- As a party of all the people, the FDP sees itself neither as a member of a political camp, nor as a majority-maker.... The FDP enters the Bundestag election of 2002 without an advance coalition commitment.... It enters the competition as a party of all the people (and) one that is on a par with the SPD and the CDU/CSU.
- Therefore, the FDP will not support someone else's chancellor candidate but instead its own leading candidate and top team.

A year later, Westerwelle reversed his position and asked for his party's endorsement as chancellor candidate. By this time, he appeared to have consolidated his leadership of the party and there seemed to be no threat of a challenge from Möllemann. A few weeks earlier, Cornelia Pieper had been advertised with great success as the future premier of Saxony-Anhalt. The great victory in the eastern state seems to have been decisive for Westerwelle's decision to go for the supposed electoral bonus linked to a formal chancellor candidacy. The delegates who came to the party congress at Mannheim in May 2002 gave overwhelming approval. Only two voted against naming Westerwelle to be the FDP's *Kanzlerkandidat*—its first in history.

This designation had long been claimed by the leading candidate of the CDU/CSU and the SPD respectively. Its importance had been enhanced at least since 1961, when Willy Brandt ran as the SPD chancellor candidate while Erich Ollenhauer remained that party's leader. The title thus had traditional legitimacy, even though it was not legally defined and recognized. Until 2002, the FDP and the other small Bundestag parties had never tried to lay claim to the title. In effect, as Möllemann liked to point out, the Free Democrats had until then deferentially accepted that their party could at best hope to be a junior cabinet partner in a coalition government headed by a chancellor designated by one of the *Volksparteien*.

Gerhard Schröder was surely not the only one who, on hearing the news about Westerwelle's candidacy, called it "a joke."[20] It was not quite that. By claiming the title for Westerwelle, the party asserted its claim to be on "an eye-to-eye level" with the SPD and CDU. The controversial candidacy brought the small party some additional publicity, but it was not taken for full by German public television. Despite his pleas, backed by unsuccessful court appeals, Westerwelle remained excluded from the two televised debates between the chancellor candidates, a forum in which Westerwelle's stage presence could well have scored some points for his party.

On first sight the repeated assertion that the FDP is not a party of a certain income class or occupational group appears curious. It can be traced to Westerwelle's general concern to move away from his party's association with privilege and wealth. More particularly, it reflected his reaction to the lingering embarrassment of a notorious campaign gaffe by the Liberals. In 1994 the FDP had made an ironic reference to itself as the *Partei der Besserverdienenden* (party of higher income earners) in the first draft of its election program. The phrase immediately caused offense and met with ridicule. It has dogged the party ever since, with both media and political rivals gleefully recalling this self-characterization at election time. The FDP tried eagerly to heal the self-inflicted wound. It pointed out that the formulation "higher income earners" was borrowed from a controversial SPD minimum tax proposal and set in quotations marks to indicate its ironic and forensic usage by the FDP. The phrase had been scrapped early, well before the adoption of the final election program. All these explanations made no dent in a collective memory that sometimes raised the phrase to the level of a former FDP slogan. Its longevity can be attributed to the fact that the verbal slip contained more than a grain of truth and thus seemed unwittingly self-revealing, in view of the small party's traditional voter base and policy orientation.[21] Westerwelle thus faced an uphill battle in his determination to overcome an elitist appearance in favor of a more inclusive image of the FDP as a "party of all the people."

The Campaign: Reaching for the 18

Strategy 18 foresaw a Bundestag campaign handled by "professionals," as had been the case with the Landtag campaign in North Rhine-Westphalia two years earlier. Goergen, who had conceptualized the new strategy, was an important link between the two campaign groups. The party headquarters in Berlin reported enthusiastically on the work of the planners, now renamed "Team 18." The financial constraints were considerable, for the party was able to set aside only 5 million euros for the campaign, or about one-fifth the sum available to each of the *Volksparteien*, as estimated by a leading FDP strategist.[22] In this respect, as in so many others, parity of status was a long way off for the Free Democrats.

An example of the team's product is the glossy brochure, *On the Road to 18*, directed at party activists.[23] It stressed the need to convey a dynamic image of the party that should be contrasted with that of "the competition." The first two sentences, to be repeated endlessly during the campaign, pronounced the "decisive difference" between the three old parties: "The Free Democrats create [*gestalten*], CDU/CSU and SPD administer [*verwalten*]." Echoing Goergen and Möllemann's views on political communication, the brochure emphasized the need to convey clear messages that employ "talking pictures ... not pictures of talkers." And it practiced what it preached, mixing pictures of campaign posters with a relatively short, direct text. The posters were all in some way sassy or provocative, such as one of a male dressing down to his briefs to satisfy the tax man. Another was written in Chinese with a smaller German text pointing out that every fourth child in German schools feels "that way" (presumably bewildered) when attending German language classes. A curious reader would learn the translation of the message: "If we are in the next government, we will lower taxes, improve the school system, and make sure there is more employment."

The goal of *18* became a mantra during the campaign. The number was intoned or displayed alone or together with a refurbished FDP logo (minus the three dots) wherever the party presented itself. It appeared in the FDP's bright yellow-and-blue colored posters, letter heads, Web sites, flags, stickers, caps, T-shirts, cigarette lighters, balloons, wine labels and at least one lamp shade located in Westerwelle's *Guidomobil*. The federal party manager and campaign coordinator, Beerfeltz, welcomed the visual inundation with the number and pointed earnestly to its symbolic meaning: "The 18 is ... more than the so-called 'running gag' of the campaign. It is the FDP's metaphor for the claim to a complete transformation of the party system in Germany."[24]

The script included the basic elements of a traditional campaign. As always, the FDP took pride in presenting a detailed election program, 88 pages in length, which had been debated, revised and approved by the Mannheim congress.[25] Again following convention, the party waited to issue its mercifully shorter election call (*Wahlaufruf*), in which the FDP managed to state its main positions in four pages. For really light reading, the party provided a separate list of "18 Good Reasons to Vote FDP." The recurrent theme was less state, more society.

The party's economic and financial reform proposals earned high marks from some business-oriented publications.[26] They included a proposal for a lower and simpler income tax, based on only three progressive levels (15, 25, and 35 percent). That would make the top rate 7 percent lower than the 42 percent rate to which it was scheduled to fall by 2005 under the current reforms. The party further demanded significant cuts in subsidies to aging industries, such as coal mining. Its labor market reforms included a move away from the industry-wide bargaining system toward a company-based one. The program also stressed the need for higher investment in education and research to take Germany well above the average in the OECD. The key promises were summed up in the slogan "More Net Pay. More Education. More Work."

The FDP's strategy had started out with a rejection of the "third force" status, but the party's practical efforts became increasingly concentrated on replacing the Greens in that position. In other ways, too, the FDP was finding it necessary to work within the existing system that it wanted to transcend. There remained some important differences to the conventions of past campaigns. For the first time since 1969, the FDP abandoned its practice of officially announcing in advance its preferred coalition option. Instead the Free Democrats emphasized their "equidistance" from the *Volksparteien*, making it clear that they would be open to bids from both, even when the odds seemed to favor a coalition with the Christian Democrats. They also abstained from the usual practice of mounting a special campaign for the crucial second vote, and on at least one widely displayed poster specifically asked for "both votes." By positioning the FDP as a "constructive" protest party of the center, "a party of all the people," the Free Democrats wanted to broaden its electoral appeal and attract disaffected voters even among lower income earners. This catch-all approach gave rise to self-ironic references to the "vacuum cleaner party."[27] There were none of the desperate survival pleas, so prominent in the last two Bundestag campaigns.

Westerwelle personified the party's "go-getter" attitude, as suggested in the party slogan, "Machen. Machen. Machen." He spiced up the campaign by adding an array of gags that some critics disdainfully referred to as slapstick (*Klamauk*). Yet Westerwelle's flamboyance was a key factor in keeping the media interested in the FDP. He was a frequent guest on the German talk shows, and it was primarily his repertoire of antics that earned the Free Democrats the label of "the fun party." What other prominent politician would have made an unannounced nightly visit to the "Big Brother Container," a German reality television show? Or inscribe a luminous 18 on the soles of his shoes and raise them to the camera for maximum national exposure during one of his many television interviews? He took a special interest in the plan to drive through Germany for six summer weeks in the yellow-and-blue *Guidomobil*, a huge, rebuilt camping bus. The itinerary included all of the sixteen states and was reportedly 8,000 kilometers long. It included 80 stops in towns and villages, at summer festivals, sports events, and camping places where Westerwelle sought contact to voters and reporters, and then usually left the vehicle for the comforts of a local hotel.

The FDP remained curiously low keyed on two topics that together helped shift the electoral balance of power in favor of the governing Red-Green coalition. One was the unexpected political decision by Chancellor Schröder to break with tradition and disagree with the United States on its policy toward Iraq. It took some time for the FDP to digest his outspoken refusal to let Germany join a U.S.-led military intervention in Iraq. The other topic was the natural catastrophe that hit Saxony and Saxony-Anhalt in midsummer. Like everyone else, the FDP campaigners were surprised by the August floods along the Elbe and its tributaries. But whereas the leading political rivals used the occasion to draw positive attention to themselves and their parties, Westerwelle continued on his *Deutschlandreise*. He did eventually visit the stricken area, but the press seemed only to notice his belated and brief presence there. It would have been possible to cut short his tour and let his huge vehicle be used as a shelter for a homeless family or donated to a charity for the benefit of the flood victims.[28] Somehow his talent for the dramatic gesture failed him in this instance.

Möllemann and Westerwelle: Testing the Limits of Catch-All Politics

A very different problem had dogged the FDP's campaign since the spring of 2002. It grew out of allegations that Möllemann, in his pursuit of the *18*, was seeking to attract ultra-right voters by engaging in a series of gestures, statements and actions directed against Israel and a leading member of the Jewish community in Germany. Any appearance of anti-Semitism in public life is a serious matter in today's Germany, and Möllemann's prominence as a Free Democrat ensured that it would tarnish the reputation of the FDP as well. Next to the party leader, no one had been so active in the early phase of the campaign as Möllemann. Westerwelle's failure to stop his deputy early and decisively gave the impression of weak leadership, or worse. By pure coincidence, the Möllemann affair overlapped with a literary anti-Semitism debate that was triggered by Martin Walser's new novel, *Death of a Critic*. The two affairs differed considerably, but they became intermingled in the debate that followed.[29]

German political observers have long speculated that the existentially vulnerable FDP could one day be tempted to reinvent itself as a more broadly based protest party of right-wing populism.[30] They have usually presented Jörg Haider's Freedom Party in Austria as a possible model for the transformation of the FDP, but recently some have added Pim Fortuyn's Party in the Netherlands as a more likely libertarian alternative. There has been no convincing evidence that ultra-right tendencies are of more than marginal significance in today's FDP. Nevertheless, Möllemann managed to feed such speculation in an opinion column that regularly appeared under his name in *Neues Deutschland*, where it served as a foil for some very different political ideas advanced by Gregor Gysi, the outspoken left-socialist politician of the PDS. On May 27, Möllemann's column, widely believed to have been ghostwritten by Goergen, seemed to welcome the recent electoral advances by the parties of Haider and Fortuyn as representing the "emancipation of the democrats."[31] It referred vaguely to "a wave of awakening self-confidence among the people of the nations and states of Europe." Claiming that Möllemann had here revealed his true colors as a far-right politician, the newspaper announced that it would publish no more of his columns. It did grant him a response that left matters no less obscure than before. Möllemann insisted that he had been misinterpreted: "Whoever disparages my column ... as 'Haiderization' cannot read." He went on to portray Haider and Le Pen as political pied pipers who had profited from the failure of the democratic parties.

These obscure remarks were published in a former Communist newspaper that is not widely read outside former East Germany. They caught attention because they came at a time when Möllemann was already entangled in another controversy. As president of the German-Arab Society, Möllemann had for years been an outspoken critic of Israel's policy toward the Palestinians. In early April 2002, he referred to the *intifada* suicide bombers as resistance fighters who were opposing foreign occupation. At the end of April he encouraged the political transfer to his FDP Landtag group of a naturalized Syrian-born deputy, Jamal Karsli, who had left his own Green Landtag group after a reprimand for accusing Israel's army of using "Nazi methods." Karsli had lambasted Israeli policies on other occasions, and he now spoke of a Zionist lobby that controlled much of the media.

Karsli's departure from the Greens was politically useful to Möllemann. By reducing the shaky government majority in the Düsseldorf Landtag to five, it revived his hope of leading the Free Democrats into a governing coalition with the SPD in that important state. But the ready acceptance of Karsli by the FDP Landtag group gave rise to a storm of critical reactions. Hildegard Hamm-Brücher, the best known woman in the party and a member since 1948, was one of several prominent Liberals who joined the protest and called for Karsli's ouster. Unhappy with Westerwelle's response, she waited until after the election to submit her formal resignation from the FDP.

The controversy took on a new dimension after Michel Friedman joined the fray by criticizing Möllemann's remarks on the Middle East. Well known as a confrontational television talk show host, Friedman also served as deputy head of the Central Council of Jews in Germany. In a response to his critic, Möllemann managed to include a personal swipe at both President Sharon and Michel Friedman. His convoluted remark essentially blamed them for swelling the ranks of anti-Semites in Germany.[32] Coming in the early stage of an election campaign, these and other remarks and gestures by Möllemann seemed designed to draw attention among far-right voters.

During the latter half of May and into the first week of June, the FDP was in partial disarray as it tried to extricate itself from the controversy. Many leading members of the old guard wanted the exclusion of Karsli from the FDP, but Westerwelle only came to that position belatedly. First he concentrated on a defense of Möllemann's right to be critical of Israel's policies—which was not really at issue. On a previously planned short visit to Israel in late May, Westerwelle encountered high-level outrage over the events in Germany and looked distinctly uncomfortable in the news photos. Karsli remained in the FDP Landtag group until 6 June, when Möllemann finally let him go after receiving an ultimatum from the party leader.

In addition to the Jewish community and a largely critical media, the FDP had faced other expressions of disapproval that culminated in a large protest demonstration before the party's Berlin headquarters in early June. The criticism was no longer directed only at Möllemann, who responded by pointing to thousands of supportive letters he had received, but also at the party and its leader. The controversy inevitably found an echo in the campaign. One of the most indignant reactions came from Joschka Fischer, the Green foreign minister, who decried what he saw as a flirtation with anti-Semitism among his main political rivals. But chancellor candidates Schröder and Stoiber also expressed reservations concerning the suitability of the FDP as a coalition partner (Schröder) or Möllemann as a cabinet member (Stoiber). A survey of business leaders showed a sharp deterioration in the FDP's public appearance (*Auftreten*) between May and June: The percentage of those who judged it to be "bad" or "very bad" had gone from 14 to 54 during the month when the Karsli affair played out.[33]

At the beginning of the affair, Westerwelle vastly underestimated the political and moral trade-offs involved in Möllemann's forays into far-right territory. The party leader unnecessarily stirred misgivings by declaring that the FDP would serve democracy by seeking to attract politically homeless people from across the Left-Right spectrum. In addition to previous non-voters, he specifically named former supporters of the PDS and the far-right *Republikaner*. Westerwelle's own campaign rhetoric focused on mainstream voters, while his antics seemed primarily addressed to the young. But the party leader had made a poor appearance in dealing with Möllemann. Neither Westerwelle nor the FDP recovered their former élan before election day.

Until June, the poll ratings had placed the FDP well ahead of the Greens, and it was widely assumed that the FDP would be part of the next government. The FDP never came anywhere close to 18 percent, but it managed to reach low double-digit poll standings before they tumbled several points in the aftermath of the Karsli Affair to around 8 percent. That is where they stayed until 22 September. By the end of the campaign, they were close to those of the Greens, whose stock had increased, as voters seemed to pay renewed attention to their environmental and pacifist messages. The two major parties and their chancellor candidates came increasingly to dominate the campaign.

As so often, Möllemann turned out to be good for yet another surprise. In the last days of the campaign, he resurrected the controversy of the summer in a flyer that he had printed and sent to some 8 million homes in North Rhine-Westphalia. The front of the folded sheet presented a photo of Möllemann, identified as "one of us" (*einer wie wir*). It promised "straight talk" (*Klartext*) and "courage," but the back contained only a familiar political ad urging that both votes be cast for the FDP. On its inside page, however, the flyer departed sharply from the party's campaign script in order to pursue Möllemann's own feud. Showing Friedman in an unflattering photo, it described him as defending Prime Minister Sharon and trying to brand Möllemann as "anti-Israeli" and "anti-Semitic." Another photo showed Sharon and identified him with sending tanks into refugee camps, ignoring Security Council resolutions, and rejecting a separate Palestinian state. By contrast, Möllemann was presented as working for a peace settlement in the Middle East based on secure boundaries for Israel and a separate Palestinian state.

With the flyer, Möllemann revived the dispute with Friedman and, more clearly than before, connected it to the election campaign. For the FDP, it was no longer possible to simply distance itself from the willful actions of its deputy leader. Political consequences were inevitable, even though they were delayed until after the election. There were additional questions raised by the flyer that would be debated in the months that followed. One of them dealt with how the flyer's printing and mass mailing had been financed. That question soon opened the door to judicial investigations of Möllemann's apparent access to unreported political funds that had been spent in both his Landtag and Bundestag campaigns.

German pollsters seem to agree that this intervention, unlike the controversy of May and June, came too late to affect the outcome of the election in any significant way. It served to emphasize that Möllemann had his own political agenda and would pursue it at will. The flyer took the rest of the FDP leaders by surprise, although a few higher staffers appear to have received some indications, including a written warning, about Möllemann's plan in advance.[34] It was, in other words, not a complete secret that Möllemann intended to make some kind of last-minute move before election day. In the last two hectic campaign weeks, however, no one seems to have looked into the matter.

With his final unilateral campaign move, Möllemann had made himself a convenient scapegoat for the party's troubles. He was effectively kept away from the party's final campaign rally. Proud to the last, he stepped down from the deputy leadership right after the election and then, over a period of several months, from various other party offices before the FDP could complete the formal measures required to remove him. In March 2003, he left the party in advance of his formal exclusion.

The Election Result

On 22 September 2002, the FDP failed to achieve any of its proclaimed campaign goals. It won 7.4 percent of the vote on the crucial second ballot, leaving the party far below the *18*. It was also denied the consolation of a lower double-digit figure. No matter how one interpreted the goal of parity with the two *Volksparteien*, there could be no credible claim that the FDP had narrowed the status gap. Westerwelle's chancellor candidacy now seemed more fanciful than ever. It is as unlikely to be repeated soon as his *Deutschlandreise* in a *Guidomobil*.

Among the small parties, the Greens retained their position as "third force" and majority-maker in the Red-Green coalition government. They won their biggest share of the vote since first entering the Bundestag (8.6 percent) and widened their distance to the FDP slightly. With the virtual disappearance of the PDS, the Bundestag now returned, at least for the time being, to a four-party system—but one in which the FDP continued to be in the fourth place, without the leverage to function as majority-maker. The rough Left-Right alignment of the Bundestag parties continued, even as the balance between the two sides became almost even. Schröder's left-of-center government managed to stay in office, despite the SPD's own losses and the CDU/CSU's gains over 1998.

Given the almost even Left-Right balance in the post-election Bundestag, the question inevitably arose, whether it had been wise for the FDP to announce its "equidistance" from the two *Volksparteien* and thus keep its coalition options open. An officially stated preference for co-governing with the CDU/CSU need not have resulted in a zero-sum exchange of supporters between the two former coalition partners. Some voters oriented toward the other parties, especially the SPD, might have been drawn into a wider and more complex exchange, once the governing alternatives had been more clearly defined by such an advance alignment. The net result could have provided a coalition of Christian and Free Democrats with the small margin needed for a parliamentary majority.

A closely related question could be asked about the FDP's abandonment of a "second vote" campaign, as part of its strategy of autonomy (*Eigenständigkeit*). Since the 1972 Bundestag election, when the beleaguered Free Democrats successfully appealed to supporters of other parties to split their tickets and cast the all-important second vote for the FDP, the Liberals have repeatedly sought to attract such "borrowed votes" (*Leihstimmen*). They had not done so in this election, and that helps explain their advance of 2.8 percent on the first ballot (to 5.8 percent), compared to only 1.2 percent on the second ballot (to 7.4 percent). The resulting gap of just 1.6 percent between the first and second vote is the party's lowest since 1976, when it was 1.5 percent. In that year, the small party had sought to widen and stabilize its electoral base by increasing its share of *both* votes.[35] The result was not positive, and the FDP returned to a second-vote strategy in every Bundestag election that followed until 2002, when the emphasis on autonomy led to its abandonment. It would not be surprising to see the FDP return to a second-vote strategy in future elections.

When Möllemann and Goergen tried to explain why their party's reach had far exceeded its grasp, they did not fault the strategic concept. Instead, they pointed to the failings of many Free Democrats who had not fully understood or supported *Project 18*. Goergen publicly announced his resignation from the FDP and expressed his loss of faith in political parties altogether. Half a year after the election, Möllemann presented his book, *Klartext*. He had borrowed the title from his controversial election flyer, and once again the promise of "straight talk" remained unfulfilled.[36]

In the last days of October 2002, Westerwelle completed his own analysis of the election outcome. It was joined to a future perspective and became the basis for an internal party discussion on the first weekend in November.[37] Westerwelle was forthright in acknowledging that the party had failed to realize its goals. But he managed to find some good news as well. First, the FDP had gained disproportionately in the eastern states. In all of them, the FDP had cleared the 5 percent hurdle in 2002, after failing to do that in any of them in 1994 and 1998. As a result, the East-West divide in the party's electoral support had practically disappeared (6.4 percent in the East, 7.6 percent in the West). In that sense, the FDP could again claim to be an all-German party, in contrast to the Greens who had remained below 5 percent in every one of the eastern states (4.7 percent in the East, 9.4 percent in the West). Second, Westerwelle argued that the FDP now had a broader base of voters who identified with it, as measured by the advance in the FDP's share of the first vote. Here the Liberals had also pulled slightly ahead of the Greens. Third, he stressed the growing symmetry in the electoral support for the FDP, whose voters came more than ever before from across the socioeconomic spectrum.

Somewhat surprising was the FDP's electoral advance among workers, including the unemployed, offset in part by losses among some of its traditional middle class voters. The new supporters were not numerous, but they fit into Westerwelle's vision of the FDP becoming an inclusive "party of all the people." He also noted two group discrepancies in voter support for the Liberals. The FDP was once again a party supported more by males (8 percent) than females (6.9 percent), resulting in a gender gap of 1.1 percent. In fact, the gender gap among FDP voters was probably somewhat bigger (1.4 percent) than Westerwelle's report indicated.[38] The most striking variation came with the age factor. Generally speaking, the FDP had been more successful in attracting younger voters than older ones. In the group over 60 years of age, only 5.8 percent had backed the Liberals. Among voters under 30, 10 percent had voted FDP— or nearly as many as had supported the Greens. Westerwelle reasoned that one factor could have been the FDP's "unconventional and provocative campaign style" which had attracted younger voters and turned off some older voters.

Westerwelle reminded fellow Liberals of the high point reached by the party in April, with its electoral triumph in Saxony-Anhalt, followed by the party congress at Mannheim in May. He singled out Möllemann's role in the anti-Semitism controversy as the main factor in the FDP's loss of support after midsummer. He recognized that Schröder had played the Iraq card to his own party's advantage. But he also acknowledged that the chancellor's leadership role in the August floods had provided an additional boost for the SPD.

In the end, Westerwelle defended the basic innovations brought by *Strategy 18*. Its essence had never been the number 18, he now emphasized, but the decision to become an autonomous party in the major league rather than an auxiliary party in the minor league. He defended the decisions to have the FDP refrain from stating a clear coalition preference or adopting a "second vote" campaign, but he indicated that such choices should be governed by situational factors. Presumably, the same logic applied to any future chancellor candidacies for the party. Most important, while Westerwelle reiterated his belief that the German party system was undergoing change, he now pictured the process as a slow transformation rather than an imminent upheaval: "The party system changes more slowly in Germany than in Europe, but it changes like that in Europe."[39]

Observers of German party politics have questioned Westerwelle's political judgment in the enthusiastic pursuit of *Project 18*. After the election, he conceded on more than one occasion that he had made mistakes and "today" would have done some things differently. His regret at having tolerated or defended some of Möllemann's political escapades now made Westerwelle unforgiving toward the offender and adamant that he be excluded from the party. Möllemann's tragic death in a parachute jump in June 2003 shocked Westerwelle into a temporary inner withdrawal from the political game that has meant so much to him. On his return, he appeared more subdued than before. Inevitably there was talk of his replacement as party leader, but this time there was no obvious successor candidate. Any FDP leader would face a formidable set of challenges in a party that the Bundestag election of 2002 left politically divided, financially almost broke, and morally tainted. While the political charge of "Haiderization" has largely petered out, it has been followed by press reports about a new political funding scandal that this time could implicate the financially strapped FDP, primarily through Möllemann's alleged campaign slush funds.

In the absence of Möllemann and Goergen, Westerwelle *revividus* remains curiously attached to the belief that the small and vulnerable FDP will become a major player in German party politics. He continues to envision its transition from a condition of "klein aber fein" to one of "gross und famos"—like the Liberal sister parties in some neighboring countries.[40] From this perspective, the FDP's problems in the 2002 election represent temporary setbacks on a bumpy road to a transformation of the party system.

Yet the disappointments connected with *Project 18* could serve as a corrective to the temptations of further political make-believe. The FDP clearly cannot force or steer a realignment of the German party system to fit its wishes. Nor is there any guarantee that the FDP will be among the ultimate winners, or indeed survivors, of any transformation that may take place.

In the Bundestag election of 2002 the FDP engaged in a highflying attempt to defy political gravity. Its vague political vision of becoming an inclusive liberal *Volkspartei* was rooted in wishful thinking, supported by a dubious neo-Whig interpretation of German political development. Its lighthearted campaign was *Begleitmusik* to an earnest but unrealistic goal. Before committing itself to another adventure in political levitation, the FDP might consider an alternative future. It could do worse than start with an honest assessment of the potential for its own reinvention as a small but vigorous coalition party.

Notes

I am grateful to many people in Germany, including many active Liberals, who have been willing to inform me about the FDP and other political parties. The responsibility for any errors of fact or interpretation lies with me. My research on German party politics has been generously supported by California State University, Long Beach.

1. See Jürgen W. Möllemann, *Klartext. Für Deutschland* (Munich: Bertelsmann, 2003), and Fritz Goergen, interview in *Report Mainz*, 28 October 2002, "Katerstimmung – die Wahlkampfmanager von CDU und FDP," transcript, pp. 4–6. See also Goergen, "Projekt 18. Der Erfolg und seine Kinder und ihr Erfolg," *Frankfurter Allgemeine Zeitung*, 12 November 2002.
2. "The Project" in British Liberal politics is discussed by David Walter, *The Strange Rebirth of Liberal England* (London: Politico's, 2003), pp. 152, 163, 172, 180–186.
3. For examples, see the speeches by Möllemann and Westerwelle at the party congress in Nuremberg on 16 June 2000, and Möllemann's article, "Eine FDP für das ganze Volk," *Frankfurter Allgemeine Zeitung*, 3 July 2000.
4. Jürgen Möllemann, speech on 16 June 2000, manuscript, pp. 1–17.
5. Guido Westerwelle, speech on 16 June 2000, manuscript, pp. 1ff.
6. Hans-Jürgen Beerfeltz, "Die 18 und der Charakter der FDP," *Liberal*, September 2002, p. 5.
7. The party's planning group, first known as "Campaign 2002," began its work on 12 September 2000. See Westerwelle's report to the party's presidium two days later.
8. See *Geschäftsbericht FDP 2001/2003*, FDP-Bundesgeschäftsstelle Berlin, 2003, p. 48. The party added 14,300 new members between May 2001 and the end of 2002. The net growth was less than one-third as large, from 62,721 in December 2000 to 66,560 two years later. One-quarter of the FDP membership belonged to Möllemann's state party in North Rhine-Westphalia.
9. Friedrich Naumann Stiftung, *Informationen aus der Meinungsforschung*, 11/2000 (23.11.2000), section 11, pp. 1–4.
10. For a list and brief commentary on some recent scandals in North Rhine-Westphalia, see Pascal Beucker, "Clement hat sich durchgemogelt," *die tageszeitung*, 9 May 2000.
11. For a selective account by an insider, see Goergen, "Projekt 18."
12. This account draws on the daily German press as well as my observation of the last week of the FDP election campaign in Bonn, Cologne, Düsseldorf, and Dortmund.
13. Jürgen Möllemann, speech to the 2000 party congress, 16 June 2000.
14. See the FDP membership publication, *die liberale depesche*, "Wahlergebnisse," May 2001, p. 3. For informative reports on the congress, see several articles by Majid Satter in the *Frankfurter Allgemeine Zeitung*, 3, 4, and 5 May 2001.

15. See his long letter of 24 April 2001 on behalf of *Project 18*. It is the third in a series sent to leading Free Democrats, many of them delegates to the annual congress in May of that year.
16. There were 469 votes in favor of Westerwelle's amendment, 173 votes against, 8 abstentions. For Möllemann's bitter account of the Düsseldorf congress along with the contents of his prepared speech for which he substituted spontaneous remarks, see *Klartext*, pp. 140–147.
17. My rough-but-rhyming translation of the German original: "Auf jedem Schiff, das dampft und segelt, gibt's einen, der die Sache regelt," to which Westerwelle added: "und das bin ich!"
18. *Strategie 18%*, Beschluß des Bundesparteitags, Düsseldorf, 4–6 May 2001. For more details, see the document, *Der Weg zur 18* (FDP: Berlin, several editions, 2002), pp. 1–27.
19. The two documents differ only slightly from each other in contents: *Auf dem Weg zur 18*. Konzept für den FDP Bundesvorstand am 18.02. *Auf dem Weg zur 18*. Beschluß des FDP Bundesvorstands vom 18.02.2002.
20. *The Economist*, 18 May 2002, p. 54.
21. See my chapter, "The Free Democratic Party," in *Germany's New Politics: Parties and Issues in the 1990s*, ed. David Conradt, Gerald R. Kleinfeld, George K. Romoser, and Christian Søe (Providence: Berghahn Books, 1995), pp. 175–176, 199–200 (note 11).
22. For the basic budget figure, see Beerfeltz, "Die 18," pp. 8, 11. The comparative estimate comes from Stefan Kapferer, head of the party's "Strategy and Campaigns" section in the party headquarters. The figures were confirmed in my interviews with both, June 2002.
23. *Auf dem Weg zur 18. Machen. Machen. Machen. 18 FDP* (Berlin: FDP, 2002).
24. Beerfeltz, "Die 18."
25. *Bürgerprogramm 2002. Programm der FDP zur Bundestagswahl 2002*, pp. 1–88.
26. They are described as towering above the proposals of the other parties in "FTD-Wahlempfehlung," *Financial Times Deutschland*, 16 September 2002. Yet the chief editor went on to recommend a vote for the Christian Democrats, after raising questions about the top candidates representing the FDP. He specifically mentioned Möllemann and Westerwelle as flawed or weak leaders.
27. Heard in the party headquarters in 2002 during my June interviews there. Another self-ironic reference to the *Partei der Besserverdrossenen* (instead of *Besserverdienenden*) seemed to carry a double meaning at a time when the FDP was portrayed as the "fun party."
28. Other suggestions can be found in Hans Vorländer's delightful and insightful essay, "Die FDP – Ein Lehrstück medialen Illusionstheaters," *Forschungsjournal Neue Soziale Bewegungen*, January 2003, pp. 89–92.
29. The mingling of the two affairs is evident in many of the contributions gathered by a former member of the Schröder government and rushed to publication before the September election: Michael Naumann, ed., *Der Neue Antisemitismus-Streit* (Munich: Ullstein, 2002). The central character of Martin Walser's novel, *Tod eines Kritikers*, resembles Marcel Reich-Ranicki, Germany's renowned literary critic. The debate about the novel began in the *Frankfurter Allgemeine Zeitung*, 29 May 2002.
30. Peter Lösche and Franz Walter, *Die FDP. Richtungsstreit und Zukunftszweifel* (Darmstadt: Wissenschaftliche Buchgesellschaft, 1996).
31. Jürgen W. Möllemann, "In die neue Zeit," *Neues Deutschland*, 27 May 2002.
32. John Hooper, "Germany's Liberal Party Flirts with the Far Right," *The Guardian*, 28 May 2002.
33. The survey was taken by the Business Monitor of *Handelsblatt*. The findings were reported to the party after the election by Guido Westerwelle, *Aufbruch 2006*, p. 7.
34. "Projekt Größenwahn," *Der Spiegel* 45/2002, pp. 22–38.
35. The subject is further explored in my chapter, "The Free Democratic Party: Two Victories and a Political Realignment," in *Germany at the Polls: The Bundestag Elections of the 1980s*, ed. Karl H. Cerny (London: Duke University Press, 1990), p. 119.

36. Möllemann, *Klartext*, p. 236 and elsewhere. Möllemann charged that Westerwelle and his closest advisors had never "believed " in *Project 18*. Among the other nonbelievers, he named the most prominent members of the party. Similarly, Goergen claimed that merely a handful ("two, three, four") had truly understood and believed in his strategic concept. Among the *cognoscenti*, he named only Möllemann. Possibly Westerwelle had also understood, but Goergen was no longer sure that he had. See his interview, "Katerstimmung." Also Goergen, "Projekt 18."
37. The next few paragraphs draw on parts 1 and 2 of Guido Westerwelle's report, *Aufbruch 2006: Die FDP als Bürgerpartei für das ganze Volk,*" Berlin, 30 October 2002.
38. The federal statistical office reported later that the FDP's support level had in fact been 8.1 percent among men and only 6.7 percent among women. Statistisches Bundesamt, *Wahl zum 15. Deutschen Bundestag am 22.9.2002*, Heft 4, p. 72. There are some other minor differences between the figures used in Westerwelle's report and the later official figures.
39. Guido Westerwelle, *Aufbruch 2006*, p. 3.
40. "Westerwelle bleibt dabei: Die FDP muß groß sein," *Frankfurter Allgemeine Zeitung*, 14 October 2002.

Chapter 7

THE PDS IMPLODES

Gerald R. Kleinfeld

Like a punch-drunk boxer, reeling across the ring, the PDS leadership is not certain which blow led to the knockout, but all the hopes and forecasts of 2001 were dashed on 22 September 2002. The PDS lost its status as a Bundestag caucus (*Fraktion*) and is now represented by only two deputies.

Was it the decision to join the Berlin state coalition with the SPD? The resignation of Gregor Gysi? The floods in eastern Germany? Or, and also, was it the pre-emptive strike by the Schröder-Fischer government against American President George W. Bush, injecting anti-Bush rhetoric into the election campaign and insisting that Germany would not ever do what Bush had not asked it to do—send troops to a war against Iraq. This move by Schröder took the "peace" issue away from the PDS.

Certainly, it was all of these and more. Redrawing the election districts in Berlin, as a part of reducing the huge size of the Bundestag, took away traditional safe districts that would have provided the PDS with the cushion in German election law that allows any party which gains three directly elected deputies automatic *Fraktion* status in lieu of meeting the 5 percent minimum national vote. Had they won the same number of districts they held four years earlier, they would have been in with more seats, but still below 5 percent. A very bad election campaign strategy did not help. Eastern Germans deserted the PDS in droves, and the western option never materialized. How did this all come to pass, and what might it mean for the future?

The Campaign

The situation in mid-2001 seemed to provide a good starting point for the national PDS campaign. The Schröder-Fischer government looked tired, and out of ideas. The economy was in very bad shape and getting worse. Unemployment had risen, instead of falling, as the chancellor had promised. The

---

Notes for this chapter begin on page 151.

East of Germany was in perhaps worse shape than it had been since unification. The economy was stagnant, unemployment was high and growing, underemployment, instead of full-time employment, had spread, confidence was down and people were emigrating to other regions. This was a ripe political environment for the PDS. With the German public disappointed in the SPD-Green coalition, and the threatening possibility of a Union-Liberal takeover, the PDS thought that it could campaign successfully against both the government and the Opposition.

But the party decided to shoot itself in the foot. It began by announcing, at virtually every opportunity, that it would block a Stoiber victory, if necessary, by voting in the Bundestag to re-elect Schröder.[1] At the same time, the PDS Land chief in Brandenburg claimed that he could imagine a Land government coalition with the CDU.[2] In an interview, Ralf Christoffers revealed himself to be a pragmatic reformer, who could easily have been accepted into the SPD.[3] But what was the PDS prepared to offer the eastern voter? Or the western voter? Aside from a re-elected Schröder, did the PDS have its own realistic plan?

A good part of the discussion within the PDS since the last Bundestag election had been about the direction of the party.[4] The difference of opinion was not only of strategy, but also of ideology. And it was not merely a division into left and right, or between two camps, but among many. When the floods of summer came, and people looked to the state for assistance, where did the PDS stand? The splintered party could only proclaim in its posters, "Let Jobs Rule the Land. More Jobs!" How? From where?

One group, the reformers, was centered on mainly younger party members who had received a good education during the German Democratic Republic, and were just about ready to begin their rise within the SED when the GDR collapsed. This group, which can be called the "young cadre," was largely excluded by choice and sentiment from the other parties in the republic. Their future was now in the PDS, and to have a future the party had to succeed. Their concept of reform meant a variety of left-socialism similar to some of the Scandinavian models, but certainly to the left of the SPD but reconciled with the Federal Republic.[5] They were not at all united in what this left-socialism might mean, and they were not clear, either, how far it differentiated itself from communism. But they were survivors, and were determined to survive. Whatever their socialism meant, it did not necessarily mean to be reconciled to the prevailing economic winds. These individuals had their greatest strength in the higher party administration, though not in the apparatus itself, or the membership. The reformers were not only divided on ideology, but also on strategy. Lothar Bisky, who was to be returned to the party leadership in 2003, refused to consider the PDS a protest party, and tried for a while to maintain a positive approach to solving Germany's problems.

A second group was the doctrinaire neo-communists centered on such key figures as Angela Marquardt. Also young, and even younger, these were ideologues who hewed fairly closely to communist doctrine. A third group, by far the largest, and including the vast majority of the party membership, were the orthodox Marxist survivors of the GDR. Coming ideologically close to the Young Communists, and emotionally not willing to abandon them, these members were backward looking, socially conservative, but politically and economically left. Old, and growing older, in a party whose average age among members was over sixty, they wanted to justify their past and not to accept any more of the present than necessary.[6] A fourth group, the bureaucrats, people who had found places in the new Germany but were still Marxists, was mainly concerned with keeping their positions. It had been more than a dozen years since the "*Wende*" (the collapse of the GDR), and the power of the PDS in the East had brought opportunities for many to hold government and civil service posts as well as other positions in the new party apparatus. These people did not wish to lose what over 20 percent of the eastern vote had provided them—political perks and position. A fifth group was the successful businesspeople who had made it in the new Germany, and had been SED members before 1990 but continued to vote PDS because this was "home." They were more pragmatic on some issues, but needed the party to justify their pasts. Essentially, the old members could vote any leadership out, would not abandon the Young Communists, and did not identify with reform or with the new Germany. Thus, the reformers could at best try to pacify them while trying to find an image that would appeal to new voters. If they failed to attract new support, especially in the western part of the country, the PDS would gradually disappear as the older members passed on.

The PDS was the successor of the SED, the Socialist Unity Party of the German Democratic Republic (GDR), formed by the union of the Communists and Social Democrats under Soviet Russian occupation. Its core membership were the former members of the SED, now a dozen years older than they were at the demise of the GDR. The western membership was a motley collection of former Communists, leftist radicals of varying stripes, and disaffected former members of the Greens and SPD.[7] In the East, the PDS had almost 90,000 members, more than all of the other parties combined. In Germany, party membership is more significant than in the United States, and it represents a greater commitment. The PDS membership was not only committed to the party, it understood the party to be its representative in the new Germany. Already, in the early 1990s, analysts observed the advancing age of PDS members, and predicted the eventual demise of the party. By 2002, they were older still, with the average age over sixty, and many lived in the past.

At an election rally in September 2002, a small group of American professors settled on to benches in Berlin awaiting a speech by Gregor Gysi, the party's most exciting speaker. On the benches in front and in back of them were gray-haired senior citizens. The conversation between the two groups was amicable, as the party loyalists asked about the fate of Gus

Hall, and the relative strength of the American Communist Party, and why it never seemed to have attracted more supporters. The Americans felt strangely transported into a time warp, until the atmosphere changed as Gysi began to speak and the party's younger leadership made its appearance—among them Petra Pau, the "Power Frau." The seniors applauded vigorously, but neither Gysi nor Pau really represented them. The vote-getters did not necessarily share the values of the seniors, but they did need to respect their sympathies. The seniors were the still the backbone of the membership, and the leadership needed to go beyond them to capture new voters.

The PDS membership and the PDS electorate were quite different. As former, and future party leader Lothar Bisky claimed, the PDS did not want to view itself as a protest party. But it was, and more. In the West, the PDS inherited a vastly different array of members and voters, ranging from former members of the DKP (the Communists) to various hues of leftist radicals and a few disaffected Greens and Social Democrats. Lately, more of the latter were coming to the party, but not enough to make much of a difference. Several times it was necessary for the more homogeneous and better organized easterners to pressure the western groups into following a common path. But as the 1990s drew to a close, there were finally signs that new organization had reached the West, and a more structured adherence to the PDS seemed on the horizon. Still, there were few victories in the former western Germany, and the PDS failed to gain 5 percent of the vote in the key Land elections it contested. In the East, the 90,000 members were overwhelmed by the party's total vote. Many other former members of the SED, and former adherents of the GDR government and its institutions, including the State Security forces, regularly voted PDS. This was a loyal electorate, more closely tied to the PDS than voters for other parties, and it gave the PDS a firm basis of support. But like the members, these people were graying, and even dying. It was necessary for the PDS to reach beyond them, into the next generations.

The PDS considered itself the protector of the German Democratic Republic's (GDR) functionaries, that vast party and state *apparat* whose world collapsed in 1989–1990. Its honorary chairman, Hans Modrow, was the very personification of that effort. In fact, the loyalty of these voters stretched beyond their current lifestyles and economic status. Many were businesspeople, having entered the world of market economy. A good number were *Beamte*, civil servants in the local, regional, and Land bureaucracy. One of the main achievements of the PDS since 1990 was to place its people in the machinery of the state, and this was a key reason for party adherents to advocate coalition rule with the SPD. They could use that to place their people. Other voters included younger people, attracted often by the spirited election campaigns since 1990 that had often shown a very modern face, and featured quirky posters, catchy slogans, and speeches that were sometimes witty, always challenging, and roundly populist. The true nature of the party's program and its specific recipes for dealing with Germany's many problems were diffuse, even hotly debated within the party itself, and never straightforward. Still, it was clear that the party challenged the system, did not accept the market economy, and yet often had competent people in various elected posts, people who could be pragmatic on local issues in ways that others might not be. It was, of course, the only totally "eastern" party, and enjoyed much sympathy as the supposed representative of eastern interests against the more populous and wealthy West, where there were less unemployed, and where those who were employed earned higher wages.

From the beginning the dichotomy of East and West bedeviled the party. In the West, it was an opposition party, but not merely an opposition party, a system opposition party. That meant that it really did not accept the idea of a market economy, even a social market economy. And it was still uncomfortable with the functioning of a multiparty environment. In the East, it was that as well, but also a governing party—in Berlin, for a time in Saxony-Anhalt, and in Mecklenburg-West Pomerania. On top of that, it was also a governing party through thousands of elected officials in local government on many levels. In the West, it was insignificantly small, less than 2 percent and, in most regions, less than 1 percent of the vote. All of its attempts since 1990 to become a national party had failed. As the campaign for the 2002 Bundestag opened, the PDS remained what it had been since 1990—a full-fledged party in the East, where it often attracted more votes than the SPD, and an insignificant minority in the West. The party leadership needed once again to develop a national election strategy that bridged that gap while capitalizing in the East on its "regional" character. However, the PDS had two new wrinkles in that seemingly perennial problem: Berlin, and its show horse, Gregor Gysi.

The city of Berlin was a beneficiary and a victim of German unification. It was a beneficiary in that it became the capital of the unified country, with all that entailed. This included massive investment in public buildings and a newly resident bureaucracy, but also the policing and security structure for a capital city. It was a victim in that the former federal subsidies to western Berlin were eliminated, but not the large superstructure that had been created over four decades. Nor did Berlin replace Frankfurt as a business center, and it did not even have a truly functional international airport. All that remained in Frankfurt. Further, eastern Berlin sorely needed renovation and enhanced city services, but had a disproportionate percentage of retired SED cadre and a weak industrial and retail base. Unemployment was high, and easterners were paid less than their western neighbors, as was the case throughout eastern Germany. The city administration, a coalition between the CDU and SPD, was divided on how to approach the huge municipal problems, and the specter of corruption fell heavily on several politicians as a major bank threatened to collapse. With the PDS polling an average of 40 percent in eastern Berlin elections, there were few options for a replacement coalition. The Greens in the western part were notoriously radical, more so than their counterparts in the rest of the country, while the FDP also had a different tradition. It could be more right wing than the party in the rest of the country. The Berlin municipal elections punished the CDU, which was identified with the banking crisis and corruption, and made it unlikely that the SPD would coalesce with them under an SPD governing mayor, so negotiations began for a "traffic light coalition" (Red-Green-Yellow, SPD-Greens-FDP). When it became clear that the Greens and FDP could not resolve their differences, the SPD was forced to turn to the PDS for a Red-Red coalition. The PDS agreed, and Gregor Gysi, who had stepped down from his position of leadership among the PDS in the Bundestag, became deputy mayor.

The wandering of Gysi from the Bundestag to deputy mayor, and then in frustration and disappointment out of that position, was both a symptom and a cause of the emerging difficulties of the PDS. Gysi was never as popular among the membership as he was among the voters, but he was a brilliant orator and could galvanize support as he mercilessly pilloried the major parties for their failures, real or imagined. He could be spectacularly populist, totally irresponsible, and courageously unpredictable. In the Bundestag, he could neither lead nor represent a united party behind himself. The PDS was virtually excluded by its small size and the anti-communist attitude of many deputies from a major role in the country's legislation, and Gysi became a voice crying in the wilderness between elections. Nor did the party leadership trust him and follow his lead. After years of frustration, he resigned his Bundestag seat. However, when the Red-Red coalition in Berlin became unavoidable, he re-emerged and became deputy mayor. It was an unfortunate choice for him, and for the party. He became a curious pleader for traditional investment, development, and unpopular budget cuts.[8] Instead of enacting higher spending for various social causes, the PDS was hemmed in. The party was forced to buy into a budget-paring administration, weakening its stance as a populist opposition force. It even backed the expansion of Schoenefeld Airport into a new mega-airport, Berlin-Brandenburg, a white elephant that mobilized thousands of eastern Germans to defend themselves against the noise of countless jets taking off and landing over their homes. The ordinary folk, the people, rose up against the PDS, an uncomfortable spectacle for the ex-Communist Party. The planners advertised everywhere the inevitability of their mega-airport, but legal action brought it to a screeching halt. Enmeshed in the civil and budgetary chains of Berlin, the PDS lost much of its advertised glamour as a fresh force that had emerged from the old SED. It seemed to many of the old guard as a party that had lost its way. The newer voters did not recognize the party that had advertised how different it was from the others. Gysi was unrealistic and unbelievable as a pseudo-capitalist deputy mayor. In addition, the number of deputies in the German Bundestag was finally scheduled to be somewhat reduced from the swollen figure that had emerged out of unification. Redistricting in Berlin no longer respected the former East-West boundaries, and previously safe PDS seats now were uncertain. When the federal election would come, the PDS began to question whether it could count on its previously safe Berlin seats, a healer against failing to earn the 5 percent minimum popular vote.

The party's continued toleration of an SPD government in the state of Saxony-Anhalt was also becoming a negative for the PDS's national image. Here the so-called Magdeburg Model meant that a minority SPD government ruled the Land, with the negotiated support of the PDS deputies. In this de facto coalition, the PDS technically remained an opposition party, but bore responsibility for government decisions and legislation it could not determine. Initially, this had seemed to be a wise compromise, which would put the responsibility for failures on the SPD, while preserving the ability of the PDS to criticize the state government. However, the economy of Saxony-Anhalt under performed even in comparison to other eastern Länder. As one American professor stood on a railroad platform in Wittenberg waiting for a train, he took up a conversation with an unemployed worker. The Land government came in for serious criticism, but there was much admiration for the CDU *Landesvater* (a term of more-or-less endearment, describing a governor as "father-figure" of the Land), Governor Bernhard Vogel, in neighboring Thuringia. Unemployment was not low in Thuringia, but it was clearly lower than in Saxony-Anhalt, and Thuringia gave the impression both of progress and achievement. This diagnosis was typical, and boded ill both for the SPD Land government and its PDS partner. It was difficult for the PDS to capitalize on the mistakes and failures of a government to which it was tied. This was not lost on the party membership, or on its leadership. It was also not lost on the voters.

At the April 2002 state election, the PDS paid a price for its toleration of this unpopular SPD minority government. While the combined vote of the "pure" opposition parties, the Christian Democrats and the Free Democrats, jumped from 26 percent to 41 percent, support for the PDS actually declined.

The Magdeburg Model was not tried in Mecklenburg-West Pomerania, where Land elections were to take place on the same day as the Bundestag elections. There, the local PDS leader, Helmut Holter, and his colleagues had decided on a formal coalition with the SPD. Land Minister-President Harald Ringsdorff was determined to stay in office, for which he needed the PDS, but he asserted boldly the primacy of his party and tried to put the PDS in the shadows wherever possible. Alas, for the PDS, they helped. Holter's band contained not a few misfits, and shoplifting was not an attractive activity for a prominent Landtag deputy and party member. Embroiled in a number of personal problems, the PDS in Mecklenburg-West Pomerania hardly earned a reputation for solid attention to the needs of the Land. On the other hand, Holter and others continually reinforced their devotion to some of the older SED traditions and ideas, thus confusing potential noncommunist supporters. While local issues were still a strong suit for the PDS in that Land, the party made many errors, allowed the voters too much insight into the nature of the party itself and its leadership, and developed a reputation for feathering its nest in a grand manner. PDS adherents avidly sought civil service jobs and burrowed into the administration from one corner of the Land to the next, hardly being contested by the SPD, whose membership was far too small by comparison to provide a genuine opposition. Ringsdorff did not raise this as an issue, contenting himself with the prospect of shifting the relation of forces, gaining relatively more votes in the next election for the SPD within the coalition. Unless the FDP emerged as a reasonable force, the CDU would have to have an absolute majority to unseat him, and he expected that the Land elections would not produce that. On the other hand, Ringsdorff was not any more successful than his colleagues in Saxony-Anhalt, and the local economy went from bad to worse. With Kohl and the CDU no longer governing on the national level, he could not blame Berlin, where the Social Democrats under Schröder and the Greens under Fischer, were responsible for national economic policy. Therefore, Ringsdorff blamed the Americans for the poor Mecklenburg-West Pomerania economic results. It was American economic policy, economic liberalism, and monetary and fiscal policy that had brought such misfortune. While the PDS supported this contention in all of their utterances, this made it somewhat difficult to differentiate themselves from Ringsdorff's criticisms. They did not hesitate to attack Berlin, but their support of an SPD-led government in which they were a coalition partner blunted their own criticisms. Efforts to break ranks in the Bundesrat, the federal upper house where the states, or Länder, represented their interests, were opposed by the Social Democrats and brought scant result.

Thus, as 2002 opened, the PDS was in far worse a situation than it seemed.[9] What it is important to remember here is that the PDS had really weakened before Chancellor Schröder and Mother Nature, in the form of floods in the East, had set their sights on them, and before the Iraq controversy erupted, and that growing internal divisions and rethinking had set in when it came to the questions of participation in government on the Land level. It was easy afterwards for some observers to look at the chancellor's actions and the fears of American military action in Iraq as weaning eastern voters from the PDS. This was wrong, except in that these developments contributed to a trend under way. The PDS dropped in the polls to under 4 percent in February, and never recovered.[10] A study published in May by the PDS-close Rosa Luxemburg Foundation openly admitted that the party was hemorrhaging voters in Mecklenburg-West Pomerania, and that the Red-Red cooperation in Saxony-Anhalt was on its last legs and would not be re-elected. The party, wrote Michael Chrapa, needed to find a real profile.[11]

Among the critical issues within the party was this problem of participating in governing coalitions. This was not generally a serious question in the first years after unification, particularly on the extremely local level of town councils. It became so as the party began redefining itself and the struggles continued among the various wings. of the party. This is not just a theoretical issue. It goes to a basic question of jobs in a country where unemployment in the western regions is generally twice that of the United States, and in the eastern Länder where it is even higher. Where unemployment has reached over 25 percent, jobs of any kind are important, and government jobs are even more so. They pay well, and have excellent pensions. Further, they allow influence in societal development, particularly when they are in fields such as education, the education ministry, or in justice, administration, and so on. Thus, for its own philosophies, the PDS has a vested interest in gaining firm footholds in certain ministries, all across the board, not only in jobs. On the other hand, as a jobs-placement organization, the PDS is also extremely active, taking care of its own in good Chicago-ward style politics. A problem with this is the compromising of ideology. This is a rub for the party.

While it is theoretically possible to have system-opposition and to undermine from within, it is also possible that serving the beast corrupts the server. It works both ways, and can also be perceived by the public in that way.

To be in the best position to place party loyalists in the bureaucracy, the PDS has to support an SPD government. While the SPD has the same problem in reverse, generally in the East being forced into either leading a coalition with the PDS or being the junior partner in a coalition with the CDU, that is not the issue for this chapter. An SPD tied to the PDS has its own difficulties. But a PDS that is tied to SPD governments is tied to the governmental decisions the other party might take. It makes little difference to the voters, as is increasingly evident, whether the PDS is under a "Magdeburg Model" or a full coalition. The public is aware of it. Stagnant growth, high levels of unemployment, and serious problems of low business investment in high tax regions, are issues the public expects the government to address. More than the SPD, the PDS is vulnerable on questions of business investment and unemployment. Accusing the United States only goes so far. Sooner or later, the public asks about Brussels, the European Central Bank (ECB), and even Berlin.

The PDS was also hurt in Berlin by the inability of the local and national economy to sustain the high level of social expenditures that had characterized the German Model. The SPD, governing in Berlin, was forced to address those issues in the election campaign. The PDS, governing only in Länder, was able to afford the luxury of criticism from the left.

The state of the German economy in 2002 placed severe tests on the PDS. Germany was becoming less and less competitive as a high-cost producer of goods. German work rules were so inflexible that businesses were reluctant to hire new workers, and unemployment crept ever higher, above the figure that the Schröder-Fischer government had said it would tolerate. ECB rules meant that the government could not depend upon the Bundesbank to create favorable interest rates. The American economy, which had helped to carry Europe and Germany, could no longer sustain such demands in the aftermath of the September 11 tragedy and the very substantial tax cuts of the Bush administration. Backing and filling, the national government was being forced to consider a revision downward of social expectations. The opposition, but especially the FDP, supported such cuts in social programs. In addition, the demographic pyramid in Germany was standing on its head. There were fewer and fewer young workers for an increasing number of older citizens receiving pensions. Demographers reckoned that the population of Germany would drop from 82 million to 55 million by the middle of the new century. Flamboyantly, the PDS represented a blind eye to these truths, as it railed especially against the FDP and told the people that they could escape all of that with a policy of increasing socialism in the German society. Since unification, the PDS had been backing away from its initial forced effort to flirt with a social market economy toward a return to the ideas of socialism. Now, in 2002, such a direction flaunted every economic indicator and all economists' data, not to mention every global demographer. To those for whom the PDS did not seem an anachronism already in the early 1990s, such a probability loomed more evident at the beginning of the new millennium.

But Germans generally feel more comfortable with a party that knows where it is going, and which appears to be united in going there. Despite all of its factions, the PDS had generally presented such an image reasonably enough to a large enough group of people throughout the 1990s. By 2002, this was no longer possible. The party appeared to disintegrate before the eyes of the voters. It was enough to lose Gysi, that acid-tongued smilingly brilliant public figure, whose quips and wit were so characteristic that he felt the need to inform the public that he really had some useful ideas, and entitled one of his books "More Than Just Impudent Comments." But at the same time, in 2001 and 2002 it slapped down strongly the group of people called the "new cadre," the leaders of a more youthful generation who had grown up since 1990 and represented a sense of leftist socialism. The party's so-called hope of the future, these younger leaders had hoped to push it from the image of representing the old SED to being a new national political force to the left of the SPD, while at the same time remaining the chief advocate of the East.

Their eventual rejection by the old-line members was evident to the general public in both East and West. The new cadre became increasingly isolated in the party, as those who favored the old orthodoxies became disenchanted with both the conditions of the German economy and the responsibility of their own party. Far from following the younger leadership into an integrated, but leftist, role in German politics, the membership reared its head in rebellion. The policy of participating in government was abandoned.

Lothar Bisky was replaced by Gabrielle (Gaby) Zimmer, a lackluster functionary whose election speech resonated with the cries of the oldest members. It was precisely because she offered nothing new that she was elected. With the new cadre marginalized, the search for an agenda and a program became even more necessary, but proved just as elusive as in the months before. Disorientation, indecision, wavering, all became ever-more-evident characteristics of the PDS in 2002.[12] When Gysi returned to the fold, not as a Bundestag member but as vice mayor of Berlin, he seemed just as witty and intelligent, but no longer credible. In government, he failed. He made great personal appearances, but found no success, and was derisively called "the red economic liberal."[13] After a few months, he dropped out again. While this was going on, the PDS prepared for the Bundestag election. The election campaign of 2002 was a disappointment, but not only because of some accidental events such as the floods or the Iraq issue. From the beginning, the PDS campaign was poorly conceived and organized. The PDS has "stumbled into a loss of credibility," charged Harald Werner, member of the party executive.[14] "We are lacking in vision," claimed the 29-year-old PDS party leader in Berlin.[15]

In May, at a meeting in Halle to discuss election strategy, Zimmer declared, "We are not yet in the 2002 Bundestag."[16] Having made it in 1998 with 5.1 percent of the votes and enough direct seats to ensure representation in any case, Zimmer explained that it would be tough. She also went on to explain that an alliance with the SPD in eastern Länder or municipal councils made it impossible to carry out "real changes." PDS caucus chief in the Bundestag Roland Claus, thundered that nobody would get them out of the Bundestag. They were now in, permanently. Together, they promised that the PDS 2002 election campaign would be fought under the slogan of "Social Justice instead of Self-Enrichment." Zimmer insisted that they would prove themselves to be the only party genuinely struggling for social justice and for peace. Gysi gave an impassioned speech, and claimed that the PDS would become the "third strongest force" in German politics.[17] In an interview with the author, party manager and election strategist Dietmar Bartsch claimed that the party would do well and had good prospects.[18]

Little wonder that the election slogans—once sharp, incisive, witty, and successful—now had a bitter and hollow ring. In Bavaria, a PDS pamphlet showed the "Last Supper" with politicians replacing the disciples. Some citizens in this Catholic region angrily shouted at PDS representatives setting up their party's campaign tables in Munich. One flyer, supposedly supporting women's rights, showed a pregnant woman lying on a sofa while her husband read to her from a newspaper that medicines are tested on men. "Only on men?" the pregnant lady shrieks. What would voters think of a flyer showing a retired couple speeding on a motorcycle past the Egyptian pyramids, while one says to the other, "What'll we do with next month's pension check?" Or a bumper sticker showing an office secretary with a desk full of papers and three pairs of hands, frantically observing to her impatient boss, "I don't need work; I need MONEY!" Or a postcard proclaiming: "Generation X, Golf, Red!! Whose world is the world? If you want to know more about equal opportunities and peaceful conflict resolution—PDS." How about a huge poster showing a young man and young woman kissing, with the legend in large type: "Make the East strong!" Years ago, the PDS had a similar poster with a young man and young woman kissing, but the legend said "the first time—PDS." Now, THAT was clever. What does the kissing couple have to do with eastern Germany? In 2002, the PDS used a bumper sticker that proclaimed "08/16—PDS." No genius thought that one up. It seemed that public opinion was right. A unified party makes a better campaign image. The advertising and slogans were far below the previous PDS standards, and lacked a unifying theme. They also seemed vague, such as "Social Justice?—in our country the rich grow richer and the poor poorer." While sporting traditional class appeals to the downtrodden, that slogan scarcely even convinced the already convinced. Probably the most imaginative was a poster that proclaimed "Umsteuern." This has a double meaning. It can either mean to change direction, or it can mean change the tax structure. Both meanings work, because the secondary legend was the demand to reintroduce the luxury tax. In a country where most citizens were beginning to feel that they were overtaxed, this also had, unfortunately, a secondary—and not helpful—meaning. Yet another tax?

The campaign continued with the usual condemnation of neo-liberalism, warnings against big business, and urgings that people vote for a party that always promoted peace—the PDS. Our kind of European Union, as the PDS asked voters to endorse, was too vague.

Lurching through the election campaign, the PDS was then caught further off stride when the summer floods came to eastern Germany. These summer floods were more extensive and a greater catastrophe than any in one hundred years. It seemed that everything was washed away in Thuringia, Saxony-Anhalt, and Saxony. Huge areas of eastern Germany (the floods had started in Bavaria, but were much worse in the East) were completely under water: whole valleys, farmland, and central cities. Highways disappeared. Lengthy stretches of railroad track were destroyed. Homes were flooded. Many regions looked like lakes. The pictures on television were heartbreaking. Gerhard Schröder saw his opportunity. Speeding to the worst flood scenes, the chancellor appeared as a gift from heaven. He promised that the STATE would help. To easterners, a natural expectation, but something they had grown less accustomed to hearing, certainly not from opposition parties claiming that the individual should help himself. Not having made dramatic gestures to the East before, Schröder now seized the opportunity. The army arrived. Troops helped.

For the voters of the PDS, the dreaded military was now a helpful ally in the war against water. The PDS was caught flatfooted. Here was an SPD chancellor promising to help the East with the full power of the national government. Already awash in their own troubles, the PDS leaders had no magic answer to this indication of federal largesse, and of federal, and western, concern. Slogging through the mud, the chancellor made the appearance as pater familias.

The next body blow was struck by the Bush administration. In August, his vice president, Richard Cheney, suggested that there might be an American assault on Iraq to overthrow President Saddam Hussein. In a preemptive strike during the last weeks of the election campaign, Schröder announced that Germany would not participate in a war against Iraq. More than that, he snubbed the United Nations (though that was overlooked) by claiming that Germany would not assist in such a war even if the United Nations sanctioned it. Germany was for peace! The East erupted in sympathy for the chancellor. Rushing to eastern campaign locations, Schröder immediately boosted his leftist credentials by promising huge, cheering crowds that his plan to revive the German economy would never, under any circumstances, involve introducing "American methods and American conditions." The citizens of the East roared their approval. The PDS could not outdo in anti-Americanism such flamboyant promises by the sitting chancellor. They could not race to his left and claim that they opposed "American capitalism" any more strongly. Their invectives against neo-liberalism could not compete with the chancellor's condemnation of the American business system.

Some in the chancellor's party carried the invective against American President Bush further, with Minister of Justice Herta Däubler-Gmelin allegedly comparing him to Adolf Hitler and describing the American system of justice as "evil." Others joined happily in the fray. The PDS almost disappeared from the news reports and seemed only to echo the criticism, which was both of the United States and its government. The chancellor's repudiation of the minister was delayed, and not especially sharp. Eastern voters were unsure what to make of it all. However, the PDS did not shine during the last election weeks. Too much action was elsewhere. Rallies betrayed a sense of gloom. Too many traditional voters were looking anew at the SPD, the party of peace.

Trying to win voters by explaining that they were against war, while the chancellor and his foreign minister were demonstrating their opposition to war with concrete policies, had a hollow ring. "No blood for oil" sounded like something the SPD or Greens were saying. Against the specter of the right wing—a CDU/CSU/FDP coalition—the PDS was also not credible. Its slogan—"Stop Stoiber!"—plastered on many posters, little handout cards, and everywhere they could find a place, raised the wrong questions. After all, if one wanted to stop Stoiber, would one not vote Red-Green? Why, then, PDS? In fact, if what one wanted to prevent a change in government and a new coalition in power, a vote for the PDS might not do it, but one for the SPD or Greens could.

The Results

The election itself was a disaster for the PDS, all across the board. In 1998, the PDS elected four Bundestag deputies directly and a total of 36 deputies were assigned the party in accordance with its having reached the minimum 5 percent level. It had actually reached 5.1 percent. In 2002, with the Bundestag having fewer total seats, and Berlin having been redistricted, the PDS elected only two deputies directly, both in Berlin, and achieved a total vote of 4 percent. The two seats in Berlin were won by Dr. Gesinne Lötzsch in election district 87, Berlin-Lichtenberg, with 39.6 percent of the votes in the first vote, and by Petra Pau in election district 86, Berlin-Marzahn-Hellersdorf, with 37.7 percent of the first vote. Thus, the party dropped below the 5 percent minimum needed to participate in the proportional distribution of seats from the party list, and the minimum needed to reach *Fraktion,* or caucus, status.[19] It virtually disappeared from the national scene. Instead of the jubilation that had taken place at the election evening party in 1998, there was gloom, and the sense of impending doom. The PDS lost everywhere, and all over the East. In the East, the PDS also lost in every age group, including the senior citizens, its bulwark. Only 79.1 percent of the electorate turned out to vote, against 82.2 percent in 1998, but the drop in turnout in the East was greater. It ranged from a low of 68.8 percent in Saxony-Anhalt, where the PDS had supported the SPD government, to a high of 74.8 percent in CDU-ruled Thuringia. The PDS lost votes in comparison with 1998 in every western Land, except the Saar, where the party increased its vote by 0.4 percent of the total. In Hesse, the party had had high hopes. They achieved only 1.3 percent of the vote. Leading the state election list for the PDS in Hesse was Luc Jochimsen, former chief editor of Hessian state radio and a typical example of leftist intellectuals in the West who had become PDS. Jochimsen, interviewed after the election, was distraught. "We had hoped to win more votes than in 1998,... but we have to draw the conclusion that the PDS has just not found any support in the West."[20] In the East, the PDS had reached 21.6 percent of the total vote in 1998, but gained only 16.1 percent in 2002.

Table 7.1 presents the PDS party vote in the eastern states in 1998 and 2002. In general, the PDS followed the trend of the smaller parties, having a very slight edge of male over female voters, but had its greatest numbers in the age group from 45 to 59 (5 percent) of the total. On the other hand, 21.1 percent of voters in the East over 60 years old still voted PDS, the largest age group for the party. But 72.5 percent of the oldest voters in the East sided with either the SPD or the CDU. The PDS gained only 11.2 percent of the younger voters, the most crucial beginning group for them. The

TABLE 7.1 PDS Support in the Eastern States, 1998 and 2002 (percentage)

	1998	2002
Land		
Berlin	13.4	11.4
Mecklenburg-West Pomerania	23.6	16.3
Saxony	20.0	16.2
Saxony-Anhalt	20.7	14.4
Thuringia	21.2	17.0

PDS actually lost its greatest numbers in those voters under 30, and a large percentage by those under 45.[21] The PDS lost in the East more than a third of their voters who were white-collar workers, previously one of the most important PDS voting groups.[22] Nevertheless, fully 44 percent of the PDS voters described themselves as having white-collar jobs; 33 percent, blue-collar.[23] Whereas the CDU attracted more Catholic voters than Protestants and the SPD more Protestants than Catholics, the PDS stood out in this category by attracting mostly atheists, those professing no religion.[24] Only the Greens appear to have had a similarly high percentage as the PDS of voters who had attended university.[25]

At the same time as the Bundestag elections, there were also Landtag elections in Mecklenburg-West Pomerania, where the PDS was in coalition with the SPD. Since the incumbent SPD-PDS government was so unpopular, the CDU tried to win an absolute majority. Riding Schröder's coattails, the SPD forged ahead. The PDS sank like a rock from 24 percent to 16 percent.

After the elections, the PDS licked its wounds and tried to recover. Bisky was returned in office to replace Zimmer, but the damage was not over.[26] The party had not been able to come up with a unifying program, nor to find a place in the West or the East. The few votes it accumulated in some western university towns represented little more than the temporary flirtations of leftist youth, and no incoming tide. The election defeat caused both recriminations and reconsiderations in the East. There was no scarcity of internal criticism, but no unity on what went wrong or what to do. All of the divisions that had existed for years had now come out. It did not help that the German economy failed to recover after the elections, but went into recession.

The election reopened the issue of whether the PDS should go into coalitions with the SPD or not. Many in the party believe that it is hurt by such alignments. Others believe that staying out ensures the success of others. For the SPD, before 2002, it was clear that their party would be in a dilemma: a coalition with the PDS seemed to mean that they would be forced to govern to the left of their members and voters. After 2002, it became clear that this might be the case, but that a coalition also might turn out to be an embrace of death.

After the 2002 election, the possible demise of the PDS became a subject of serious debate, even within the party itself. The party's internal divisions are severe. The viewpoints are often diametrically opposed to one another. Their prescriptions for the national economic future are increasingly unrealistic. The new cadre is not powerful enough to lead the party into becoming a more leftist version of the SPD, and the membership is too unwilling to let that happen. It still is an eastern party, still reflective of eastern concerns, but the mantle is passing in the eastern SPD and CDU to a new generation. In some respects, it is happening with the FDP, too, particularly in Saxony. This new generation is clearly eastern, and has grown to power in unified Germany, working within the system and making local decisions. The PDS has lost its theme of exclusiveness, whether it seeks to retain it or not. The loss of Bundestag caucus status removes the PDS from credibility on the national scene, if ever it had that before. The two Bundestag deputies can be little more than an afterthought. Western expansion is fairly well dead. But now, the PDS is a much-weakened third force in the East, as well, and speculation has begun to center on the attraction of younger voters to the SPD or the CDU. The PDS has begun a process of decline, and there is little evidence to suggest that it would be able to turn itself around. Luc Jochimsen, who lead the state party list for the PDS in Hesse, remorsefully predicted that "in four years,… without a caucus status in the Bundestag, we will be in an even weaker position than we were this year,… [people will ask] do we need a leftist party in Germany."[27] Surely, too, those who did not want Stoiber, and the CDU, voted for Schröder. If so, why through the PDS and why not directly the SPD?

Richard Schröder, a Social Democrat and former leader in the East German *Volkskammer*, who has been a sharp-eyed analyst of eastern politics, opined that the PDS would gradually fall apart. Eighty percent of the eastern Germans had not voted PDS, he observed. Without Gysi and a real Bundestag representation, they would sink to the level of an eastern state parliament and communal party, and never again return to the Bundestag. Time is against them. Even Gysi knows, Schröder observed, that his departure had contributed to the election disaster.[28] "What was the PDS," asked the *Berliner Zeitung*.[29] "Gregor Gysi and his colorful band. Even younger voters of today find that a bit comical." But for a while, Gysi gave a number of eastern Germans the feeling that they were somebodies, "witty, clever, eloquent, [Gysi] made them feel proud that they had such a politician, who knew how to handle himself in TV talk shows and beat out the westerners there … that increased their self-esteem, and the majority of the eastern voters longed for a fillip to their self-esteem." It was something, the only party in the East who understood easterners, and which could demonstrate a continuing success, from election to election. It was over. What was fascinating was the reaction of the westerners to the flood, remarked the newspaper. They helped! They helped without asking for a thank you or for anything. They were just there. The easterners found a united Germany had been there for them. The PDS, which had lived for a considerable part on the East-West differences, suffered under that. The flood hurt. "The PDS without Gregor Gysi is the real existing PDS," copying the standard phrase of the GDR, the land of the "real existing socialism." Young voters laughed as they heard Gaby Zimmer's remarks on the election disaster, sounding like some self-important teacher right out of the GDR. Finally, the newspaper termed her "Zimmer ohne Aussicht" (Room without a View), a play on words that showed the hopelessness of her position. The *Frankfurter Allgemeine Zeitung* compared the PDS to the BHE (Bund der Heimatvertriebenen und Entrechteten), the party of refugees from the territories surrendered to Poland and the Soviet Union, which gradually disappeared as the refugees integrated themselves into western Germany.[30]

But Gysi's evaluation of the PDS without Gysi failed to hit the point as sharply as Richard Schröder. He told the *Süddeutsche Zeitung* that all this proved was the "personalization of politics," that individuals, not issues, drove the election.[31] To which, the newspaper editorialized, "even if Stoiber had pressed himself much more forward as the Union parties' leader, it would not have worked." Of course, the venerable newspaper missed part of the point. Stoiber was not that much of a plus for the opposition, and the more he pushed, the less likely he would gain more votes. Still, Gysi was certainly wrong. He was only part of the reason for the party's collapse. That decline was evident before 2002. It was evident in the failures of the PDS during 2002, in the nature of the party, in the developments since 1990, in the issues of 2002 from the economic situation to the floods and to the peace campaign. Neither the floods alone nor the Gysi withdrawal, nor the peace campaign of Schröder caused the collapse of the PDS in 2002. It was the inner contradictions, which had themselves helped lead to Gysi's frustration and resignation, the man the party itself continually refused to acknowledge as having been their strong attraction, that played a major role. In what form can the PDS survive? Will it dissolve like the BHE? This is now being fought out within the party itself.

Notes

1. *Die Welt*, 30 April 2002, p. 4.
2. *Der Tagesspiegel*, 28 April 2002.
3. Interview with the author, June 2002. Also see "Grossmutters grosser Mund. Die SPD schnappt nach dem Klientel der PDS," *Frankfurter Rundschau*, 30 September 2002, p. 2.
4. For a more complete discussion of the early successes of the party and its internal issues, see my chapters in two earlier volumes, *Germany's New Politics* (Providence: Berghahn Books, 1995) and *Power Shift in Germany* (New York: Berghahn Books, 2000), which analyze the federal elections of 1994 and 1998, respectively.

5. Operationally, according to the Green leader, Reinhard Bütikofer, this meant that the PDS position on most issues was: SPD+Green+15 percent. Interview, Berlin, 20 September 2002.
6. "The PDS is a party without young people. Three-fourths of its members were already in the SED [in the German Democratic Republic]. Of possibly 83,000 members, only 3 percent are under 30 years old, and ... 68 percent are pensioners or near pension age." *Frankfurter Allgemeine Zeitung*, 5 October 2001.
7. They were constantly battling one another. See "Streit in Hamburgs PDS beigelegt?" in *Neues Deutschland*, 2 May 2002, p. 5.
8. The party's newspaper pilloried Gysi for being "accommodating" to the business community. See "Einspruch Genosse Senator," in *Neues Deutschland*, 30 April 2002, pp. 10–11.
9. "The PDS expects to win at least five directly elected Bundestag seats." in *Neues Deutschland*, 29 April 2002, p. 5.
10. Forschungsgruppe Wahlen, *Bundestag 2002*, p. 33.
11. *Junge Welt*, 30 May 2002, p. 5.
12. Susanne Scheerer, writing in the *Frankfurter Allgemeine Zeitung* on 28 May 2002, observed that Gysi had been shouted down, that the leftists in the party were taking up cudgels against the reformers, and that the party, known for its discipline, was now in trouble.
13. "Der rote Wirtschaftsliberale," in *Frankfurter Allgemeine Sonntagszeitung*, 2 June 2002, p. 8.
14. *Neues Deutschland*, 31 May 2002, p. 2.
15. *Berliner Zeitung*, 31 May 2002, p. 22.
16. *Frankfurter Allgemeine Zeitung*, 26 May 2002, p. 3.
17. *Die Welt*, 28 May 2002, p.2.
18. Interview, Dietmar Bartsch, June 2002.
19. Unless otherwise noted, all such data herein represent the final vote tally and are taken from the report of the *Bundeswahlleiter* at http://www.Bundeswahlleiter.de.
20. Quoted in *Junge Welt*, 27 September 2002, p. 2.
21. Forschungsgruppe Wahlen, *Bundestag 2002, Analyse*, p. 55.
22. Ibid., p. 59.
23. Ibid., p. 61.
24. Ibid., pp. 65ff.
25. Ibid., p. 72.
26. But Bisky was already "the tired integration-uncle of the PDS." See *Berliner Morgenpost*, 27 September 2002, p. 25.
27. Jochimsen interview, cited from *Junge Welt*.
28. *Der Tagesspiegel*, 24 September 2002, p. 6.
29. *Berliner Zeitung*, 24 September 2002, p. 9.
30. *Frankfurter Allgemeine Zeitung*, 24 September 2002, p. 12.
31. *Süddeutsche Zeitung*, 24 September 2002, p. 17.

Chapter 8

LADIES' CHOICE
Returning the Schröder Government to Power in 2002

Mary N. Hampton

A major German newspaper ran the following headline in the 2002 election: "Are Women Schröder's Last Chance?"[1] The answer was yes. An Associated Press poll taken early in the election cycle, in March 2002, showed that Chancellor Gerhard Schröder's best electoral chances were with women's votes: 40 percent of female respondents would vote for the chancellor and 29 percent for Edmund Stoiber.[2] Those numbers began to shift in Stoiber's favor by midsummer. However, by the end of August, and only after Schröder responded quickly to the flooding in eastern Germany and raised the issue of resisting a war on Iraq, the Red-Green coalition rallied enough of the its sagging support among women and enough of the undecided female vote to win.[3] In short, the female vote was critical in returning the Red-Green coalition to power in its razor-thin victory over the CDU/CSU/FDP.

The rise of women into power positions in the German political system has helped bring women and their issues to the forefront of electoral politics. Their steady march through the halls of power picked up momentum in 2002. Both in parliamentary representation and in party politics, women are playing increasingly important and prominent roles in Germany. Equally revealing of their influence was the fact that so-called women's issues became central campaign foci for all parties as women became a critical campaign target audience. The major party candidates actually made women and their concerns, such as work, central features of their campaigns, as all tried openly to garner as much support as they could among female voters. Especially interesting in the campaign was the fact that Stoiber and the center-right parties constructed an earnest strategy to win back female support, which had dropped precipitously over the last decade. His strategy might have worked had not the Iraq war and flooding issues intervened at summer's end.

Notes for this chapter begin on page 166.

Another striking example of the influence women have gained in German politics was their visibility as public personalities and media stars in the 2002 campaigns. For example, the candidates' wives assumed campaign roles in an unprecedented manner. Karin Stoiber and Doris Schröder-Köpf became constant companions of their respective spouses and developed into media figures during the campaign, and each did her part to rally the party faithful while trying to reach out to more women. Other women became stars as the candidates attempted to show their support for and popularity with women.

In short, women have arrived at center stage in German politics, and this phenomenon became acutely visible in the 2002 election year, with women taking the stage from center-left. That said, the prominence of women's issues on the political agenda also revealed the many political roadblocks that continue to hinder women from achieving success in work place related politics. Thus, relative to other political systems, Germany scores well in the public sector regarding numbers of women present in government, parliament, and in important party positions. However, German women still suffer in the private sector from a traditional social system and mindset that forces them to choose between raising families and pursuing careers. On these types of indicators, Germany scores much lower than many other European countries. For example, compared to France, Germany boasts many more women in Parliament, but on the issue of adequate child care facilities that enable mothers to work, France scores much higher than Germany.[4] Therefore, the increasing political power held by women will be necessary to pull down the societal walls and break through the glass ceilings that continue to constrain them in the pursuit of balancing careers and families, and in creating a work place that is fairer on issues such as equal pay.

How Women Voted: Taking Political Center Stage Left

The trend since the unity election of 1990 has been for German women, and especially younger women, to vote Red-Green. In 1998, that trend was critical to the SPD/Green coalition in achieving its electoral victory.[5] The steady erosion of support for the CDU/CSU/FDP by 1998 led each of the right-of-center coalition parties to search for ways of returning women voters to their fold. The CDU/CSU actually gained marginally in 2002 among women voters compared to the 1998 election, while the SPD lost a percentage point. Yet, the gains for the center-right among women were too small to buck the trend and turn the tide. Once again, a majority of women voted for the SPD/Greens, while a majority of men voted for the CDU and CSU. SPD voters were 52 percent female and 48 percent male. Green voters were 55 percent female and 45 percent male.[6] In such a tightly contested election, women voters therefore made the critical difference in ensuring that the Schröder government retained power. Figure 8.1 details the voting patterns of women over the last several electoral cycles.[7]

Age was an important factor in determining how women voted. As figure 8.2 shows, the center-left parties achieved their best results among young and career age women voters, while the center-right parties clung to a small advantage in the over-60 age group: 49 percent for the center-right parties to 47 percent for the center-left parties. In all age groups up to age 60, the SPD/Greens scored substantially better than their center-right rivals.[8]

FIGURE 8.1 Female Vote for CDU/CSU-FDP vs. SPD-Green, 1990–2002

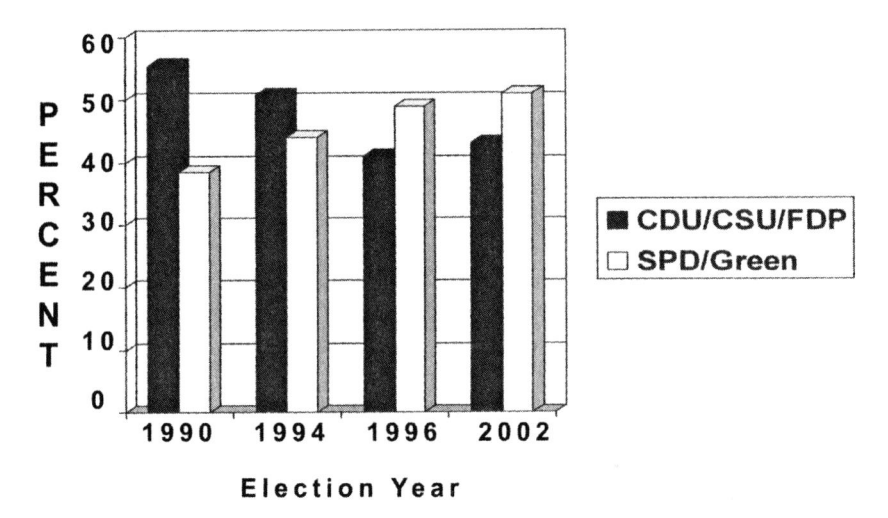

FIGURE 8.2 Female Party Vote by Age, 2002

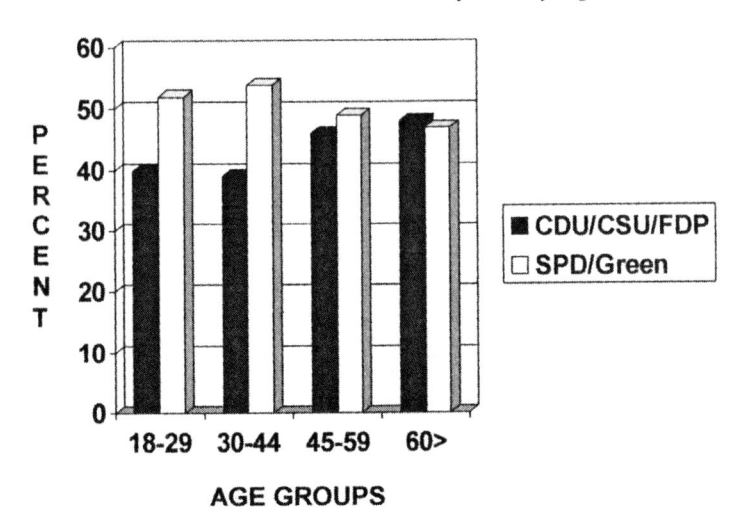

The East-West divide among women voters continued, but was less pronounced than in the other federal elections since unification. The biggest gains among women for the SPD came in the East. Here the party gained a full 9 percent over 1998 results, while female voting for the CDU remained unchanged.[9] The Greens also gained in the East with women voters, getting 5.2 percent of their vote and helping the party to pass the 5 percent hurdle in the eastern states.[10] The PDS became the big losers in the East among women voters. In no category of women voters did the PDS receive near 20 percent, and the party dropped below the 5 percent electoral hurdle nationally. The only reason the PDS has any presence in the 15th German Parliament is because two of their women candidates, Petra Pau and Gesine Lötzsch, got elected through the direct mandate system.

The last-minute issues of the war and the flooding probably saved Schröder, and they played particularly well in the East. Traditionally the eastern states lagged behind the German West in supporting a close alliance with the United States, and it was in the East where most of the summer flooding occurred. Coming in the last weeks of the campaign, the salience of those two issues helped to marginalize the PDS and decrease momentarily the centrality of the public's most important concerns, which had been unemployment and economic security, problems which continue to affect women in the East more negatively than any other group in Germany. The importance of the war and flood issues for women voters will be further explored later in this chapter. Soon after the election, polls showed that economic concerns quickly returned to the top slot, accompanied by a precipitous drop in the popularity of Schröder and his coalition government. Likewise, the first state elections in 2003, disastrous for the SPD, revealed the continued vulnerability of the governing coalition on economic issues.

The Rise of the "Power Frau": Women in German Politics

Women have been gaining steadily in acquiring positions of power and electoral seats in the German political system over the last two decades. The efforts of Social Democratic women such as Elisabeth Selbert to empower women in the 1950s, and to codify equality of the sexes into the Basic Law were important in the immediate postwar German political environment. However, the 1950s actually saw women's primary societal role emerge as being the domestic caregiver and homemaker, while it solidified men's role as the breadwinner.[11] The center-right parties were particularly keen to construct this paradigm in shattered postwar West Germany, viewing women's domesticity as "normal."[12] As I have argued elsewhere, the role of women in East Germany evolved very differently, and adapting to the western model after unification is an ongoing process with multiple problems for women in the eastern zones.[13]

The social movements that exploded on the West German scene in the 1970s fueled the growth of feminist, emancipation, and equality demands placed on the political system. The policies of the Greens in the early 1980s systematically adopted elements of the societal movements. The party spearheaded the charge to empower women in the West German political system and in party politics, and the mainstream political parties were thereafter compelled to work harder at winning women to their ranks.[14] By introducing quotas in party positions and advocating them in the workplace, and by constantly highlighting women's issues, the Greens helped women achieve power at a quicker pace than would have otherwise been true. Part of the Greens success among many women voters continues to be the party's emphasis on quotas and equality. Fully 75 percent of German women support quotas and the Greens continue to lead on the issue.

The 2002 election revealed that women are becoming increasingly visible as power-wielders in German party politics.[15] The current Red-Green coalition boasts six women in cabinet positions, up from four in the 1998 government. The cabinet is approaching parity between men and women.[16] The Green Party is now co-chaired by a man and a woman. The CDU leader, Angela Merkel, has grown into her power position since assuming it in 2000 after Helmut Kohl's and then Wolfgang Schäuble's political demise. Her assumption of party leadership represented the first time a woman held such a powerful job in German politics. Some argue that replacing Merkel with Stoiber as the candidate for chancellor in 2002 hurt the coalition's chances. Others argued that running with a woman and one from the East was an even less attractive strategy for the coalition than running with a Bavarian who was seen as more conservative than much of the CDU mainstream. Given the center-right's defeat in its one and only prior decision to run with a Bavarian from the CSU, Franz Josef Strauß in 1980, the decision in 2002 was a gamble.[17] In the face of defeat, many observers now argue that Merkel could make a formidable opponent for Schröder as a candidate in the next election. One SPD politician ironically observed after the election: "Frau Merkel would be more difficult for the SPD: she is a woman, comes from the East, and has a modern image."[18] In any case, Merkel wasted little time after the election in reclaiming the mantle of CDU party and coalition parliamentary leadership, and immediately spawned a policy and programmatic debate inside the coalition about the future.[19] Reflective of Merkel's refurbished power was the subtext of a headline that ran in the well respected German newspaper, *Die Zeit*, just after the election was over: "Angela Merkel captures the strongest power position in the Union since Helmut Kohl."[20]

The percentage of women in the German Parliament after the 1998 federal election was 30.9 percent, an increase of around 10 percent just since 1990.[21] That percentage increased again for the seventh time in a row with the 2002 election outcome. Women now make up 32.2 percent of the parliament, putting Germany seventh in the world and well ahead of the international average of 14.7 percent. The percentage of German women in Parliament far outpaces the numbers for France, which has only 12.3 percent female members of Parliament, and most other European countries. The United States also lags far behind Germany in fifty-sixth place.[22]

In keeping with the trend that has been emerging over the last decade, the left and left-of-center parties have the highest percentage of parliamentary members who are women, and the number would have been even higher in 2002 had the PDS made it over the 5 percent hurdle. Fully 58 percent of the Green Party's members of parliament are women, the highest of any party. The SPD follows with 37.8 percent of its parliamentary members being women. The CDU/CSU is quite a distant third with 21.3 percent women.[23]

The Media Campaign: Women as Stars and Personalities

Just as the Greens really started the march of women through the German political system and the higher profile it accorded women's issues, so too did they produce the first post–World War II female political and media superstar, Petra Kelly. Until her tragic death in 1992, Kelly proved through the 1980s that women could stand on their own both as savvy media celebrities and as smart political party representatives. Today, a number of German women have found the spotlight as political stars in their own right and others as media stars for the party. This phenomenon was especially evident in the 2002 election cycle.

The first set of female media stars of the 2002 campaign turned out to be the wives of the candidates. While Schröder has resented and tried to stop the media coverage of alleged marriage difficulties in the post-election period, there was no doubt about his and Stoiber's willingness to highlight their marriages and spouses as positive advertisement during the campaign. Interesting to note was the fact that each major candidate prized the presence of his wife in the campaign, and each used the image of his wife to portray certain perceived strengths about himself. At one point, an author in the conservative German newspaper, *Die Welt*, asked, "tradition vs. modernity?" and "motherhood vs. emancipation?"[24] To a large extent, Karin Stoiber was presented as the traditional woman, who valued stable family life and traditional values. She was the stay at home mom in the small Bavarian town of Wolfratshausen, who raised the children, cooked, and tended the house while her husband rose through the ranks of the CSU. She stayed at her husband's side during the campaign and spoke of her children and grandchildren. At one point, it was said that, "she is the incorporation of the saying 'behind every successful man is a strong woman.'"[25]

Doris Schröder-Köpf, from her hyphenated last name to her stylish demeanor, was the picture of the modern woman, the woman of the New Politics. Before marrying Schröder, she was a divorced single mother who had a successful career as a journalist. One observer noted that, "there has never been a more influential political wife." Over the course of Schröder's tenure, Doris Schröder-Köpf has written political pieces, such as one advocating Turkey's admittance to the European Union, and one concerning the Union's enlargement. She even edited a book about politics aimed at a juvenile audience. The book, *The Chancellor Lives in the Swimming Pool; or How Policy Is Made*, was published early in 2002, and can be seen as indicative both of her political savvy and her appeal to younger women and families.[26]

In short, the two women represented, or were depicted as representing, the clash of two competing and dichotomous models, or ideal types.[27] On the one hand was the traditional woman who marries and stays at home, and on the other the modern woman who works, marries, divorces, has children, marries, etc. Both were at times portrayed as independent, but in very different ways. The kind of independence displayed by Karin Stoiber was that of a strong woman inside a strong marriage. For Doris Schröder-Köpf, independence was expressed through her life story of working, raising a child alone, and then entering a marriage where she retained important aspects of her independence.

Of course, both of these images reflected what the candidates wanted projected about themselves as well: Stoiber was traditional, stable, resolute, and a bit stiff; Schröder was modern, flexible, and media savvy. The problem for Stoiber, however, was that these images reinforced some of the problems he was perceived as having with women, and that the center-right has had with women for a decade. Stoiber often appeared stiff and even awkward around women. One observer in Die Welt opined, "There it was, the suspicion: does he fear strong women?"[28] Stoiber's political team tried throughout the campaign to offset that image by having him appear in various formats with women. Most notably, he appeared at a media soaked gala in Munich two days before the election alongside German superstar, sex symbol, and "super woman," Veronica Ferres.[29]

While the traditional values pitch played to important parts of the electorate, especially to older voters, it did nothing to move the CSU/CDU closer to recapturing a majority of women voters along the New Politics frontier, and it made easier the SPD/Green's attempts to paint him as the out of touch conservative. As I discuss below, Stoiber did try to counter that image among younger women through a number of policy initiatives and political actions, such as naming Katherina Reiche, a young, educated, single mother as his candidate for to head the German Family Ministry.

Other women that became media stars were various candidates standing for office and certain women selected as potential cabinet members for the parties. One of the very visible candidates was Green candidate Anna

Lührmann, who won election at age 19, making her the youngest member of Parliament. Another Green political-media star was Renata Künast, the minister for consumer protection. According to Infratest polling, upwards of 58 percent of the German electorate hold her in high regard.[30]

The CSU/CDU had its own set of campaign stars besides Angela Merkel, such as Katherina Reiche. As mentioned above, Stoiber named her as his candidate for the German Youth, Women and Family Ministry. She is young, 29 years old, an unmarried mother of two from the former East, a biochemist, and a member of Parliament. The political move was strategic and very controversial within the CSU's conservative ranks. With her appointment, Stoiber hoped to appeal to younger women and eastern women, both voting blocs that have evaded the right-of-center parties. Reiche was what Karin Stoiber was not: she was the woman of the New Politics, not the perceived traditional representative of "Kinder, Küche, Kirche" (Children, kitchen, church).[31] As Reiche observed, "traditional (family) values have changed."[32] Stoiber's choice caused a real stir in his party and was criticized especially by the conservative wing of the CSU, and by institutional bulwarks of conservative values such as the Catholic Church. At one point, Stoiber actually considered trying to detach the Family from the Youth, Women, and Family Ministry, which would have made Reiche minister for youth and women, while a more traditional appointee would have overseen the Family Ministry. In the end, he did not take this path.[33]

Another center-right female star was Hildegard Müller. Again, she is youthful at 35, a long-standing member of the CDU's Youth Union, and a lynchpin for Stoiber's appeal to younger women. She was one of the members of the "Stoiber team" whose task it was to reach out to women between 25 and 45 years of age.[34] Known for standing up to Kohl before his resignation, Müller was seen as an independent player who would bring much to Stoiber's team, and appeal especially to many younger Union women who were loyal to Merkel.

The Issues for Women: Work, Family, Image

All parties attempted to insert "women's issues" into their campaigns. From the SPD's media event in the spring of 2002, called "One Hundred Strong Women,"[35] to the CSU/CDU's ongoing campaign strategy of targeting women voters through an emphasis on "family policy," all parties in 2002 recognized the power of women voters and set out to win them over. First, German women voters were in the majority. Some 31.9 million women voted, which was a full 2.9 million more than men voters.[36] In any election, that is a sizable group; in closely won elections, such as those held over the last decade in Germany and the United States, that represents a voting block of major significance.

Second, it was quite clear from early in the campaign that if the SPD/Greens had an electoral advantage, it was with female voters.[37] The trend of women voters deserting the conservative parties for the SPD and Greens has been accelerating since the 1980s, and the CDU's loss among women voters in 1998 was pivotal in Schröder's first victory. As mentioned above, it was first the Greens and then the SPD that began in the 1980s to forge policies meant to both attract and empower women voters. The right-of-center parties generally continued being perceived as the traditional parties. Thus, in the scheme of post-materialism, or what Russell Dalton calls the New Politics, the left-of-center parties have taken a strong lead in German politics in appealing to younger and better-educated women.[38]

The most prominent themes that ran through each party's campaign included working moms, tax policies related to families, discrimination against workingwomen, and a more symbolic politics of the traditional vs. the modern.

The Campaign of Symbolism

In the campaign of symbolism, the "woman problem" facing the CDU/CSU from the 1998 election remained that of overcoming the image of being too traditional in the face of the real issues today's women face. Because the 2002 campaign really typified more than previous German campaigns the triumph of the media and sound bite campaign, the politics of symbolism and personalities were critical, and nowhere more so than along the gender divide. The left-of-center parties attempted throughout the campaign to paint Stoiber and his coalition partners as relics of the past. Stoiber's age was consistently painted as synonymous with "old" policies. To that end, SPD and Green campaign rhetoric was peppered with remarks like that of one SPD activist who observed that, "Stoiber is the candidate of old men."[39] Schröder himself tied the Christian Democrats symbolically to "old men," when he opined that, "Women in German should be able to live the way they want not the way some old men in the [CDU/CSU] think they should live."[40] The comments were provocative, but the voting statistics revealed that the center-right opposition parties indeed received their most sizable voting block from men over sixty, while the SPD/Greens won among women, especially among young and middle age voters.[41] In a similar vein, Schröder and others in his coalition spoke of the CDU/CSU family policies as being "reactionary," and "aimed at keeping mothers chained to the kitchen."[42] Regarding specific family policies advocated by Stoiber, which I address below, Schröder would on occasion make remarks like, "This is a dusty, antiquated and totally out of date image of the family," one that "draws more from the era of the Kaiser than from our own."[43]

Policies Aimed at Women and Work

Women make up 42 percent of the German work force yet they continue to face a number of work barriers.[44] Women and the work place remains a real problem in Germany and include a cluster of policy issues. Discrimination against women continues, with women continuing to make about 20 percent below what men earn. In the public sector, women make 77 percent of what men earn; in the private sector, women earn only 73 percent of what their male colleagues make.[45]

The central policy issue seen as vital to women's interests was that of the work-family dilemma. German women, more so than many of their European counterparts, have for decades been forced to choose between having and raising a family, or working outside the home. Relative to other European states such as Denmark, France, and Belgium, Germany has very restrictive childcare policies when it comes to accommodating working mothers. There are very limited childcare opportunities for children under three years old, and where they do exist, they normally close at noon. Only about 5 percent of German children have spots in nursery schools. Likewise, the fact that school ends at 1:00 P.M. in Germany means that mothers must be home or find transportation from school and supervision for children all afternoon.[46] Only about 13 percent of German schools have facilities for students after school hours in the afternoon. These embedded practices have been campaign issues for the last several election cycles. In 2002 they became hotter issues than ever before.

Policies related to women and the work place have become all the more critical in Germany and other European states such as Spain and Italy because of the continued trend of negative population growth. As was felt especially by East German women after unification, but also by German women as a whole, women continue to be forced into choosing between having families and working because of state and societal policies still practiced that deny women adequate child care help. The infrastructure does not exist, and women are still constrained by societal attitudes that advocate women staying home with the children. Isabelle de Pommereau observes, Germany's "hausfrau" model for women who are married "isn't yielding the expected results. Germany's birthrate has dropped ominously since the 1970s and is now among the lowest in the industrialized world, threatening the labor pool and the economy." Indeed, while half of Germany's university graduates are women, only 15.7 percent of German women with children under six years old work full time even though, "twice as many would like to." That statistic is particularly revealing when compared to comparable statistics for France and Sweden, where 40 percent of French women with small children work full time, and more than 50 percent do in Sweden.[47]

Another striking statistic reveals the dilemma for women. One study examining gender and the work place showed that while 97 percent of the men who reached leadership positions were either married or in a stable relationship, 40 percent of the women in similar jobs neither were in such relationships nor had children.[48] Another study found that only 10 percent of managers are women with children.[49] In short, many women who do work full time are choosing not to have children. Thus, the issue of workingwomen has become both political and politicized.[50]

Both the SPD/Greens and the CSU/CDU knew about the gender gap going into the 2002 election, and the right-of-center parties attempted to win women back through various tactics and policy pronouncements. Learning from the 1998 campaign, Stoiber and the CSU/CDU intentionally set out in this last federal campaign to craft policies aimed at appealing to women on the matter of the childcare-work tradeoff. Stoiber attempted to build a campaign that would both bring in new women voters, as he revealed with naming Reiche as his candidate for family minister, and keep the traditional conservative values in the party's program. His symbolic gestures, such as showcasing Reiche, were aimed more at the former, while his substantive policy recommendations seemed more anchored in the traditional approach. That the SPD and Greens maintained the drumbeat of casting Stoiber and his policies as "old" showed up in this regard too. The Greens' co-chair, Claudia Roth commented on Stoiber's choice of Reiche during the campaign, noting that the CSU election team had added a young face. Yet she followed this observation by remarking that Stoiber "has looked very old in the last few days."[51]

The center-right's campaign tried to support the right of women to work and raise a family. Angela Merkel was pivotal in seeing to it that "compatibility between work and family" became an important objective. That said, Stoiber's substantive centerpiece policy proposal offered financial aid to stay-at-home mothers to help raise their children. His plan was to pay families with children 600 euros per month until the age of three, then decrease the payment as the child ages. Stoiber advocated this policy as part of his "Marshall plan for families."[52] While this was seen by many as a forward-looking policy for the center-right, the center-left continued to beat the drum about Stoiber's anachronistic approach by pointing out statistics such as the fact that Bavaria has more stay-at-home moms than anywhere else in Germany, and that only 1.4 percent of children in Bavaria are in child care.[53]

As soon as the election was over, debate about reforming the parties to capture young women and eastern women voters once again commenced, especially in the CDU.[54] As many have observed, part of the problem with the right-of-center's continued appeal to the traditional family model is that the model itself has been undergoing radical transformation, and especially among young women. For example, whereas for years the percentage of German women that were childless hovered at around 10 percent, that figure is now at 30 percent, and some predict it to go as high as 40 percent by 2020. Second, German divorce rates are nearing United States levels. The rate of divorce in Germany rose 2.5 percent from 1997–1998 to around 46 percent; the United States still leads the way with over 50 percent.[55] Third, despite the continued entrenchment of conservative and traditional views concerning marriage in Germany, unmarried cohabitation is also on the rise. In short, what is called the pluralization of life choices in Germany leaves the CSU's appeal to traditional family values playing less well among large swaths of the public as the makeup of families themselves continues to change.[56]

It was significant that the SPD forged an electoral campaign from the beginning that was intended to keep the female voters in the left-of-center column. Schröder's campaign worked hard on the work/family issue. First, Schröder capitalized on policies already put in place by his government that are working woman- and family-friendly. For example, under Schröder's leadership, child support by the federal government has been raised three times and tax relief for families with children has been increased. State spending on families increased from about 40 billion euros per year in 1998 to around 53 billion by the time of the 2002 campaign.[57] While Schröder backed off some from his 1998 pledge to introduce quotas aimed at enhancing women's chances in the work force, his government has supported "soft" quotas, where companies are encouraged by the government to introduce quota systems and mentoring programs for women. Many corporations have followed the "soft" model, including Daimler Chrysler, Lufthansa, Deutsche Bank, Telekom, Proctor and Gamble, and Bosch.[58] The SPD has also introduced a mentoring system within the party.

The SPD therefore showcased itself as the "family-friendly" party, proposing during the campaign to spend 4 billion euros (as a start) to establish new childcare facilities in Germany.[59] This policy was directly aimed at the problem working women face because of inadequate or nonexistent childcare facilities. Alongside this proposal, Schröder advocated introducing all day supervision in schools, a program to be operationalized and funded in his next four-year term.

The Schröder government had already introduced a monthly federal payment to families of 150 euros per child. The campaign pledge was to increase that sum to 200 euros a month. The SPD was careful to advertise the payment "as a bonus, not a subsidy to stay at home." In short, Schröder's campaign sought to enhance the working opportunities for women through better childcare, and to lighten the financial load of family maintenance through payment of the "bonuses."[60]

War and the Deluge: The Last-Minute Surge for the SPD

Much ink has been spilled over the issue of Schröder's anti-war positioning during the last month of the campaign. The chancellor's decision to challenge an American president openly on security issues during a national campaign was unprecedented. Many have taken Schröder to task regarding the possible damage to the transatlantic relationship caused by his continued defiance about supporting a war against Iraq. He has also been criticized, especially by the opposition CDU/CSU, for making a campaign issue out of a critical security policy that affects one of Germany's most important allied relationships.

Those considerations aside, Schröder's stance of resistance was pivotal in helping him and the Red-Green coalition eke out their narrow electoral victory. Public opinion polls taken during and after the election showed that both men and women remained firm in rejecting German participation in a war against Iraq, even in the event that Saddam Hussein be caught lying about the disposition of Iraq's weapons.[61] Politicizing the issue helped Schröder capture some of the large pool of undecided voters toward the end of the campaign.

Looking more closely at public opinion data, the anti-war strategy was particularly successful with women voters, and it is likely that Schröder had them in mind when he pursued the policy. Surveys taken throughout 2002 showed women to be even more negatively disposed than men toward war in general, and specifically with Iraq. A widely held view is that women are generally more opposed to war than men, and especially among women who are mothers.[62] Former Chancellor Helmut Kohl furthers the claim in raising the fact that a generation of German women still remembers the losses of the last world war, but he is critical of Schröder for rekindling those fears.[63]

An Emnid poll taken in April 2002 measured German willingness to go to war under six different circumstances and across a number of identity categories, including that of gender. In only one of the six categories, that of homeland defense did a majority of women (62 percent) say that war was justifiable. While some majority of male respondents answered that war was justifiable in order to unseat illegitimate regimes (54 percent), or to ensure international stability (51 percent), female respondents rejected both scenarios (36 and 37 percent, respectively).[64] Both of those categories could be interpreted to include the willingness to go to war with Iraq.

If one looks back to German public opinion and the war in Kosovo, which presents a totally different case than that of Iraq, a majority of Germans supported NATO's intervention throughout the spring of 1999. The support never dropped below 50 percent. That said, it is again interesting to note that women tended to support the war less than did men. In an Allensbach poll from May 1999, a number of war-related questions were posed to a group of 14 to 19-year-old males and females. On all of the questions, support for the Kosovo war and war in general was higher among the males. For example, while an overall 53 percent believed that the NATO intervention was justified, 62 percent of the male respondents said the air war was justified, while only 44 percent of the females agreed. In a similar vein, 59 percent of the females answered that war should be avoided, while only 37 percent of the males agreed.[65] Thus, from Kosovo in 1999 through Iraq in 2002, German women are less likely to support war than are men.

The second political golden egg laid for Schröder during the last phase of the campaign was the flooding that affected especially the eastern parts of Germany. The coalition's efforts at disaster relief resonated especially well with women voters in the East. Further helping the Red-Green parties among women was the fact that the natural disasters highlighted especially the environmentalist identity of the Greens and gave them extra political mileage in criticizing the opposition's environmental policies.

Conclusion

The closeness of the 2002 election increased the importance of specific voting blocs including women. They were wooed by all major parties, and their issues became centerpieces for each campaign. Work, family, taxes, retirement: all of these issues resonated in very particular ways with women voters. Beyond the strategies developed by the major parties to appeal to them, 2002 also made clear the real advances women continued to make in the German political system. They advanced to become major players in the parties and attained parliamentary seats in larger numbers than ever. An equally compelling story from the election was the emergence of women as media stars. There can be little doubt that these trends will continue and that the arrival of women at the center of German politics has changed the landscape permanently.

Notes

For their help, I would like to thank Helga Welsh, John Yekulis for his comments and help on the charts, and especially Christian Søe for his helpful suggestions.

1. "Sind die Frauen Schröder's letzte Chance?" *Welt am Sonntag*, *Die Welt Online* (accessed 16 June 2002).
2. Peter Zander, "Die Charme-Offensive," *Die Welt*, 22 June 2002.
3. Fully 30 percent of women voters were still undecided in their preference in early September 2002. The war and flooding issues clearly intervened to tip some of those voters toward the governing coalition. See "Women's Issues a Focus in German Election Campaign," *Deutsche Welle*, http://dw.world.de (accessed 19 September 2002).
4. Catherine Rama, "Less Than Two in 10 Parliamentarians in World Are Women," *Global News Bank*, http://infoweb11.newsbank.com (accessed 21 September 2002).
5. Mary N. Hampton, "Reaching Critical Mass? German Women and the 1998 Election," in *Power Shift in Germany: The 1998 Election and the End of the Kohl Era*, ed. David P. Conradt, Gerald R. Kleinfeld, and Christian Søe (New York: Berghahn Books, 2000), pp. 155–177.

6. Dieter Roth and Matthias Jung, "Ablösung der Regierung vertagt: Eine Analyse der Bundestagswahl 2002," in *Aus Politik und Zeitgeschichte. Beilage zur Wochenzeitung das Parlament*, 9 December 2002, p. 15.
7. For data represented in figures 8.1 and 8.2, see statistics and analysis in *Bundestagswahl: Eine Analyse der Wahl vom. 22. September 2002*, Berichte der Forschungsgruppe Wahlen, Mannheim no. 108, and Der Bundeswahlleiter, *Erste Ergebnisse der Repräsentativen Wahlstatistik zur Bundestagswahl 2002*.
8. *Bundestagswahl: Eine Analyse der Wahl vom. 22. September 2002*, Berichte der Forschungsgruppe Wahlen, Mannheim no. 108.
9. "Scharfe Kontraste zwischen Ost und West, Nord und Süd," *Die Welt Online* (accessed 9 September 2002).
10. "'Superstars': German Green Party and the Election 2002," Bündnis 90/Die Grünen, http://www.gruene.de.
11. See Hanna Schissler, "'Normalization' as Project: Some Thoughts on Gender Relations in West Germany during the 1950s," in *The Miracle Years: A Cultural History of West Germany, 1949–1968*, ed. Hanna Schissler (Princeton: Princeton University Press, 2001), pp. 359–375.
12. Schissler, "'Normalization' as Project"; Elizabeth Heinemann, "The Hour of the Woman: Memories of Germany's 'Crisis Years' and West German National Identity," in Schissler, *The Miracle Years*, pp. 21–56.
13. Hampton, "Reaching Critical Mass?"
14. Ibid., pp. 166–167.
15. For a detailed and interesting description of many of the current "power Frauen" in and around the coalition government, see Joyce Mushaben, "Girl Power: Women, Politics and Leadership in the Berlin Republic," unpublished manuscript, 2002.
16. The six female ministers in Schröder's cabinet include Ulla Schmidt (SPD) at Health and Social Services; Edelgard Bulmahn (SPD) at Education and Research; Heidemarie Wieczorek-Zeul (SPD) at Development/Foreign Aid; Renate Künast (Greens) at Consumer and Agriculture; Brigitte Zypries (SPD) at Justice; and Renate Schmidt (SPD) at Family, Women, and Children. See "Das neue Schröder-Kabinett," *Spiegel Online*, http://www.spiegel.de (accessed 16 October 2002).
17. For a discussion of the CDU's agreeing to have Strauß run in 1980 as the coalition's candidate, see David P. Conradt, *The German Polity*, 7th ed. (New York: Addison, Wesley, Longman, 2001), pp. 114–115. Interestingly, many moderates and liberals in the CDU agreed to Strauß being the candidate only because they concluded that they did not have a chance against the SPD's popular Helmut Schmidt anyway. Having let Strauß run and lose, any commitment they may have felt to him and the conservative CSU was thereby met and finished.
18. Matthias Machnig, quoted in "Sündenbock und IM Cohiba," *Spiegel Online* (accessed 1 January 2003, 30 December 2002).
19. For a revealing look at Merkel's ascendancy after the election, see Matthias Geis, "Jetzt spricht die Chefin," *Die Zeit*, Politik 40/2002, http://www.zeit.de; "With Stoiber Out, Merkel Is on the Rise," *Current Affairs*, 24 September 2002; *Deutsche Welle*, "Sorge vor Spaltung der Union," *Welt am Sonntag*, 6 October 2002.
20. Geis, "Jetzt Spricht die Chefin."
21. Hampton, "Reaching Critical Mass?" p. 155.
22. "German Parliament Sports Young Face," *Current Affairs*, http://www.dw.world.de (accessed 24 September 2002); Rama, "Less Than Two in 10 Parliamentarians"; "Kleiner, jünger und weiblicher," *Spiegel Online*, http://www.spiegel.de (accessed 23 September 2002).
23. "German Parliament Sports Young Face," *Current Affairs*.
24. Inga Griese, "Familienbilder," *Die Welt, Welt Online*, http://www.welt.de/2002/01/19 (accessed 19 January 2002).
25. "Stand By Your Man," *Deutsche Welle*, 26 June 2002.

26. Ibid. The German title for Köpf-Schröder's book is *Der Kanzler wohnt im Swimmingpool Oder wie Politik gemacht wird*. The translation in the text is mine.
27. Some observers argued during the campaign that the two women were not as different as the media messages suggested.
28. Zander, "Die Charme-Offensive."
29. Ibid.
30. "'Superstars': German Green Party and the Election 2002."
31. See discussion in "Who's an Expert on Family Values?" *Deutsche Welle*, http://www.dw-world.de (accessed 4 July 2002).
32. Reiche, quoted in "Who's an Expert on Family Values?"
33. "Who's an Expert on Family Values?"
34. Jens Tartler, "Hildegard Müller: Stoibers Angebot an die jungen Frauen." *Financial Times Deutschland*, 9 August 2002.
35. On the "One Hundred Strong Women," see "Sind die Frauen Schröder's letzte Chance?"
36. See "Frauen Wählen mit dem Herzen," *Welt am Sonntag*, *Die Welt Online* (accessed 15 September 2002).
37. See discussion of the two candidates and their differing skill level with women in Severin Weiland, "Zwei Männer streiten um die Frauen," *Spiegel Online* (accessed 19 September 2002).
38. See Russell Dalton, *Citizen Politics*, 3rd ed. (New York: Chatham House, 2002), p. 163. On the key role of the Greens in forging ahead with a New Politics agenda in the 1980s, see Andrei Markovits and Philip Gorsky, *The German Left: Red, Green and Beyond* (Cambridge: Cambridge University Press, 1993).
39. Matthias Machnig, quoted in "Sind die Frauen Schröder's letzte Chance?"
40. "Schröder Likens Stay-at-Home Moms to Kaiser's Era—Vows Child Care Increase," *Global News Bank*, Deutsche Press-Agentur, 29 May 2002.
41. The CSU/CDU won 47 percent of the over-60 male vote, its highest percentage; the SPD got its best result, 42.8 percent, from women between 18 and 24; the Greens got the most support from women between the ages of 35–44. Interestingly, older men made up the highest voting block.
42. "Schröder Battles Weak Poll Ratings at Election Congress," *Global News Bank*, Deutsche Press-Agentur, http://infoweb11.newsbank.com (accessed 2 June 2002).
43. "Schröder Likens Stay-at-Home Moms to Kaiser's Era—Vows Child Care Increase."
44. Stephanie Halasz, "Working Mums Focus of German Poll," CNN.com, http://Europe.cnn.com (accessed 28 August 2002).
45. "Der grosse Unterschied," *Süddeutsche Zeitung*, http://www.süddeutsche.de (accessed 9 October 2002).
46. Hampton, "Reaching Critical Mass?" pp. 170–173.
47. Isabelle de Pommereau, "Hot Campaign Issue in Germany: Working Moms," *The Christian Science Monitor*, 11 July 2002.
48. Renate Schmidt, "Der Quark steht im Kühlschrank," *Welt am Sonntag*, 17 March 2002.
49. "The Politics of Raising Children," *Deutsche Welle*, http://www.dw-world.de (accessed 2 April 2002).
50. Pommereau, "Hot Campaign Issue in Germany."
51. Claudia Roth, quoted in "Who's an Expert on Family Values?"
52. "The Politics of Raising Children," *Deutsche Welle*, http://www.dw-world.de (accessed 2 April 2002).
53. Ibid.
54. For example, see the interview with CDUer Friedrich Merz, "Wir hatten keine Strategie," in *Die Welt*, 27 September 2002. He specifically bemoans the fact that the party no longer reaches many young women with its programmatic family policies.
55. "Neuer Scheidungsrekord in Deutschland," transparent.com, http://www.transparent.com/newsletter (accessed October–November 1999).

56. "The Politics of Raising Children"; Guido Geist, "Die klassische Familie unterliegt in Deutschland einem tief greifenden Wandel," *Die Welt*, 13 July 2002.
57. "More Cash for Social Welfare, Vows Schröder in Election Speech," *Deutsche Press-Agentur*, 18 April 2002.
58. "Breaking through the Glass Ceiling," *Deutsche Welle*, http://www.dw-world.de (accessed 2 February 2002).
59. "Schröder Likens Stay-at-Home Moms to Kaiser's Era—Vows Child Care Increase."
60. Halasz, "Working Mums Focus of German Poll."
61. See survey taken by Emnid, January 2003. Seventy-one percent of German respondents continued to be against war with Iraq, including under circumstances in which Hussein was dishonest. See http://de.news.yahoo.com/030117/3/36ehq.html.
62. See "Frauen wählen mit dem Herzen." See also an interview with Helmut Kohl, conducted after the 2002 election, in which he also avers that women are more anti-war than men because of the personal burdens of loss. "Lassen Sie uns über Frauen reden …," *Die Welt*, 18 January 2003, *Die Welt Online*.
63. "Lassen Sie uns über Frauen reden."
64. Emnid poll from 19–20 April 2002, http://www.chrismon.de/ctexte/2002/6/6-umfrage.html.
65. Allensbach poll of 14- to 19-year-olds appeared in *Die Zeit*, http://www.Zeit.de/1999/21 (accessed 20 May 1999).

Chapter 9

DOGS THAT DID NOT BARK
German Exceptionalism Reconsidered

David F. Patton

Just six years ago, center-left parties were ascendant throughout much of Europe, governing in 13 of the 15 member countries of the Europe.[1] At this time, there was much talk of a revitalized European left that had moved beyond the statism of traditional social democracy in order to find modern solutions to current problems. At a symposium held at New York University in September 1998, Bill Clinton (as a "New Democrat"), Tony Blair (leader of "New Labour" and an outspoken proponent of a "Third Way"), and Italy's Romano Prodi praised the virtues of pragmatic, less ideological approaches to markets, the welfare state, law and order, and education. In June 1999, Tony Blair and Gerhard Schröder ("New Center") jointly released a white paper that distanced their politics from that of traditional social democracy and optimistically proclaimed: "Let the policies of the Third Way and the New Center be the new hope for Europe."[2]

What a difference an electoral cycle makes! By early summer 2002, most of the center-left governments, with the notable exception of Tony Blair's Labour Party in Great Britain, had been swept out of office. Rather than presage a fundamental shift in partisan loyalties, the coming of the center-left appeared to be little more than a passing fad that had largely passed. In its place, center-right governments assumed power across the continent, dislodging center-left parties in consecutive elections in Denmark, Italy, Portugal, France, and the Netherlands. By mid-2002, conservatives governed in 10 of the 15 European Union states. In Germany, Chancellor Gerhard Schröder (SPD), whose politics of the *Neue Mitte* (New Center) resembled that of Blair's New Labour, appeared headed for electoral defeat as his Red-Green coalition (SPD-Greens) trailed badly in the polls just months prior to the Bundestag elections on 22 September.

Yet the Red-Green alliance won in Germany, in part because two trends that had contributed to the end of center-left rule elsewhere were

---

Notes for this chapter begin on page 183.

conspicuously absent: namely, Germany was spared an upsurge in right-wing populism and a splintering on the Left. These products of protest, on the Right and on the Left, had hastened the defeat of center-left governments elsewhere. Why they did not arise in the Federal Republic is the analytical puzzle of this chapter. Certainly the objective conditions in Germany seemed right for both developments. In 2002, Schröder and his Red-Green coalition faced a hostile political climate not dissimilar to that of other European Union democracies where center-left governments had been recently voted out of office. To understand this apparent German exceptionalism, we will briefly consider factors specific to Germany. The chapter concludes by arguing that another transnational tendency, namely, the growing electoral importance of individual politicians rather than parties, helps explain what at first glance may appear as German exceptionalism.

The Rise of Right-Wing Populism

Since the mid-1980s, right-wing populist parties have gained entry to most national parliaments in Western Europe by drawing upon the widespread anti-foreigner sentiment, disillusionment with the political establishment, and anger over high taxes and excessive regulation.[3] These parties of protest have thrived at a time of high unemployment and a perceived crisis of the welfare state which, the rightists argued, has been exacerbated by immigration. They have mobilized an eclectic group of voters ranging from the petty bourgeoisie to industrial workers by combining xenophobia with a program of radical deregulation and welfare state reform.[4] This so-called third wave of the postwar European far right has encompassed anti-immigration parties with varied programs and practices. The Vlaams Blok was separatist and openly racist, while the Freedom Party of Austria and Swiss People's Party attacked power-sharing in their respective countries.[5] Nonetheless, as Hans-Georg Betz has shown, "the current wave of radical right-wing populist movements and parties represents a transnational phenomenon whose rise to political success has occurred contemporaneously and shares common traits."[6] Betz characterizes today's parties as *radical* because they oppose the current welfare system and the present political system (although they support representative democracy), as *right wing* because they reject social equality and the integration of foreigners and other outsiders, and as *populist* because they exploit the frustration of the general public. They distinguish "themselves both from the backward-looking, reactionary politics of the traditional extremist right (i.e., neo-fascist and neo-Nazi) as well its proclivity for violence."[7]

Over the past decade, right-wing populist parties have recorded some spectacular gains at the polls.[8] The Freedom Party of Austria (FPÖ), whose share of the vote dramatically increased after Jörg Haider leadership of the party in the mid-1980s, won over 27 percent in the 1999 parliamentary elections, up from the nearly 22 percent it had garnered in 1995. In neighboring Switzerland, Christoph Blocher, the charismatic leader of the Swiss People's Party (SVP), successfully transformed the SVP into Switzerland's largest vote-getter by defending Swiss traditions and history (such as neutrality and its role in World War II) and by taking a hard line on asylum, immigration, and multiculturalism. The SVP's share of the vote jumped from 12 percent in 1991 to 22.5 percent in 1999. Both the Austrian Freedom Party and the Swiss People's Party won over workers who had grown disenchanted with politics-as-usual in their respective countries.[9]

In Scandinavia, a region often associated with tolerance and social justice, right-wing populists have acquired significant levels of support in recent years. The Danish People's Party (DF), led by Pia Kjaersgaard, improved its share of the vote from 7.4 percent in 1978 to 12 percent in 2001 by staking out positions critical of immigrants, political asylum, the functioning of the Danish welfare state, and the process of European integration.[10] In Norway, the anti-foreigner Progress party, headed by the plain-speaking Carl I. Hagen, garnered nearly 15 percent of the vote in 2001 parliamentary elections. In Scandinavia, "the common denominator of the Nordic parties was and is dissatisfaction with the social and economic policies of the established parties as well as their domestic policies and policies on immigration. They are therefore a channel for resentment in their countries."[11] Likewise in the Netherlands and to an even greater extent in the Dutch-speaking region of Belgium, the xenophobic right wing amassed a sizeable following among the working class by linking immigration to social and economic problems. The far-right Flemish Bloc (VB) won just under 10 percent of the Belgian vote in 1999 (and a much higher share in Flanders), while the anti-foreigner List Pim Fortuyn (LPF), led by Pim Fortuyn ("the Netherlands is full") until his murder in spring 2002, received 17 percent of the vote in the 2002 Dutch parliamentary elections.[12]

Other notable successes of right-wing populism included the second coming of the Italian media mogul Silvio Berlusconi in 2001 and Jean-Marie Le Pen's startling second-place finish (16.9 percent) in the first round of the French presidential elections in spring 2002. In Portugal, the Popular party, led by Paulo Portas, displaced the Communists as the third largest party by campaigning against immigration and multiculturalism.

In the past few years, right-wing populist parties have become acceptable coalition partners in several European democracies. A controversial step was taken by the center-right Austrian People's Party (ÖVP), which joined in coalition with Haider's Freedom Party of Austria (FPÖ), much to the dismay of the member-states of the European Union. In contrast to the Europe-wide protests that followed the FPÖ's entry into government, the members of the European Union quietly tolerated the right-wing coalition in Italy between Berlusconi's Forza Italia, Gianfranco Fini's post-fascist National Alliance, and Umberto Bossi's xenophobic Northern League.[13]

By mid-2002, Austria, Italy, Denmark, the Netherlands, Portugal, and Switzerland had governing cabinets that either included or were tolerated by populist parties of the Right.[14]

Right-wing populism surged as center-left governments in Europe struggled with high unemployment, an overburdened welfare state and a sluggish economy. Many Europeans blamed immigrants for crime, the crisis of the welfare state, joblessness, and poor public education. According to surveys taken in spring 2000 in the member states of the European Union, 30 percent of those polled expressed the view that immigrants are disproportionately involved in crime; less than half indicated that immigrants enrich the European Union culturally; and nearly one-fifth of those polled stated that immigrants from Muslim countries should not be accepted into the European Union at all.[15] Since the terrorist attacks on 11 September 2001, European publics have grown even more hostile to immigration, linking newcomers from Muslim countries with Islamic fundamentalism and terrorism. To disillusioned voters, the much-acclaimed Third Way seemed to bring about more of the same. They therefore turned in increasing numbers to the right-wing populist parties that promised radical solutions.

The success of these parties has hurt the center-left in two ways. First, the right-wing populists made significant electoral inroads among the industrial working class, the traditional constituency of social democracy. Second, as the center-right parties became more willing to cooperate with right-wing populist parties, the center-left parties were forced into the opposition in Austria, Denmark, the Netherlands, and Portugal.

In 2002, Germany seemed like fertile ground for right-wing populism. Notes Frank Decker, "with reference to the 'demand side' one can hardly account for the weakness of right-wing populism."[16] Like other democracies in Northern Europe, Germany had an extensive welfare state burdened by mounting costs. Although the German economy was the largest in Europe, it had grown at a sluggish rate in recent years and earned the moniker, "the sick man of Europe." Germany, like other Europe member states, was also plagued by a high rate of joblessness that had reached nearly 10 percent nationwide and 18 percent in eastern Germany by mid-2002. Germans also faced high levels of taxation and cuts in social services. Taken together, these unfavorable economic factors, coupled with little optimism about the future, created the potential for right-wing populism in the Federal Republic.

Furthermore, many Germans resented the large population of foreigners that lived within their country's borders. At around 9 percent, the share of foreigners in Germany was among the highest in the European Union. The unemployment rate among foreigners was disproportionately high, while foreigners made up a third of Germany's prison population.[17,18] As was common throughout Western Europe, many Germans blamed foreigners for crime, unemployment, problems in the schools, and the growing costs of the welfare state. Foreign residents, particularly those of Muslim background, were commonly criticized for their alleged unwillingness to accept the culture of Germany. The events of September 11 compounded the fears of many Germans, especially once it became known that three of the pilots of the hijacked planes, including the alleged ringleader, had studied at a technical university in Hamburg.

If Frank Decker is right and the "demand-side" cannot explain the weakness of right-wing populism in Germany, then it is necessary to look at the "supply-side." At the start of 2002, there were several candidates that might mobilize anti-foreigner resentment in the upcoming the election campaign. These included the openly racist National Democratic Party of Germany (NPD) and the Republicans (REPs); a new conservative populist party (the Party for a Rule of Law Offensive, widely known as the Schill Party) that was led by the former judge Roland Barnabas Schill ("Judge Merciless"); the Free Democratic Party, whose vice-chairman Jürgen Möllemann was suspected of right-wing populism; and Edmund Stoiber (CSU), the chancellor candidate of the Christian Democrats, who as premier in Bavaria had opposed multiculturalism and championed law-and-order policies.

The least likely to succeed were the NPD and the REPs. The NPD had peaked in the late 1960s when they held 61 seats in seven state parliaments and nearly crossed the 5 percent threshold necessary to enter the Bundestag in 1969.[19] Thereafter it steadily declined, gravitating toward the extreme right and the status of a splinter party. In the 1990s, its then chairman, Günter Deckert, was jailed for Holocaust denial. Following Deckert, Udo Voit opened the party up to German skinheads, endangering the very existence of the NPD which now faced a possible ban due to its alleged anti-democratic activities. The party has floundered at the polls, receiving 0.3 percent of the vote in the 1998 parliamentary elections. The Republicans had risen to prominence in the late 1980s by pitting "German interests" against those of foreign workers, asylum-seekers, and other newcomers to the Federal Republic. In the late 1980s, led by the charismatic former television journalist Franz Schönhuber, the REPs entered state parliaments in Baden-Württemberg and Berlin. They remained in the state parliament of Baden-Württemberg after winning 10.5 percent and 9.1 percent of the vote in 1992 and 1996 respectively. Despite these successes, the REPs could not fashion a breakthrough at the national level along the lines of the Front National in France. They received just 1.8 percent in the Bundestag elections in 1998. The German People's Union (DVU), led and financed by the millionaire publisher Gerhard Frey, was another xenophobic party that had enjoyed some success in state elections, especially in eastern Germany. In 1998, it had received 12.9 percent of the vote in Saxony-Anhalt; this marked the highest share ever recorded by a right-wing populist party in the Federal Republic. However, the DVU lacked the party organization to unify the racist right in Germany and did not participate in the Bundestag elections of 2002. In short, the parties of the German extreme right, in part because of their fragmentation, stood little chance of an electoral breakthrough in 2002 or even of surpassing the combined 3.3 percent captured in 1998.

In early 2002, the newly formed Schill Party appeared likely to benefit from the growing unease about crime in Germany. This textbook example of a one-issue party had won a sensational 19.4 percent of the vote in the Hamburg state elections of 23 September 2001 by promising law and order in a city afflicted with Germany's highest crime rate. Roland Schill pledged to cut the crime rate in half by toughening sentences and increasing the police presence in Hamburg.[20] In its program, the Schill Party steered clear of nationalism and overt racism, yet nonetheless tapped into latent xenophobia by underscoring the link between foreigners and crime. It praised the zero tolerance approach of New York City mayor Rudolph Giuliani.[21] Led by an adroit political entrepreneur with democratic credentials whose grandfather was murdered by the National Socialists, the Schill Party did disproportionately well among Hamburg's workers, many of whom had earlier voted for the SPD.[22] This fits the pattern of right-wing populist parties on the continent that have acquired strong working-class support. After the election, the CDU and the FDP formed a governing coalition with the Schill Party, despite the latent xenophobia of the latter. Roland Schill became Hamburg's minister of the interior.

The Schill Party faced several obstacles to national success in 2002. First, it lacked the personnel to expand the party organization to other federal states without risking infiltration by opportunistic right-wing extremists. Second, it had benefited from the peculiarities of Hamburg, characterized by Schill as the "German capital of crime," and had no clear strategy for southern Germany, which was held up by the party to be something of a role model. Third, the reputation of Ronald Schill, so integral to the success of the party, soon suffered. Once in office, Schill naturally could not keep the promises and threats that he had made during the campaign, such as halving the rate of crime, castrating sex offenders, or massively building up the Hamburg police force. His party proved to be inexperienced at governance and internally divided. Complicating matters further, Schill was soon embroiled in a scandal surrounding his alleged use of cocaine. These charges were especially damaging to Schill as a former judge and self-proclaimed law-and-order politician. Notwithstanding these problems, the Schill Party nonetheless possessed a well-known leader and a campaign issue (public safety) that resonated with many Germans, especially after September 11.

In 2002, the FDP dabbled in populism in an effort to attract new voters. It after all had headily declared that 18 percent of the vote was its electoral goal, a far cry from the 6.3 percent it had garnered in 1998. Jürgen Möllemann, its flamboyant vice-chairman, sought to transform the FDP into a catch-all party (*Volkspartei*) that would rival the CDU/CSU and SPD. For this to happen, the FDP would need to move far beyond its core clientele of doctors, dentists, professors, and lawyers and attract disaffected lower middle class and working class voters. Would it embrace right-wing populism, as had the FPÖ in Austria and Blocher's SVP in Switzerland?

In spring 2002, Jürgen Möllemann defended Jamal Karsli whose virulent attacks on Israel had led Karsli to switch from the Greens caucus to the FDP caucus in the state parliament of North Rhine-Westphalia.[23] Möllemann criticized Israeli policy and blamed Ariel Sharon and Michel Friedman, the deputy chairman of the Central Council of German Jews, for causing more anti-Semitism in Germany. Like right-wing populists in other countries, Möllemann claimed to speak for the little man and chastised the establishment: "In a panic, Schröder, Merkel and company want to deny our ability to govern. This only makes the voters even more scornful since they alone decide who is fit to govern."[24] Möllemann went so far as to welcome the defeat of the established parties (often at the hands of right-wing populists) throughout Western Europe: "The historians will later write that a wave of growing self-confidence among the people shaped nations and states at the start of the new millennium. One nation of democrats after another has come of age and forced the political class to renew itself from head to toe."[25] The leader of the FDP, Guido Westerwelle, also maintained that criticism of Israel must be allowed in a democracy and that Friedman bore responsibility for the controversy over anti-Semitism that had erupted in Germany.

The political scientists Hajo Funke and Lars Rensmann have made the case that Möllemann and Westerwelle were deliberately pursuing a right-wing populist strategy, along the lines of Jörg Haider in Austria. To Funke and Rensmann, right-wing populists parties are distinguished by three features: they invoke ethnic nationalism or anti-Semitism; they present themselves as willing to challenge 'politically correct' assumptions, taboos, and business as usual within a liberal democracy; and they view themselves as the vanguard of an anti-elitist mass movement that challenges the establishment.[26] Funke and Rensmann have reasoned that Möllemann and the FDP satisfied all three criteria.

In early 2002, Edmund Stoiber, the Bavarian premier and the chancellor candidate of the center-right Christian Democrats (CDU/CSU), appeared to be a established politician that might turn to populism in order to tap into anti-foreigner sentiment in Germany. On the issue of crime, which many Germans associated with foreigners, Stoiber (CSU) could point to Bavaria's tough law-and-order policy and boast of a rate of crime that was among the lowest in the Federal Republic.[27] During the 1990s, Bavaria had increased camera surveillance of public places, computer dragnets, and police searches (often of racial minorities) without due cause for suspicion. Under Stoiber, Bavaria deported more foreigners in 1998 than any other German state; it also opposed dual citizenship, the initial Red-Green proposal to establish a German policy of immigration, and multiculturalism. Its hard line appealed to many Germans concerned about the impact of immigration on unemployment and crime. Would Stoiber seek to exploit these concerns by making immigration and multiculturalism a major campaign issue?

Since the CSU had governed Bavaria for decades, it could hardly present itself as anti-establishment, although it should be noted that the Swiss SVP had done so despite being in government for years. Nonetheless, Stoiber had sharply criticized the European Union for the sanctions on Austria after Jörg Haider's xenophobic Freedom Party joined the government in Vienna. Moreover, he was on record, although more than a decade earlier, as having objected to a "racially mixed society" (*durchrasste Gesellschaft*). In an interview in early 2002, the German Nobel Laureate Günter Grass went so far as to assert: "In the form of the candidate [i.e., Stoiber] something looms that we already have in several European countries. It is not without reason that Haider and Berlusconi are true friends of Mr. Stoiber. In fact, a continuation of a development threatens us that we can observe in Italy and Austria."[28]

In short, Germany appeared to offer favorable conditions for an upsurge in right-wing populism. In fact, the Schröder government had proven less adept at reducing unemployment than the Jospin government in France and the Kok government in the Netherlands, both of which nonetheless lost votes to right-wing populists in spring 2002. Moreover, like their neighbors, many Germans resented immigrants, linking foreigners to crime, unemployment and welfare state fraud. That Schill had recorded an unprecedented electoral success in Hamburg soon after September 11 suggested that the fear of terrorism was playing into the hands of those willing to play the populist card. In Germany, the controversies surrounding dual citizenship (ultimately rejected) and the immigration law (sent back to the drawing board) reflected a society deeply divided on the issues of immigration and newcomer integration. In short, on the demand side, Germany appeared to satisfy the requirements for a backlash against foreigners. What about the supply side? As seen, there were several potential beneficiaries of right-wing protest, whether the xenophobic small parties, the conservative Schill Party, the FDP under the opportunistic leadership of Westerwelle and Möllemann, or Edmund Stoiber whose CSU had long opposed liberal asylum laws, a policy of immigration and multiculturalism.

Fragmentation on the Left

The splintering of the center-left has received far less attention than the rise of the right-wing populists in Europe. Yet it played a part in the defeat of center-left governments in France, the United States, the Netherlands, and Norway. In France, Prime Minister Lionel Jospin of the Socialist Party failed to finish first or second in the initial round of the

French presidential elections and therefore did not qualify for the runoff election. While the attention of the world understandably focused on the shocking second place finish of Le Pen (16.9 percent), who finished just three percentage points behind President Chirac (19.9 percent), an equally important story was that the Left had splintered. Trotskyites Arlette Laguiller (Workers Struggle) and Olivier Besancenot (Revolutionary Communist League) together garnered nearly 10 percent of the vote; two Green parties split 7.5 percent of the vote; the radical republican Chevénement secured 5.3 percent, and the candidate of the Communists won 3.4 percent. Because of this fragmentation, Jospin finished third with just 16.2 percent of the vote. This set the stage for Chirac's easy victory over Le Pen. In the ensuing parliamentary elections, the government parties suffered bruising setbacks. The Socialists' share remained at around 24 percent yet they lost over 100 seats in the assembly. Support for the Greens dropped by nearly a third (from 6.8 percent to 4.4 percent), while the Communists' share was cut in half (i.e., 9.9 percent to 4.9 percent). The three center-left parties together mustered just one-third of the total vote in 2002; in 1997, they had collected two-fifths.

In the 2000 presidential election in the United States, Ralph Nader of the Greens took decisive votes away from Al Gore in Florida and in New Hampshire, thereby ensuring George Bush a paper-thin victory in the electoral college. In the Netherlands, Wim Kok's governing Labor Party not only lost votes to the anti-foreigner List Pim Fortuyn, but also to the left-opposition Socialist Party that increased its share from 3.5 percent to 5.9 percent. In Norway, the Labor Party fell from power in fall 2001 in part because the opposition Socialist Left party improved its share of the vote from 6 percent in 1997 to 12.4 percent in 2001 and its number of seats in parliament from nine to twenty-three. When the governing social democratic parties shifted toward the center, they created an opening on the Left for parties in opposition. These parties generally defended welfare statism and criticized the government for failing to deal with unemployment.

In late 2001, it looked as if the German Social Democrats and Greens would lose votes to the Left. They had come under heavy criticism for their support of the U.S.-led wars in Yugoslavia and Afghanistan and for their economic policies. In the Berlin elections of fall 2001, the Party of Democratic Socialists (PDS) received over 22.6 percent of the vote in the city (and nearly 48 percent in East Berlin) by opposing the war in Afghanistan.[29] According to polling data gathered in early 2002, 26 percent of the voters in eastern Germany indicated that they would vote for the PDS were Bundestag elections held on the coming Sunday.[30] If the PDS were to record significant gains in the September elections, it would all but assure that Red-Green would not have a majority in parliament.

German Exceptionalism Reconsidered

On 22 September, the German Social Democrats and Greens bucked the transnational trends by not losing support to the populist right or to the left-wing opposition. In fact, the extreme right-wing parties in Germany suffered a crushing defeat and lost 70 percent of the support they had won in 1998.[31] The Republicans and the NPD received just 0.6 percent and 0.4 percent respectively. The more moderate Schill Party (PRO) garnered a mere 0.8 percent of the vote, a far cry from the nearly 20 percent it had won in Hamburg in September 2001. The abysmal performance of the right-wing populist parties stands in sharp contrast to their success throughout much of Europe.

The FDP increased its share of the vote from 6.3 percent in 1998 to 7.4 percent in 2002. Party leaders however had set their sights on a far better outcome and had to accept a result that was nowhere near their proclaimed goal of 18 percent. In spring 2002, polls had put the FDP at over 10 percent and ahead of the Greens, yet the party finished with less support than the rival Greens. It is notable that the FDP achieved its best results (9.3 percent, up 2.1 percentage points from 1998) in Möllemann's home state of North Rhine-Westphalia.[32] To Stöss and Neugebauer, " Möllemann's populist scandal-strategy was by all accounts successful in his homeland."[33] Nonetheless, on the whole, his effort to begin to "haiderize" the FDP likely cost the party more votes among liberals than it secured among right-wing protest voters.[34] After the election, Westerwelle and the FDP blamed Möllemann for their party's disappointing performance. They called for a return to liberal principles and stripped Möllemann of his leadership posts within the party.

Stoiber and the CDU/CSU managed to increase their share of the vote substantially, especially in southern Germany, and they did so without resorting to anti-immigrant appeals. Stoiber ran a moderate campaign that steered clear of the populism of Haider, Blocher, or Berlusconi. Despite his earlier controversial pronouncements and positions, he did not make immigration and multiculturalism central campaign issues. Christian Democratic gains can in no way be viewed as resurgent right-wing populism. As in neighboring democracies, the primary social democratic party, in this case the SPD, witnessed an erosion of its support among the industrial working class.[35] Yet unlike in France, the Netherlands, Belgium, and Austria, industrial workers defected to the center-right rather than to the radical right.

Likewise, left-leaning voters did not abandon the SPD and Greens in favor of left-wing protest parties as had happened in France, Holland, the United States, and Norway. In fact, the SPD and Greens together sustained a loss of just 0.5 percentage points. The SPD, for just the third time in the history of the Federal Republic, received more votes than the CDU/CSU, while the Greens improved nearly 2 percentage points to 8.6 percent. The

PDS, as the main socialist opposition party, not only did not benefit from a "vacuum" on the Left created by the centrist policies of Red-Green, but lost 4.6 percentage points in its stronghold of eastern Germany and 1.1 percentage points overall.[36] As a result, the PDS failed to cross the 5 percent threshold needed for entry into the Bundestag.[37]

There are a number of reasons why the parties of right-wing populism floundered in Germany in 2002, yet flourished elsewhere in Europe. These included factors specific to the political institutions and culture of the Federal Republic.[38] For instance, the 5 percent cut off for entry into parliament is higher in the Federal Republic than in most other European democracies. This makes it more difficult for right-wing populist parties to acquire a foothold in parliament, which can serve as a springboard to further success.[39] German federalism may also help explain why the far right has had such limited success in national politics. Unlike in the more unitary states of Europe, German voters appear to signal their protest (i.e., letting off steam) in state elections, which are considered less important, while refraining from protest voting in the Bundestag elections.[40] This sheds light on the fact that the Republicans and the DVU have achieved success at the state level yet not at the national level. Because of the crimes of National Socialism, right-wing populist parties are on the defensive in Germany, having to distance themselves from the extreme right if they are to attract voters. This is however difficult to do since neo-fascists seek to infiltrate these parties, thereby dividing and further discrediting the Right.[41] Because the Federal Republic practices "militant democracy" (*streitbare Demokratie*) by limiting the rights of those opposed to the constitutional order, right-wing populist parties face government surveillance, and, as in the case of the NPD, a possible ban. Since public officials cannot be members of extremist political organizations, far right parties in Germany are cut off from the many well-connected, educated professionals in the public sector. Finally, the far right in Germany has remained much more fragmented than in Austria, Denmark, Norway, France, and Belgium, where one party has assumed a clear position of leadership.[42]

In 2002, German right-wing populist parties faced an especially difficult environment because of Edmund Stoiber's solid conservative credentials on issues of immigration, multiculturalism, and public safety. Möllemann likely took additional votes from the far right parties. Given the extremely tight race in 2002, disgruntled voters who might have preferred to vote for the law-and-order Schill Party were reluctant to do so since protest votes were perceived as helping Schröder.

This logic also hurt the PDS. Many on the Left who were disappointed with Red-Green policies nonetheless wanted above all to prevent Stoiber from becoming chancellor. As the race went down to the wire, the SPD and Greens argued that a vote for the PDS would strengthen the right wing. Because they had ruled out the possibility of an SPD-Greens-PDS coalition, they argued that the return of the PDS to the Bundestag decreased the likelihood of an SPD-Green majority since the seats in parliament would be divided amongst five rather than four parties. Two other campaign developments that were specific to Germany bolstered the Red-Green coalition and undermined the PDS. In August 2002, Schröder took a strong stance against any German military contribution to an American-led invasion of Iraq. Whereas in 2001 the PDS had prospered by opposing the war in Afghanistan, it was now the SPD that reaped the electoral benefits of an anti-war position. Second, Schröder and the SPD picked up electoral support in the East, again at the cost of the PDS, by responding energetically to the disastrous flooding of the Elbe in summer 2002.

Certainly, factors unique to Germany's culture and institutions, as well as those factors specific to the election campaign of 2002, help account for the fact that Germany, unlike its neighbors, did not experience an upsurge in right-wing populism, fragmentation on the Left, or the defeat of a government unable to solve the problem of mass unemployment. Yet rather than overstate German exceptionalism, it is important to note that the German outcome was wholly consistent with broader transnational trends in at least one important way. Namely, the personal popularity of individual politicians played a key role in the election. This personalizing of politics, whereby voters are swayed by prominent personalities rather than by party organizations and platforms, has acquired importance not just in Germany, but in many other parliamentary systems as well. It shaped the German results and raises doubt about the extent of German exceptionalism.

Throughout Europe, right-wing populist parties have depended upon their leaders. Dynamic, even charismatic politicians, such as Le Pen, Haider, Blocher, Berlusconi, Pim Fortuyn, and Pia Kjaersgaard, spearheaded right-wing populism in their countries. When the Danish populist Mogens Glistrup, who had founded the Progress party in the early 1970s, fell into disrepute, his party's fortunes plummeted. The same occurred to the List Pim Fortuyn in Holland after the assassination of its namesake and will likely befall the Freedom Party of Austria after Haider and the Front National after Le Pen. Sweden does not have a significant party of right-wing populism, yet neighboring Denmark and Norway do, in large part because the right-wing populist party of Sweden (New Democracy) has not managed to fill the now empty shoes of its popular leadership duo of the mid-1990s.[43] Likewise, the German populist right has lacked a charismatic leader, along the lines of Haider, who could unify the fractured far right and also appeal to a broader electorate. Jürgen Möllemann, who was flamboyant and dynamic on the campaign trail, did not have sufficient influence within his party to shift the FDP toward a consistently aggressive, right-wing populism that had found success in other countries. Instead, Möllemann's strategy divided the party leadership and in so doing cost the FDP on election day.[44] If Möllemann had been the unchallenged leader of the FDP, then he might have had more success with his broadsides against Israeli and German Jewish leaders.

Unlike the FPÖ, the FDP does not have a potential leader on the horizon who has the capacity not only to become a "clarion of the people," but to re-shape the party in his own image.[45]

Personal popularity also helps explain developments on the Left. Unlike Al Gore, Lionel Jospin and Romano Prodi, Gerhard Schröder was a much more dynamic candidate than his opponents. In this regard, he more closely resembled the personable Tony Blair, who in 2001 easily defeated the Conservatives and the far from telegenic William Hague. In contrast, Edmund Stoiber had a rather wooden delivery and technocratic image that was closer to the persona of Al Gore or Lionel Jospin than the more folksy Chirac, Clinton or Schröder. This proved a liability in talk shows and in the two televised debates. Stoiber, a southern Catholic with a record of aggressively advancing Bavarian interests, had much less appeal in northern and eastern Germany. Like William Hague, whose party performed miserably outside of England, Stoiber had difficulty attracting support across all the regions of Germany.

In addition to Schröder, the Red-Green government was blessed with other highly effective campaigners. The Greens took advantage of the personal popularity of Joschka Fischer (the foreign minister) by featuring him whenever possible. They also benefited from the broad name recognition and skillful campaigning of Renate Künast, Jürgen Trittin and Christian Ströbele. In short, the German Greens were endowed with several prominent politicians that distinguished the party from its French counterpart in government. In this age of personalized politics, the PDS was hurt by the fact that it did not possess media savvy leaders with name recognition and broad public appeal. Throughout the 1990s, the exceptional political talent of Gregor Gysi had lifted the party's fortunes. It was Gysi in fact who had anchored the PDS's victory in the Berlin elections of fall 2001. He delivered his party a bad blow, however, when he quit politics in summer 2002 in the wake of a scandal involving the private use of frequent flier miles accrued on state business. Rather than focus on one prominent leader, the PDS unsuccessfully featured several less well-known politicians in its campaign.

In closing, the growing personalization of politics is a tendency found across Europe. In this regard, the Federal Republic is quite "normal" in comparative perspective.[46] Yet whereas this transnational phenomenon has bolstered parties of right-wing populism and undermined center-left governments in recent years, it contributed to Schröder's victory on 22 September 2002.

Notes

1. Spain and Ireland were the two exceptions. See "A Continent Drift—to the Left," *The Economist*, 3 October 1998, pp. 59–60.
2. The German version, "Der Weg nach vorne für Europas Sozialdemokraten," is reprinted in *Blätter für deutsche und internationale Politik* (July 1999): 887–896, quot. on p. 896.
3. Spain, Great Britain, and Germany are notable exceptions.
4. See Hans-Georg Betz, *Radical Right-Wing Populism in Western Europe* (New York: St. Martin's Press, 1994); Herbert Kitschelt, *The Radical Right in Western Europe: A Comparative Analysis* (Ann Arbor: University of Michigan Press, 1995); Michael Minkenberg, *Die neue radikale Rechte im Vergleich: USA, Frankreich, Deutschland* (Opladen: 1998); Frank Decker, *Parteien unter Druck: Der neue Rechtspopulismus in den westlichen Demokratien* (Opladen: 2002).
5. See Marc Swyngedouw and Gilles Ivaldi, "The Extreme Right Utopia in Belgium and France: The Ideology of the Flemish Vlaams Blok and the French Front National," *West European Politics* 24, no. 3 (July 2001): 1–22. Hans-Georg Betz, "The Populist Right in Austria and Switzerland," *Politik* 16 (Summer 2001): 4–6.
6. Betz, *Radical Right-Wing Populism in Western Europe*, p. 23.
7. Ibid., pp. 3–4. This section is drawn from my review essay on *Radical Right-Wing Populism in Western Europe* in *The Stanford Humanities Review* 5, no. 2 (1997): 298–302.
8. "Europe's Far Right: Toxic but Containable," *The Economist*, 27 April 2002, pp. 47–48.
9. Betz, "The Populist Right in Austria and Switzerland," pp. 4–6.
10. Carsten Schlüter-Knauer, "Die Bedeutung des Rechtsrucks in Dänemark," *Die Neue Gesellschaft/Frankfurter Hefte* (March 2002): 152–156.
11. Lisbeth Weihe-Lindeborg, "Mit Glistrup fing es an. Rechtspopulismus in Skandinavien," *Die Neue Gesellschaft/Frankfurter Hefte* (March 2002): 156–160.
12. In the 1999 regional elections to the Flemish council, the Flemish Bloc received 15.5 percent of the vote and finished in third place ahead of the main social democratic party of Flanders.
13. See Roland H. Wiegenstein, "Berlusconi oder: wie man demokratische Institutionen demoliert," *Die Neue Gesellschaft/Frankfurter Hefte* (March 2002):147–152.
14. Klaus Dräger and Andreas Weir, "Dritte Kraft statt Dritter Weg," *Freitag*, 28 June 2002, p. 7.
15. See Thomas Fuller, "Foreign Workers Face Turning Tide," *International Herald Tribune*, 24–25 December 2002, p. 1.
16. Frank Deckert, "Perspektiven des Rechtspopulismus in Deutschland am Beispiel der 'Schill-Partei,'" *Aus Politik und Zeitgeschichte*, no. 21 (May 2002): 22–31, quot. on p. 23.
17. In 1999–2000, among the foreign labor force in Germany 13.2 percent of the women and 14.9 percent of the men were unemployed, while among German nationals on average 8.4 percent of women and 7.3 percent of men were jobless. Fuller, "Foreign Workers Face Turning Tide," p. 4.
18. Ibid.
19. See Richard Stöss, *Rechtsextremismus im vereinten Deutschland*, 3rd ed. (Berlin: Friedrich-Ebert-Stiftung, 2000), pp. 49–51.
20. See Joachim Raschke and Ralf Tils, "CSU des Nordens: Profil und bundespolitische Perspektiven der Schill-Partei," *Blätter für deutsche und internationale Politik* (January 2002): 49–58; Decker, "Perspektiven des Rechtspopulismus in Deutschland am Beispiel der 'Schill-Partei'"; Harald Bergsdorf, "Gegner oder Partner? Schill als Problem der Volksparteien," *Die Neue Gesellschaft/Frankfurter Hefte* (March 2002): 160–164.
21. Bergsdorf, "Gegner oder Partner?" p. 162.
22. Ibid., p. 163.
23. Karsli had claimed that "the Israeli army utilized Nazi methods" against the Palestinians; that Israel "poisoned the drinking water" of the Palestinians; and that there was "a concentration of thousands of imprisoned Palestinians in large camps where they had

numbers tattooed on the hand." He also claimed that there was a powerful Jewish lobby that controlled the media and silenced influential politicians. Hajo Funke and Lars Rensmann, "Wir sind so frei. Zum rechtspopulistischen Kurswechsel der FDP," *Blätter für deutsche und internationale Politik* 7/2002 (July 2002): 822–835.

24. Quoted in Funke and Rensmann, "Wir sind so frei," pp. 824–825.
25. Quoted in ibid., p. 825.
26. Quoted in ibid., p. 822.
27. This section is drawn from David F. Patton, "Laptops and Lederhosen," *Aufbau*, 5 September 2002, pp. 8–9.
28. "NDR Pressemitteilungen. Im ersten TV-Interview zu seinem neuen Buch: Grass vergleicht Stoiber mit Haider und Berlusconi. Sendung: 4. Februar, 22.30 Uhr im NDR Fernsehen," http://www.ndr.de/ndr/derndr/presse/archiv/200202041.html (accessed 22 January 2003).
29. In the 1999 elections in Berlin, the PDS had received 17.7 percent of the vote.
30. Richard Stöss and Gero Neugebauer, "Mit einem blauen Auge davon gekommen. Eine Analyse der Bundestagswahl 2002," *Arbeitshefte aus dem Otto-Stammer-Zentrum*, no. 7 (Berlin 2002), p. 31.
31. Dieter Roth and Matthias Jung, "Ablösung der Regierung vertagt: Eine Analyse der Bundestagswahl 2002," *Aus Politik und Zeitgeschichte*, no. 49–50 (2002): 3–17. In 1998, the DVU, NPD, and Republicans had received 3.3 percent of the total vote and 5 percent of the eastern vote. In 2002, the NPD and the Republicans together received a scant 1.7 percent in the East and just 1 percent overall.
32. The FDP also received 9.3 percent of the second ballots casts in Rhineland-Palatinate.
33. Stöss and Neugebauer, "Mit einem blauen Auge davon gekommen," p. 44.
34. Ibid., p. 27.
35. The SPD lost 8 percentage points among industrial workers in western Germany. Stöss and Neugebauer, "Mit einem blauen Auge davon gekommen," p. 46.
36. The SPD gained 4.7 percentage points in the East.
37. Since the PDS won two districts of eastern Berlin outright, it has two deputies in the Bundestag.
38. Decker, "Perspektiven des Rechtspopulismus in Deutschland am Beispiel der 'Schill-Partei,'" pp. 23–25.
39. Parties represented in the national parliament receive more state funding and can more easily reach a national audience.
40. Decker, "Perspektiven des Rechtspopulismus in Deutschland am Beispiel der 'Schill-Partei,'" p. 24.
41. Roger Karapin, "Radical-Right and Neo-Fascist Political Parties in Western Europe," *Comparative Politics* 30 (January 1998): 213–234, esp. 225–226.
42. For instance, see Uwe Backes and Cas Mudde, "Germany: Extremism without Successful Parties," *Parliamentary Affairs* 53 (2000): 457–468.
43. Weihe-Lindeborg, "Mit Glistrup fing es an. Rechtspopulismus in Skandinavien," p. 157.
44. Dieter Oberndörfer, Gerd Mielke, and Ulrich Eith, "Analyse der Bundestagswahl vom 22 September 2002," *Frankfurter Rundschau*, 27 September 2002.
45. Markus Klein and Kai Arzheimer, "Liberalismus, Rechtsradikalismus und Rechtspopulismus in Deutschland und Österreich. Bestandaufnahme und Zukunktsszenarien," in *Wahlen und politische Einstellungen in Deutschland und Österreich*, ed. Fritz Plasser et al. (Frankfurt am Main: Peter Lang, 1999). Accessed on the Internet at http://www.politik.uni-mainz.de/kai.arzheimer/fpoe/fpoe.pdf.
46. Moreover, the Federal Republic has joined a "mini-wave" that began with the Swedish elections of September 2002 and encompassed ensuing elections in Germany, Austria, and the Netherlands. In each case, the center-left performed strongly, while the right-wing populist parties sustained heavy losses.

Chapter 10

THE POISONED RELATIONSHIP
Germany, the United States, and the Election of 2002

Stephen F. Szabo

The biggest surprise of the 2002 German election was the importance of the German-American relationship to the electoral outcome. Pollsters, academics, journalists, politicians and the general public all expected the election to turn on domestic issues, especially on economic policy, unemployment and perhaps immigration and law and order. While exit polls confirmed that economic issues remained central to most voters, the crisis in German-American relations over the issue of Iraq was crucial with key swing voters and helped tip the narrow balance of victory for the Red-Green coalition. The current crisis, and the relationship is still in crisis, reflects both the short-term effects of the Bush-Schröder dispute and longer-term secular changes that were in play before the dispute, but have been accelerated by it.

The Schröder-Bush "Poisoned Relationship"

When George W. Bush came to power, Gerhard Schröder had been chancellor for a little over two years. Schröder, like Bush, came to office with little experience or interest in foreign policy. Not only was his power based on local and national politics, he knew that elections were not decided by foreign policy issues. However he soon learned the difference between being a governor and party leader and being chancellor, as foreign policy issues now consumed, by his own estimate, about half of his time.[1] By the time the attacks on New York and Washington, D.C., had occurred, Gerhard Schröder was no longer a foreign policy neophyte.

While the German Social Democrat had developed a good if not warm relationship with the Democrat Bill Clinton, the start with George W. Bush was a rocky one. On the chancellor's first visit with the new president

---

Notes for this chapter begin on page 202.

shortly after his inauguration, Bush embarrassed him and his Green coalition partners by having his National Security Advisor Condoleeza Rice announce that the Kyoto treaty was dead a half-hour before the two leaders met. This was followed by a series of blunt unilateral declarations from the new team in Washington denouncing a series of multilateral initiatives including the Chemical and Biological Weapons Treaty, the International Criminal Court, and the ABM treaty. It was clear that the neo-conservative president and the "Third Way Chancellor" were going to have problems.

When the attacks on New York and Washington occurred on 11 September 2001, the chancellor immediately declared the "unlimited solidarity" of his government for the United States, and supported the invocation of the self-defense clause, Article 5, of the NATO treaty. He did this both because of his sympathy for the victims and because he understood that any hesitation on his part would isolate Germany from the United States and provide an opening to the Christian Democrats to accuse his government of being anti-American. He also believed that by providing support, Germany would gain the right to be consulted and thus could exercise a moderating influence on American policy.[2] He followed up by forcing a vote of no confidence in November, which his government barely won, authorizing the use of German forces in Operation Enduring Freedom in Afghanistan. The Red-Green government deployed over 3,900 ground forces to the theater of operations. This was the high point of German-American cooperation during the Bush II administration.

The Bush administration decided not to make much use of this newfound support to bring Germany and NATO more fully into the war on Al Qaeda, but opted to go it mostly alone in the war in Afghanistan.[3] Clearly, one of the lessons of Kosovo for the American military and political leadership was to avoid another war by committee. The selectively multilateral phase of its diplomacy ended with the president's State of the Union speech in January 2002, when he expanded the war on terrorism and used the term "Axis of Evil." German hopes that the administration would follow a coalition strategy began to be replaced by concerns about American unilateralism, which were prevalent before September 11. These worries mounted as talk of war with Iraq increased in Washington.

The chancellor continued his support of the U.S. strategy after the State of the Union speech. On the plane returning to Berlin from Washington after his meeting with Bush in February 2002, Schröder told some of his aides that Germany could not play the same role it had played during the Cold War and that it had to make a military contribution. This was consistent with his fundamental belief that he had when he became chancellor, that the country's foreign role should match its economic power and its growing geopolitical importance. This new self-assurance (*Selbstverständlichkeit*) was a leitmotif of Schröder's chancellorship and implied Germany both taking on more international responsibilities and being taken more seriously by key states.[4]

Schröder told a German journalist in February, "I know that a German chancellor cannot travel to the United States in the next twenty or thirty years if we withdraw our tanks from Kuwait."[5] Yet even at the time of that summit meeting, the chancellor had serious concerns over the intentions of the Bush administration on Iraq. He made his reservations about an intervention known during his February visit to Washington, telling the president and his advisors that any military action would have to be successful. He followed up in March stating that any military participation by Germany would be done only with a United Nations mandate.[6]

Schröder had hoped to forge a common European position with the goal of enhancing Europe's power and role and thus acting as a moderating influence on the Bush administration, but he failed in this attempt at the Barcelona European Union summit in March. He then realized that London and Paris were more interested in aligning with the U.S. than in shaping a joint European policy.[7]

When the American president came to Berlin in May 2002, the meeting and the president's visit went well. When they turned to the topic of Iraq, it was only briefly discussed. The president told the chancellor, in effect, you know my position and I will keep you posted. There was an implicit agreement that neither would make a war with Iraq an issue before the German election.[8] As the summer deepened, two major developments changed this situation and led to the crisis in the larger relationship.

First, Schröder made a tactical decision sometime in July regarding his strategy in the election campaign. In the spring he had told the leadership in his party that the SPD would fight the campaign alone and not in coalition with the Greens. This changed in midsummer when he became desperate. All the tactics he had tried, including the attempt to paint his opponent, Edmund Stoiber of Bavaria, as a right-wing extremist, had failed. While he remained personally popular, his party and his coalition were trailing badly in the polls. He was searching for an issue. Suddenly two emerged, the devastating floods in eastern Germany and the mounting prospect of a war with Iraq.

The chancellor quickly sensed that the floods, which had raised his standing as a leader in the East, gave him the opportunity to get enough votes in the former East Germany to sink the neo-Communist Party of Democratic Socialism below the 5 percent minimum vote hurdle and thus consolidate the Left within the SPD-Green coalition. Iraq played into this strategy because of the combination of pacifism and nationalism, which could be mobilized. Polls had shown that eastern voters were less attached to the relationship with the United States than were western voters and had more concerns about war and NATO. This combination of frustration and opportunism led to his injection of Iraq, and, by implication, the Bush administration, into the campaign at the end of July.

Both Schröder and Foreign Minister Fischer had already picked up a great sense of uneasiness among crowds at campaign rallies both about a war and about the perceived recklessness of Bush. The audiences they addressed responded strongly to any assertions about not being pulled into a war in Iraq. In an election speech delivered in Hanover on 5 August, followed by an interview with *Die Zeit*, he openly criticized the lack of consultation of the Bush administration and the need for a German way. He began to use charged phrases such as "reckless adventure" and "German Way," and made it clear there would be no German military contribution to a war against Iraq, even though the Bush administration had not asked for one. Schröder in effect said no to a question that was not being asked. However, for the chancellor, the point was not what Germany might do militarily, but rather the perceived adventurousness of the Bush administration among German voters.

As a politician with a well-developed sense for power and for divining the public mood quickly, Schröder began to build on the responses from his audiences. He escalated his rhetoric and became more emphatic about Germany's rejection of Bush's Iraq plans. Early on, in late July, his national security advisor, the veteran diplomat, Dieter Kastrup, urged him to weigh his words carefully. The chancellor responded that he understood the meaning of what he said, but added: "I have to win the election." After that, Kastrup was not again consulted on the issue, and domestic political advisors played a larger role, although it is clear that this was a decision made by Gerhard Schröder based on his political instincts. This was a political more than a strategic decision, and there was never any full strategic discussion within the government, including within the Chancellery and the Foreign Office.

In addition, he and his foreign minister had expended a lot of political capital and taken substantial risks to support both the war in Kosovo and in Afghanistan. The chancellor knew that while his coalition had gone along with these policies, many had done so reluctantly and without conviction. He knew that opposition was growing within the SPD and the Greens, and this issue gave him a way to recapture his base.

Very close to this time, in mid- to late August, leading figures in the Bush administration began to escalate their rhetoric on war with Iraq. This was done in response to growing questions and criticism of the proposed policy by leading Republicans, such as Representative Dick Armey, Senators Chuck Hagel and Richard Lugar, as well as traditional realists in the party who had been in the first Bush administration. These included James Baker, Lawrence Eagelburger, and Brent Scowcroft. This questioning, coupled with growing concerns being raised by Democrats in the House, put the Iraq hawks on the defensive. In order to regain the initiative, the leading and most influential hawk, Vice-President Richard Cheney gave a tough speech in late August in Nashville, Tennessee to a veterans group making it sound as if war was going to happen. This speech had the effect, in the words of one high German official, of kicking the ball to the government. It was a decisive event.

The chancellor became enraged as he had, contrary to the agreement with Bush, not been informed on developments and learned everything he knew from the media. He believed he had worked for three and a half years against an anti-U.S. pacifist streak within his own coalition, and was angry that this was the thanks he got from Washington. He was not convinced that Bush had made the case for war and was worried about the principle of preemption and the problems it posed for international law. If the United States could preempt, why not India or Pakistan? This sharply unilateralist speech went against the deep multilateralist grain of the German strategic culture. The speech also shifted the emphasis from controlling weapons of mass destruction (WMD) to regime change, and this was seen as new in Berlin.

There was disagreement in the chancellor's office and the Foreign Office over whether the speech should be seen as representing the president's thinking. Schröder's top foreign policy advisor, Dieter Kastrup, did not see it as a major change in tone or substance, and the chancellor requested no serious analysis of the speech. When German Ambassador Wolfgang Ischinger, in Washington, tried to convey this to the chancellor, he was informed that Schröder was on the campaign trail and could not take a call of this nature on an insecure line. Cheney's speech was clearly manna from heaven from Schröder's perspective, and it allowed him to argue that the promise to Bush not to make Iraq an issue in the campaign was based on the goal of controlling WMD and not on the goal of regime change. This was now seen to have been broken by Cheney.[9]

Karsten Voigt, the coordinator for German-American relations in the Foreign Office, contends that whether the Cheney speech was United States policy or not is irrelevant, because in a parliamentary election, candidates are asked by their voters about their positions, and they must respond simply. Support for the Bush policy on Iraq had been sliding and the Cheney speech as well as others by Rumsfeld immediately intruded themselves into the German campaign. Thus the U.S. view that Schröder was saying no to a question he was not asked, that is for a military contribution to a war on Iraq, is not relevant as parliament would have to decide on participation in a war and the electorate wanted to know where candidates stood on this issue. What was new in this case in comparison to others, in which German chancellors were in a difficult position because of perceived American belligerence, was that Schröder did not maneuver but simply said no.

The situation was still seen in Washington as largely campaign induced. When the president met with Joschka Fischer as well as with one of Fischer's state secretaries, the former Ambassador to the U.S., Jürgen Chrobog, in New York at the UN, right around the time of his speech there on 12 September, he asked both, "When is your damn election over?" Here again there is a divergence in German and American portrayals of the tone of Bush's comment, with German officials describing it as a light comment while American officials relate that it reflected real anger from the president. Then came the last weekend of the campaign and the comparison made by Schröder's minister of justice, Herta Däubler Gmelin, in which she compared Bush's tactics to those of Hitler, on the grounds that he, like the Führer, tried to divert people from domestic problems with foreign policy adventures. Besides the fact that this was historically inaccurate in that Hitler's domestic policies were popular and that the comparison better fit the Schröder campaign, the fact that a German politician would compare an American president to Adolf Hitler set off an outraged reaction in the United States. It was this, as much as Schröder's statements on Iraq, that prompted National Security Advisor Condoleezza Rice to describe the relationship as "poisoned," a term which was repeated by Secretary of Defense Donald Rumsfeld.[10]

The chancellor was upset by what his justice minister had said, but he was only two days away from an election and could not afford to lose yet another minister from his government so close to the voting. He had just recently fired his defense minister over a personal scandal and had already lost a large number of ministers in his four-year term. He sent a letter to the president in which he stated his regret and indicated that she would not return to his new government, but the letter was viewed by the White House as simply justifying what had happened rather than apologizing for it. The letter was not seen by the Foreign Office before it was sent, and some in the chancellory had argued for a stronger reaction including a personal telephone call to the president. The chancellor declined to follow this advice.

The president is someone who places great value upon loyalty. He had never forgiven those Republicans who had turned against his father when he had run for re-election. As he described himself, he has a tendency to be emotional and to place great emphasis upon personal relationships.[11] It was hardly surprising that the two politicians had never been close as they were polar opposites. Ideologically, they were far apart, and their personal histories could not have been more different. As one of the chancellor's closest advisors put it: "They were never on the same wave length. Bush is very American, and Schröder never developed a deep understanding of what makes the U.S. tick."

The American president was born to privilege, both in wealth and in politics. In his formative years he simply lived off his name and his father's connections. The chancellor was raised in a one-parent household. His father was killed in World War II soon after he was born, and his mother was a cleaning lady. He got to the top strictly on his own through determination and an acute sense for tactics and power.

So it did not take much for this forced relationship to go bad. Bush and his foreign policy team appreciated the support Schröder provided after September 11, even risking his government over it, and so the relationship while not close, fit the parameters of a good working one. This quickly turned to outright distrust and worse in the summer of 2002 on the part of Bush. Schröder did not have such strong emotions. He is a man without a center, without strong convictions or close friends or personal relationships. He changed political partners just as he changed wives.[12] As one journalist who has followed Schröder for over twenty years described his view on personal relationships put it: "'Personal relationships to other leading politicians,' said Gerhard Schröder, are 'helpful, but are not the precondition for successful foreign policies.... Personal relationships cannot be more important than interests. That is what dominates.'"[13]

He does not carry a grudge, yet will not simply cave in to placate Washington, especially if he believes this will weaken him at home. As one German official put it, it is absurd to think that Schröder's generation will go to Washington to get the okay from the United States. From this perspective, the White House has been too emotional about Germany. "For Condi Rice and others, there was a 'love affair' based on their experience in German unification. They still think of Germany as West Germany and ignore the one-quarter of the population that lives in eastern Germany. Germany is not simply a continuation of West Germany."[14]

One clear result of the election campaign of 2002 is that the personal relationship between the two top leaders was deeply, probably irreparably damaged. This damage is deeper in Washington than in Berlin, largely because of the personality of George W. Bush and his highly personalist approach to foreign policy. This approach is partly a trait of amateurism in foreign policy, not surprising for someone who never took much interest in the larger world or in foreign policy and of someone who is proudly non-intellectual and ahistorical.[15] But it is also part of a foreign policy style of the Bush administration, which believes in toughness and prefers to be feared more than loved. The White House and the Pentagon leadership wanted to send a message, not only to Germany but to other nations as well, that there is a cost for opposing the administration, in part to punish but more to deter any future opposition.

Iraq and the German Electorate

While the personal clash of leaders was important, it was hardly a unique event in the postwar German-American relationship. The personality conflict at the highest levels does not seem any more severe than that between young President Kennedy and the aging Adenauer or between Jimmy Carter and Helmut Schmidt, who once characterized the American president as being as difficult to pin down as nailing jello to a wall. Schmidt also had his problems with Reagan, while Nixon once was heard to say of Brandt, "Good God, if this is Germany's hope then Germany doesn't have much hope."[16]

What then is new about 2002 compared to previous scrapes and strains in the broader relationship? Friedbert Pfleuger, a leading foreign policy specialist of the Christian Democratic Union has said that, "This time and for the first time, the government was not in danger of yielding to the street, it was fueling the street."[17] If "the street" refers to public opinion, then it is clear that Schröder was responding to a broad sense of uneasiness and concern about the Bush administration as well as its policy on Iraq.

The real question is why and to what extent Schröder's position resonated with the wider public, including a majority of the Christian Democrats. After all, Edmund Stoiber was not supportive of a war against Iraq either, although he made the important qualification that he would respect a United Nations mandate. He lost the crucial second television debate to Schröder in large part on this issue, as he tried to state conditions and qualifications while the chancellor simply said no to any German military participation. It is important to determine in answering the question of why the German public responded as it did, the extent this was a simple policy difference and the extent to which it was what Henry Kissinger labeled "a kind of anti-Americanism (which) may have become a permanent temptation of German politics."[18]

Iraq and the United States as Electoral Themes

While it is no surprise that most Germans (82 percent) viewed unemployment as the most important issue facing the country on election day, what is new is that terror and war ranked second (15 percent) along with concerns about the economy as the most important problem facing Germany.[19] Iraq only became a campaign issue in August and in the television debates.[20] The seizure of the theme of opposition to German military participation in a war against Iraq was, along with the flood issue, one of the two reasons that Schröder was able to turn the campaign tide in his direction. He played on a strong public consensus against military involvement that was already apparent in a Politbarometer survey in early August, which indicated that 81 percent of the public opposed the country's participation in a military intervention in Iraq.[21] On election day, 46 percent of respondents were opposed to any participation of German troops in Iraq whatsoever, while 50 percent supported such a participation only with a United Nations mandate.[22]

This concern over Iraq did not mean that German voters did not take terrorism seriously or that it did not support the American war against it. A Pew Global Attitudes Project surveyed attitudes in forty-four countries during the summer of 2002 and found that 70 percent of German respondents favored the U.S.-led war on terrorism. A German Marshall Fund survey taken at about the same time in June 2002, that is before it became a major campaign issue, found that 63 percent of those questioned in Germany believed that terrorism was an extremely important threat to the country.[23] While lower that the proportions found in U.S. samples, these figures were in the mainstream of European opinion.

Yet while there was and remains general support for the United States in this area, there is also a general European and German perception that

Washington disregards the views of others in carrying out its policies. In the Pew survey, only 53 percent of Germans believed that American foreign policy considers the views of others, while 45 percent believed it did not. While high compared to other European samples (only 44 percent of Britons, 36 percent of Italians, and 21 percent of French believed the United States considered others in its policies), it reveals a strong pool of those with concerns about American unilateralism. Furthermore, the percentage of those having a favorable opinion of the United States has dropped over the two years of the Bush administration and stood at 61 percent in Germany (as compared to 75 percent in Britain, 70 percent in Italy, and 63 percent in France).[24]

Berlin's concerns with the Bush administration's approach toward Iraq were about both its perceived unilateralism but also about the fear of war that remains within certain elements of the German population, especially among older women.[25] As Dieter Roth has discussed in chapter 2, the Iraq issue had a number of positive effects for the SPD campaign. It shifted attention away from economic issues. Second, it mobilized the SPD and Green constituencies, many of whom were deeply skeptical about the use of military force and of the motives of the Bush administration in Iraq and elsewhere. Third, it not only helped gain the votes of many women voters, but is also appealed to voters in the East (especially PDS voters) who were either pacifist or simply did not trust the United States and who tended to equate its role in Germany with that the Soviet Union played in the GDR. Finally, it also allowed Schröder to take advantage of his leadership edge over Edmund Stoiber and to lead in an area where the chancellor always has an advantage over a challenger, security policy.[26] The renewed emphasis upon the leadership question at the end of the campaign reinforced the normal reluctance of German voters to change leadership so soon into the term of a new chancellor.

The voters believed that the SPD was better able to deal with Washington than was the CDU (40 percent believed that the SPD was better in this problem area as compared to 27 percent naming the CDU). As the Forschungsgruppe Wahlen report on the election results concluded, "in no other policy area is the competence of the parties to deal with the issue so striking as in this one."[27] On the personal level, Schröder had a comfortable lead over Stoiber in the confidence of the electorate in his ability to represent German interests. A majority (52 percent) thought that the chancellor was better able to realize German interests in foreign policy as compared to 21 percent who gave the edge to the challenger (21 percent thought there was no difference between the two on this dimension).[28]

Anti-American or Anti-Bush?

Anti-Americanism can be defined as opposition to what America stands for in contrast to what a particular American government does. A cultural or political critique, which is continuous across administrations, regardless of their partisan orientations or policies, reflects deeper seeded stereotypes and images of America as a polity and society, and when persistently negative can be characterized as anti-American.

There is no doubt that the election results were a rebuke of the Bush administration's approach to the Iraq issue. The reaction Gerhard Schröder and other politicians of the Red-Green government received when they raised concerns about the Bush policy toward Iraq in the summer of 2002 were largely the result of growing German and European worries about the policies followed by the American government after the tragedy of September 11. Polls found large majorities of Germans opposed to a war with Iraq, even with United Nations support. An analysis of the 2002 election conducted by the Forschungsgruppe Wahlen (FGW) found that 50 percent of the public believed that Germany should participate in a war against Iraq only with a United Nations mandate while 46 percent opposed such participation in all cases.[29] While about two of every three Social Democratic supporters opposed war in any case, 40 percent of Christian Democrats were also opposed.

In many aspects, these concerns about Bush are typical of all of Western Europe and are not uniquely German. The Pew Global Survey conducted in the fall of 2002 found concerns about the unilateralism of the Bush administration to be widespread.

The Pew study also revealed that a reserve of goodwill continues to exist toward the United States throughout Europe. FGW data also confirm that this is the case in Germany as well. About 52 percent of Germans continue to view the United States as Germany's most important partner followed by about 41 percent who see France in this role. The Christian Democrats remain more pro-U.S. in this measure with 63 percent viewing Washington as the most important partner followed by 51 percent of the SPD supporters and 42 percent of the Greens. Germans also continue to report that they "like" Americans with about 72 percent of western Germans saying they do compared to about 57 percent of easterners. These proportions did not vary significantly from those reported in 1991.[30]

While popular anti-Americanism is clearly an important factor in other parts of Europe, especially France (as well as in the Arab world and in Mexico), it is low in both eastern and western Germany. Attitudes in the former East Germany are clearly more reserved and skeptical toward the United States given the different political socialization of that part of the political culture. In this respect eastern Germans are distinctive from other former members of the Soviet bloc such as Poland, Romania, and Hungary, who are strongly pro-American.

The Bush Problem

The two Bush administrations represented polar opposites in their approach to the world and their reception in Germany and Europe. Bush I's approach was one of traditional realists, limited in both aspirations and commitments. It shared a basic worldview with Europeans who believed that realistic management of problems was far less dangerous than utopian attempts to rid the world of all evil. Bush II and its leading and most ideological voices reawakened the fears and stereotypes Germans had of the Reagan administration of a rather reckless and dangerous America that used the terms "evil empires" and "axis of evil" loosely.

It is not surprising that these should be especially German fears given the impact of war and what the reliance on force had meant in recent German history. Both the total devastation of World War II and the deliberate efforts of American governments after that war to eradicate all vestiges of militarism and nationalism in postwar Germany have made all Germans especially sensitive to the prospect of war. Furthermore, Germans have difficulties understanding the American sense of invulnerability, which existed before September 11, and the resulting traumatization of post–September 11 American society. Many fear that this trauma will be utilized by the Bush administration for its own ends, just as Hitler took advantage of the German trauma in the Weimar period. Finally there is also the fear that America will follow Germany's false path because of the hubris of unchallenged power.[31]

The strongly unilateralist style of the Bush II also contrasted sharply with the coalition approach of Bush I. While one person's unilateralism is another's leadership, it is clear that the style of Bush II, at least the leadership style of the White House and the Pentagon, has been characterized by the approach of Secretary of Defense Rumsfeld, who stated that "it is less important to have unanimity than it is to be making the right decisions and doing the right thing, even though at the outset it may seem lonesome."[32] This style could not be more ill suited to dealing with a newly unified and sovereign Germany led by a government which has described its foreign policy as one based more on German assertion of its interests. The statements of leading figures in the SPD-Green government from the chancellor and foreign minister on down—that Germany will not "click its heels" in obedience to the United States or that it is not a satellite, through comparisons of the American ambassador, Daniel Coats, with the former Soviet ambassador to the GDR, Abrassimov, or of President Bush with Caesar Augustus of the Roman Empire—are all symptoms of this new psychology. Even a leading figure of the Christian Democratic opposition, Wolfgang Schäuble, in reference to the snub administered by Rumsfeld to Defense Minister Struck at the NATO defense ministers meeting in Warsaw just after the German election, said: "The way in which Rumsfeld handled Struck was not the way that adults deal with each other. A Great Power must act in a generous way."[33]

The America Problem

While George W. Bush and the more vocal and conservative elements of his administration have served as a catalyst, the critique of Bush has fed a larger critique of America. The Forschungsgruppe Wahlen polls found a link between a "liking" of Americans and support for participation in a war on Iraq with a United Nations mandate. Of those who don't like Americans, 71 percent would not support a war on Iraq under any circumstances, while 47 percent of those who like Americans take a similar view on Iraq.[34] While this poses a chicken or egg problem for the analyst, there is probably a good deal of interaction between the two variables. Those with a critical image of America are likely to be critical of its policies. But those who are favorably inclined, in this case the majority of Germans, may experience cognitive dissonance and be forced to modify either their image of Bush or of America. The latter seems to be happening as many, especially younger, Germans are beginning to develop a more critical or differentiated view of the United States as a society.

While Europe and the United States continue to be closer to each other than to any other part of the world, signs of a divergence are growing. The Pew and Marshall Fund surveys as well as the World Values survey conducted by the University of Michigan, reveal some important divergences within the West. In Germany these trends are apparent in the following areas. A vast majority (70 percent) of Germans believe that U.S. policies widen the global economic divide. And although there is widespread approval of American popular culture and admiration for American technology, only about one-fourth (28 percent) believe that the spread of U.S. ideas and customs is good while about two-thirds (67 percent) think this is bad, a number second only to those found in France. Germans, like most Europeans, are divided even over American ideas about democracy, with 47 percent answering they like them and 45 percent saying they do not.

Gerhard Schröder's use of the term "German Way" referred not to foreign policy but to social and economic models: "The term 'German Way' has nothing to do with international politics. What was meant is the balance between capital and labor we have created domestically.... This is what we call 'Modell Deutschland.' This phrase should make it clear that what has developed in Europe is not only a single market, but also a type of social interaction."[35]

His use of the term "amerikanische Verhältnisse" or American conditions, is also meant to distance the German social democratic model from that of the "Anglo-Saxon" model of Reagan, Thatcher, and now Bush II. This aversion is reflected in German public opinion, which rejects this model. As the Pew survey put it: "In Germany and five of six Eastern European countries surveyed, broader attitudes concerning the role of government are linked to opinion of the U.S. approach to democracy. People who say it is up to the government to ensure that no citizens are in need tend to reject American-style democracy. By contrast, those who favor a more minimalist government role favor the American form of democracy by higher margins."[36]

While these concerns have been heightened by the wave of corporate scandals in the United States, they reflect a more traditional German ambivalence about America as a social and economic model. German views of America have "tended towards extremes of admiration or condescension,"[37] German immigrants to America reported back that it was either the land of opportunity and riches (a land of unlimited opportunities) or "an uncultured, artificial, heartless and mechanistic society."[38] These views were shaped by the very different milieu of German society with its emphasis on social stability and welfare over the risks of individual achievement and failure. The Bismarckian social state stood in contrast to the America of the Robber Barons and the Gilded Age. While influenced and tempered by ideology and social class, there remains a broader sense of a social economy in Germany than in post-Reagan America.

Finally, these surveys, find significant and growing differences between Americans and Europeans on secularism, patriotism and views of the international order. As a summary of the findings concludes, "What is different now? Two things. The first is that the values gap may be widening a little and starting to affect perceptions of foreign policy interest on which the transatlantic alliance is based. The second is that, in the past, cultural differences have been suppressed by the shared values of American and European elites—and elite opinion is now even more sharply divided than popular opinion."[39]

This is the case in Germany. What has been happening is a gradual divergence between the United States and Germany, fueled by longer terms forces and accelerated by policy differences between the Bush and Schröder governments.

Long-Term Forces of Change

A Clash of Strategic Cultures

The German elite and public would be very uneasy about any serious consideration of the use of military force in any case. The German strategic culture since 1945 has been based not upon pacifism, but upon a very limited basis of legitimacy for the use of force. Germany is not a pacifist country and has consistently followed a policy, which has been based upon a balance of power as the basis for peace. Adenauer's policy of strength, Brandt's *Ostpolitik*, Schmidt and Kohl's willingness to deploy intermediate range nuclear missiles were all grounded on this key prerequisite. Originally the consensus on German rearmament and entry into NATO was based on integration of German forces into a multilateral system and the limitation to defense of NATO territory. During the Cold War, force was seen as a deterrent and the deterrence aspect was modified with the détente component in the Harmel formula adopted by NATO in 1967.

With the end of the Cold War, the definition of the legitimate use of force was gradually expanded both by the Kohl government and then by the Red-Green coalition, to include use of force out of the NATO territorial area so long as it had a multilateral basis for both legitimization and for deployment. The Balkan wars created a new justification for military action based upon humanitarian values, in these cases to prevent "ethnic cleansing." The growing Europeanization of Europe also provided another rationale, namely, the need for Germany to make contributions to a credible European Security and Defense Policy (ESDP). The public has gone along with these modifications to a strategic culture, which moved, from one of "a culture of reticence" to one of limited, multilateral engagement.

The nationalism of the Bush administration and its emphasis upon the use of force went against the fundamentals of the German political and strategic culture. If the administration had begun with a multilateral approach focused on the issue of WMD and Iraq's violations of United Nations sanctions rather than coming to that position in September, much less porcelain would have broken and the summer storm would have been postponed.

Strategic Divergence

The developments of 2002 were manifestations of a deeper structural change, which had begun with German unification but accelerated after September 11. The strategic glue that held the alliance together is much weaker than it was during the Cold War. Germany and Berlin are no longer divided, and the American security tie is no longer existential to Germany. As Joseph Joffe put it: "Alliances die when they win.... Germany no longer needs American strategic protection; at least the rent Berlin is willing to pay for this shelter has plummeted."[40]

A similar trend can be seen in another close ally of Washington and that is South Korea. Although it remains a divided nation with a threat on its border, a majority of the South Korean public is reported to believe there was little or no chance of an attack from North Korea. As two American correspondents observed regarding the U.S.-Korean divide, "the divide has deeper roots involving this country's (South Korea) rapid passage to affluence and its perception that its distant ally is heavy handed and insensitive, particularly with regard to North Korea."[41] In addition, the desire for freedom of action and maximum flexibility in the United States has fostered a similar preference in Germany.[42] For the first time in fifty years the vitality of the transatlantic circle of German policy is now in question.

The Berlin Republic and Generational Change

These changes in the international environment have been accompanied by changes in the political and strategic culture of Germany. The election of 2002 confirmed that the Berlin Republic had now replaced the Bonn Republic. This was evident in the role of eastern voters in the election outcome. Schröder's use of the Iraq issue succeeded in moving enough former PDS voters to the SPD column to save the election.

But beyond this new volatility, the breaking or challenging of a number of taboos were signs of a changing political and strategic culture. Not only was the Bonn tradition of staying as close to Washington as possible shaken, but the primacy of the Franco-German engine and of European solidarity was as well. The challenge of Jürgen Möllemann to the taboo of anti-Semitism and criticism of Israel, while ultimately unsuccessful, was another indication of change, as was the growing treatment of Germans as victims of World War II as evidenced in the raising of the issues of the Benes decrees and the publication of *Im Krebsgang* by Günter Grass, a novel which describes the sinking of a ship carrying German refugees from the East at the end of World War II.[43]

This changing self-view coincided with the coming to power of the first fully postwar generation, the so-called 68ers. Gerhard Schröder and Joschka Fischer were prominent activists against the United States in their youth and have shaped a view of America, which, while not antagonistic, remains critical of its global role. The leadership of this generation on the Left came of age in opposition to American policy, not as Kohl and Schmidt's generation, in support of it. As a recent column in the *Financial Times* put it: "Former Chancellor Kohl's government was very much one of technocrats with socially conservative values. With Gerhard Schröder's SPD, the 68 generation came to power; former student activists, civil rights campaigners, and Baader-Meinhof defense lawyers are all present in the upper echelons."[44]

The fact that Schröder was willing to use criticism of the U.S. administration in his recent campaign, and received a positive response from much of the electorate, not to mention the more critical references made to Washington by other leading figures in the SPD, indicates the difference between this generation and that of Kohl as well as the changing generational make up of the public. This is part of a "double-double generational break." The first is the double break of both leaders and the public in Germany and the second is the generational breaks between Germany and the United States, which also has a new set of leaders with weaker links to Germany.[45]

Not only do the 68ers have an ambivalent view of America, but its view of Europe is quite different from that of the Kohl generation. Schröder was the first chancellor who did not feel emotionally bound to the postwar consensus.[46] His relation to Europe is entirely pragmatic and instrumental, unencumbered by the emotional and historically driven commitment to Europe of both Adenauer and Kohl.

The 68ers have made an impact in the areas of environmental policy and immigration law and they have broadened the growing consensus of the limited and multilateral use of force by Germany. They remain, however, sandwiched between the founders generation, which shaped the Federal Republic after World War II and the Gen-Xers, and 89ers who will soon follow them.

The generations coming behind them, the Gen-Xers, or as Peter Merkl labels them, the third postwar generation, are a transitional cohort. Their views were shaped by the oil crises of the 1970s and the shocks of the 1980s. They were the first to come of age during the "limits of growth" era, the first since 1945 to experience lower expectations of growth. They were shaped by ecological issues and the great missile debate of the 1980s, both in East and West. Their image of America was one of Reagan and of a certain United States recklessness. For example, they credit Gorbachev more for the end of the Cold War than Reagan. When the Wall came down they were more wary in the West than the Kohl generation and in this regard shared the skepticism of Oskar Lafontaine and his generation. The eastern generation was on the cusp between those who would benefit from unification and those left behind.[47]

The 89ers, the fourth postwar generation, and those who follow, were shaped by a great historical event, the end of the Cold War and the unification of Germany. They have also came of age in a time of slow economic growth and talk of Germany as the new sick man of Europe. Unlike the 68ers who used the past against their fathers, this group has a much weaker link to, and feeling of responsibility for, that past. They feel that while the past cannot be forgotten, they should not continue to be held responsible for the crimes of previous generations and that in some respects, the past "was often used as a pretext for inaction."[48]

These will be the leaders of the new, "normal" Germany. They tend to be pro-European, with about half wishing that the EU would develop into one state. They tend to favor enlargement to the East. "Europe is a reality for the young."[49] They also regard Germany's new role in a pragmatic way without any ideological blinkers. About 42 percent want to see the country speak up for its interests in the world more, and a third want to see Germany have more influence. About a third want to maintain current levels of cooperation with the U.S., with about a fifth each wanting either to decrease or increase it. A clear relative majority supports the international involvement of the Bundeswehr.

What is occurring in Germany is predicted by the interactive model of generational change, which sees social and political change coming from the interaction between generations, with succeeding generations reacting against the values of the previous one so that there is a cyclical nature to social and political change. In this case, the reaction of the younger generations against the 68ers is interesting and may lead to a more centrist and pragmatic Germany once their successors assume power. The more assertive approach to foreign policy, what Schröder called for as a "new self-confident German foreign policy," finds resonance with the younger generations.

Conclusion: A Watershed Year

All of this leads to the conclusion that the German-American relationship has been fundamentally changed by the events of 2002. While the personalities and regimes involved may have been the direct catalyst of change, the longer-term trends at work are leading to a new, more neutral and less emotional or special relationship.

The dispute over Iraq was really about a growing confidence gap, which is emerging on both sides due to a changing strategic landscape, accompanied by a major change in generations. The fact is that the foundation of the German-American relationship over the past five decades had been the common threat faced by both countries in the form of the Soviet Union. Once that threat disappeared and Germany and Berlin were united, the existential nature of the relationship was gone and with it the strategic glue which held it together.

For the United States, Germany and Europe are no longer the cockpit of conflict. Threats are now more acute in the Persian Gulf and East Asia, while Europe, with the exception of the Balkans, has become increasingly stable. There was still work to be done in Europe associated with ending the division left by the Cold War, but American attention had already begun to shift even before September 11.

The Germans, in contrast, have become even more fixated on Europe and on the reconstruction of the East after unification. While the United States remains an important partner, the transatlantic dimension of German policy has been steadily eclipsed by the European one in the past decade. The Berlin Republic is not Bonn and it is not led by the generation that had shaped the Bonn Republic, but rather by one shaped in protest against American policies in Vietnam.

This all means that even though the working relationship is back on track, things will never be the same again. The relationship is now "business like," but it is no longer cordial. Schröder and Bush are resigned to working with each other, but they will not have a close relationship based on trust. The Bush administration is unlikely to call for Germany to be a "Partner in Leadership" as did the first President Bush in Mainz in 1989. Worse yet, they will not share a common perception of threat or a strategy to deal with it.

The weakening of the strategic relationship is being accompanied by a divergence on social and political values, a divergence, which is no longer, held in check by a broader strategic purpose of empathy. This evolution will mean that Germany will once again find itself in a more fluid security environment and that the Atlantic pillar of its overall strategy has been substantially weakened.

Notes

This chapter was researched and written while the author was a Bosch Fellow at the American Academy in Berlin. He would like to thank both the American Academy and the Bosch Stiftung for their generous support of this research.

1. See Jürgen Hogrefe, *Gerhard Schröder: Ein Porträt* (Berlin: Siedler, 2002), pp. 199, 208.
2. Ibid., pp. 209–211.
3. In a principles' meeting held on 30 September 2001, which the president did not attend, the issue of using a broader coalition came up. National Security Advisor Rice turned to the allies who were clamoring to participate. Getting as many of them invested with military forces in the war was essential. The coalition had to have teeth. She did not want to leave them all dressed up with no place to go. "'The Aussies, the French, the Canadians, the Germans want to help,' she said. 'Anything they can do to help....' But [Secretary of Defense] Rumsfeld didn't want other forces included for cosmetic purposes. Some German battalion or French frigate could get in the way of his operation. The coalition had to fit the conflict and not the other way around. [CIA Director] Tenet turned to Germany ... 'the best thing the Germans can do is to get their act together on their own internal terrorist problems and the groups that we know are there,' he said. He was worried about more German-based plots." Bob Woodward, *Bush at War* (New York: Simon and Schuster, 2002), pp. 179–180.
4. Hogrefe, *Gerhard Schröder*, p. 208; also based on an interview with Michael Inacher, 8 November 2002.
5. Interview with Inacker.
6. Hogrefe, *Gerhard Schröder*, pp. 211–212.
7. Ibid.
8. In fact, the Christian Democratic opposition came to believe that Schröder had given Bush a letter stating that he would support a war on Iraq, but there is no credible substantiation for this suspicion. The U.S. ambassador to Berlin, Daniel Coates, also believed that there was a clear agreement by Schröder not to oppose openly the Bush policy on Iraq.
9. The Cheney speech seems to be widely regarded in Berlin as a key event, although this is not a unanimous view. In an interview with the *New York Times*, Schröder stated in reference to the Cheney speech: "How can you exert pressure on someone by saying to them: Even if you accede to our demands, we will destroy you? I think this was a change of strategy in the United States—whatever the explanation may be—a change that made things difficult for others, including ourselves.... [C]onsultation cannot mean that I get a call two hours in advance only to be told, 'We are going in.'" (Steven Erlanger, "German Leader's Warning: War Plan is a Huge Mistake," *New York Times*, 5 September 2002, p. A9.) One key advisor to the chancellor believed that there was no reason for the Germans to complain, as not much had been going on regarding Iraq and no one in the chancellory was concerned enough to ask the American side what was going on: "No one was asking why aren't these guys calling or calling Condi to find out what was going on." He felt that the speech had not represented a change in substance

and that no in-depth analysis of it was made within the chancellory. When asked in the *New York Times* interview about whether Cheney spoke for the president, the chancellor responded: "I am not qualified to say. The problem is that he has or seems to have committed himself so strongly that it is hard to imagine how he can climb down." Whatever the case, the speech was an ideal opportunity for Schröder to escalate his opposition to American policy on Iraq.

10. As Rice put it: "How can you use the name of Hitler and the name of the president of the United States in the same sentence? Particularly, how can a German, given the devotion of the U.S. in the liberation from Hitler? An atmosphere has been created that is in that sense poisoned." Quoted in Steven Erlanger, "Germans Vote in a Tight Election in Which Bush, Hitler and Israel Became Key Issues," *New York Times*, 22 September 2002, p. 14.
11. See the description of the importance of the personal relationship in Bush's dealings with Russian President Putin in Woodward, *Bush at War*, p. 119.
12. See a penetrating description and analysis of Schröder in Jane Kramer, "The Once and Future Chancellor," *New Yorker*, 14 September 1998, pp. 58–71.
13. Hogrefe, *Gerhard Schröder*, p. 215.
14. Interview with the author, December 2002.
15. This president came into office with the least amount of experience in foreign policy since Harry Truman, and without Truman's Washington experience. In fact, he seemed to have almost no interest or curiosity in the world. One observer labeled this a "principled provincialism": "Here is someone who by age 13 was mingling in the country club set of Houston, who then went on to Andover, Yale and Harvard Business School—and did so in the age of cut-rate international air fares—and yet he rarely traveled abroad." Philip Taubman, *New York Times Sunday Magazine*, 14 January 2001, p. 30.
16. "Freund oder Feind," *Der Spiegel* 40 (2002): 118.
17. Quoted in John Vinocur, "U.S. and Germany Still Estranged," *International Herald Tribune*, 20 November 2002, p. 1.
18. Henry A Kissinger, "The 'Made in Berlin' Generation," *Washington Post*, 30 October 2002, p. A23.
19. These data are taken from the exit polls conducted by Forschungsgruppe Wahlen and reported both in *Bundestagswahl: Eine Analyse der Wahl vom 22. September 2002*, no. 108 (Mannheim: Forschungsgruppe Wahlen, 2002): pp. 10–11, and in Dieter Roth and Mathias Jung, "Ablösung der Regierung vertagt: Eine Analyse der Bundestagswahl 2002," *Aus Politik und Zeitgeschichte* B49–50/2002 (9 December 2002): pp. 3–17.
20. *Bundestagswahl*, p. 42.
21. Roth and Jung, "Ablösung der Regierung vertagt," p. 12.
22. *Bundestagswahl*, pp. 48–49. Only one month after the election, those numbers shifted slightly more in favor of participation with a United Nations mandate. "Der Kanzler verliert seinen Vertrauensbonus," *Süddeutsche Zeitung*, 19–20 October 2002, p. 7.
23. *What the World Thinks in 2002*, The Pew Global Attitudes Project (Washington, D.C.: The Pew Research Center for the People and the Press, 2002), p, 58; http://www.people-press.org; *Worldviews 2002* (Washington: The German Marshall Fund of the United States, 2002), p. 24.
24. *What the World Thinks in 2002*, pp. 53, 58.
25. The rejection of German participation in a war against Iraq was stronger among women than men and was especially pronounced among women over the age of 60, two-thirds of whom rejected German participation. Roth and Jung, "Ablösung der Regierung vertagt," p. 12. See also Wolfgang Hartenstein and Rita Müller-Hilmer, "Die Bundestagswahl 2002: Neue Themen – neue Allianzen," *Aus Politik und Zeitgeschichte* B49–50/2002 (9 December 2002), p. 23.
26. Roth and Jung, "Ablösung der Regierung vertagt," pp. 12–13.
27. Ibid., p. 12. Confidence in the SPD's handling of relations with the United States dropped from 41 percent in September to 34 percent in October, but with only 27 percent having

confidence in the CDU's policy toward the United States. *Bundestagswahl*, pp. 48–49. The month after the election figures from the FGW can be found in "Der Kanzler verliert seinen Vertrauensbonus," *Süddeutsche Zeitung*, 19–20 October 2002, p. 7.
28. *Bundestagswahl*, p. 38.
29. Ibid., p. 49.
30. Dr. Dieter Roth of FGW reported the data to a conference on anti-Americanism sponsored by the Friedrich-Ebert-Stiftung in Washington on 16 December 2002.
31. Gustav Stresemann, foreign minister during the Weimar period, once commented that it was remarkable how consistently American ideals corresponded to the United States' material interests. See Ulf Poschardt, "Lieben oder hassen wir die Amerikaner?" *Welt am Sonntag*, 9 September 2002.
32. Quoted in Philip H. Gordon, "Bridging the Atlantic Divide," *Foreign Affairs* 82, no. 1 (2003): 80.
33. Quoted in Poschardt, "Lieber oder hassen."
34. Dieter Roth, Ebert conference of 16 December 2002.
35. "Am Ende der ersten Halbzeit," *Die Zeit*, 15 August 2002, p. 3.
36. *What the World Thinks in 2002*, p. 64.
37. Hans W. Gatzke, *Germany and the United States: A Special Relationship?* (Cambridge, Mass.: Harvard University Press, 1980), p. 48.
38. Ibid., p. 32.
39. "Living with a Superpower," *The Economist*, 4 January 2003, p. 20.
40. Josef Joffe, "The Alliance is Dead. Long Live the New Alliance," *New York Times*, 29 September 2002, section 4, p. 3.
41. Howard W. French and Don Kirk, "Amid Mounting Protests, U.S.-Korean Relations Reach a Low," *International Herald Tribune*, 12 December 2002, p. 4.
42. Gunter Hellmann, "Der deutsche Weg. Eine politische Gratwanderung," *Internationale Politik* 44, no. 9 (2002): 5.
43. As Hellmann observed: "The children of Hitler's children have even gained moral capital in the last few years. The increased uncovering of dark chapters in the history of neighbors (in contrast to what is seen as an exemplary working over of the disturbing German history) and the current discovery of the suffering in the history of flight and relocation after World War II are seen as placing the Germans, for the first time, morally in a non-minority category." Ibid., p. 6; Günter Grass, *Im Krebsgang* (Göttingen: Steidl, 2002).
44. Rachel Seiffert, "Generation Gap," *FT Weekend*, 21–22 September 2002, p. 1.
45. "Joschka Fischer was nineteen years old when he threw stones at the police in Stuttgart. In essence, the street protesters of then, who are today in the highest positions of government, have repeated their resistance against an American war, organized and directed from the White House and Pentagon." "Freund oder Feind," *Der Spiegel* 40 (2002), p. 113. For more on the "double generation break," see Werner Weidenfeld, "Abschied von Adenauer," *Die Welt*, 1 June 2002, p. 3; Jochen Thies, "Die Ringen um eine neue Weltordnung," *Aus Politik und Zeitgeschichte*, no. 25 (2002): 3; and Kissinger, "The 'Made in Berlin' Generation," p. A23.
46. Michael Thurmann and Constanze Stelzenmüller, "Mit Gewehr, aber ohne Kompass," *Die Zeit*, 27 September 2002, p. 1.
47. See Peter Merkl, *German Unification in the European Context* (University Park: Pennsylvania State University Press, 1993), pp. 40–50.
48. Seiffert, "Generation Gap," p. 1.
49. *Jugend 2002*, p. 9.

Chapter 11

GERMAN POLICYMAKING AND THE REFORM GRIDLOCK

Helga A. Welsh

Introduction

Electoral rhetoric usually highlights the need for change, combined with the need to safeguard cherished achievements; the 2002 campaign in Germany was no exception. But clear ideas and focus were mostly absent from the politicians' speeches; leaving aside the last few weeks when floods in some parts of eastern Germany aroused civic mindedness and the Iraq debate captured public attention. "Never before in the history of the Federal Republic," journalist Heribert Prantl commented in July 2002, "had there been an electoral campaign in which topics appeared so quickly and vanished equally quickly."[1]

German voters had not yet cast their votes, but the verdict seemed clear: at least in the short run, the reform blockage that has gripped the Republic for more than decade would continue. According to the authors of the lead story "A Stalled Republic" in the weekly *Der Spiegel*, it was almost as if politicians had draped a curtain over the country's urgent political problems.[2] The *Spiegel* journalists were not alone in unmasking the paralyzing effects of political parties and interest groups on efficient policymaking. The lamenting about reform gridlock in Germany surely must count as one of the major media themes during 2002. For example, the weekly *Die Zeit* featured for most of pre-election 2002 a series of articles, "Agenda Deutschland." Identified as the "German sickness," reluctance toward reform was critically analyzed, finding both the public as well as the political class to blame. The perception of paralysis combined with hectic activity has prevailed for some time.[3]

Public opinion remains divided over whether the Federal Republic of Germany is prepared to take on the challenges of the future. Party identification has become more fluid, and public opinion reacts accordingly:

Notes for this chapter begin on page 217.

less than two months after the September 2002 elections, public support for the SPD had fallen with unprecedented speed to record low levels.[4] Political observers pondered with bewilderment why the re-elected government under Chancellor Gerhard Schröder seemed just as unprepared as it was in 1998 to tackle problems that have gripped the country for some time. Declining labor productivity and persistent low economic growth rates; a budget deficit that violated the provisions of the European Union's stability pact in 2002; an aging population whose pension funds are endangered; educational deficiencies; structural mass unemployment; and spiraling costs associated with upgrading as well as maintaining crucial aspects of the cherished social welfare state plague Germany.[5]

The term *Reformstau* (reform gridlock) has come to symbolize one of the most pressing issues in German politics. The term was initially coined to refer to the last years of Helmut Kohl's chancellorship, when the difficulty of getting things done in a timely and efficient manner became glaringly evident. But have matters really changed? To engage in reform—that is, to pass policies that alter the form and function of certain policies—remains exceedingly difficult. Harold L. Wilensky used the term "policy paralysis" to refer to a situation in the United States when "(1) both elites and masses favor a policy or program, and (2) other countries have acted successfully, and (3) there is no action in the U.S. for long periods, say 25 or 30 years."[6]

Wilensky's definition of paralysis provides a fitting point of departure to describe phenomena that are typically described as gridlock, blockage, deadlock, or paralysis; I use the terms interchangeably to refer to the German situation. Modifying Wilensky, I state that reform paralysis can be identified when (1) important segments of the elite and the public advocate policy or program change; (2) other countries that faced similar reform pressures have been successful in implementing new policies; and (3) attempts at passing new policies have failed or been watered down to such an extent that, within a short period of time, the same or similar policy issues re-emerge with renewed urgency.

Applied to Germany, the need for reform in many policy areas such as the labor market, pensions, education, and health care is hardly questioned. German preference for evolutionary, piecemeal change has characterized past policy restructuring, but, at this juncture, many argue, more than tinkering with the system may be required to meet the challenges of the future. More and more scholars ask why the country seems less capable than some European neighbors of "seizing upon reform proposals and transforming them into effective solutions."[7]

What explains the coincidence of widespread reform rhetoric and persistent reform reluctance in Germany? In responding to this question, I briefly review the main political and institutional features of policymaking in Germany. I emphasize that far from paralyzing all policy reforms, they provide opportunities for change and persistence; adaptations have taken place to circumvent existing barriers and to respond to a changing political landscape. Institutional features, however, are only part of the puzzle. Political resources—that is, the level of elite and societal support for reform initiatives—are of equal importance. The reform debate focuses on policy issues that are closely related to Germany's socioeconomic system of *Modell Deutschland* and thus go to the heart of post–World War II identity. Politicians and voters alike are tied to those policies and have, therefore, been slow to reframe the discourse.

Reform Gridlock and *Modell Deutschland*

Simultaneously driven and constrained by globalization and Europeanization, German performance as measured by indicators ranging from educational achievements to financial stability no longer ranks first in relation to other countries but, at best, reflects a middle position and decline. Comparison with other countries has become an important reference point in political discussions. Due to Germany's economic importance and its exposed political and economic role in Europe and within the European Union, what goes wrong not only matters to Germans but to a wider international audience.

The difficulty of initiating and implementing major policy change is obviously not limited to Germany, yet, here, the complex mesh of structural and psychological obstacles to the efficient adjustment of certain policies has probably led to more political and scholarly soul searching than elsewhere.[8] Postwar West Germany was a remarkable success story; now, not past accomplishments but the future viability of the system is in question. In other words, the marked deficiencies in solving urgent problems are eroding Germany's political identity as a societal and economic model.

In lamenting the reform gridlock, political analysts have focused on distinct, critical policies. While gridlock suggests that the visions of the political parties are quite different and that little-to-nothing gets done, the picture is more multifaceted. On daily political matters even in such crucial areas such as foreign policy, the major parties strikingly share attitudes and approaches and important changes have taken place in the last decade. Topics ranging from the introduction of the euro to the enlargement of the European Union have not roused serious disagreement or affected electoral campaigns.[9]

Both the much-criticized Kohl and Schröder governments can claim important policy accomplishments.[10] They include steps toward reforming the welfare state and the process of German unification, a new citizenship law, tax, and pension reforms, and a revised system of fiscal burden sharing among the federal states. Thus, questions about gridlock are more particular: why are some reforms accomplished while others fail, and why do the many incremental policy adjustments necessitate a reform of the reform within a short period of time? A major part of the explanation lies in the strong identification of the political elite and the public with the German postwar success story, the *Modell Deutschland*.[11]

Modell Deutschland stands for a specific form of neo-corporatist policy that relies on a complex yet consensual interrelationship of the major German political and economic institutions. For the first forty years after its creation, it was seen as a foundation of social peace and labor productivity. Built on a wide network of social provisions, it guaranteed a flexible response to economic and social challenges, individual security, and economic growth. For example, the educational system fulfilled its mandate to provide skilled workers through structured vocational training. Even when substantial changes were made, the basic institutions of the social model remained intact and thus could be "viewed as the same institutions."[12]

Exactly this kind of system is now under fire. Just as the existing welfare system relies on the interrelationship of labor market regulations and elaborate social provisions that cover both the work force and those outside of it, reforms are interdependent. In practice, however, pension, health care, and labor policies are segmented, making comprehensive and coherent reform proposals difficult to achieve.

The social welfare system is a particularly sensitive topic; Germans are proud of their model social market economy, and the achievement of "social peace" is a highly prized commodity. When asked about sources of pride in the Federal Republic's system, social peace ranked highest in both the East and the West, followed by economic strength.[13] And although most Germans are attached to the benefits of the welfare state, eastern Germans are so in particular.[14]

Post-unification developments undermined the system's institutional foundations and added considerable financial strain. For example, the economic consequences of German unification cannot be ignored when explaining the employment predicament of the 1990s or the pension conundrum.[15,16] In addition, such changing demographics as low birth rates and increasing life expectancy and high social insurance contributions that add to labor costs have destabilized the success of the German social and economic system with equal force.[17]

The Political Landscape

Politicians and journalists cry out for a move from policy initiation to implementation, but scholarly assessments are often more differentiated. They emphasize that policymaking is difficult but not unfeasible.[18] Manfred G. Schmidt summarized the four main factors that complicate policy steering processes: a large number of veto players; staggered elections at the national and Land level that foster permanent electoral campaigning; the judicialization of politics that inflates the political role of the Federal Constitutional Court; and a prominent political legacy (*Erblast*). Political legacy refers not only to path-dependent processes that lock in existing policies or, at the very least, create disincentives for change and discourage citizens' expectations but also to financial constraints and frustrated hopes associated with unification. Despite difficult framework conditions, Schmidt argues, political steering is possible: to get things done, veto players are skirted, informal politics surges, and political strategizing that aims to satisfy both entrenched party clientele and a wider electorate is common.[19]

Traditionally, consensus and bargaining are fundamental to the German postwar political system. The institutional design deliberately disperses power and involves multilevel negotiations among various political actors; the key role in politics and policy devolves to the political parties. For the past fifty years, institutional change was guided by the incentive of stability, and, in the words of one observer, "change and adaptation occurred essentially silently, unplanned and mostly *without reform impulse.*"[20] The dominant tendency, according to Ludger Helms, was concentration and centralization, "complemented by what could be called 'informalisation' of the governmental decision-making system."[21]

The political party landscape in Germany has changed due not only to the addition of new actors (Alliance 90/The Greens and Party of Democratic Socialism) but also to the reduction in fundamental ideological differences between the major parties, SPD and CDU/CSU. In addition, voters have become more willing to switch sides. Taken together, the main political parties are running neck to neck. Indeed, in 2002, less than 7,000 votes (out of more than 39 million) separated SPD and CDU/CSU. When election results are that narrow, every vote is important, and no societal group is asked to make major sacrifices. German parties are welfare state parties, and SPD and CSU/CSU seek electoral support from the political center.[22]

The German political system, often characterized as "negotiation democracy," emphasizes compromise and bargaining, yet the media—and politicians—highlight conflict in order to reduce complexity and to mobilize voters. Differences on economic, social, and value-related policies, such as family policy, are often not nearly as pronounced as the official rhetoric suggests. Political agendas with many points in common allow package deals, but parties tend to exaggerate their differences when deemed necessary for political advantage. Multilevel decision-making and bargaining procedures behind closed doors lack transparency, and their results are difficult to transmit to the electorate, yet easily accessible policy recommendations are a prerequisite of a modern mass-media-driven society. The tension between the complexity of the decisions that have to be made and the need to translate them into palatable sound bites favors key political players with privileged media access; the personalization of politics was particularly evident in the 2002 election.[23]

Critics of parties' attitudes toward reform have found important allies in the federal presidents. Using the "soft power" associated with their office, German federal presidents increasingly have behaved as the "conscience of the nation."[24] Their addresses have focused on the role of political parties, reform gridlock, and the resultant disenchantment with political life. In 2002, Federal President Johannes Rau asked political parties to be less self-centered and more worried about their societal roots. He criticized voting patterns in the Federal Council that put partisan interests above specific Länder interests.[25] Richard von Weizsäcker, during his presidential tenure and to this day, highlights the lack of political leadership among the parties and their unwillingness to openly discuss unsolved problems. Germany may be a status-quo society, but Von Weizsäcker states, the political parties can and must lead their clientele in new directions.[26] In 1997, then-Federal President Roman Herzog pointed to societal paralysis and the loss of economic dynamism and outlined the cycle that leads from reform initiatives to failure.[27] All three presidents have remarked critically that staying in power seems more important for political parties than advancing necessary but difficult reforms.

To blame the political parties exclusively for gridlock, however, would be shortsighted. Wolfgang Rentzsch reminds us that political parties "do not cause blockages, but rather help to overcome them," although he admits that they are sometimes slow in doing so or even fail.[28] The political class reacts to mass sentiment and thus confronts a paradox. As one commentator argued, Germans "say they want reforms, but then rebel against the measures needed to achieve them."[29] Jonathan Rauch's finding for the United States that "[t]he electorate is at war with its government (and with itself) because it demands both the security of entitlements and the effectiveness of experiment"[30] applies in equal measure to Germany.

In 1998, public opinion data suggested reluctance toward reform yet a desire for change in leadership.[31] Four years later, Chancellor Schröder repeatedly referred to the difficulty of gaining sufficient legitimacy to pursue reform policies. Asked whether a perceived crisis can accelerate reforms, he reacted cautiously. People in rich democracies are afraid, he argued, that change will deteriorate their standard of living.[32] Since the great majority of Germans still lives in comfortable and secure circumstances, it is hardly surprising that change is viewed with anxiety, and that crisis-talk does not match their personal experience. The policy predicament is summarized by a leading SPD Party strategist: "The competition between the large people's parties will be decided with regard to the question of who will more successfully combine transformation with stability, progress with maintenance, change with security."[33] While the analysis is accurate, implementing it may also be difficult.

Policymaking in Germany emphasizes incremental change and multilevel decision-making (*Politikvernetzung*), for example, in the form of cooperative federalism and consensus seeking. In tandem with the decline of the German model, institutional disincentives for reform have been singled out for widespread attention. Prominently at issue is the interplay between the Federal Council (Bundesrat) and the Federal Parliament (Bundestag), and the need for coalition government at the national and, with few exceptions, the Land level. Heightened partisan conflict has sparked new interest in the reform of the federal system and questions about the effectiveness of second chambers more generally.[34]

The Federal Council's power has increased to the point that 55 to 60 percent of bills require the approval of both houses of parliament, where increasingly shifting majorities have necessitated intense bargaining and search for compromises. In historical context, the Federal Council is not a graveyard for bills; however, times of greater conflict coincide with divided parliamentary majorities and the political will to deliberately use the Federal Council to weaken the coalition in power.[35] The role of political parties comes into play once again. The enforced cooperation of the major parties is most evident in the role of the Mediation Committee (*Vermittlungsausschuss*), whose 32 members are appointed in equal numbers from the Bundestag and Bundesrat. For example, between 1983 and 1990, when CDU/CSU and FDP held majorities in both chambers, the Mediation Committee took action in nineteen cases but its involvement went up considerably after the ruling coalition lost its dominant position in the Federal Council in 1991; 166 bills were discussed between 1990 and 1998. Ultimately, 144 were signed into law after the Committee came up with a compromise.[36] In reality, in order to move forward, divided government favors, and programmatic similarities among the major parties make possible, covert grand coalition arrangements.

Institutional arrangements can slow down or obstruct legislation for change. In the 1990s, the shift from a three to a five-plus party system made coalition building less predictable and policy outcomes more varied. The multitude of different coalitions at the Länder level may have made governing at the national level more complex but also opened up new avenues for bargaining. Conflict over financial redistribution has become more pronounced since the addition of the so-called new states in the East. Who is "rich" and who is "poor" among the Länder matters more today than ever; coalitions based on financial strength or weakness have added a new strategic layer to decision-making. They also opened avenues for "blackmailing" votes in the Federal Council. In particular, the so-called grand coalitions between CDU and SPD at the Land level have sparked package deals in the Federal Council that permitted tax and pension reforms during the first Red-Green coalition but also created intense conflict over divergent votes in the case of immigration reform in 2002.

In addition to the Federal Council, the Federal Constitutional Court has proven another important challenge to reform initiatives. Ever since its inception in 1951, political parties have used the powers of the court as an important opposition tool and to dispute legislation. Indeed, even the threat of "going to Karlsruhe" has become an almost expected ritualistic response when major reform initiatives have been passed.[37] In recent years, the partnership law for gays and lesbians (2001), the immigration and integration law (2002), and amendments to the framework law on higher education (2001 and 2002) were all legally challenged by the opposition forces.

The political class—in Germany and elsewhere among post-industrial societies—is often accused of being too dependent on interest groups, of not wanting to offend important clientele. In short, getting things done the old way is too comfortable. The number of interest groups has grown significantly, from 635 in 1974 to 1,673 in 1998, and so has their potential for mobilization; often, one social force tries to obstruct the other.[38] In 1997, then-Federal President Herzog outlined in his famous *Ruck-Rede* a ritual that regularly kills reform initiatives. It starts with a policy proposal that asks for some sacrifice from an interest group, which ultimately leads to its postponement. Almost immediately, "collective indignation" arouses opposing opinions among the parties. All kinds of counterproposals and activism emerge, and the population is uncertain as to what constitutes the best solution. In the end, according to Herzog, the status quo prevails.[39]

When traditional channels are blocked, policy actors tend to look for ways to overcome the gridlock. Resorting to new and old forms of informal politics is one reaction to increasingly complex decision-making procedures: governing has become the art of nurturing various policy networks. As many political actors as possible are incorporated into the decision-making process in order to anticipate and/or to defuse potential opposition and more and more "rounds of consensus," such as expert commissions, are created.

Informal politics has received renewed attention in recent years, but its role and codes of conduct are not new to German politics. Already in 1984, Helmuth Schulze-Fielitz identified informal arrangements: proportional rules within parliament, political parties, and society, and informal cooperation procedures.[40] Informal politics has since become part of every chancellor's toolbox, and the mechanisms surrounding the formation and functioning of national coalition governments have been given particular attention.[41] In the 1980s, Kohl's informal policy coordination was not only a form of coalition management but also a vehicle to control the unruly Länder. After the CDU/CSU and FDP coalition lost its majority in the Federal Council, Kohl embraced a new strategy that, at times, included the opposition parties and the major social partners, that is, labor unions and employers associations.[42] The change of government in 1998 did not end the surge in informal politics; it simply entered a new phase. Hailed by journalist Gunter Hofmann as "consensus via tolerant embracing," Chancellor Gerhard Schröder's policy style has allegedly replaced Kohl's system of "consensus via authoritarian integration."[43] According to Matthias Machnig, political analyst and SPD strategist, commissions "shall bring competence to the government, make it more difficult for the opposition to digress, and at times, help to conquer crises."[44] The head of the Federal Chancellery under Schröder, Frank Walter Steinmeier, referred to Schröder's incorporation of many actors in decision-making as "'innovative consensus' beyond the traditional ideological ditches." By pointing to the temporary nature of those arrangements, Steinmeier rejects claims that they are part and parcel of corporatist decision-making.[45] He also differentiates them from "ritualized" ways to incorporate different actors in the lawmaking process.

Apart from individual assessments, it is obvious that most major policy initiatives in the last few years involved "rounds of consensus" or expert commissions. Commissions are everywhere: at the level of the national government, its individual ministries, the parliament, and the Federal Presidency. Nobody knows the exact number, but estimates refer to approximately 600 consulting bodies at the federal level and 1,000, if the Länder are included.[46] To be sure, only very few receive national attention: among them were the commission on the reform of the armed forces under the chairmanship of Richard von Weizsäcker, the immigration commission led by Rita Süssmuth, the commission to reform the labor market, named after its leader, Peter Hartz, and a commission to reform the pension, health, and nursing insurance systems, chaired by Bert Rürup. The choice of chairpersons reveals a distinct preference for expertise and reputation and downplays partisan affiliation.

As a result, governmental action is increasingly characterized by the addition of new actors, many of whom are set apart by their transience, circumscribed goals, and wide ideological and institutional diversity. A style of informal governing has emerged that emphasizes consensus and diffuses political influence and accountability at the expense of traditional policy actors. These informal arrangements are important tools in setting the agenda, and they influence the public discourse. But innovative consensus-building measures are inadequate when elite and public support are lacking.

Benchmarking and International Comparison

International comparisons have become an important benchmark in the discussion of how to reform certain aspects of the German economic and social welfare system. The Anglo-Saxon economic model remains an ambiguous and sensitive reference point for many continental Europeans. Chancellor Gerhard Schröder has repeatedly argued that "American circumstances," meaning high levels of low-paying jobs, less job security, and fewer social benefits, are not the solution to Germany's unemployment woes. He cautioned that foreign critics of German economic performance recommend transposing Anglo-Saxon ideas to Germany, which, according to Schröder, cannot work.[47]

Comparisons with other European countries that are in similar need of reform and share institutional and cultural characteristics are a different matter, even if some critics, particularly in the popular media, often neglect important distinctions, such as the size of the German economy, the continued economic burden that unification entails, and qualities unique to the German social state. With increasing frequency, however, both inside and outside of Germany, international comparisons have come to the forefront of the scholarly and the political debate. Why, for example, have the Netherlands and Denmark been able to make greater inroads in reforming the welfare state, while Germany remains at the sidelines? Two lines of argument have emerged. One focuses on the importance of reframing the discourse, the other on the ability to revive patterns of social partnership in order to adjust critical policies.

Public resistance to reforming the welfare state is widely shared across Europe, but values, no matter how persistent, are not immune to adaptations. Using Jacob Torfing's concept of path-shaping behavior, Robert Henry Cox argues "issues can successfully be reformed when they build upon existing social values, sometimes recasting values to make them relevant to the proposed reform."[48] He contends that exactly this neglect of public discourse severely hampered welfare reform efforts in Germany, in contrast to the Netherlands and Denmark.[49] Vivien Schmidt highlights the importance of discourse "as both a set of ideas about the necessity and appropriateness of reform and an interactive process of policy construction and communication" for recent successful welfare reforms. In her view, in Germany "meaningful reform" was "stymied by the lack of a successful coordinative discourse among the social partners and the often contradictory communicative discourse of government and opposition in the frequent elections."[50]

Efforts to reframe discourse invite opposition in most political settings, and Schmidt remarks that acting against the majority can be costly at election time for reformers. Nevertheless, a shared perception of crisis can also unify policymakers. In other European countries, crisis united major parties, but in Germany, efforts to reframe the discourse on most problems continued to separate the SPD on one side and CDU/CSU on the other. For example, during the last two electoral campaigns, promising the reversal of some previously instituted policy changes became commonplace. In 1998, the SPD assured voters that it would overturn some reforms implemented under the Kohl government, in particular, the reduction in sickness pay and important elements of the pension reform of 1997 that were supposed to become effective in 1999, and it did. The same strategy was pursued during the 2002 campaign, when the opposition candidate for chancellor, Edmund Stoiber, pledged to repeal some policies that had been introduced under the Red-Green coalition government. Hardly any reform package has passed in recent years without major resistance by the main opposition party—in the Federal Parliament, the Federal Council, the Federal Constitutional Court, and sometimes even all three of them.

However, change has not been completely absent from the German political discourse. In contrast to foreign observers, Martin Seeleib-Kaiser argues that a "dual transformation of the welfare state" has taken place incrementally within the last 25 years. In his view, new "interpretative patterns" have emerged. As regards disability, pension, and unemployment benefits, the state has stopped guaranteeing the standard of living of previous wage earners, while expanding its role in providing family policies.[51] Just as in the area of welfare state reform, the policy steps surrounding the diversification and internationalization of higher education, shaped by a diverse advocacy coalition, have been incremental, yet they have the potential for substantial change in the long run.[52]

In a similar vein, the immigration paradigm has changed.[53] The proposed immigration and integration law, the first of its kind in Germany, has been endorsed by a wide-ranging alliance of societal, economic, and political groups, although the CDU/CSU voted against it in the Federal Council and successfully challenged its constitutionality in the Federal Constitutional Court on procedural grounds. Still, gone are the days when political elites can proclaim that Germany is not a country of immigration. Furthermore, the most recent pension reform moved away from sole reliance on pay-as-you-go, state-financed contributions and introduced privately funded contributions. Thus, the perception of paralysis is at times misleading. Change does take place, but the pace is slow and relies on piecemeal steps.

Welfare reform has received particular attention in the last decade, and tripartite negotiations among European governments and their social partners have been reinvigorated, but, once again, Germany seems to differ in its lack of successful concertation from the Netherlands and Italy, although not in this instance from France.[54] In Germany, neo-corporatist arrangements involving social partners have not led to the expected recalibrations in labor relations; the Alliance for Jobs (*Bündnis für Arbeit*) has failed to make any headway toward reform. The reasons are manifold. Roland Czada, for example, emphasizes that substantial differences in the economic performance of the eastern and western part of Germany have eroded the *Modell Deutschland* and broken down neo-corporatist policies.[55] During the heyday of *Modell Deutschland*, according to Czada, consensual conflict mechanisms and authority structures bridged tensions to initiate changes, but the old balance of political players no longer exists. The political landscape has become more heterogeneous and thus more divided.[56] Old mechanisms no longer work in the traditional way; new ones are emerging but their shape has not crystallized.

Bernhard Ebbinghaus and Anke Hassel emphasize the continued organizational power of the German trade unions in the workplace and the collective bargaining system that explains decreased pressure to "make deals" with the government.[57] Kenneth Dyson comes to a different conclusion. For him, it is exactly the weakened authority of the employer organizations and the trade unions in post-unification Germany that have undermined *Modell Deutschland*. In such an environment, the major players' interests are in preserving benefits for their clientele, not in making concessions.[58]

Conclusion

Rich Western democracies are challenged to meet society's high expectations in providing continued prosperity and security in view of financial constraints and a changing demographic composition. How the political elites address or fail to address crucial questions about welfare, labor market regulations, pensions, and immigration contributes to political frustrations and declining public trust in political institutions.

In many unforeseen ways, German unification catalyzed policy transformations. International competition added urgency to the reform project of the treasured *Modell Deutschland*. German policymaking, I have shown, accentuates negotiation and compromise against a background of partisan quarreling and blockage. This mode of interaction highlights institutional and mental impasse and entitlement thinking and favors incremental change that is often exceedingly slow.

However, policymaking is far from paralyzed. Germany's foreign policy has evolved in significant ways, and new policy directions have been outlined in citizenship, immigration, pension, and labor market reforms. Despite all the warnings about a "stalled society," Germany has accomplished much. As the December 2002 edition of the *The Economist* points out:

> For quality of life and protection of the weak, [t]his country remains at the top of the league. Its welfare system is enviably generous. Its environmental and health standards are high. Its sense of civic virtue ... remains pretty solid. Public discourse is vigorous but dignified. Germany is an eminently civilised country with a solidly entrenched democracy.... If compromise and consensus slow down growth but deliver civil serenity, then let us—say many Germans—pay the price.[59]

Still, the same authors also point to the "fading luster" of some aspects of its economic and educational system. Increasingly, signs indicate that the economic and social systems have arrived at a crossroads, and the sluggishness of the policymaking process has become a major obstacle. Just how much and how radical a policy innovation is needed is still open to question, but the calls for leadership have become louder since the 2002 election.

Notes

1. Heribert Prantl, "Schröders letzte Chance," *Süddeutsche Zeitung*, 20–21 July 2002, p. 4.
2. *Der Spiegel*, 21 September 2002, p. 39.
3. Wolfgang Fach asserts: "Much happens but nothing changes; much fails but there are no consequences," in "Die zerstreute Republik," *Blätter für deutsche und internationale Politik* 43 (1998), p. 931 [author's translation].
4. Forschungsgruppe Wahlen, *Bundestagswahl. Eine Analyse der Wahl vom 22. September 2002*, Berichte der Forschungsgruppe Wahlen, Mannheim no. 108, 47–48; and *Politbarometer* 11 (2002) (Repräsentative Umfrage – KW 46).
5. Roland Berger, "Zehn Schritte zum Wohlstand," *Die Zeit*, Politik 21/2002 (online version).
6. Harold L. Wilensky, *Rich Democracies: Political Economy, Public Policy, and Performance* (Berkeley: University of California Press, 2002), p. 693.
7. Fritz W. Scharpf, "Die gefesselte Republik," *Die Zeit*, Politik 35/2002 (online version).
8. Nearly 80 percent of Germans felt that too much lamenting was characteristic of political debates. *Modell Deutschland?* (Mannheim: Institut für praxisorientierte Sozialforschung, no. 1084, August 1997).
9. Charles Lees, "'Dark Matter': Institutional Constraints and the Failure of Party-Based Euroscepticism in Germany," *Political Studies* 50, no. 2 (2002): 244–267.
10. See, for example, Manfred Schmidt, "Politiksteuerung in der Bundesrepublik Deutschland," in *Jenseits des Regierungsalltags. Strategiefähigkeit politischer Parteien*, ed. Frank Nullmeier and Thomas Saretzki (Frankfurt am Main and New York: Campus, 2002), pp. 27–28; see also Christine Margerum Harlen, "Schröder's Economic Reforms: The End of *Reformstau*?" *German Politics* 11, no. 1 (April 2002): 61–80.
11. For a related discussion, see Ben Lieberman, "From Economic Miracle to Standort Deutschland: Exchanging Economic Metaphors in the Federal Republic of Germany," *German Politics and Society* 18, no. 2 (Summer 2000): 30–65.
12. Lutz Leisering, "Germany: Reform from Within," in *International Social Policy: Welfare Regimes in the Developed World*, ed. Pete Alcock and Cary Craig (New York: Palgrave, 2001), p. 178.
13. *50 Jahre Bundesrepublik Deutschland. Ergebnisse einer repräsentativen Bevölkerungsumfrage* (Mannheim: Institut für praxisorientierte Sozialforschung [IPOS], no. 1169, May 1999).
14. Edeltraud Roller, "Erosion des sozialstaatlichen Konsenses und die Entstehung einer neuen Konfliktlinie in Deutschland?" *Aus Politik und Zeitgeschichte* B 29–30 (2002): 13–19; see also Roller, "Shrinking the Welfare State: Citizens' Attitudes Towards Cuts in Social Spending in Germany in the 1990s," *German Politics* 8 (1999): 21–39. The greater attachment (and thus higher expectations) of Germans (and once again, in particular, eastern Germans) compared to British citizens toward the welfare state is emphasized by Steffen Mau, *Patterns of Popular Support for the Welfare State: A Comparison of the United Kingdom and Germany* (Berlin: Wissenschaftszentrum, FSIII 01-405).
15. See, for example, Ludger Lindlar and Wolfgang Scheremet, *Germany's Slump: Explaining the Unemployment Crisis of the 1990s* (Berlin: DIW Discussion Paper no. 169, June 1998).
16. Bert Rürup, "The German Pension System: Status Quo and Reform Options," in *Social Security Pension Reform in Europe*, ed. Martin Feldstein and Horst Siebert (Chicago and London: University of Chicago Press, 2002), pp. 137–163.
17. Tina Baier, "Im Land der Greise," *Süddeutsche Zeitung*, 15 November 2002 (online version).
18. Cf. Everhard Holtmann and Helmut Voelzkow, eds., *Zwischen Wettbewerbs- und Verhandlungsdemokratie. Analysen zum Regierungssystem in der Bundesrepublik Deutschland* (Wiesbaden: Westdeutscher Verlag, 2000).
19. Manfred G. Schmidt, "Politiksteuerung in der Bundesrepublik Deutschland," in Nullmaier and Saretzki, *Jenseits*, pp. 23–26.
20. Roland Czada, "Reformloser Wandel. Stabilität und Anpassung im politischen Akteursystem der Bundesrepublik," in *50 Jahre Bundesrepublik. Rahmenbedingungen – Entwicklungen*

– *Perspektiven*, ed. Thomas Ellwein and Everhard Holtmann (Opladen and Wiesbaden: Westdeutscher Verlag, 1999), p. 400, emphasis in original.
21. Ludger Helms, "Introduction: Institutional Change and Adaptation in a Stable Democracy," in *Institutions and Institutional Change in the Federal Republic of Germany*, ed. Ludger Helms (New York: St. Martin's Press, 2000), p. 8.
22. Herbert Kitschelt, "The German Political Economy and the 1998 Election," in *Power Shift in Germany: The 1998 Election and the End of the Kohl Era*, ed. David P. Conradt, Gerald R. Kleinfeld, and Christian Søe (New York and Oxford: Berghahn Books, 2000), p. 218.
23. Cf. Edgar Grande, "Charisma und Komplexität. Verhandlungsdemokratie, Mediendemokratie und der Funktionswandel politischer Eliten," *Leviathan* 28, no. 1 (March 2000): 122–141.
24. Dr. Michael Jochum, "Die Macht, die aus der Marktlücke kommt. Der Bundespräsident als Soft-Power-Institution," *Frankfurter Allgemeine Zeitung*, 1 July 2000, p. 11.
25. Bundespräsidialamt, Pressemitteilung: Erklärung von Bundespräsident Johannes Rau zur Ausfertigung des Zuwanderungsgesetzes am 20. Juni 2002 im Schloss Bellevue in Berlin, http://www.bundespraesident.de (accessed 5 July 2002).
26. Interview with von Weizsäcker in *Süddeutsche Zeitung Magazin*, no. 27 (5 July 2002): 16–23.
27. "Durch Deutschland muss ein Ruck gehen." Ansprache von Bundespräsident Roman Herzog im Hotel Adlon am 26. April 1997: http://www.glidenet.org/herzog1.htm (accessed 18 August 2001).
28. Wolfgang Rentzsch, "Party Competition in the German Federal State: New Variation on an Old Theme," *Regional and Federal Studies* 9, no. 3 (Autumn 1999): 181.
29. "World in 2000," Special Issue of *The Economist*, p. 58.
30. Jonathan Rauch, *Demosclerosis: The Silent Killer of American Government* (New York: Times Books/Random House, 1995), p. 240.
31. For an interesting insider account of the SPD campaign of 1998, see Malte Ristau, "Wahlkampf in der Mediendemokratie: Die Kampagne der SPD 1997/98," in *50 Jahre Empirische Wahlforschung in Deutschland. Entwicklung, Befunde, Perspektiven, Daten*, ed. Markus Klein et al. (Wiesbaden: Westdeutscher Verlag, 2000), pp. 467–468.
32. "Am Ende der ersten Halbzeit." *Die Zeit*, Politik 34/2002 (online version).
33. Matthias Machnig, "erfolgsbedingungen fuer modernisierungspolitik: grundlinien einer reformpolitik fur sicherheit und wandel," in *Sicherheit im Wandel. Neue Solidarität im 21. Jahrhundert*, ed. Franz Müntefering and Matthias Machnig (Berlin: Berliner vorwärts Verlagsges.mbh, 2001), p. 251. With reference to Zygmunt Baumann, Machnig highlights the multiple meanings of the German term *Sicherheit* in the English language: security, certainty, safety (252–253).
34. See, for example, Adrian Vatter, "Politische Institutionen und ihre Leistungsfähigkeit. Der Fall des Bikameralismus im Vergleich," *Zeitschrift für Parlamentsfragen* 1 (2002): 125–143, and the commission work sponsored by the Bertelsmann Foundation. Hans-Wolfgang Arndt et al., *Entflechtung 2005. Zehn Vorschläge zur Optimierung der Regierungsfähigkeit im deutschen Föderalismus* (Gütersloh: Verlag Bertelsmann Stiftung, 2000).
35. Klaus von Beyme, "Institutionelle Grundlagen der deutschen Demokratie," in *Eine lernende Demokratie. 50 Jahre Bundesrepublik Deutschland*, ed. Max Kaase and Günther Schmid (Berlin: Edition Sigma, 1999), p. 29; see also Thomas König, "Von der Politikverflechtung in die Parteienblockade? Probleme und Perspektiven der deutschen Zweikammergesetzgebung," in Kaase and Schmid, *Eine lernende Demokratie*, pp. 63–85.
36. Statistical summaries are accessible from the Internet site of the Federal Council, http://www.bundesrat.de (accessed 10 November 2002).
37. The conditions under which opposition parties have been more or less successful are analyzed by Klaus Stüwe, "Das Bundesverfassungsgericht als verlängerter Arm der Opposition?" supplement to the weekly newspaper *Das Parlament* B 37–38 (7 September 2001), pp. 34–44.
38. Martin Sebaldt, "Interest Groups: Continuity and Change of German Lobbyism since 1974," in Helms, *Institutions*, p. 189.

39. "Durch Deutschland muss ein Ruck gehen" (n28).
40. Helmuth Schulze-Fielitz, *Der informale Verfassungsstaat. Aktuelle Beobachtungen des Verfassungslebens in der Bundesrepublik Deutschland im Lichte der Verfassungstheorie* (Berlin: Duncker & Humblot, 1984).
41. The most recent addition to this literature is Michaela Richter, "Continuity or *Politikwechsel*? The First Federal Red-Green Coalition," *German Politics and Society* 20, no. 1 (Spring 2002): 1–48. See also Wolfgang Rudzio, "Informelle Entscheidungsmuster in Bonner Koalitionsregierungen," *Regieren in der Bundesrepublik*, vol. 2 (Opladen: Leske & Budrich, 1991), pp. 125–141; Waldemar Schreckenberger, "Informelle Verfahren der Entscheidungsvorbereitung zwischen der Bundesregierung und den Mehrheitsfraktionen: Koalitionsgespräche und Koalitionsrunden," *Zeitschrift für Parlamentsfragen* (1994): 329–346; Philip Manow, "Informalisierung und Parteipolitisierung – Zum Wandel exekutiver Entscheidungsprozesse in der Bundesrepublik," *Zeitschrift für Parlamentsfragen* (1996): 96–107.
42. Gerhard Lehmbruch, *Parteienwettbewerb im Bundesstaat. Regelsysteme und Spannungslagen im Institutionengefüge der Bundesrepublik Deutschland*, 2nd exp. ed. (Opladen and Wiesbaden, 1998), pp. 160–175.
43. Gunter Hofmann, "Das System Schröder. Kohls Erbe: Wo die Konsensdemokratie funktioniert und wo sie an ihre Grenzen stößt," *Die Zeit*, 6 July 2000.
44. Matthias Machnig, "Strategiefähigkeit in der beschleunigten Mediengesellschaft," in Nullmaier and Saretzki, *Jenseits*, p. 175.
45. Frank Walter Steinmeier, "konsens und führung," in Müntefering and Machnig, *Sicherheit*, p. 265.
46. "Wer hat da am Rat gedreht?" *Die Zeit*, Politik 35/2002 (online version).
47. Interview with Schröder, "Notfalls auch mit Zwang," *Die Zeit*, Politik 49/2002 (online version).
48. Robert Henry Cox, "The Social Construction of an Imperative: Why Welfare Reform Happened in Denmark and the Netherlands but Not in Germany," *World Politics* 53 (April 2001): 463–498.
49. Ibid., p. 476.
50. Vivien Schmidt, "Does Discourse Matter in the Politics of Welfare State Adjustment?" *Comparative Political Studies* 35, no. 2 (March 2002): 169, 182.
51. Martin Seeleib-Kaiser, "A Dual Transformation of the German Welfare State?" *West European Politics* 25, no. 4 (October 2002): 25–48.
52. Helga A. Welsh, "Disentangling the Gridlock of Reform: Higher Education in Germany," The Program for the Study of Germany and Europe Working Papers Series, Harvard University 02.7 (2002).
53. See Kay Hailbronner, "Reform des Zuwanderungsrechts. Konsens and Dissens in der Ausländerpolitik," supplement to the weekly newspaper *Das Parlament* B 43, 19 October 2001, p. 7.
54. Bernhard Ebbinghaus and Anke Hassel, "Striking Deals: Concertation in the Reform of Continental European Welfare States," *Journal of European Public Policy* 7, no. 1 (March 2000): 44–62.
55. Roland Czada, "Vereinigungskrise und Standortdebatte. Der Beitrag der Wiedervereinigung zur Krise des westdeutschen Modells," *Leviathan* 26 (1998), p. 52.
56. Roland Czada, "Nach 1989. Reflexionen zur Rede von der 'Berliner Republik,'" in *von der Bonner zur Berliner Republik. 10 Jahre Deutsche Einheit*, ed. Roland Czada and Hellmut Wollmann (Opladen: Westdeutscher Verlag, 2000), pp. 13–45.
57. Ebbinghaus and Hassel, "Striking Deals," p. 59.
58. Kenneth Dyson, "The German Model Revisited: From Schmidt to Schröder," *German Politics* 10, no. 2 (August 2001): 151.
59. "An Uncertain Giant: A Survey of Germany," *The Economist*, 7 December 2002, p. 4.

Chapter 12

CAN GERHARD SCHRÖDER DO IT?
Prospects for Fundamental Reform of the
German Economy and a Return to High Employment

Irwin Collier

> If we are not successful in significantly lowering the unemployment rate, then we would neither deserve to be re-elected nor would we even be re-elected.
>
> — Gerhard Schröder, *Der Spiegel*, 23 August 1998

In 1998 Gerhard Schröder had the luxury of running against the economic record of the last years of Kohl government. Candidate Schröder was quite aware that later in 2002 he would have to run on his own economic record. The German electorate yearned for a substantial reduction in unemployment, but all it got was an insignificant change. When Gerhard Schröder first became the federal chancellor in September 1998, the number of unemployed was 3.97 million. Four Septembers later in 2002, the number of unemployed had declined to only 3.94 million.

One prong of the 2002 election strategy of the Schröder team to deal with its unemployment problem was to attempt to shift the blame for the continued labor market stagnation to the weak state of the world economy. The other prong of the strategy was to appoint a blue-ribbon commission for the reform of the German system of employment offices. The commission claimed and perhaps even believed itself that its 13-module reform package would be capable of reducing the number of unemployed by half and that this goal could be achieved by the end of 2005. One can easily sense just how desperate the Schröder re-election campaign staff must have felt regarding the vulnerability of their unemployment flank in the months before the 2002 elections.

However, history was to smile on the Schröder campaign as nature and international politics provided well-timed and much needed distractions

---

Notes for this chapter begin on page 252.

from the country's unemployment problems. The flood of August 2002 in East Germany was the sort of crisis needed to demonstrate that this federal chancellor could lead and dispense federal favor at will, while the international tensions over the growing Iraq crisis provided an opportunity for striking a pose for peace.

A Triad of Economic Problems

The German proverb that misfortune seldom arrives alone completely captures the essence of present economic difficulties. The chronic failure to achieve the full utilization of the nation's productive resources, in particular as seen in the high levels of unemployment we observe, is but one of three interrelated economic problems facing Germany. The second problem is that the mainsprings of the postwar revival seem to have run down, vibrant economic growth has become a memory and is not part of the historical experience shared by the young generation. Nothing less than the strength of the underlying trend of Germany's ability to generate real income growth over the future long run is the issue. The third economic problem involves the sustainability of its tax-transfer programs and systems of social insurance. Schröder's Germany, much like Kohl's Germany before it, is in very serious trouble on all three counts and there is a growing sense that the day of reckoning is nigh.

The best way to get a sense of the scale of Germany's economic problems is to place them within a longer historical or broader international context. The urgency of large steps becomes much clearer once the magnitude of the problems is truly grasped.

The upward trend in unemployment has taken close to a full generation to get where it is today (figure 12.1). Instead of roughly symmetric up- and downward fluctuations in the number of unemployed around a flat average number of unemployed, Germany has experienced an unrelenting upward ratcheting of unemployment from recession trough to recession trough. While some of the increase in unemployment can be seen to be reduced in each subsequent economic upturn, no economic recovery since the mid-1970s has been adequate to stabilize unemployment, much less reverse the upward trend that can be easily constructed by connecting either the peaks or the troughs in figure 12.1. The high unemployment experienced in the East German states can be seen to have acted as a disproportionate upward shift to the trend and underscores the chronic increase in unemployment. Rather than reversing the trend, the Schröder government in its second term has also fallen victim to the trend increase in unemployment.

One of the problems of suffering a chronic condition is that the deterioration can be so gradual as to go unperceived. Gerhard Schröder's case for reform was strengthened considerably following the announcement of

FIGURE 12.1 Unemployment in Germany (thousands)

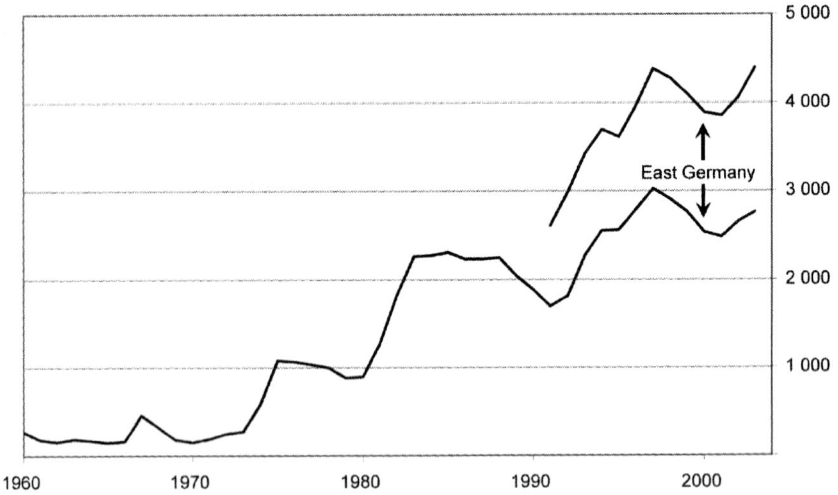

Source: Sachverständigenrat zur Begutachtung der gesamtwirtschaftlichen Entwicklung, *Jahresgutachten 2002/03: Zwanzig Punkte für Beschäftigung und Wachstum*, table 2. The international and national tables are downloadable as Excel files at http://www.sachverstaendigenrat-wirtschaft.de/gutacht/02_anhe.zip.

Note: The unemployment data were updated using data from the Herbstgutachten der wirtschaftswissenschaftlichen Forschungsinstitute, published in *DIW Wochenbericht* 43/2003, http://www.diw.de/deutsch/publikationen/wochenberichte/docs/03-43 .pdf. Unemployment data through 1990 were calculated according to existing German definitions of unemployment; beginning in 1991, the numbers were calculated according to the harmonized EU definition of unemployment.

the results of the OECD's Program for International Student Assessment (PISA) in December 2001. Germany was unceremoniously lumped into a group of nations found to be statistically significantly *below* the average of the OECD countries.[1] Less than a year later, the president of a major economics institute, Professor Hans-Werner Sinn, brought home a similar point with regard to Germany's relative economic growth performance.[2] *Schlußlicht* (tail lamp) was able to replace the metaphor of the *Reformstau* (reform gridlock) as the recurring theme of television talk shows and newspaper editorials.

An examination of the average growth rates for the last decade in the EU-15, U.S. and Japan, shown in figure 12.2 reveals an enormous variance from high-flying Ireland to the liquidity-trapped Japan. Alas it is true. The last place of the EU-15 for average economic growth goes to Germany. It is small consolation that the sick man of Europe has only managed to hobble slightly faster than the sick man of Asia.

Having looked back in time and across much of the European continent, there is more bad news if we look into the German future as far as

FIGURE 12.2 Real GDP Growth in the EU-15, Japan, and the United States, 1991–2004

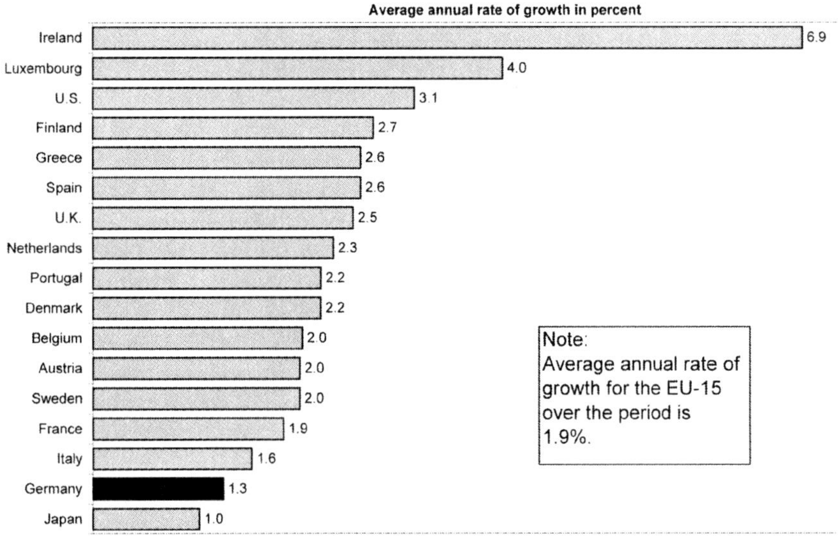

Average annual rate of growth in percent

Ireland	6.9
Luxembourg	4.0
U.S.	3.1
Finland	2.7
Greece	2.6
Spain	2.6
U.K.	2.5
Netherlands	2.3
Portugal	2.2
Denmark	2.2
Belgium	2.0
Austria	2.0
Sweden	2.0
France	1.9
Italy	1.6
Germany	1.3
Japan	1.0

Note: Average annual rate of growth for the EU-15 over the period is 1.9%.

Source: Author's calculations using data from: Sachverständigenrat zur Begutachtung der gesamtwirtschaftlichen Entwicklung, *Jahresgutachten 2002/03*, table 3. Updated using forecasts from Arbeitskreis Konjunktur, Grundlinien der Wirtschaftsentwicklung 2003/2004. *DIW Wochenbericht* 1–2/2003, http://www.diw.de/deutsch/publikationen/wochenberichte/docs/03-01.pdf.

professional demographers claim to be able to see. Figure 12.3 reveals the workings of a demographic infernal machine that certainly has the potential to destroy existing unfunded systems of public pensions, health care insurance and insurance for long-term care. Plotted in figure 12.3 are the historical as well as projected number of senior citizens (defined as those 65 years of age and older) and juniors (below the age of 20 years), both relative to the population in the working ages between 20 and 64 years of age. Similar trends are witnessed across the world so it is useful to put the German demographics in a comparative context. At the present time, Germany's senior ratio is higher than 49 of the 50 U.S. states. While one is not surprised that Florida is, statistically speaking, grayer than Germany, most people are surprised to learn that within only a couple of years, the senior ratio in Germany will actually pass that of Florida. These demographic trends pose problems for the sustainability of all systems of social insurance that are funded on a pay-as-you-go basis, that is, the benefits paid out in a calendar period equals the contributions paid in by contributors during the same period. Either social insurance contribution

FIGURE 12.3 Junior and Senior Citizen Ratios (relative to population 20–64 years)

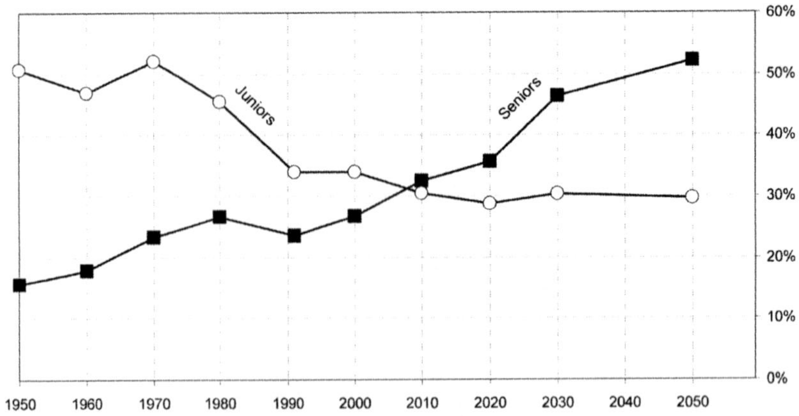

Source: Calculated from data in the ninth coordinated population forecast (Variant 2) as published in table 14 of Sachverständigenrat zur Begutachtung der gesamtwirtschaftlichen Entwicklung, *Jahresgutachten 2002/03*.

rates need to be raised or entitlements cut for beneficiaries in order for such systems to stay in balance, as the ratio of beneficiaries to the population paying into the system gets larger. This demographic trend is of central importance for pensions and long-term care systems and it is an important part of the story for the future development of aggregate health care costs (there is also a medical cost explosion worth worrying about). To the extent that unemployment benefits for older workers continue to be exploited, as a bridge to span the gap between active employment and pension eligibility, bad demographics in the future will add pressure on the unemployment insurance system as well.

While the litany of high unemployment, low growth and unsustainable systems of social insurance is bad enough, it is the interaction of all these problems that makes anything short of a broad fundamental reform of Germany's economic and social institutions unlikely to break the existing bad trends. High unemployment reduces contributions into the pay-as-you-go systems of social insurance. This puts upward pressure on the social contribution rates (figure 12.4), and higher nonwage labor costs help to push up the cost of labor, weakening the demand for German workers. Dismal growth means that the natural increase in the demand for labor derived from the growth of production falls behind the reduction in the demand for labor as a consequence of productivity growth, that is, low growth rates are jobless growth rates. Social entitlements outrunning contributions either push up the nonwage labor costs or force additional government spending to offset the shortfall (requiring budget cuts in

FIGURE 12.4 Social Insurance Rates in Germany (1970–2003)

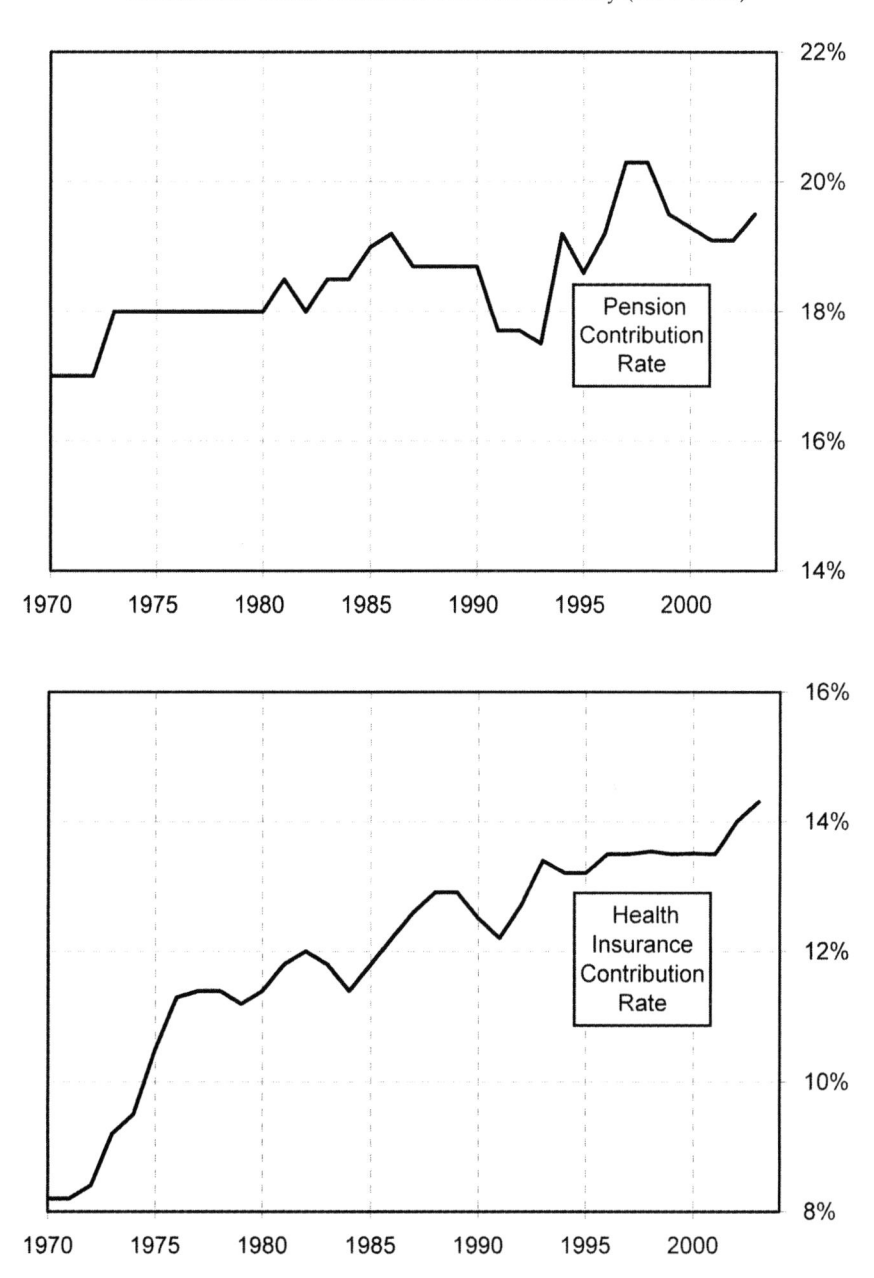

(Continued on next page)

FIGURE 12.4 Social Insurance Rates in Germany (1970–2003) *(cont.)*

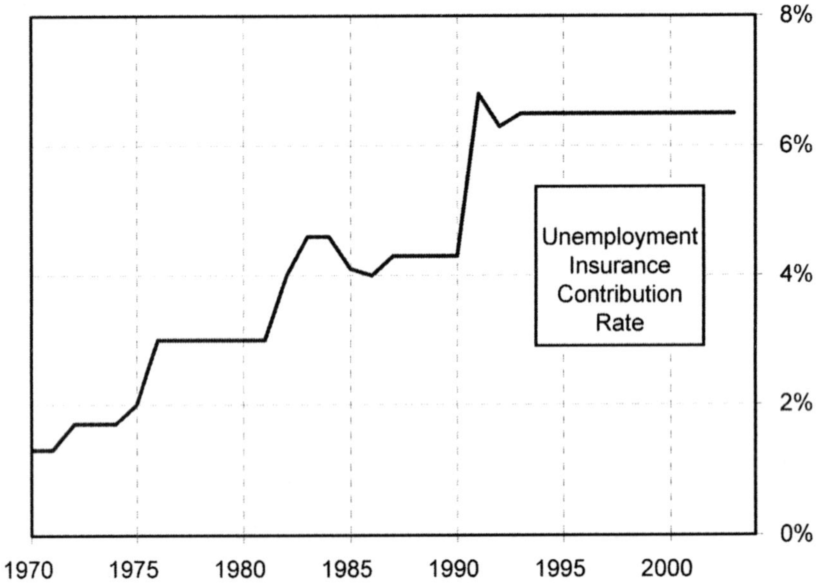

Unemployment Insurance Contribution Rate

Source: Contribution rates for the statutory pension system, public health insurance system and unemployment insurance system from tables 69*, 75*, and 78*, respectively, of Sachverständigenrat zur Begutachtung der gesamtwirtschaftlichen Entwicklung *Jahresgutachten 2002/03*. Current values for the parameters of the social insurance systems are available at http://www.sozialpolitik-aktuell.de/neuregelungen_rechengroessen.shtml.

other programs or tax increases). These last adjustments will simply aggravate unemployment or growth problems, when not both.

Since the 2002 election the unemployment problem has worsened with the number of unemployed expected to average 4.4 million over the first half of the second Schröder term[3] and the sustainability of many of the core social policy institutions of Germany's social-market economy are almost as much as in doubt as when Gerhard Schröder first took office. The Red-Green coalition has found itself in a precarious position regarding the economic policies needed to solve the country's long- and short-term problems: they will be damned by voters sooner if they do (cut and restructure social entitlements) *and* will be damned by voters later if they do not (reduce unemployment).

The Schröder government knows that it needs genuine economic success in the form of a definite break for the better and 2003 has turned into a year of major and minor reforms for the labor market as well as for its pension, health, and long-term care systems. For the German Left, 2003 has been something of an *annus horribilis* as one sacred cow after another has been led to legislative chambers. Bismarck's famous analogy between the making of laws and the making of sausage is no less apt today. The slaughter of a sacred cow is not a pretty sight. This does not spare us the necessity of examining the proposed reforms in order to judge their ultimate contribution to solving Germany's economic problems that will have an impact on Gerhard Schröder's political future and more importantly his historical legacy.

Thinking about Unemployment

Rather than rush into a top-ten list of Gerhard Schröder's labor market reforms, a quick survey of basic labor market theory is useful in providing a framework to help us answer the ultimate question of whether all the changes will really add up to a significant reduction in unemployment. There are two complementary ways of approaching the issue of unemployment. Each captures an important aspect of the labor market. The first approach uses the traditional concepts of supply and demand. Unemployment is seen as the result of having "the" wage too high to clear "the" labor market. The second approach views the labor market as a place where a process of matching individuals (everybody is special) to jobs (no two jobs are exactly alike) takes place. Unemployment comes from the fact that it takes time for those seeking jobs and those hiring to actually find each other.[4] We can consider the Schröder labor market reforms of 2002–2003 by considering their impact on labor demand, labor supply and the matching process, respectively.

While there are die-hard Keynesians of the old school who continue to believe that Germany's unemployment problems are completely independent of the cost of labor and that the high unemployment is solely a matter of an inadequate aggregate demand for goods and services, a glance at figure 12.5 and figure 12.6 reveals that the data do show a definite negative relationship between real wage growth and the demand for labor in the manufacturing sectors of Germany, France and the United States. The real hourly labor compensation indexes computed for these countries from official country data by the U.S. Bureau of Labor Statistics include wage costs and nonwage costs such as social insurance contributions, vacation, and holiday pay and they have been adjusted for changes in the purchasing power of nominal wages using an index of consumer prices.[5] The indexes of hours in manufacturing are shown because they capture the actual volume of labor that is demanded at the hourly real compensation rate seen in figure 12.5. Comparing the two figures with each other, one can appreciate the dilemma of union leaders in France and Germany. They have enough power to negotiate a high real wage growth, but given the high wages, they lack the power to force employers

FIGURE 12.5 Hourly Labor Costs in Manufacturing
(West Germany, France, and the U.S.)

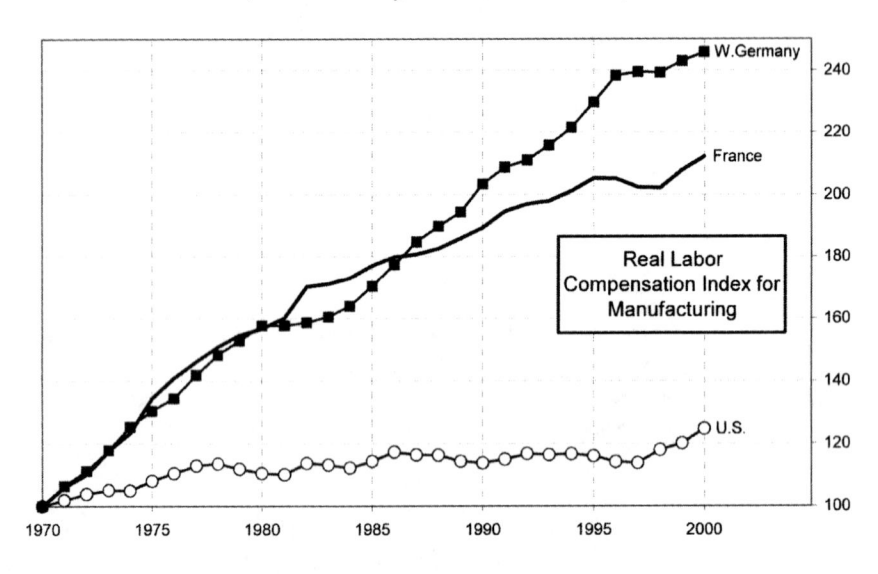

Real Labor Compensation Index for Manufacturing

FIGURE 12.6 Aggregate Hours in Manufacturing
(West Germany, France, and the U.S.)

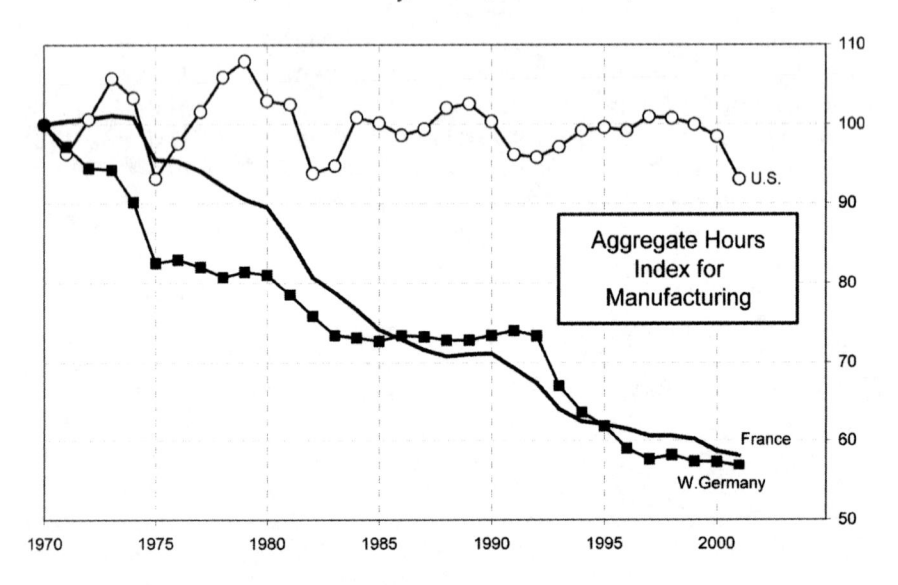

Aggregate Hours Index for Manufacturing

Source: Source of comparable data on aggregate manufacturing hours and hourly compensation index: U.S. Department of Labor, Bureau of Labor Statistics, Foreign Labor Statistics Program, http://www.bls.gov/fls/home.htm.

to maintain, much less expand payrolls. In comparison we see that the slow wage growth in U.S. manufacturing where unions are weak was accompanied by an expansion in the volume of labor employed. High real wage growth in French and German manufacturing and the fall in aggregate hours is not a statistical artifact. One presumes that the unemployed in France and Germany have a preference for labor demand to grow as it has in the United States while the "insiders" with jobs in France and Germany can look back at the real wage increases rather sanguinely—it is nice to still have a well-paid job. The lie that German unions have lived by (*Lebenslüge*) is that their high wages are the purchasing power that guarantees the employment of others. The reality is that their wage policies have played a critical role in the story of why there are not nearly enough jobs to go around. Almost all of the attention in public debate has been limited to the role of nonwage labor costs rather than on the much larger share of total labor costs accounted for by wage costs. It appears that the laws protecting the wage cartels of organized labor and organized associations of employers are one sacred cow that continues to ruminate in peace during the fury of the politics surrounding the Schröder government's Agenda 2010.

The relationship of unemployment and the supply side of the labor market can be illustrated using images of floors and wedges. The fundamental principle of a market economy is that exchange is *voluntary*—people will not work if they do not choose to work and they will not be hired if employers do not choose to hire them. The notion that unemployment is always and everywhere involuntary is an oversimplification that may be warranted when discussing pathological cases such as the Great Depression or for particularly depressed areas in the new states of Germany, but misses much of the reality in normal times, good, and bad. The question for labor supply is what are the options that the unemployed have to choose from?

The "floor" in question is established by the value of time in nonmarket activities (which include paid employment in the "black" economy) and social entitlements that replace lost wages. As the advice columnist might ask "Are you better off with work, or without it?" Even without a statutory minimum wage, there is an effective floor for wages at which employers can effectively hire workers that is in part determined by a country's system of income support for its unemployed. It is impossible to force someone to accept a low-paying job, if they feel it is not a better alternative to some combination of work at home, work in the informal economy and receiving unemployment compensation. Similarly it is equally impossible to force employers to hire people when this effective wage floor exceeds the value of a potential worker's productivity in the new job. Hence, safety nets can stabilize the income of low-skilled unemployed workers while at the same time they destroy the demand for low-productivity workers.

The image of the wedge captures the economic difference between what you see on your gross pay statement with what you get to spend once taxes, social insurance contributions and unemployment or welfare benefits cuts are figured in. Relevant for the employer is the gross number and relevant for the person deciding the value of going to work is what is left over, which because of the partial or total loss of social entitlements upon accepting employment can be considerably smaller than what we normally think of as take-home pay. Consider the extreme case (which is much closer to the reality experienced by low-skilled long-term unemployed than "extreme" might suggest) of a 100 percent implicit tax on market work, i.e., an unemployed worker sees the choice as no job vs. working with no difference in household net income. *Homo faber* might choose to work instead of remaining unemployed, but *homo sapiens* in Germany would choose the safety net. Part of Germany's unemployment problem is that it has allowed a confiscatory implicit tax rate on market work for its unemployed, low-skilled population.

The wedge for a normal working family (one member of the household has an average full-time job in industry, the other earns 33 percent of the average, two children) in several countries can be seen in table 12.1, which is based on OECD calculations, with German data updated by the ifo-Institut in Munich. The table gives the *marginal* burden on labor value-added of taxes and social insurance contributions together so that one is able to compare just how much of a bill for labor service, e.g., for a house painter, succeeds in becoming net income for someone providing that service.[6] The marginal burden of taxes and social insurance contributions in

TABLE 12.1 International Comparison of Shares of Marginal Value-Added by Labor for Taxes, Social Insurance Contributions, and Increase in Worker Income (in percentage)

	Wedge				
	Value-added tax/sales tax	Employer contrib. to social ins.	Employee contrib. to social ins.	Income tax	Net increase in labor earnings
Germany*	13.8	15.0	15.0	22.9	33.3
Sweden	20.0	19.8	4.2	17.0	39.0
Denmark	20.0	7.2	0.0	33.3	39.5
France	17.1	24.2	7.9	10.0	40.8
U.K.	14.9	9.3	7.6	16.7	51.6
U.S.**	5.7	6.7	6.7	19.2	61.7

*West Germany, 2004.
**Detroit, Michigan.
Source: Hans-Werner Sinn, *Ist Deutschland noch zu retten?* (Munich: Econ Verlag, 2003), p. 300), using OECD and ifo-Institute estimates.

Germany puts it at the top of the table, even ahead of Scandinavian countries known for their large public sectors.[7]

The second framework for analyzing unemployment regards people searching for jobs and vacant jobs "searching" for people as a matching problem. Thus, a spell of unemployment is seen to be the time it takes an unemployed worker to search and find (or be found) and policies for reducing unemployment focus on shortening the length of unemployment spells.

The idea that an economy's labor market can be seen as a place where heterogeneous job vacancies are matched to heterogeneous workers seeking new jobs goes back at least to the 1940s when William Beveridge proposed to define full employment for an economy as the state when the number of vacancies slightly exceeds the number of people seeking work. Because of costs to searching for both sides of the labor market, the matching process takes time and unfilled jobs and unemployed workers will coexist at any point in time.

The plausibility of such a definition comes from the memory of signs "We are hiring" at factory gates during times of growing economic prosperity and growing lines of people seeking work or unemployment benefits at the local labor office during times of recession or depression.[8] More important for understanding much of the labor market reform discussion in Germany is the implicit inverse relationship suggested in this definition between the number of jobs seeking workers and the number of workers seeking jobs. Plotting job vacancy rates together with unemployment rates on a graph, economists have named the pattern they observe a "Beveridge Curve."

When one looks at the data on vacancy rates and unemployment rates in Germany (figure 12.7), it is clear that the reality is more complex. Connecting the annual dots, one discovers a series of "Beveridge Loops" rather than a simple Beveridge Curve with a strong and simple inverse relationship between the two rates. Fortunately one does not have to torture this data too hard to have it tell us a tale involving at least three different Beveridge Curves: 1976–1984, 1985–1994, and 1997–2000. The movements down and to the right along any given Beveridge Curve occur during an economic downturn when we observe more unemployed workers chasing fewer unfilled vacancies, whereas movements up and to the left take place during an economic expansion with more unfilled vacancies chasing fewer unemployed. What is overlooked in the simplest formulation of the Beveridge Curve is (1) that structural change in the economy could increase the mismatch between those out of work and the growing new industries seeking workers with significantly different skills and training; and (2) institutions of social insurance that provide income support for longer periods and at a higher levels generate incentives to take longer to look for work and hope for better alternatives. Either or both stories would be sufficient to explain the outward drift of the German Beveridge Curve.

FIGURE 12.7 Beveridge Curve in Germany (1976–2002)

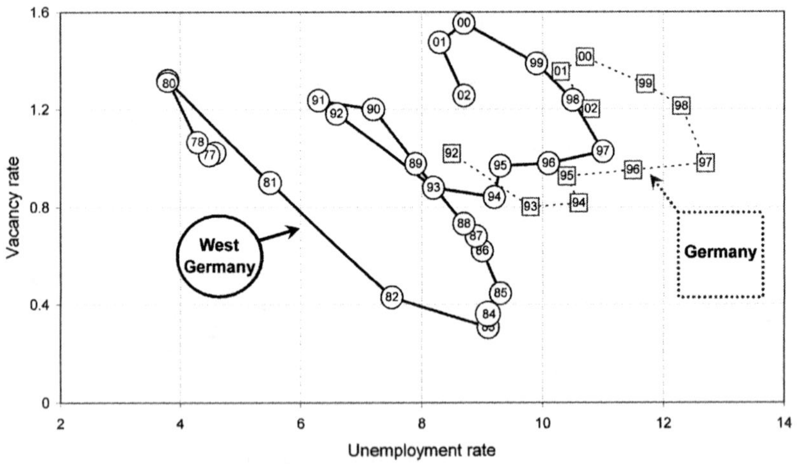

Source: Data, Federal Labor Office (Bundesanstalt für Arbeit); stock of job vacancies (*Bestand an gemeldeten Stellen*), http://www.pub.arbeitsamt.de/hst/services/statistik/aktuell/iiia4/zr_stellen_ab_1976b.xls; unemployment rates (*Registrierte Arbeitslose*), http://www.pub.arbeitsamt.de/hst/services/statistik/aktuell/iiia4/zr_alo_qu_west_ostb.xls.

Note: The vacancy rate was obtained by dividing the published stock of job vacancies by the number of non-self-employed workforce (*abhängige Erwerbspersonen*). The non-self-employed workforce is the denominator for the unemployment rate. Thus, the non-self-employed workforce for the vacancy rate was calculated by dividing the published unemployment rate into the number of registered employed in the table cited above.

Something else that we see from the figure 12.7 is that adding the East German post-Wall labor market to the story of the Beveridge Curve does not really change the qualitative movements along the Beveridge Curve. However, unification (unsurprisingly) added an extra rightward shift to the relationship on top of the large shifts that occurred over the fifteen years before unification and the shift observed in West Germany during the decade of the 1990s.

About Face, Forward March

Considering that the first Schröder government began business by undoing relatively modest economic reforms that had been passed during the last years of the Kohl era, the shift into high gear with respect to economic reform going into the second Red-Green government becomes all the more remarkable.[9,10] Even the timid Riester reform of 2001 that brought the beginnings of government supported individual retirement accounts only managed to take a relatively simple concept (some of your saving now for retirement would be subsidized) and added enough layers of regulation to turn a surefire retirement product into a less than popular way to save. In short, at the beginning of 2002 nobody really expected a reform year like 2003 from a government that seemed to think that all Germany really needed was a crackdown on "pseudo-self-employment" (that is, the subcontracting of work to people who are formally self-employed but only working for a single client) in the interest of keeping businesses and individuals from working around the statutory systems of social insurance to avoid paying contributions.

But that was all before a Federal Accounting Office report to the Federal Ministry of Labor in January 2002 in which five employment offices under suspicion had been found to have falsely or incorrectly reported job placements in 70 percent of 5,100 cases. Even the most cynical critics of government waste were shocked at the degree of the misreporting. No wonder Germany was suffering such high unemployment when clerks in the labor offices are able to overcook the books like this! It was of no matter that the little tail of the Federal Labor Office was not wagging the big dog of unemployment. This scandal forced Gerhard Schröder's reform hand at the start of his re-election year.

If voters could not be shown evidence of a turnaround in the German labor market in 2002, it was at least necessary to offer a promise of coming full-employment attractions. Given the utter failure of roundtables such as the unsuccessful Alliance for Jobs to rise above the level of a heated *Stammtisch* debate of regulars in the neighborhood pub, the Schröder government sought refuge in a blue-ribbon commission.

The Hartz Commission

The 15-member Commission for the Reduction of Unemployment and the Reorganization of the Federal Labor Office was constituted on 22 February 2002 under the chairmanship of Dr. Peter Hartz, Labor Director on the Board of Management of Volkswagen. The commission included management consultants, company human resource managers, union and employer association representatives, communal politicians, and a couple of academics. Unlike the Rürup Commission that would be named at the end of the year to prepare reform proposals for the social insurance system, the Hartz Commission charged into the economic reform fray without the benefit of a single professional economist which helps to explain that the final report presented in August 2002 was as far from being dismal as it was from being scientific. The early claims of the commission that its proposals could reduce unemployment by two million people by the end of 2005 seem rather absurd with the advantage of hindsight one year later. Going into the final month of the 2002 federal election, the promise of the Hartz Commission reform proposals seemed merely incredible.

The 13 modules of the final report of the Hartz commission were primarily designed to transform a government bureaucracy that processed unemployment claims and administered the unemployed into a new kind of public service agency committed to the reduction in the time it takes to match a person looking for work to a job. Part of the accelerated matching would come about from requiring advanced notice of impending cases of unemployment to be given to the local labor offices so that job placement activity could be initiated before a spell of unemployment would even begin and early filing requirements imposed upon the unemployed themselves. Another part of the accelerated matching would be the result of proposed simplifications in procedures that would release more of the 90,000 employees of the Federal Labor Office from routine administrative tasks so they too would be available for helping the unemployed find jobs. Yet the overwhelming impression one takes away from a reading of the Hartz Commission's detailed proposals for the implementation of this structural transformation of low-keyed paper shufflers into dynamic headhunters in the service of the unemployed is that management consultants are actually worse than their reputation.[11]

While the mandate for the Hartz Commission was mostly limited to the organizational restructuring of the Federal Labor Office, some of its final recommendations in fact go beyond proposals to improve its core function of finding jobs for the unemployed to include proposals to expand opportunities for work free of the scent of public make-work projects. Personal Service Agencies as independent units in the new JobCenters are to become active in the market for temp jobs.[12] Mini-jobs with reduced social insurance contributions are seen to serve the dual purpose of bringing some unreported jobs out of the shadows and creating new jobs in an expanded low-wage sector. The *Ich-AG* program (roughly "Me, Myself & I(nc)") is to provide a supported entry into small-time self-employment as an option for the unemployed.[13]

The consolidation of unemployment assistance for the long-term unemployed with public assistance for able-bodied persons in working age has turned out to be one of the more controversial recommendations of the Hartz Commission because it involves the reduction of unemployment assistance to the lower public assistance benefits. Also controversial are recommendations for making it increasingly costly for recipients of unemployment benefits to refuse an offer of work judged suitable for them.[14] It could even turn out that reducing the size of the unemployment benefit for the long-term unemployed (a key element of the income floor discussed above) and the toughening of the sanctions for noncompliance could make a significant difference in the labor market choices made by the unemployed.

Contemplating the rightward drift of the Beveridge Curve in figure 12.7, it was perhaps only natural to dream of pushing it back in a grand act of labor market reform (i.e., for the same number of vacancies having fewer unemployed). The Hartz reforms have been sold as a package that is in effect supposed to shift the Beveridge relationship back to where it was some twenty years ago. There are plenty of good reasons for transforming the Federal Labor Office from a government agency that exists "to administer the unemployed" (matching them to their unemployment entitlements) into a public service agency that provides the service of job placement. However, expecting to achieve a substantial reduction in unemployment through an administrative reform of the Federal Labor Office is like having a director of a cruise ship with 80 percent widows and 20 percent widowers who thinks that the way to get many more couples dancing would be to keep widowers in close proximity to the dance floor. Germany has a problem with a shortage of job vacancies relative to the demand for jobs by the unemployed. Most of the Hartz reforms promise little more than a more effective way to manage that shortage.

The Hartz Commission helped Gerhard Schröder defuse the scandal in the Federal Labor Office in time for his re-election and it helps us mark a turning point in the reform rhetoric of the Schröder government. It also provided a model for the Greens who extracted a concession for their willingness to sign off on the increase in the contribution rate for the statutory pension system that their SPD coalition partners badly wanted: there would be a new blue-ribbon commission, one that would recommend reforms needed for the financial sustainability of the social insurance system.[15]

The Rürup Commission

On 21 November, the 26 members of the Commission for the Financial Sustainability of the Social Security Systems were officially named by Minister for Health and Social Security Ulla Schmidt.[16] Professor Bert Rürup, an expert on the economics of pensions (not infrequently referred to as the "Pension Pope" by the German press) and a member of the Council of German Economic Experts, was appointed the chair of the new commission. In addition to several academic heavyweights in the fields of public finance and social policy, the Rürup Commission had ample representation of members from the governmental-social complex and union representatives such as the outspoken Dr. Ursula Engelen-Kefer, deputy chair of the DGB. Conspicuously excluded were representatives from associations of health providers. The Commission first met officially on 13 December 2002 and was originally expected to deliver its final report to the government in October 2003.[17]

The mixture of policy positions brought into the Rürup Commission by its members was extremely volatile from the start. In less than one month from its first meeting Rürup had to publicly scold a few of his fellow commission members for talking out of school.[18] The next months would be far worse when leaks to the press from the Rürup Commission began to upstage the chancellor's efforts to set his own reform agenda. At the end of March 2003 Gerhard Schröder lost his patience with the Commission (it was not his child after all) and explicitly threatened to disband it if the members continued to debate in public directly or indirectly before their report was complete.

In late April 2003 the commission presented an interim set of recommendations which included a proposal to begin increasing the retirement system's "normal retirement age" from age 65 to age 67 in one month increments beginning in 2011. This would be one of two key elements in stabilizing the pension contribution rate in 2030 at a level of no more than 22 percent. The Commission was able to justify this step as matching the expected increase in the longevity of the population over the same period of time. The second element is a so-called sustainability factor added to the pension index formula to adjust future pension increases (downward!) for adverse changes in the age composition of the population as well as for changes in labor force participation. The bottom line for pensions and contribution rates from the combined impact of these changes along with the maximum use of the Riester pension accounts assumed by the Rürup Commission can be seen in table 12.2.

The calculations of the Rürup Commission indicate just how difficult it turns out to be to get nonwage labor costs back under control once things have taken a dramatic demographic turn for the worse. At the present time the joint employer-employee contribution rate for someone with average earnings of 2,435 euros per month (gross) is 19.5 percent. The so-called standard pensioner who has worked 45 years and earned exactly the average of all covered employees in each of those 45 years is 1,170 euros per month which is equal to 48 percent of that average monthly paycheck of average employees paying into the pension system now.

The Rürup Commission has assumed full participation in the Riester pension reform by everyone. Furthermore, by increasing the working life of the cohort that retires in 2030 by 1.7 years, a combination of a public pension from the Rürup reformed system together with a private Riester pension would result in retirement income equal to 48.1 percent of the forecasted average gross monthly labor income of covered employees in 2030. So from the point of view of the relative position of the newly retired household in 2030, things would look much like they do to the newly retired pensioner in 2003.[19]

We can see from table 12.2 that there would be a 4.7 percentage point increase in the contribution rate forecast from a simple scenario of keeping the current system as it is in 2003, subject to the constraint of the balance between revenues and expenditures that characterizes the pay-as-you-go system. If the Rürup Commission's recommendations that the working years be extended and the sustainability factor be included in calculating future pension increases are both implemented, the increase in nonwage labor costs accounted for by pension contributions will increase only 2.5

TABLE 12.2 Pension Reform Scenarios à la Rürup

	2003	2030
Pension contribution rates		
Current law	19.5%	24.2%
Reform Scenario	19.5%	22.0%
adding to reform scenario		
4% Gross Riester pension contribution	23.5%	26.0%
2.8% Net Riester pension contribution (after subsidy)	22.3%	24.8%
Standard monthly pensions		
(in constant prices of 2003)		
Current law (45 years of contributions)	1,170 €	1,496 €
Reform Scenario (45 years of contributions)		1,429 €
Reform Scenario (46.7 years of contributions)		1,482 €
Riester pension		233 €
Total retirement income =		1,715 €
Pension from 46.7 years + Riester pension from 4% contribution		
Gross Relative Pension Ratios		
(standard monthly pensions divided by		
average gross monthly labor income)		
Current law	48%	41.9%
Reform Scenario (45 years of contributions)		40.1%
Total: More working years + Riester pension		41.6%
Reform Scenario (46.7 years of contributions)		48.1%
Average gross monthly labor income		
(at prices of 2003)	2,435 €	3,567 €

Source: Bundesministerium für Gesundheit und Soziale Sicherung, *Nachhaltigkeit in der Finanzierung der Sozialen Sicherungssysteme. Bericht der Kommission*, Berlin, August 2003.
Note: Estimates are for an insured employee receiving average earnings in every working year.

percentage points. This is just over half of the increase for a continuation of the status quo rules.

The 2.2 percent difference (i.e., 4.7 percent increase without Rürup reforms less 2.5 percent increase with Rürup reforms) can be decomposed as follows: the sustainability factor in calculating the size of future pension increases accounts for 1.4 percent of the difference, the increase in the notional retirement age of 67 accounts for another 0.6 percent, and the proposed shift of pension increases from 1 July to 1 January of the following year is worth 0.2 percent.

A forty-year-old with average earnings reading the Rürup Commission's report whose goal is to have a pension equal to slightly half of average labor earnings in 2030 will have to start putting 4 percent of labor earnings aside for the Riester pension quite independent of whether all the pension recommendations of the Rürup Commission are carried out or not. Expressed in terms of intergenerational burdens, the 2.2 percentage point reduction of nonwage labor costs for the active generation in 2030 will cost our average forty-year old worker 1.7 years of working to a later retirement. This is not really the stuff of a senseless demolition of the social market economy, though one would hardly guess it judging from the reaction of the union representatives in the Rürup Commission who refused to sign off on the recommendations.

The Rürup Commission was not even able to come to a majority opinion on the issue of health insurance reform. In the end the Commission proposed two competing models of reform for the political system to choose from. The first model, called a citizens' insurance (*Bürgerversicherung*), was the brainchild of the health economist Professor Karl Lauterbach, a member of the Council of Health Experts and trusted advisor to Minister Ulla Schmidt. The proposed citizens' insurance would involve an expansion of the present statutory health insurance system to absorb the career civil service and self-employed who would be compelled to join the wage and salary employees currently in the system. Furthermore health insurance premiums would be assessed on rental and interest income as well as on labor income. The ability to opt out of the statutory health insurance system to obtain private insurance at a sufficiently high income would be abolished. Rürup favored the second model, the flat-rate insurance premium with redistributive corrections through the tax system to prevent economic inequities. Under the first model, the health insurance portion of the wedge between gross and net labor income would become smaller and grow more slowly over time whereas the second model would eliminate that portion of the wedge with health insurance contributions not influencing on the margin decisions to work or to hire.

Which of the two models will be closer to the course actually attempted by the Red-Green coalition remains to be seen. With the experts divided, policymakers have little choice but to trust their political instincts. A "citizens' insurance" has a natural ring to it that appeals to the vast majority of Red-Green voters without even getting into details. It promises what appears to be equality: no special treatment for the career civil service and no escape into private health care for those with very high incomes or the self-employed. It promises what appears to be solidarity: not just labor income up to the present level but income from assets and higher labor incomes would become subject to health insurance contributions. And perhaps most important, it is recognizable to everyone inside and outside of the current system. With regard to the problem of the upward creep of nonwage labor costs, the citizens' insurance proposal promises only temporary relief at best. The bad demographic trend will reassert itself later with rising contribution rates on labor income again becoming a problem.

The competing proposal of flat-rate health insurance premiums with adjustments in the income tax system to prevent unwanted distributive consequences is at a competitive disadvantage in several ways. The trouble with this model is that it combines the disadvantage of a clumsy name (*System pauschaler Gesundheitsprämien mit steuerfinanziertem Einkommensausgleich*) with unfamiliarity. It is almost as though the economic engineers never thought of consulting with artistic social designers to create a social insurance product that functions, attractively fits with the other social policy "appliances" and is user-friendly. This is a pity, since the Rürup proposal represents a bold way of eliminating the wedge of health insurance contributions in labor costs altogether. It also would signify an equally audacious shift in social policy that would attempt to separate the issue of income distribution from issues of an allocative nature.[20] However, one knows from the example of the negative income tax that it can take a long time for the work of academic scribblers to be accepted in the polite company of those who actually decide policy.

The ultimate choice between these two long-term health insurance reform proposals is like the ultimate choice on the normal age of retirement, both are decisions that will have little impact on the course of unemployment over the next five years. To win the 2006 Bundestag elections, Gerhard Schröder will need to worry more about reviving the German labor market. Sustainability is good, electability is better.

Agenda 2010

The Agenda 2010 was announced by Gerhard Schröder in his speech before the Bundestag on 14 March 2003. The agenda is a package of policy proposals aimed at achieving full employment by the end of the first decade of the twenty-first century, reviving economic growth and re-establishing financial sustainability for social insurance institutions. A few months later the SPD signed off on the Agenda 2010 at its June party conference with 90 percent of the delegates approving the resolution.[21] Because of the enormous public attention given both the Hartz and Rürup Commissions, there were few surprises in the reform measures found in the Schröder reform agenda. And yet it has become clear, as its parts have been molded into legislation that the whole of the Agenda 2010 marks the beginning of a serious willingness to redefine the German social market economy.

Reduction in the Duration of Unemployment Compensation Benefits

One important deviation from the Hartz proposals is that Agenda 2010 included a significant reduction in the duration for the full unemployment benefit. There is widespread agreement among economists that an entitlement to a long duration of unemployment compensation will have an impact on the intensity of job search and the willingness of an unemployed person to accept a job offer. For these reasons the duration of full unemployment benefits (unemployment compensation) is being significantly reduced to a maximum of twelve months (exception: workers above the age of 55 will be eligible for a longer duration of 18 months).[22] This change reverses a trend that began in the mid-1980s that eventually led to a 32-month entitlement for unemployment compensation for a 57 year old. Many businesses were able to exploit this long benefit duration to work out early retirement packages that enabled them to shed older employees with the unemployment insurance system "sharing" in the cost of the early retirement package.

Consolidation of Long-Term Unemployment Assistance with Public Assistance

Unemployment compensation serves as the first line of defense for falling household income in the event of unemployment, providing benefits (60–67 percent of last net pay) that permit a smoothing of a household's consumption. The second line of defense in Germany after unemployment compensation is exhausted has been a secondary unemployment benefit, unemployment assistance, which is lower than the unemployment compensation (unemployment assistance is 53–57 percent of last net pay) though higher than public assistance. Like public assistance, unemployment assistance has been means-tested and is of unlimited duration. Both public assistance and unemployment assistance function as safety nets to catch the long-term unemployed. The essential difference has been that unemployment assistance was the net for recipients of unemployment compensation to fall into once they had exhausted their benefits, whereas public assistance remains the lowest social safety net to catch everyone else. From a functional standpoint this distinction has separated people of working age and capable of work into those reporting to the local employment offices (where job placement, training, advice was provided) and those reporting to the welfare office which can only refer clients to the employment offices for placement assistance. From a fiscal standpoint the unemployment assistance benefits were paid from the unemployment insurance system (responsibility of the federal level of government) and the public assistance benefits were paid for by local governments so consolidation of the two programs has significant implications for the division of social responsibilities in the German federal system as well.

The consolidation of unemployment assistance and public assistance for all able-bodied people in working age paying a benefit equal to that of public assistance has been designated "unemployment compensation II." One presumes the name of the previously higher paying benefit was chosen to paper over the de facto reduction in benefits entailed for recipients. In addition unemployment compensation II would come with stricter sanctions for the refusal to accept a job placement from the employment office. Reasonable exemptions are to be granted for retirement assets or owner-occupied housing in determining eligibility for the unemployment compensation II to avoid creating unwanted disincentives for saving. Limits to allowable labor earnings not subject to automatic benefit reductions are also to be expanded so as not to undermine incentives for accepting minor work.

This reduction in the unemployment benefit for the long-term unemployed together with a strengthening of sanctions for refusal to accept a job placement constitute an even greater change in the terms on which unemployed can be hired than the reduction in the duration of unemployment compensation. Should experience prove that the resulting labor incomes are such as to result in a working poor, then we can expect the scholarly discussion on wage-subsidies to finally spill over into further labor market reform.[23]

Employment Protection

This item provided Gerhard Schröder some embarrassment since it forced him to admit that his government had made a mistake in reversing the Kohl government's relaxation of the employment protection laws for small businesses (those between six and ten employees). By reintroducing the old threshold for the full application of employment security laws to five employees, an enormous barrier for a business with fewer than five employees to expand had been put back in place. Should such a small company hire enough to have even one new employee above this threshold, the entire force of employment protection laws would apply to all employees, both old and new.[24] The proposal in the Agenda 2010 is to make this threshold more gradual so that the hiring of a couple of workers on fixed-term contracts would not immediately have consequences for the contract terms of the employees already there.

A reduction in the list of social criteria to govern the selection of employees for discharge when staff reductions become unavoidable will make it easier for businesses to keep younger and/or high performance employees on the payroll during hard times for the firm. Also measures are being introduced to help avoid the necessity of going to a labor court when someone is dismissed from a job through established procedures for severance pay in lieu of legal redress. To the extent that these reforms actually help to reduce the costs of adjustment of a firm's workforce to changing conditions, we can expect a greater willingness to hire new people. It would be wrong however to underestimate the ability of the labor courts and labor lawyers to protect the inflexible status quo here.

Long-Term Unemployed

For structurally disadvantaged regions (i.e., particularly for most of the new states), public works programs in those regions will be continued. The Agenda 2010 established a large-scale program in which federal and local levels are to cooperate in creating public works jobs for the long-term unemployed that will include opportunities for retraining.[25] The program which will run through the summer of 2005 is expected to support about 100,000 long-term unemployed over the age of twenty-five.

This item in the Agenda 2010 amounts to little more than a meager bone thrown to the eastern states. In fact voices in the East are becoming louder that national policymakers are yet again failing to address the specific circumstances of East German unemployment. In a recent interview Saxony's premier, Georg Milbradt, provided a disturbing assessment of what the Schröder reforms really mean for the eastern states:

> The most you can say for Hartz reforms up to now is that they are good for the sunny day problems of the West. They don't address the special situation in the East of significantly higher structural unemployment and structural job shortages. Cutting unemployment assistance, which is paid for by the federal government, to the level of public assistance is a pure fiscal operation. The federal government will save money but that doesn't create a single job in the East. This has to be changed. Incidentally, the federal government is going to pay itself a larger share of turnover taxes as compensation for consolidating public assistance and unemployment assistance. It will actually come out ahead in the deal. The federal government will be pulling more money out of the East than it will be saving the local governments here in public assistance. In the East there are many recipients of unemployment assistance and few people receiving public assistance relative to the West. So East Germany would be forced to take a double hit from the current Hartz reforms.[26]

Pensions

The Rürup Commission's recommendation for the introduction of a sustainability factor in determining future pension entitlements (i.e., lowering future pension entitlements in the interest of preventing an explosive increase of contribution rates paid by future working generations) was included in the Agenda 2010 passed by the SPD party conference. However, the Schröder government has backed away from the commission's recommendation to increase the normal retirement age for the statutory pension system to 67 years. Instead the Red-Green coalition will look for ways to increase the effective age of retirement to bring it in line with the current normal retirement age of sixty-five.[27]

Miscellaneous Other Measures

Liberalization of master craftsman regulations. Earlier in 2003 the government approved a plan that would abolish the mandatory apprenticeship and master craftsman certification in 65 skilled trades. Previously a journeyman who did not have the master craftsman certificate was not allowed to set up an independent shop. This liberalization is limited to skilled trades such as tailoring or tile laying where no issue of public safety could be put forward for the restriction.[28] These changes have a symbolic importance that go beyond their actual economic impact. Preindustrial institutional remnants in a post-industrial economy are quaint in the way trolleys in San Francisco are quaint. However, the master craftsman regulations serve no purpose other than the restriction of supply of services to protect the incomes of the master craftsmen, and they need to yield the right of way to competition in markets for goods and services.

Vocational training. Should German business collectively not offer sufficient opportunities for young people to enroll in apprenticeship training, a fine is being considered for those companies lacking apprenticeship programs. The Schröder government hopes that this can be organized through the skilled trade associations but failing a satisfactory result, legislation is threatened. While this sounds like a measure to combat youth unemployment pre-emptively, it is more likely just a sop for the left wing of the SPD to show that the government is as willing to stick it to businesses as it is to the long-term unemployed.

Sick pay. The insurance costs for sick pay beginning in the seventh week of illness will be shifted to the employee entirely, resulting in a saving for the employer. This change will result in a 0.4 percent increase in the health insurance payment for employees participating in the statutory health care system. One of the difficulties in cutting back on the benefits provided by the statutory health insurance system is identifying blocks of benefits that are not intricately part of the core of basic health services. Since this benefit has nothing to do with health care per se, it was easy to isolate from the health insurance system.

Tax reductions. The planned third stage of tax cuts originally planned for 2005 are to be moved forward to 2004. As a result the initial income tax rate would decrease from 19.9 percent to 15 percent while the top rate would decrease from 48.5 percent to 42 percent. Altogether the tax cuts are estimated to increase household disposable income by 21.8 billion euros. To minimize the budgetary impact of the tax cut the government plans to also significantly cut subsidies paid to businesses and through the privatization of government-held properties.

Having discussed fiscal issues in the long-term context of the sustainability of the social security system, the East/West implications of the consolidated unemployment compensation II, and tax reform, now is a good time to consider the macroeconomic context of Schröder's economic reforms.

Traditional Monetary and Fiscal Policy Instruments: Locked Away, Not Helping Economic Reform

Germany's slide into disappointing economic performance had begun long before the Delors road map to European monetary union was agreed upon in 1989 so that losing the DM (or gaining the euro) is clearly not the root cause of most of the country's economic problems.[29] However, the loss of an independent German central bank and the addition of significant fiscal policy constraints as enshrined in the Growth and Stability Pact mean that Germany has lost a capacity for demand management that could be of considerable political use in reducing some of the unavoidable pain involved in the implementation of the labor market reforms of Agenda 2010. The problem facing the Schröder government is that the vast majority of reforms promise positive impacts that only unfold over a considerable number of years, whereas the immediate costs—for example, of a reduction in the old unemployment assistance to the new Unemployment Assistance II—need no time for their pain to be felt by those whose social entitlements have been cut. A deliberate and coordinated use of monetary and fiscal expansion that would result in a strong surge in labor demand is ruled out by the charter of the European Central Bank as well as by the deficit and debt criteria of the Stabilization and Growth Pact.[30]

In its most recent *World Economic Outlook* (September 2003), the International Monetary Fund warned of a genuine possibility that Germany could find itself in a Japanese-style deflation. Implicit in that warning was less a direct criticism of Germany than of the European Central Bank's monetary policy and of the general fiscal tightness throughout the euro area. Figure 12.8 shows the direction of monetary and fiscal policy changes for years immediately preceding Schröder's re-election for Germany and in several other advanced industrial countries. Points to the lower left indicate an expansionary impulse coming from both fiscal and monetary policies and points to the upper right indicate a more restrictive combination of macroeconomic policies. From figure 12.8 we can see that during the second half of the first Schröder government large and significant expansionary impulses from fiscal and monetary policies were taking place in the United States and the United Kingdom whereas for the entire euro area in general and for Germany in particular, fiscal and monetary policies were tighter, indeed resembling those of Japan. IMF forecasts of changes in the structural fiscal balance for 2003 compared to 2002 indicate during the first year of the Gerhard Schröder second term there was still too little help from monetary and fiscal policies to support economic expansion.

Fiscal and monetary policies can work together in the same direction or they can work at cross purposes (with respect to stimulating the level of economic activity and reducing unemployment). Unfortunately for the unemployed, there was not even the trace of a policy mix in which monetary easing by the ECB might have (over-)compensated the missing fiscal stimulus.

In Germany such views are not shared by many or indeed by most leading economists. Sinn in one of his many *obiter dicta* sprinkled throughout a quite excellent book claims that Germany's employment woes are 85 percent supply side and only 15 percent demand-side related.[31] While

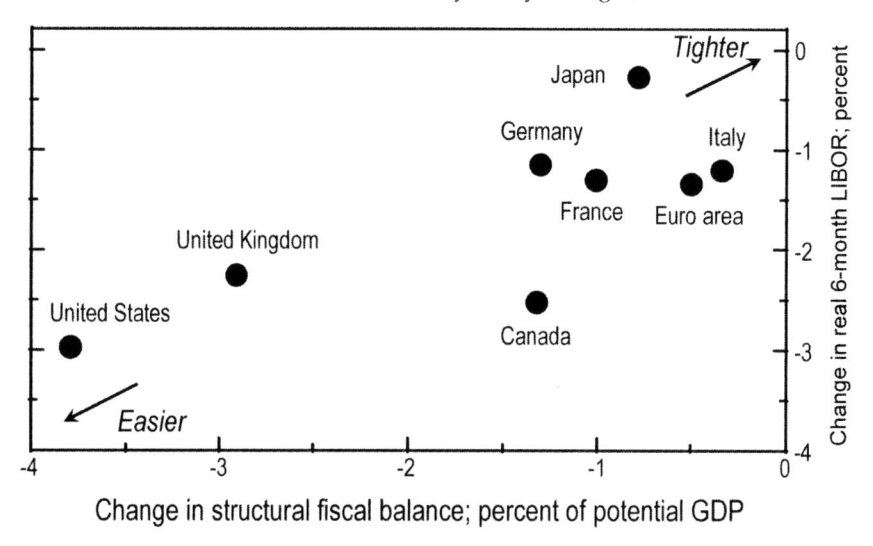

FIGURE 12.8 Fiscal and Monetary Policy Changes, 2000–2002

Change in structural fiscal balance; percent of potential GDP

Source: International Monetary Fund, *World Economic Report*, September 2003, p. 5, http://www.imf.org/external/pubs/ft/weo/2003/02/index.htm.

Note: Because tax revenues rise and fall with the ups and downs of the business cycle, whereas transfer payments from the government to individuals move in the opposite direction, changes in government budget deficits that we actually observe can confound changes in the underlying fiscal policies with changes in the fiscal balances induced by changes in the level of economic activity. Thus, economists attempt to gauge the direction of changes in fiscal policy by estimating the magnitude of changes in government budget balance were the economy at its potential output and such fiscal policy changes had been undertaken.

The *structural fiscal balance* is expressed as a percent of potential GDP to adjust for the underlying trend rate of economic growth that would cause the absolute size of the structural fiscal deficit or surplus to change without any change in the fiscal policies themselves. A movement to the left in figure 12.8 means a net expansionary fiscal impulse has been given to aggregate demand through tax reductions and/or increases in government spending (either on goods and services or on income transfers). Points to the right in the figure indicate less expansionary or even contractionary changes in fiscal policies.

Along the vertical axis of figure 12.8 we can see the change in the real six-month London Interbank Offer Rate (LIBOR). This is an average of the interest rates that major international banks charge each other to borrow U.S. dollars in the London money market and it responds quickly to the changes in the very short-term interest rates that central banks are able to determine.

the general point can be easily granted as valid (it is why this point is discussed *after* the discussion of labor market reform), it hardly follows that the government should feel itself constrained to fighting on the supply side of the labor market alone. Granting the 85:15 split, a reduction of the number of unemployed by some six to seven hundred thousand is hardly peanuts in terms of lost income and output and still worth our attention. In terms of an impact on a close election, a reduction of unemployment of this magnitude might even make the difference between winning and losing.

Independent of the issue of whether Germany should even consider expansionary macroeconomic policies to flank its economic reform agenda is the mundane question of whether the country irrevocably lost its ability to target macroeconomic policies anyway, once it agreed to surrender its DM for the euro. While monetary policy *for Germany* has indeed been irrevocably lost, Gerhard Schröder has discovered some elbowroom for fiscal policy. The monetary policy made by the European Central Bank in Frankfurt still matters for Germany, just as sun and rain matter for farmers.

The United States Federal Reserve and the European Central Bank have quite different philosophies of monetary policy as reflected in both their formal charters and in the actual implementation of monetary policy we have witnessed. The ECB sees itself (as it sees all other central banks) as solely capable of stabilizing low inflation rates with everything else being an unwarranted distraction from that task. One of the contributions of the monetarist critique of earlier forms of Keynesian policy activism was to show that gyrations in monetary policy themselves can contribute to economic instability, much as a beginning driver tends to oversteer. The problem comes when this macroeconomic insight becomes exalted to dogma much as when the microeconomic policy presumption of respecting market mechanisms is raised to a doctrine of pure laissez-faire. Thus, we have Germany riding in a monetary boat that may only be rocked for the purpose of inflation stabilization—and then only gradually.[32]

The Greenspan Federal Reserve is rather typical for the postwar Fed with an understanding of itself having a mandate to support the health of the economy in a broad sense and not being limited to a goal of a particular low rate of inflation. While illusions of having a capacity for fine-tuning the macroeconomy have been long destroyed by the valid core of the monetarist critique, there nonetheless remains in the Board of Governors of the Federal Reserve an American "ruleless" pragmatism.

These philosophical and institutional differences can be easily seen in figure 12.9 that compares the history of the very short-term interest rates that these two central banks are able to set or control quite precisely. What are positively striking are the *timing*, the *size* and the *swiftness* of the interest rate cuts engineered by the Greenspan Fed during 2001 to offset a weakening in the real economy feared to follow the bursting of the stock market bubble in the previous year. We see that the Fed struck almost a *half-year* before the ECB began to reverse its previous interest rate increases. Within a single year (2001) it brought down the Federal Funds rate about *twice* as far as the ECB was to reduce its refinancing rate in *two years*, once it began to bring European interest rates down.

For the Schröder government it is abundantly clear that the dance between European monetary and fiscal partners will continue to be one in which the ECB leads, even dancing to a different tune. If Gerhard Schröder

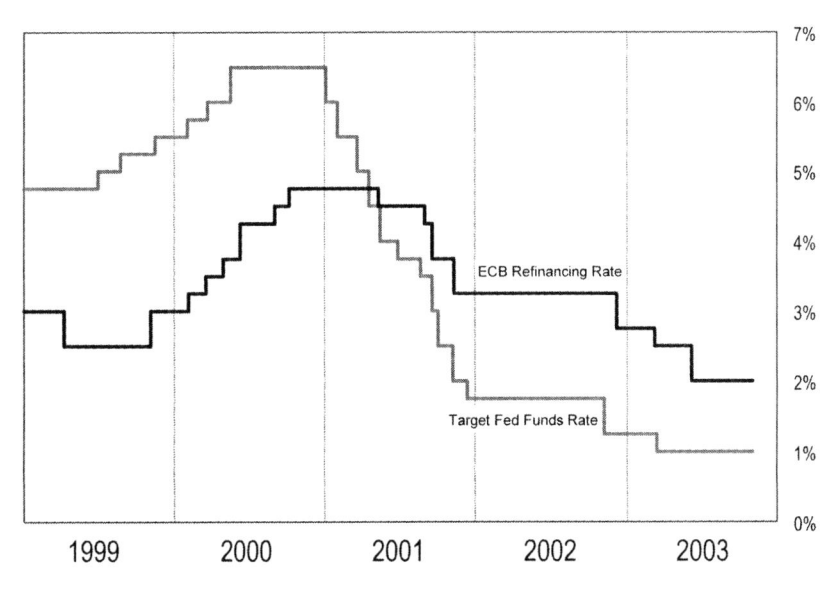

FIGURE 12.9 Very Short-Term Interest Rates: The Fed vs. the ECB

Source: Board of Governors, U.S. Federal Reserve. Targeted federal fund rate, http://www.federalreserve.gov/fomc/fundsrate.htm. European Central Bank.

Note: Rates are reported for fixed rate tenders through June 2000, after which time the minimum bid for variable rate tenders is reported, http://www.ecb.de/home/ecbinterestrates.htm..

and other euro area leaders involved in the reform of their labor markets and social welfare systems seek a way to stimulate aggregate demand, then their best bet is to be found in reforming, reinterpreting or simply defying the current restrictions of the Growth and Stability Pact.

Before examining the adverse impact of the strict interpretation and enforcement of the deficit and debt criteria of the Growth and Stability Pact, we need to remind ourselves of the legitimate intention behind having a stability pact at all that puts constraints on the acceptable sizes of public budget deficits and debt levels of the member countries of "Euroland." Episodes of high and explosive inflation are historically the result of a collapse in a government's capacity to cover its current expenses through taxation or borrowing combined with a breach in the bulkhead between fiscal and monetary policy. In its crudest and most obvious form, this involves the use of the printing press to pay for current government expenditure—the link between wheelbarrows full of fresh cash and accelerating inflation is not difficult to understand by that point. Essentially the same thing can go on when government debt levels become so high that the interest on the debt plus other kinds of government expenditure come to exceed the tax system's capacity to generate real tax revenue and the finance ministry's capacity to borrow.[33] In such a situation, pressure grows for the central bank to "monetize" the new debt (i.e., create new money through the act of buying the government bonds that no one else wants to buy). Independent central banks do not have to do this, but even proudly independent central banks are themselves only the creation of a political system that under sufficiently extreme circumstances could rescind that independence. Thus, the idea behind the Growth and Stabilization Pact criteria—government deficits in a year are not to exceed the value of 3 percent of the value of gross domestic product, and the national debt shall not exceed 60 percent of the value of the gross domestic product—is to provide a credible bulkhead against such future fiscal pressure that might ever threaten the independence of the European Central Bank.[34] One is hardly surprised that people who fear the scourge of high inflation more than the misery of high unemployment would want to set such thresholds "on the safe side" rather than risk being sorry at the loss of monetary policy independence of the ECB.

The practical problem in the use and implementation of the deficit and debt criterion is that the legal and administrative mind seeks to impose thresholds where the economist sees a relatively smooth continuum. Civilization as we know it will not end should the euro area have average deficits greater than 3 percent of GDP and/or average national debts greater than 60 percent of GDP for an extended period. The irony of course is that it was Germany that had insisted upon such membership criteria for joining the euro and as a condition of membership in the euro area. Thus, there is a certain justice in the present situation of Germany sharing the stocks with fellow offender France (see figure 12.10).

The trouble comes when one tries to implement these criteria in the short-run. The deficit criterion in the Growth and Stability Pact is expressed in terms of actual deficits so that an economy falling into a recession will see its deficit naturally begin to increase as tax revenues fall and government transfers for the poor and unemployed can be expected to increase when times get tough. Should the economy cross below the deficit line as have France and Germany in figure 12.10, the terms of the Growth and Stability Pact demand that fiscal belts be tied tighter which is a *pro-cyclical* fiscal policy rule.[35] Thus, a strict literal interpretation of the Growth and Stability Pact demands that the fiscal authorities of member countries of the euro area kick their economies when they are down. While this may sound too foolish to be true, it is too true.

Fortunately in this case it just might turn out that the worst implications of the stability pact are offset by a countervailing tendency for bad laws to become as laxly enforced. The fact that Germany and France together have been walking on the wild side of the deficit criterion for several consecutive years has made it likely that a somewhat looser interpretation of the Stability and Growth Pact has been established as a precedent (i.e., that countries will have considerably more time to get their fiscal affairs in order consistent with the intent of the pact rather than being

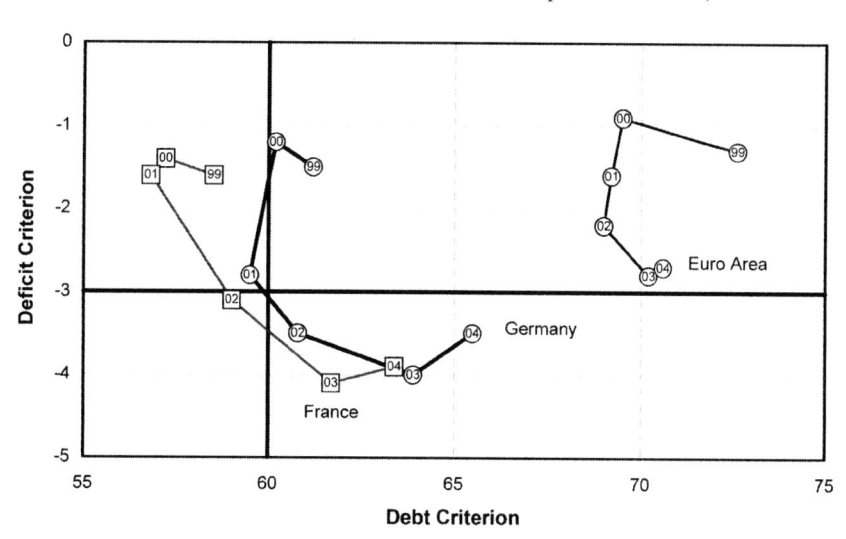

FIGURE 12.10 Fiscal Indicators of the Growth and Stability Pact: Germany, France, and the Euro Area, 1999–2004 (percent of GDP)

Source: Herbstgutachten der wirtschaftswissenschaftlichen Forschungsinstitute, published in *DIW Wochenbericht* 43/2003, table 2.1, http://www.diw.de/deutsch/publikationen/wochenberichte/docs/03-43.pdf. Arbeitskreis Konjunktur, Grundlinien der Wirtschaftsentwicklung 2003/2004. *DIW Wochenbericht* 1–2/2003, table 2.3, http://www.diw.de/deutsch/publikationen/wochenberichte/docs/03-01.pdf.

forced to step hard on the fiscal brakes just to achieve one of the criteria within a few years). Gerhard Schröder has shown less than an overwhelming commitment to the timely satisfaction of the stability pact criteria, which has given critics inside his coalition as well as in the opposition an apparent fiscal failure to harp on. Here Schröder's pragmatism works out to Germany's benefit in avoiding an unnecessary tightening of an already tight fiscal straitjacket.

Germany's "transgressions" against these criteria have been met with surprising understanding by the European Commission that believes them to be in large part merely a manifestation of the economic aftershocks from unification rather than evidence of a member state about to undermine confidence in the euro. Nonetheless, the letter of the Stability and Growth Pact being what it is, these concessions represent little more than a stay of execution for German public budgets.

Hopeless Cause or Cause to Hope?

Gerhard Schröder's second term has surprised many both inside and outside of his party with its active economic reform agenda. Given the length of time it has taken Germany to get itself into a hole of high unemployment, low growth, and unsustainable systems of social insurance, it will take a lucky series of reform chancellors to get the economy back running with the global leaders again. Theoretically, it only takes one chancellor to mark the change in course and this could be Gerhard Schröder's opportunity to be remembered as more than the spoiler of the Kohl era. At the danger of oversimplification but in the interest of brevity, all possibilities about the near future of economic reform can be consigned to one of two scenarios. To end on the happier note, we begin with the pessimistic scenario first.

Scenario I: Too Slow, Too Little, Too Late

One only need be reminded about the never ending drama of getting German shopping hours to correspond to the life rhythms of modern German households to realize just how long institutions such as unions, churches and associations of mom-and-pop stores can put up fanatic resistance to even the most obvious and simple reform.[36] Gerhard Schröder has had to overcome parliamentary barricades erected by the ideological street fighters of his own party at every fork in the reform road. With his parliamentary majority threatened more than once in 2003, Schröder has felt himself compelled to repeatedly play the threat-of-stepping-down card, which tends to lose credibility with use.

The critical concession wrung out of the Hartz IV proposals by Schröder's intraparty opposition was the establishment of de facto minimum wages for the Unemployment Assistance II recipients placed into local jobs by the new Federal Labor Service. The qualification "at prevailing local wages" was added to the characterization of jobs that the unemployed must be willing to accept under penalty of benefit loss for placement refusal. The purpose of this qualification is to shield the wages of those employed from downward pressure due to wage competition from the unemployed. Unfortunately it is precisely wage flexibility for those hard-to-place cases that is required to get the long-term unemployed back into jobs.

Counter to a recommendation of the Rürup Commission, one that was fully supported by Minister for Health and Social Affairs Ulla Schmidt, Gerhard Schröder tabled the gradual future increases in the notional pensionable age from 65 to 67. While such a decision can and most certainly will be reversed in time (the demographic problem is not about to leave us), it is a bad portent when such a modest reform proposal suffers the fate of an unlucky trial balloon.

Once one begins to contemplate the inherent technical difficulties in any major health-care reform—difficulties that are further compounded by the competing interests of health care providers, the institutions that administer public and private health insurance, and the pharmaceutical industry it is easy to see how the Rürup Commission was unable to come up with a clear majority recommendation. Reforms to date do nothing more than shift entire blocks of health benefits out of the public health insurance system (e.g., crowns, bridges and dentures) and add minor co-payments (the 10 euros quarterly office visit fee) cut costs or enhance revenues of the system without addressing the underlying problems that will continue to drive contribution rates up over the coming decades.

Finally the same facts of demography that endanger the workings of the unfunded systems of social insurance are working against reform. As the relative weight of the population continues to those in or nearing the retirement phase of the life cycle, the natural constituency for defending existing pension, health, and long-term care entitlements at the expense of long-term sustainability is growing. Elected politicians tend to see reform windows opening sporadically whenever there happens to be a year between major national or regional elections. However, it could be the case that further delay might just result in the relevant window of reform freezing shut for a generation.

Scenario II: Reform Snowball and a Little Dumb Luck

In this scenario one can imagine that significant social policy thresholds have been crossed during 2003 that will make future reform easier. One such threshold was the decision to suspend pension increases in 2004 in order to maintain pension contribution rates. In the pay-as-you-go system, the decision has traditionally gone in the direction of adjusting contribution rates upwards to pay for mandated increases in retirement benefits. Now the political precedent has been established that the balance between inflows and outflows into the public pension system can take place through adjustments on the benefits side as well. Another threshold is seen in the decision to shorten the duration of normal unemployment benefits and to reduce the subsequent means-tested unemployment assistance benefits to the level of public assistance. This constitutes a major toughening of incentives for unemployed to accept job placements.

Quite independent of Schröder's reform agenda was the threshold crossed in the summer of 2003 represented by the failure of the IG Metall strike in East Germany to force the introduction of a 35-hour workweek in the new states. Add to this the continuous loss of union membership, the retreat of the unions in the face of major legislative defeats could even become a rout down the line with their once considerable capacity to block labor market and social reform legislation reduced to just one among many organized interests in political life.

The missing ingredient for the optimistic scenario of an acceleration of economic growth that would draw down the stock of unemployed which in turn would help to generate an increased capacity to bear the coming demographic burdens is...good fortune. A booming world economy that increases its demand for goods and services "Made in Germany" matters now as much as ever.[37] If this were to occur together with an unexpected surge in productivity analogous to that which the American economy experienced during the 1990s, then one could even imagine investment in Germany becoming a money making proposition again. Furthermore this would work to improve the fiscal indicators of the Growth and Stability Pact that could forestall needed contractionary fiscal policies to bring Germany back into compliance.

The optimistic scenario seems farfetched following an entire generation of subpar economic performance. But the fundamental weakness of the pessimistic scenario is that it sells the young generation short. There is a widespread awareness among young Germans of the nature and the extent of existing generational imbalances and of the poor performance of the economy. The success of the Schröder reform agenda will depend upon the articulation of a vision that there is more to his reforms than the mere slash-and-burn of social protection and entitlements. Gerhard Schröder will have more than enough elections between now and the Bundestag elections of 2006 to work on the articulation of his vision.

Notes

Research for this chapter was conducted during the author's visiting professorship at the Graduate School of Public Administration (GSPA) of Seoul National University, Korea during the academic year 2002/2003. An early version of the chapter was presented in a faculty seminar at the GSPA. I most gratefully acknowledge the outstanding conditions for teaching and research provided to me at SNU, in particular the time and efforts of Dean Yeon-Cheon Oh and his colleagues to integrate me into their community of scholars.

1. English language materials concerning the Program for International Student Assessment can be found at the Max-Planck-Institut für Informatik in Berlin, http://www.mpib-berlin.mpg.de/pisa/english.html.
2. Hans-Werner Sinn, "Die rote Laterne—Die Gründe für Deutschlands Wachstumsschwäche und die notwendigen Reformen," *ifo Schnelldienst* 55, no. 23 (2002): 3–32. Cf. The first chapter, "Schlusslicht Deutschland," in Professor Sinn's recently published book *Ist Deutschland noch zu retten?* (Munich: Econ Verlag, 2003).
3. See the forecasts published in the annual economic report of the Arbeitsgemeinschaft deutscher wirtschaftswissenschaftlicher Forschungsinstitute, "Die Lage der Weltwirtschaft und der deutschen Wirtschaft im Herbst 2003" in DIW, *Wochenbericht* 43 (23 October 2003).
4. An analogy with the "marriage market" can help illustrate the point. Can we explain the observed variance among people in the length of time spent in finding their mates? Dating is part of the search process for a match made in heaven. How long this search process goes on will depend upon supply considerations (how high are someone's standards?) and demand considerations (what is the demand for someone with such characteristics?).
5. Only three countries have been chosen to keep this diagram uncluttered. It is not difficult to see the same pattern with other countries.

6. There is another way to read table 12.1. It provides us with an international comparison of the temptation to avoid taxes and social insurance contributions by not reporting income for additional work. With two-thirds of the bill for labor services to split between a service provider and a customer in Germany, it is not too difficult to imagine a cash agreement on terms acceptable to both parties. The Schröder government will introduce stronger criminal sanctions for tax and social contribution evasion to go into effect in 2004 (including maximum prison sentences of 5–10 years). Poorly designed tax systems and draconian enforcement mechanisms undermine the legitimacy of any government's attempt to collect revenues for the public purpose.
7. One instinctively objects that workers are taxed more in such countries than in the United States, but they get more public service and greater social security. The point here is that from the perspective of the individual provider of labor services, the level of public provision of service and social security is perceived as given and more-or-less independent of the taxes and contributions assessed on additional income of that individual. The choice for the house painter in Germany is not "Do you want to work in Germany or the U.S.?" The choice is whether to work less, work more and pay to Caesar what is Caesar's, or work more without telling Caesar. Whatever the house painter chooses, he/she does not believe it will make much of a difference for the level of the family's health coverage, the ultimate pension entitlement, or even the quality of city services.
8. The reader is warned that it is something of a stretch to claim that a rough balance in the aggregate numbers of vacant jobs and unemployed people is a particularly meaningful way of operationalizing the notion of full employment.
9. The Arbeitnehmerkammer Bremen provides an excellent collection of materials (in German) on all aspects of German labor and social policy at their Web site: http://www.arbeitnehmerkammer.de/sozialpolitik/index.html.Its archives include complete versions of both the Hartz and Rürup Commission reports and vast quantities of background materials and documents regarding the nuts-and-bolts of the Agenda 2010 proposals discussed in this chapter. Most of the commentary comes from union sources with a definite leftist slant, so that the Web site also provides a convenient opportunity to monitor developments on Gerhard Schröder's "left-ern front."
10. For example, the threshold for the laws on employment protection were tightened to apply to businesses with more than five employees instead of more than ten employees; employees' sick pay was increased back from 80 percent to 100 percent of regular pay.
11. This is a serious charge. An illustration from the Commission's final report: "The new service quality finds its expression in the architecture and the interior design of the JobCenter. These give the 'Employment Office' a new face. The image of a corridor lined with the unemployed standing before closed doors and waiting for their 'case' to be processed will be replaced by one of an open architectural space with diverse offerings of information, events and things to do (e.g., Job-Ticker, Info-Terminals, occupational information centers, Internet-Bar, Café/Bistro, space for exhibitions)." (p. 75). Just as wonderful bicycle paths constructed in the new states have not led to blossoming landscapes in the East, so too it is unlikely that a cappuccino to die for at a JobCenter Café will do anything more than increase the quality of unemployed life.
12. As if to prove that high employment is an Anglo-American creation, but almost certainly only the reflection of the dominance of American management consultant gurus in the business, everything in the Hartz Commission recommendations appears to have been rechristened with nice English names. The *Arbeitsamt* becomes the JobCenter (pronounced "tschop-tsentah," so this does not sound nearly as foreign to German ears as one might think), the BridgeSystem for the older unemployed replaces an *Überbrückung* (a saving of two umlauts!), PersonalServiceAgenturen, JobFloater, etc.
13. One example described in a recent radio broadcast was of an unemployed woman in Brandenburg who with her husband formed an *Ich-AG* that provided mobile poodle-clipping service, traveling from village to village. Loans were arranged that allowed her and her husband to purchase a van and the necessary equipment.

14. When Minister for Economics and Labor Wolfgang Clement recently suggested that it is entirely suitable for an unemployed professor to sell sausages on the street, he was greeted with a howl of indignation at the implication that basically all work was suitable for all people who were without work. In Germany, it constitutes something of a revolution when the burden of proof of the suitability or unsuitability of a job is shifted from the employment office to an unemployed person offered a job. Happy is the land that cannot empathize with the notion of *Zumutbarkeit* in this context.
15. This political horse trade between coalition partners was reported in *Die Welt*, 28 March 2003.
16. Only one month earlier in a major reshuffling of ministerial portfolios, the former Ministry for Labor and Social Affairs had been split between the former Ministries of Economics and Health. Wolfgang Clement, former premier of North Rhine-Westphalia, joined the Schröder government as a superminister in charge of economic affairs and employment. Ulla Schmidt's ministerial domain expanded from health to include all the major systems of social insurance with the exception of unemployment insurance.
17. One sees that the Rürup Commission was an awkward fit for the Agenda 2010 timetable from the beginning. Serious reform legislation needed to be in the parliamentary pipeline by midsummer 2003 to escape being held up later due to tactical considerations related to the timing of elections in 2004. The deadline for recommendations from the commission was moved forward to June, then March, then back to the end of April so they could be fed into preparations for the SPD party conference in Berlin on 1 June. The actual final report was turned at the end of August.
18. Chairman Rürup himself had been sensitized by public criticism from the interim SPD fraction leader in the Bundestag, Ludwig Stiegler: "I am fed up that we have to put on a brave face for the membership and the voters each time the Professors start to chatter." Stiegler went on to criticize what he considered premature utterances made by Rürup on pension reform before his commission was even constituted. *Die Welt*, 5 December 2002.
19. With the following difference: the 2030 "standard pensioner" will have worked 1.7 years longer before retirement (and through the blessing of late birth, expects to have as many years in retirement as someone retiring younger in 2003). The pension will be almost 50 percent higher in real terms than it is today as well.
20. Think of a university that grants financial aid to students. One way to provide aid is to grant scholarships based on need and the other is to charge needy students less for room and board and offer them lower prices for books. The former system is administratively simpler, easier to target to the particular circumstances of the individual students and essentially leaves it to the students themselves to decide on which combinations of dorm rooms, meal plans and books give the most value for the money. The point is that it is quite possible to correct a bad income distribution without making everything depend upon on a differential treatment of those with high and low incomes.
21. An English version of the SPD party conference resolution "Courage to reform" can be downloaded from the English language pages at the official SPD Web site: http://www.spd.de.
22. To protect existing unemployment benefit entitlements, these new duration limits will only become completely effective 32 months once the new rules go into effect.
23. For example, Wissenschaftliche Beirat beim Bundesministerium für Wirtschaft und Technologie, *Reform des Sozialstaats für mehr Beschäftigung im Bereich gering qualifizierter Arbeit*, 23 July 2002.
24. "Employment protection" is partially misleading since it glosses over the additional labor costs introduced through the resulting greater inflexibility in changing a business's workforce, which tends to make new employment less likely should business improvements otherwise warrant an expansion in capacity.
25. Details can be found in the guidelines for the program: SPALAR (Sonderprogramm-Arbeit für Langzeitarbeitslose-Richtlinie), http://www.arbeitsamt.de/hst/services/afl/afl03.pdf.

26. Interview in *Leipziger Volkszeitung*, 9 November 2003.
27. Critics claim that an increase in the effective retirement age is not expected to have much of an impact because people who choose early retirement under present rules are accepting reduced pensions so that the value of lifetime benefits for early retirees do not really change significantly and are only spread over a longer period of life.
28. Electricians and opticians are still subject to the mandatory certification process, for instance.
29. For the economic reconstruction of post-Wall East Germany however, European monetary union turns out to have been one of a long list of bad policy choices. This is argued in Irwin Collier, "The Twin Curse of the Goddess Europa and the Economic Reconstruction of Eastern Germany," *German Studies Review* (October 1997): 399–428.
30. Cf. Charles Wyplosz, "The Stability and Growth Pact: Time to Rethink." Briefing Notes to the Committee for Economic and Monetary Affairs of the European Parliament (December 2002), http://www.europarl.eu.int/comparl/econ/pdf/emu/speeches/20021203/20021203_wyplosz.pdf.
31. Sinn, *Ist Deutschland noch zu retten?* p. 99.
32. There is another important difference between the two institutions. In the world of central banking reputation is a critical aspect that affects the impact of monetary policies. The European Central Bank, while being a direct descendent of the German Bundesbank (or at least bearing a strongest family resemblance), is still a fledgling institution in the history of monetary affairs. Its relatively small steps are due in at least some part to an understandable caution regarding its own future long-term reputation. It deathly fears establishing a reputation of being too easy in ratifying inflationary impulses.
33. Rational investors recognize the unsustainability of lending money to someone to pathe2interest on what they have borrowed from someone else and demand increasingly larger interest rates to compensate them for the risk of default. The rise in interest rates makes the next round of borrowing even more difficult. Every Ponzi chain letter-type scheme runs out of suckers.
34. The 3 percent and 60 percent figures were not pulled out of the air and are usually defended using the following argument. Governments are observed on average in the European Union area to spend roughly 3 percent of GDP on public investment, so that the 3 percent deficits are not a danger for stability because the benefits of the public investment will be spread into the future, as will be payments for that investment. Next assume that nominal GDP will grow 5 percent a year in the future (part of the growth is real and part is inflation but that is not important). Suppose that GDP this year is 100, national debt is 60 and the deficit is 3. Next year GDP will be 105 and debt will grow to 63 which is 60 percent of 105. Hence, the 60 percent debt criterion is consistent with a 3 percent criterion for deficits and a growth rate of nominal GDP of 5 percent.
35. The same fundamental criticism is made of rigid balanced-budget amendments by macroeconomists which amount to constraining fiscal authorities to conduct a destabilizing fiscal policy.
36. "We Germans do not believe in big bangs." Quotation attributed to an unnamed close adviser to Gerhard Schröder. *Economist*, 5 December 2002.
37. The extraordinary third quarter 2003 surge in the U.S. economy can be offered as evidence that expansionary monetary and fiscal policies do indeed make a difference and that Germany probably owes the chairman of the U.S. Federal Reserve Board, Alan Greenspan, a *Bundesverdienstkreuz*.

APPENDIX

Table A.1 Bundestag Elections since 1949—Party Percentage of the Second Vote

Year	Percent Voting	CDU/ CSU	SPD	FDP	Greens- All. 90/Gr.[1]	PDS	Other Parties[2]
1949[3]	78.5	31.0	29.2	11.9	–	–	27.8
1953	86.0	45.2	28.8	9.5	–	–	16.5
1957	87.8	50.2	31.8	7.7	–	–	10.3
1961	87.7	45.3	36.2	12.8	–	–	5.7
1965	86.8	47.6	39.3	9.5	–	–	3.6
1969	86.7	46.1	42.7	5.8	–	–	5.5
1972	91.1	44.9	45.8	8.4	–	–	0.9
1976	90.7	48.6	42.6	7.9	–	–	0.9
1980	88.6	44.5	42.9	10.6	1.5	–	0.5
1983	89.1	48.8	38.2	7.0	5.6	–	0.5
1987	84.3	44.3	37.0	9.1	8.3	–	1.4
1990	77.8	43.8	33.5	11.0	3.8[4]	2.4[5]	5.4
1994	79.0	41.4	36.4	6.9	7.3	4.4[6]	3.6
1998	82.2	35.1	40.9	6.2	6.7	5.1	5.9
2002	79.1	38.5	38.5	7.4	8.6	4.0[7]	3.0

The data in this and the following tables come from the election reports published by the Federal and State Statistical Offices in Germany as well as the reports of the Forschungsgruppe Wahlen e.V.

[1] In 1990, the Greens in the West and the Alliance 90/Greens in the East had not yet united. The Greens won 4.8 percent in the West, amounting to 3.8 percent in the enlarged Federal Republic, as listed here. The separate Alliance 90/Greens is here included under "other parties" for 1990 only: It won 6.2 percent in the East, which amounted to 1.2 percent in the entire Federal Republic. Under the special electoral arrangement for 1990, which divided the Federal Republic into two electoral areas (East and West), the eastern Alliance 90/Greens won parliamentary representation by passing the 5 percent minimum, but the western Greens did not. By 1994, a merger had created the all-German party that adopted the name Alliance 90/Greens.

[2] In 1949, including BP (Bavarian Party) 4.2 percent, Center Party 3.1 percent, DP (German Party) 4.0 percent, KPD (Communists) 5.7 percent, and independents 4.8 percent.

In 1953, including BP 1.7 percent, DP 3.3 percent, GB/BHE (a new refugee party) 5.9 percent, and KPD 2.2 percent.

In 1957, including DP 3.4 percent and GB/BHE 4.6 percent.

In 1961, including GDP (a merger of DP and BHE) 2.8 percent, and DFU (German Peace Union) 1.9 percent.

In 1965, including DFU 1.3 percent, and far right-wing NPD (National Democratic Party) 2.0 percent.

In 1969, including NPD 4.3 percent.

In 1990, including Alliance 90/Greens 1.2 percent (based on 6.2 percent in the East), and the far right-wing Republikaner 2.1 percent.

In 1994, including the Republikaner 1.9 percent.

In 1998, including DVU (German People's Union) 1.2 percent, and the Republikaner 1.8 percent.

In 2002, including the Republikaner 0.6 percent, NPD 0.4 percent, and the populist Schill party 0.8 percent.

[3] In 1949, a one-vote ballot only.

[4] Based on 4.8 percent for the Greens in the electoral region of the West. See footnote 1.

[5] In 1990, the PDS won parliamentary representation by netting 11.1 percent of the vote in the electoral area of the East. In the West, the PDS received only 0.3 percent, producing a total of 2.4 percent in the entire Federal Republic.

[6] In 1994, the PDS won parliamentary representation by scoring plurality victories in four single-member districts on the first ballot (all in eastern Berlin). That was one more first ballot victory than necessary to set aside the 5 percent minimum requirement on the second ballot for gaining proportional representation in the Bundestag. As a result, the PDS ended up with a total of 30 Bundestag seats, based proportionately on its second ballot result of 4.4 percent. The PDS won only 1.0 percent of the second vote in the West, but 19.8 percent in the East.

[7] In 2002, the PDS failed to meet the 5 percent minimum for proportional representation on the second ballot. It also failed to meet the alternative requirement of winning 3 or more seats on the first ballot. As a result, it was excluded from proportional representation in the Bundestag for the first time since Germany's reunification. It won 2 single-member district seats in eastern Berlin and therefore still has 2 representatives in the Bundestag. Had it won 3 seats (i.e., one seat more) on the first ballot, it would have been given proportional representation based on its 4.0 percent of the second ballot vote—or about 24 seats in the Bundestag (including the ones it had won on the first ballot).

Table A.2 Distribution of Bundestag Seats since 1949

Year	Percent Voting	CDU/CSU	SPD	FDP	Greens-All. 90/Gr.[1]	PDS	Other Parties[2]
1949	402	139	131	52	–	–	80
1953	487	243	151	48	–	–	45
1957	497	270	169	41	–	–	17
1961	499	242	190	67	–	–	–
1965	496	245	202	49	–	–	–
1969	496	242	224	30	–	–	–
1972	496	225	230	41	–	–	–
1976	496	243	214	39	–	–	–
1980	497	226	218	53	–	–	–
1983	498	244	193	34	27	–	–
1987	497	223	186	46	42	–	–
1990	662	319	239	79	8[3]	17[4]	–
1994	672[5]	294	252	47	49	30[6]	–
1998	669[7]	245	298	43	47	36	–
2002	603[8]	248	251	47	55	2[9]	–

[1] In 1990, under the special one-time arrangement that divided the Federal Republic into two electoral areas (East and West), the Alliance 90/Greens won parliamentary representation by passing the 5 percent minimum in the East. The western Greens fell below 5 percent that year. By 1994, the two parties had merged and taken over the name Alliance 90/Greens.

[2] In 1949, BP (the Bavarian Party) 17, the Center Party 10, DP (the German Party) 17, DRP (the German Reich Party) 5, KPD (the Communist Party) 15, SSW (a Danish minority party) 1, WAV (the Economic Reconstruction Union) 12, and independents 3.

In 1953, GB/BHE (a refugee party) 27, DP 15, Center 3.

In 1957, DP 17.

[3] In 1990, the eastern Alliance 90/Greens only. The western Greens failed to win representation in that year.

[4] In 1990, the PDS won parliamentary representation by netting 11.1 percent of the vote in the electoral area of the East. It received only 0.3 percent in the West, resulting in a total of 2.4 percent of the vote in the entire Federal Republic.

[5] In 1994, the CDU/CSU won 12 and the SPD won 4 "additional seats" (*Überhangsmandate*), an unprecedented high number. As a result, the CDU/CSU-FDP government coalition's majority margin was raised from 2 to 10 seats in a Bundestag of 672 rather than 656 seats.

[6] In 1994, the PDS won 30 Bundestag seats, based on its 4.4 percent of the second ballot vote. The 5 percent minimum was set aside, because the PDS had met an alternative requirement for proportional seating by winning three or more single-member districts on the first ballot: It had won four districts, all in eastern Berlin. The regional concentration of the PDS was reflected in the contrast between its eastern result of 19.8 percent of the second ballot vote and its western result of only 0.9 percent.

[7] In 1998, the CDU won no "additional seats," but the SPD won 13. That raised the Red-Green coalition's majority margin from 8 to 21 seats in a Bundestag of 669 rather than 656 seats.

[8] In 2002, the number of Bundestag seats was reduced to 598 (from 656). However, the SPD won four "additional seats" (one in Hamburg, two in Saxony-Anhalt, and one in Thuringia),

and the CDU won one "additional seat" (in Saxony). That raised the total number of Bundestag seats to 603, and increased the Red-Green coalition's majority margin from 6 seats (302 to 296) to 9 seats (306 to 297). In this line-up, the 2 PDS deputies have been included with the minority.

[9] In 2002, the PDS failed to pass the 5 percent threshold on the second ballot. It won only 2 single-member districts on the first ballot, excluding it from the proportional distribution of seats based on the second ballot vote.

Table A.3 East-West Differences in the Bundestag Elections, 1990–2002: Voter Turnout and Party Percentage of the Second Vote

Year	Percent Voting	CDU/CSU	SPD	FDP	Greens-All. 90/Gr.	PDS	Other Parties
1990							
Total	77.8	43.8	33.5	11.0	3.8[1]	2.4	5.4[2]
West	78.6	44.3	35.7	10.6	4.8	0.3	4.4
East	74.5	41.8	24.3	12.9	6.2	11.1	3.8
1994							
Total	79.0	41.4	36.4	6.9	7.3	4.4	3.6[3]
West	80.5	42.1	37.5	7.7	7.9	1.0	3.9
East	72.6	38.5	31.5	3.5	4.3	19.8	2.4
1998							
Total	82.2	35.1	40.9	6.2	6.7	5.1	5.9[4]
West	82.8	37.0	42.3	7.0	7.3	1.2	5.2
East	80.0	27.3	35.1	3.3	4.1	21.6	8.6
2002							
Total	79.1	38.5	38.5	7.4	8.6	4.0	3.0[5]
West	80.6	40.8	38.3	7.6	9.4	1.1	2.8
East	72.8	28.3	39.7	6.4	4.7	16.9	3.9

[1] In 1990, the Greens in the West and the Alliance 90/Greens in the East had not yet united, and it is important to keep their results separate for that year. The Greens won only 4.8 percent in the West, amounting to 3.8 percent in the enlarged Federal Republic, as listed here. The separate Alliance 90/Greens won 6.2 percent in the East, as also listed in this column. The eastern party's result translated into 1.2 percent in all-German terms, and this total has been included here under the column "other parties" in order to keep it separate from the western Greens' all-German total of 3.8 percent. Under the special electoral provision for 1990, which for this election only divided the Federal Republic into two electoral areas (East and West), the eastern Alliance 90/Greens were able to win a marginal parliamentary representation of 8 seats by passing the 5 percent minimum within their region. Having failed to meet the 5 percent minimum in *their* own region, the western Greens were excluded from the Bundestag during the next four years. Well in advance of the 1994 election, a merger had created the all-German party, which took over the name Alliance 90/Greens. If such a united party had existed in 1990, it would presumably have attracted a total of 6 percent of the popular vote within the enlarged Federal Republic and won a corresponding number of approximately 40 seats.

[2] In 1990, including Alliance 90/Greens 1.2 percent (based on 6.2 percent in the East), and the Republikaner 2.1 percent.

[3] In 1994, including the Republikaner 1.9 percent.

[4] In 1998, including DVU (German People's Union) 1.2 percent, and the Republikaner 1.8 percent.

[5] In 2002, including the Republikaner 0.6 percent, the NPD 0.4 percent, and the Schill Party 0.8 percent.

Table A.4 The Bundestag Election of 2002 in the Western and Eastern Länder: Percentage of the Second Vote by Party (1998 results in brackets)

Land	Percent Voting	CDU/CSU	SPD	FDP	Greens-All. 90/Gr.	PDS	REP[1]	Other Parties
Baden-Württemberg	81.1 (83.1)	42.8 (37.8)	33.5 (35.6)	7.8 (8.8)	11.4 (9.2)	0.9 (1.0)	1.1 (4.0)	2.6 (3.5)
Bavaria	81.5 (79.2)	58.6 (47.7)	26.1 (34.4)	4.5 (5.1)	7.6 (5.9)	0.7 (0.7)	0.7 (2.6)	1.7 (3.6)
Berlin (West only)[2]	79.4 (81.7)	32.5 (29.5)	34.9 (39.6)	8.1 (6.7)	16.6 (13.5)	3.3 (2.7)	0.7 (2.2)	3.9 (5.8)
Bremen	78.8 (82.1)	24.6 (25.5)	48.6 (50.2)	6.7 (5.9)	15.0 (11.2)	2.2 (2.4)	0.2 (0.7)	2.7 (4.0)
Hamburg	79.6 (81.1)	28.1 (30.0)	42.0 (45.7)	6.8 (6.5)	16.2 (10.8)	2.1 (2.3)	0.1 (0.6)	4.7 (4.0)
Hesse	80.1 (84.2)	37.1 (34.7)	39.7 (41.6)	8.2 (7.9)	10.7 (8.2)	1.3 (1.5)	0.8 (2.3)	2.2 (3.8)
Lower Saxony	81.0 (83.9)	34.5 (34.1)	47.8 (49.4)	7.1 (6.4)	7.3 (5.9)	1.0 (1.0)	0.3 (0.9)	1.9 (2.3)
North Rhine-Westphalia	80.3 (83.9)	35.1 (33.8)	43.0 (46.9)	9.3 (7.3)	8.9 (6.9)	1.2 (1.2)	0.4 (1.0)	1.9 (3.0)
Rhineland-Palatinate	80.0 (83.9)	40.2 (39.1)	38.2 (41.3)	9.3 (7.1)	7.9 (6.1)	1.0 (1.0)	1.0 (2.2)	2.3 (3.1)
The Saar	80.0 (84.8)	35.0 (31.8)	46.0 (52.4)	6.4 (4.7)	7.6 (5.5)	1.4 (1.0)	0.4 (1.2)	3.2 (3.3)
Schleswig-Holstein	80.7 (82.4)	36.0 (35.7)	42.9 (45.4)	8.0 (7.6)	9.4 (6.5)	1.3 (1.5)	0.1 (0.4)	2.2 (2.9)
Berlin (West and East)	77.6 (81.1)	25.9 (23.7)	36.6 (37.8)	6.6 (4.9)	14.6 (11.3)	11.4 (13.4)	0.7 (2.4)	4.2 (6.4)
Berlin (East only)[3]	75.1 (80.1)	16.0 (14.7)	39.1 (35.1)	4.5 (2.1)	11.7 (7.9)	23.2 (30.0)	0.7 (2.6)	4.8 (7.6)
Brandenburg	73.7 (78.1)	22.3 (20.8)	46.4 (43.5)	5.8 (2.8)	4.5 (3.6)	17.2 (20.3)	– (1.7)	3.8 (7.2)
Mecklenburg-West Pomer.	70.6 (79.4)	30.3 (29.3)	41.7 (35.3)	5.4 (2.2)	3.5 (2.9)	16.3 (23.6)	0.3 (0.6)	2.4 (6.1)
Saxony	73.7 (81.6)	33.6 (32.7)	33.3 (29.1)	7.3 (3.6)	4.6 (4.4)	16.2 (20.0)	1.0 (1.9)	4.1 (8.3)
Saxony-Anhalt	68.8 (77.1)	29.0 (27.2)	43.2 (38.1)	7.6 (4.1)	3.4 (3.3)	14.4 (20.7)	– (0.6)	2.4 (6.0)
Thuringia	74.8 (82.3)	29.4 (28.9)	39.9 (34.5)	5.9 (3.4)	4.3 (3.9)	17.0 (21.2)	0.8 (1.6)	2.8 (6.5)

[1] The far-right Republikaner Party.
[2] The figures for West and East Berlin come from Forschungsgruppe Wahlen, *Bundestagswahl. Eine Analyse der Wahll vom 22. September 2002*, p. 92.
[3] The figures for West and East Berlin come from Forschungsgruppe Wahlen, *Bundestagswahl. Eine Analyse der Wahll vom 22. September 2002*, p. 92.

Contributors

Clay Clemens teaches Government at the College of William and Mary. His most recent publications include *The Kohl Chancellorship* (1998, co-edited with William E. Paterson), and *NATO and the Quest for Post–Cold War Security* (1997). His articles have appeared in *West European Politics, German Politics, International Affairs* and *Armed Forces and Society*.

Irwin Collier is Professor of Economics in the Faculty of Business and Economics of the Freie Universität Berlin where he has taught courses in labor economics and social policy since 1994. He is a research fellow of the Institute for the Study of Labor (IZA) in Bonn. His research interests include current economic policy in Germany, international comparisons of living standards and income distribution, and the economic reconstruction of the eastern states of Germany. He has most recently returned from an academic year at Seoul National University where he was a visiting professor in the graduate school of public administration.

David P. Conradt is Professor of Political Science at East Carolina University. He is the author and editor of numerous books on German and European politics, including *The German Polity* (2004, 8th ed.); *Germany's New Politics* (1995); and *European Politics* (2003, 3rd ed.). He has also contributed frequently to professional journals. He has been a guest professor at universities in Cologne, Konstanz, and Dresden.

E. Gene Frankland is Professor of Political Science at Ball State University. His primary research and teaching interests are comparative politics and environmental policy. He has written scholarly articles on parliamentary recruitment, political socialization, and the Green parties of Germany, Britain, and Austria. He co-authored with Don Schoonmaker *Between Protest and Power: The Green Party in Germany* (1992). He is the co-editor with John Barry of *The International Encyclopedia of Environmental Politics* (2002).

Mary N. Hampton is Professor of National Security at the Air Command and Staff College, Maxwell Air Force Base, Montgomery, Alabama. Previously she taught at the University of Utah. She has written extensively on NATO, German foreign and security policy, women and German politics, and U.S. foreign and security policy. Most recently she co-authored an article with James Sperling entitled, "German Positive/Negative Identity in NATO and the EU," *Journal of European Integration* (Winter 2002).

Gerald R. Kleinfeld is Executive Director of the German Studies Association and Research Director of the Consortium for Atlantic Studies. He has published extensively on German-American relations, the PDS, and on the German political scene.

William E. Paterson is Director of the Institute for German Studies at the University of Birmingham. Over the past thirty years he has published numerous books and articles on German politics, elections, and European policy. His more recent works include *The Future of the German Economy* (2000); *Germany's European Diplomacy* (2000); and *Developments in German Politics 3* (2003).

David F. Patton is Associate Professor of Government at Connecticut College. His current research focuses on political regionalism in Germany. He is the author of *Cold War Politics in Postwar Germany* (1999). His articles have been published in journals such as *Politics and Society in Germany, West European Politics*, and *East European Politics and Societies*.

Dieter Roth is the Co-founder and Director of Forschungsgruppe Wahlen, Germany's leading public opinion research institute. He has directed extensive studies of public opinion and voting since 1975. His published work includes both theoretical and empirical contributions to voting and election research, and include *Empirische Wahlforschung* (1998) and *Das Superwahljahr* (1994).

James Sloam is a Research Fellow at Birmingham University's Institute for German Studies. He received his doctorate at Birmingham and is currently completing a study of Communist successor parties in Europe. He is the author of the forthcoming book, *Responsibility for Europe: The EU Policy of the German Social Democrats since 1997*.

Christian Søe is Professor of Political Science at California State University at Long Beach. He is editor of the annually revised anthology *Comparative Politics* (twenty-two editions) and writes on German party politics, with special attention to the FDP. He is one of the editors and authors of *The Germans and Their Neighbors* (1993), *Germany's New Politics* (1995), *Between Bonn and Berlin* (1999), and *Power Shift in Germany* (2000).

Stephen F. Szabo is Professor of European Studies at The Paul H. Nitze School of Advanced International Studies, The Johns Hopkins University.

He teaches in the areas of European security, European politics, and leadership, with a specialization on contemporary Germany. His publications include *The Successor Generation: International Perspectives of Postwar Europeans* (1983); *The Bundeswehr and Western Security* (1989); *The Changing Politics of German Security* (1990); *The Diplomacy of German Unification* (1992); and *Parting Ways: 9-11, Iraq and the German-American Relationship* (2004).

Helga A. Welsh is Associate Professor in the Department of Political Science at Wake Forest University. Her publications have focused on German history and politics, the unification of Germany, and democratization processes in Central and Eastern Europe. Articles have appeared in journals such as *Comparative Politics, Europe-Asia Studies, German Politics and Society, German Studies Review,* and *West European Politics*. She is one of the editors of "German History in Documents and Images," a project organized by the German Historical Institute in Washington, D.C. Her current research interests include the reform of higher education in Germany.

Index

Abrassimov, Piotr, 195
Adenauer, Konrad, 58, 191, 197, 200
Afghanistan, German troops in, 30, 45, 66, 87–88, 91, 178, 181, 186, 188
"Agenda 2010," 21–22, 52, 54, 239–243
Allensbach Institute, 35, 49, 51, 74, 77, 165
Alliance 90, 209
Alliance for Jobs, 40–41, 215
Al-Qaeda, 186
American Communist Party, 138
anti-Americanism, 193–194
Armey, Dick, 188
Austrian People's Party (ÖVP), 172

Baden-Württemberg, 7t, 9, 63, 66, 72, 89, 91, 117, 174, 261t
Baker, James, 188
Bartsch, Dietmar, 145
Beamte, 138
Beck, Kurt, 117
Beck, Volker, 100
Beckstein, Günther, 47, 72, 77
Beer, Angelika, 88, 101, 102
Beerfeltz, Hans-Jürgen, 111, 123
Berlin, 8t, 261t
Berliner Zeitung, 150
Berlin Wall, 200
Berlusconi, Silvio, 172, 177, 179, 181
Besancenot, Olivier, 178
Betz, Hans-Georg, 171
Beveridge, William, 231
Bild am Sonntag, 12, 68
Bisky, Lothar, 136, 138, 145, 149
Bittberger, Jürgen, 46
Black-Green coalition, 104
Blair, Tony, 39, 41, 170, 182
Blair-Schröder paper, 39, 56n5, 170

Blocher, Christoph, 172, 176, 179, 181
Bossi, Umberto, 172
Brandenburg, 7t, 261t
Brandt, Willy, 55, 121, 191, 197
British Liberal Democrats, 109
Brüderle, Rainer, 117, 119
Bund der Heimatvertriebenen und Entrechteten (BHE), 151
Bush, George (Bush I), 194–195
Bush, George W. (Bush II)
  on the "Axis of Evil," 186
  election of, 178
  foreign policy approach of, 52, 84, 97, 102, 133, 185–191, 203n15
  on German-American relationship, 185–202
  policy on war in Iraq, 185–201
  unilateralist style of, 186, 191, 193–195
  Western European views of, 188, 189, 193–194
Bütikofer, Reinhard, 91, 101, 102, 103

Carter, Jimmy, 191
Chemical and Biological Weapons Treaty, 186
Cheney, Richard, 147, 188, 189, 202–203n9
Chevénement, Jean-Pierre, 178
Chirac, Jacques, 178, 182
Chrapa, Michael, 142
Christian Democratic Union (CDU/CSU)
  as Black party, 30, 104
  Bundestag seats held by, 258t
  campaign strategies of, 12–13, 25–26, 42–48, 53, 54, 58–82
  characteristics of voters in, 18–19, 19t, 20, 20t
  election results of, 78–81

Note: page references with an *f* or a *t* indicate a figure or table on the designated page.

Christian Democratic Union (*cont.*)
  female voters in, 154, 155, 155f
  finance scandal of, xii, 5–6, 6f, 7t, 8t,
    9–10, 27, 41, 110, 114
  policy on citizenship law, 4, 59
  second ballot voters of, 22, 22f, 256t,
    260t, 261t
  Stoiber as candidate for, 25–26, 49,
    58–82, 174
  "Team 40+" of, 68
Christiansen, Sabine, 70
Christian Social Union (CSU)
  coalition with CDU, 62–65, 67, 68, 72,
    75–76, 77, 80
  See also Christian Democratic Union
    (CDU/CSU)
Christoffers, Ralf, 136
Chrobog, Jürgen, 189
Claus, Roland, 145
Clement, Wolfgang, 52, 54, 86, 103, 116–117
Clinton, William J., 41, 170, 182, 185
Coats, Daniel, 195
Cold War, 17, 198, 200, 201
Communist Party, 137–138
Cox, Robert Henry, 214
Czada, Roland, 215

Dalton, Russell, 161
Danish People's Party (DF), 172
Däubler-Gmelin, Herat, 52–53, 147, 190
Death of a Critic (Walser), 125
Decker, Frank, 173, 174
Deckert, Günter, 174
*Der Kanzler wohnt im Swimmingpool Oder
  wie Politik gemacht wird* (Schröder-
  Köpf, ed.), 159, 168n26
Der Spiegel, 205
Der Tagesspiegel, 83
Diepgen, Eberhard, 64
Die Welt, 44
Die Zeit, 90, 157
Döring, Walter, 117, 119
Dyson, Kenneth, 215

Eagelburger, Lawrence, 188
Ebbinghaus, Bernhard, 215
Economic and Monetary Union (EMU), 43,
  54
Economist, The, 216
economy. *See* German economy and
  employment
education, campaign issue of, 31–32, 69
Eichel, Hans, 4, 39–40, 42–43, 52, 54
89ers, 200

electoral system, ballot splitting in, 22, 22f,
  23, 33–34, 50
employment. *See* German economy and
  employment
Engelen-Kefer, Ursula, 235
Engholm, Björn, 55
environment, campaign issue of, 30, 32, 48,
  84, 92
European Central Bank, 244, 246
European Monetary System, 21
European Security and Defense Policy
  (ESDP), 198
European Union (EU)
  EU-15 in, 170, 173, 222–223, 223f
  German social policies at level of, 38, 39,
    187
  integration of Germany into, 62
  Schröder's foreign policy and, 41
  standards on deficits, 43, 74
  studies on education, 72

families, campaign issue of, 32, 158, 160
Federal Council (Bundesrat), 21
Ferres, Veronica, 159
Financial Times, 199
Fini, Gianfranco, 172
Finn, Peter, 84
Fischer, Andrea, 85, 87
Fischer, Joschka
  as foreign minister, 14, 30, 85, 187, 189
  Green party leaderships and agenda of,
    48, 50, 65, 71, 72, 78, 83, 88–89, 90,
    92–94, 96, 97, 100, 103, 127, 187, 199,
    204n45
  policy appeal and personality as candi-
    date, 33, 35, 182
Flemish Bloc (VB), 172
floods in eastern Germany, xiii, 15, 17, 21,
  28–29, 31, 32, 36, 47–49, 74, 84, 97,
  111, 146–147, 150–151, 153, 187, 221
Forsa, 49
Forschungsgruppe Wahlen (FGW), 83, 84,
  93, 96, 103, 193, 194, 196
Fortuyn, Pim, 125, 172, 178, 181
Forza Italia, 172
Frankfurter Allgemeine Zeitung, 151
Frankfurt (Oder), 43
Free Democrats Party (FDP)
  Bundestag seats held by, 258t
  campaign issues of, 4, 115–116
  campaign strategies of, 29–30, 63, 65, 80,
    179
  characteristics of voters and supporters
    of, 121–122, 124, 130

on citizenship law, 4
congress meetings of, 118–122
election results of, 128–132
membership and electoral history of, 112–122, 132n8
popular vote during inter-election period, 5–6, 6f, 7t, 8t, 9–10
Project 18 campaign strategy of, 13–14, 108–132
Project 8 of, 115
second ballot voters of, 22, 22f, 256t, 260t, 261t
Strategy 18 of, 120–121, 131
as a *Volkspartei*, xii, 109, 121–122, 124, 128, 129, 132, 175
Wiesbaden program of, 113
women voters in, 154, 155f
as Yellow party, 30
Freedom Party of Austria (FPÖ), 171, 172, 176, 177, 181
Freiburg Circle, 117
Frey, Gerhard, 174
Friedman, Michel, 126, 127–128, 176
Front National, 174, 181
Funke, Hajo, 176

Genscher, Hans-Dietrich, 118
Gen-Xers, 200
Gerhardt, Wolfgang, 112, 113, 115, 116, 117, 119
German-Arab Society, 126
German Communist Party (DKP), 138
German Democratic Republic (GDR), 136, 137, 138
German economy and employment
abolition of capital gains tax in, 40, 56n5
analyzing unemployment in, 227, 228f, 229–230, 230t, 231–232, 232f
average growth rate in, 222–223, 223f
Beveridge Curve of, 231–232, 232f
as campaign issue of, 31–33
citizens' insurance in, 238
consolidation of unemployment and public assistance, 240–241
duration of unemployment benefits in, 239–241
effects of monetary and fiscal policies on, 243–245, 245f, 246–247, 247f, 248–249, 249f
employment protection laws in, 241
Hartz Commission in, 233–235, 239
Ich-AG program in, 234
impact of unification on, 232, 232f
managing long-term unemployment in, 241–242

marginal burden of taxes in, 229–230, 230t, 231
pension reform in, 235–237, 237t, 238–239
projected senior and junior population in, 223–224, 224f
Rürup Commission of, 233, 235–237, 237t, 238–239
scandal in Federal Labor Office, 233–235
Schröder's future challenges of, 220–252
social insurance rates in, 224, 225f, 226, 226f
trends of unemployment in, 221–222, 222f, 242
German electoral
effects of reunification on districts, 2–3
"mixed" voting systems of, 2
Überhangmandate in, 2
German Marshall Fund, 192, 196
German People's Union (DVU), 8t, 118, 174
German reform and policymaking
benchmarking and international comparison of, 213–216
efficient systems of, 205–216
electoral rhetoric for, 205
emergence of informal politics in, 212–213
factors affecting process of, 208–209
Federal Constitutional Court in, 211–212
Mediation Committee in, 211
of *Modell Deutschland*, 205–216
political party systems of, 208–213
role of Bundesrat and Bundestag in, 210–211
Germany
Berlin Republic of, 199–202
Central Jewish Council in, 48, 126, 176
"citizenship law" of, 41
effects of unification on, x–xi, 2–3, 232, 232f
floods in eastern parts of, xiii, 15, 17, 21, 28–29, 31, 36, 47, 48, 49, 74, 84, 97, 111, 146–147, 150–151, 153, 187, 221
foreign populations in, xiii, 173, 215
Gen-Xers of, 200
"German Way" foreign policy of, 46, 196
immigration and integration laws of, 215
inter-election period (1998–2002) of, 3–6
limited success of right-wing populism in, 170–182
negative population growth in, 162
personalizing of politics in, 181–182
social welfare system of, 208, 215–216
strategic culture of, 197–198

Gerwien, Tilman, 84
Giuliani, Rudolph, 175
Glistrup, Mogens, 181
globalization, as "casino capitalism," 3
Glos, Michael, 68
Goergen, Fritz, 109, 115, 116, 122, 125, 129, 131
Goppel, Thomas, 68
Gorbachev, Mikhail, 200
Gore, Al, 178, 182
Göring-Eckardt, Katrin, 100
Grass, Günter, 177, 199
Great Depression, 229
Green
    Bundestag seats held by, 258*t*
    campaign strategies of, 14, 30, 94–98, 179
    characteristics of voters in, 18–19, 19*t*, 20, 20*t*, 99–100
    on citizenship law, 4–5, 95
    core values of, 92
    on ecological taxes, 85, 86, 93, 95
    election results of, 83–85, 99–104, 256*t*, 258*t*, 260*t*, 261*t*
    environmental and energy policies of, 30, 32, 48, 84, 92
    Grundsatzprogramm agenda of, 83, 91–92, 104
    membership of, 85–89
    merger with Bündnis 90, 102
    popular vote during inter-election period, 5–6, 6*f*, 7*t*, 8*t*, 9–10
    pre-electoral campaign of, 90–94
    Promis in, 90, 102
    Richtungswahlkampf strategy of, 90, 99
    second ballot voters of, 22, 22*f*, 33–34, 256*t*, 260*t*, 261*t*
    women voters in, 154–155, 155*f*, 156, 157
Growth and Stability Pact, 244, 247, 248, 249*f*, 252
Gulf War, 45
Güllner, Manfred, 49
Gysi, Gregor, role in PDS campaign, xiii, 15, 30, 48, 84, 95, 97, 125, 135, 137–140, 144–145, 150–151, 182

Hagel, Chuck, 188
Hagen, Carl I., 172
Hague, William, 182
Haider, Jörg, 60, 125, 171, 176, 177, 179, 181
Hamm-Brücher, Hildegard, 126
Harald Schmidt Show, 98
Harmel formula, 198
Hartz, Peter, 44, 49, 52, 73, 213, 233–235
Hartz Commission, 52, 54, 79, 233–235, 239, 250

Hassel, Anke, 215
Hauff, Volker, 55
Helms, Ludger, 209
Hermann, Winfried, 96
Herzog, Roman, 210, 212
Hesse, 4, 7*t*, 9, 39, 59, 61, 66, 80, 261*t*
Hitler, Adolf, 52, 116, 147, 190, 195
Hofmann, Gunter, 90, 212
Holter, Helmut, 141
Holzmann, 41
Hombach, Bodo, 39
Hoogvliet, Rudi, 94, 95, 98
Hussein, Saddam, 45, 74, 76, 147, 165

IG Metall, 54, 251
Im Krebsgang (Grass), 199
International Court, 186
International Monetary Fund (IMF), 244
Iraq
    as election issue in Germany, 20, 74, 97–98, 111, 124, 153, 164–166, 181, 187–188, 192–194
    public opinion on German troops in, 17, 32–33, 33*f*
    UN inspectors in, 77, 102
    U.S.-German policies on war in, xiv, 147–148, 185–202
Ischinger, Wolfgang, 189
Israel
    arms shipment to, 93
    policy toward Palestine, 126

Jochimsen, Luc, 148, 150
Joffe, Joseph, 198
Jospin, Lionel, 177, 182

Karsli, Jamal, 126, 127, 176, 183–184n23
Kastrup, Dieter, 188, 189
Katzenstein, Peter, 41
Kelly, Petra, 158
Kennedy, John F., 191
K-Frage, 66–67
Kinkel, Klaus, 112, 116, 117, 119
Kirsch media, 71
Kissinger, Henry, 192
Kjaersgaard, Pia, 172, 181
Klartext (Möllemann), 130, 134n36
Klimmt, Reinhard, 40
Koch, Roland, 9, 59, 60, 61, 64, 65, 67, 79, 80
Kocher, Renate, 35
Kohl, Helmut
    campaign strategies of, 12, 13, 26, 58
    defeat of, 3, 37, 157, 160
    foreign policy of, 197, 200

reform and policy accomplishments of, 53, 206, 207, 212, 214
role in CDU finance scandal, 5, 27, 41, 59–60, 63, 89, 110, 114
Kok, Wim, 177, 178
Kosovo, military intervention in, 14, 41, 45, 74, 86, 88, 165–166, 186, 188
Kubicki, Wolfgang, 115, 119
Kuhn, Fritz, 89, 90, 91, 92, 96, 100, 101, 104
Künast, Renate, 14, 87, 89, 90, 95, 98, 101, 103, 160, 182
Kurth, Undine, 93
Kyoto Treaty, 186

Labour Party (Britain), 39, 170
Lafontaine, Oskar, 3–4, 37, 38–39, 55, 59, 85, 200
Laguiller, Arlette, 178
Lambsdorff, Otto, 48
Lauterbach, Karl, 238
law and order, campaign issue of, 31–32
Leftists, 85, 91, 177–178
Lemke, Steffi, 101
Le Pen, Jean-Marie, 172, 178, 181
List Pim Fortuyn (LPF), 172, 178, 181
Lötzsch, Gesinne, 148, 156
Lower Saxony, 7t, 26ot, 53
Lugar, Richard, 188
Lührmann, Anna, 159–160

Macedonia, 45, 87
Machnig, Matthias, 212
mad cow disease, 14
Magdeburg Model, 141
Mannesmann, 40
Marquardt, Angela, 136
McCann-Erickson, 68
Mecklenburg-West Pomerania, 8t, 11, 61, 141–142, 261t
Merkel, Angela, CDU leadership of, 5, 6, 9–10, 12, 27, 47, 59–67, 70–71, 73, 77–80, 91, 95, 100, 104, 157, 163
Merkl, Peter, 200
Merz, Friedrich, 12, 60, 66, 72, 75, 80
Metzger, Oswald, 91
Meyer, Laurenz, 12, 61, 63, 66, 68
Milbradt, Georg, 242
Modell Deutschland, 196, 207–208, 215, 216
Modrow, Hans, 138
Möllemann, Jürgen
  anti-Semitic controversy by, 125–128, 130, 176, 181
  FDP campaign strategies by, 29–30, 48, 63, 73, 76, 77, 96, 125–128, 174–177, 179–181, 199

role in FDP *Project 18*, 108–111, 115–118, 119–122, 175
death of, 131
Müller, Hildegard, 160
Müller, Kerstin, 91, 100
Müntefering, Franz, 40, 43, 96
Muslim countries, immigrants from, 173, 174

Nader, Ralph, 178
National Alliance, 172
National Democratic Party of Germany (NPD), 174
National Socialists, 175
Nebenkosten, pension of, 3
Neue Mitte, 38, 39, 40, 52, 170
Neugebauer, Gero, 84, 179
New Democracy, 181
New Left, 50
New Politics, 161
Nixon, Richard M., 191
Noelle-Neumann, Elisabeth, 49, 51
North Atlantic Treaty Organization (NATO), 17, 45, 85, 86, 87, 165, 186, 197–198
Northern League, 172
North Korea, 198
North Rhine-Westphalia, 5, 7t, 25, 29, 30, 41, 44, 52, 65, 86, 103, 104, 114, 116, 127, 179, 261t
nuclear power, 4, 87, 89, 95, 101

Ökosteuer, 3
Ollenhauer, Erich, 121
Operation Enduring Freedom, 186
Organisation for Economic Co-operation and Development (OECD), 123, 222
Organization for Security and Co-operation in Europe (OSCE), 45
Özdemir, Cem, 96–97

Party for a Rule of Law Offensive, 174
Party of Democratic Socialism (PDS)
  Bundestag seats held by, 258t
  campaign strategies of, 14–15, 30–31, 135–148
  characteristics of voters in, 7t, 8t, 11, 18–19, 19t, 20, 20t, 46
  considerations for coalition with, 136, 149, 180
  dichotomy of East and West in, 139–148
  as disaster in 2002 election, 148–149, 149t, 150–151
  in eastern Germany, 48, 80
  impact of summer floods on campaign issues of, 146–147, 150–151

Party of Democratic Socialism (*cont.*)
  loss credibility and exclusiveness by, 144, 150, 180
  Magdeburg Model of, 141–142, 143
  membership and ideology of, 136–139, 148–149, 149*t*, 150–151
  old and new cadre in, 136–138, 144–146
  party collapse and failure in 2002, 50, 135–152
  popular vote during inter-election period, 5–6, 6*f*, 7*t*, 8*t*, 9–10
  as protector of the GDR functionaries, 138–139
  "6 Prozent plus X" goals of, 15
  second ballot voters for, 256*t*, 260*t*, 261*t*
Pau, Petra, 138, 148, 156
pensions, campaign issue of, 32, 235–237, 237*t*, 238–239
Pew Global Attitudes Project, 192, 193, 194, 196
Pfleuger, Friedbert, 191
Pieper, Cornelia, 118, 121
policymaking. *See* German reform and policymaking
"policy paralysis," 206–216
Pommereau, Isabelle de, 162
Porsche, 43
Portas, Paulo, 172
"power Frau," 156–158, 167n15–17
Prantl, Heribert, 205
Pries, Knut, 91
Prodi, Romano, 170, 182
Program for International Student Assessment (PISA), 222
Progress Party, 172, 181
Project 18, 13–14, 108–132

Radcke, Antje, 89
Raschke, Joachim, 84
Rau, Johannes, 210
Rauch, Jonathan, 210
Reagan, Ronald, 191, 195, 196, 200
Realos, 85, 86, 89, 91, 96, 100
Red-Green government, 4, 5, 30, 34
  during 1998–2002, 26–28, 28*f*, 29
  coalition of, 37
  election victory of, 48–55, 83–104
Red-Red Berlin government, 15
Red-Red-Green (SPD-PDS-Green), 96
Red-Yellow-Green (SPD-FDP-Green), 96
reform. *See* German reform and policymaking
Reformstau, xiv–xv, 206–216
Reiche, Katherina, 72, 73, 79, 159, 160, 163
Rensmann, Lars, 176

Rentzsch, Wolfgang, 210
Republikaner Party (REP), 5–6, 6*f*, 7*t*, 8*t*, 9–10, 127, 174, 179
Revolutionary Communist League, 178
Rhineland-Palatinate, 8*t*, 63, 66, 87, 117, 261*t*
Rice, Condoleezza, 186, 190, 191, 202n3, 203n10
Riester pension reform, 236–237, 237*t*
right-wing populism
  defined, 171
  growth in Europe of, 171–177
  limited success in German elections of, 180–182
Ringsdorff, Harald, 141, 142
Rosa Luxemburg Foundation, 142
Röstel, Gunda, 89
Roth, Claudia, 84, 89, 91, 96, 101, 102, 103, 163
Roth, Dieter, 84
Ruck-Rede, 212
Rüdig, Wolfgang, 87
Rühe, Volker, 5, 12, 64
Rumsfeld, Donald, 189, 190, 195
Rürup, Bert, 52, 213, 235
Rürup Commission, 52, 54, 233, 235–237, 237*t*, 238–239, 250
Rüttgers, Jürgen, 68

Saar, 7*t*, 39, 86, 261*t*
Sager, Krista, 100
Salomon, Dieter, 94
Saxony, 47, 86, 261*t*
Saxony-Anhalt, 8*t*, 11, 29, 71, 84, 93, 118, 174, 261*t*
Scharping, Rudolf, 17, 43, 73, 96
Schäuble, Wolfgang, xii, 5, 41, 59, 60, 61, 64, 68, 157, 195
Schavan, Annette, 72
Scherf, Henning, 102
Schill, Ronald Barnabas, 65, 70, 117, 174, 175, 177
Schill Party (PRO), 87, 174, 175, 177, 179
Schily, Otto, 47, 65, 69, 72
Schlauch, Rezzo, 90, 91, 95, 97, 100
Schleswig-Holstein, 5, 7*t*, 41, 86, 115, 261*t*
Schlötzer, Christiane, 88
Schmidt, Helmut, 53, 62, 191, 197
Schmidt, Manfred G., 208–209
Schmidt, Ulla, 87, 235, 238, 250
Schmidt, Vivien, 214
Schönhuber, Franz, 174
Schröder, Gerhard
  Agenda 2010 plan of, 21–22, 52, 54, 229, 239–243

campaign issues of, 31–33, 33f
campaign strategies of, 10–11, 187
as chancellor of first Red-Green government, 37–57
electoral response by women voters, 153–155, 155f, 156–166
foreign policy of, 185–191
on German involvement in Iraq, 45–46, 47, 74, 75, 76, 111, 124, 130, 147, 153, 164–166, 181–202
"German Way" of, 46, 196
initiative on dual citizenship by, 4–5, 59
"new center" policy of, 1, 4, 59, 170
opinion on FDP as a partner, 127
peace campaign of, 151
on personal relationships with politicians, 190–191
policy appeal and personality as candidate, 17, 17f, 18, 27, 33–34, 34t, 35, 79, 182
reform and policy challenges of, 206, 207, 210, 212, 213, 220–252
response and relief to flood victims, 21, 28–29, 31, 32, 36, 47, 48, 74, 75, 111, 130, 146–147, 153, 181, 187, 221
trend of unemployment and economy under government of, 9–10, 11, 27–28, 28f, 220–235
on Westerwelle's candidacy, 121
Schröder-Köpf, Doris, 154, 159
Schröder, Richard, 150, 151
Schulz, Werner, 91, 100, 101
Schulze-Fielitz, Helmuth, 212
Scowcroft, Brent, 188
Seehofer, Horst, 9, 64, 68, 72
Seeleib-Kaiser, Martin, 214–215
Selbert, Elisabeth, 156
September 11, 2001, events of, 15, 16, 27, 31, 44, 45, 65, 87, 91, 144, 173, 174, 175, 177, 185–186, 190, 194, 195, 201
Serbia, military intervention in, 14, 86
Serviceplan, 68
Sharon, Ariel, 48, 93, 126, 127–128, 176
Simonis, Heidi, 5
Sinn, Hans-Werner, 222, 244
68ers, 55, 200
Social Democrats Party (SPD)
Bundestag seats held by, 258t
campaign strategies of, 10–11, 25–26, 42–48, 178, 179, 193
characteristics of voters in, 18–19, 19t, 20, 20t
on citizenship law, 4–5, 59
illicit fundraising by, 42

Kampa team of, 3, 11, 49, 51, 68
labor market policy of, 44
popular vote during inter-election period, 5–6, 6f, 7t, 8t, 9–10
as Red party, 30
role in the Red-Green government, 37, 38–42
second ballot voters of, 22, 22f, 33–34, 256t, 260t, 261t
women voters in, 32, 154–155, 155f, 193
Socialist Unity Party (SED), 136–137, 138
Sommers, R., 16
South Korea, 198
Soviet Union, 201
Späth, Lothar, 51, 72, 73
Spreng, Michael, 12–13, 68, 76, 79
Stabilization and Growth Pact, 244, 248
Steinmeier, Frank Walter, 212–213
Stern, 84, 90
Stoiber, Edmund
campaign strategies of, 9, 12–13, 16, 73–77, 179, 180
as CDU/CSU candidate, 25–26, 58–82
"competence team" of, 68–69, 72
as economic problem solver, 27–28, 28f
on German troops in Iraq, 46, 47, 192
on issue of crime, 176–177, 180
as minister-president of Bavaria, 50
opinion on FDP as a partner, 127
policy appeal and personality as candidate, 33–34, 34t, 35, 62, 69, 79, 182, 214
in race as "preferred chancellor," 17, 17f, 18
view on immigration, xiii, 69–70, 180, 215
"Wolfratshausen Breakfast" at home of, 27, 67
on women's issues, 161, 163
Stoiber, Karin, 69, 72, 154, 158, 159
Stöss, Richard, 84, 179
Strategy 18, 109
Strauß, Franz Josef, 10, 12, 13, 62, 67, 70, 157, 167n17
Ströbele, Hans-Christian, 88, 91, 95, 96, 98, 99, 100, 101, 102, 182
Struck, Peter, 195
Süddeutsche Zeitung, 151
Süssmuth, Rita, 48, 213
Swiss People's Party (SVP), 171, 172, 176, 177

taxes, 6, 40, 85, 86, 93, 95
Telekom, 16
Teufel, Erwin, 63, 117
Thatcher, Margaret, 196
Thuringia, 7t, 86, 141, 261t

Torfing, Jacob, 214
"traffic light coalition," 140
Trittin, Jürgen, 85, 91, 92, 97, 101, 103, 182

Überhangmandate, 2
United Nations (UN), 32, 45, 74, 77, 102
UN World Summit on Sustainable Development, 97
U.S. Bureau of Labor Statistics, 227
U.S. Federal Reserve, 246

Vietnam, 201
Vlaams Blok, 171
Vodafone, 40
Vogel, Bernhard, 141
Voigt, Karsten, 189
Voit, Udo, 174
Volkswagen, 44, 73
Volmer, Ludger, 97
von Weizsäcker, Richard, 210, 213
voters
  class and religion of, 18–19, 19t, 20, 20t
  in eastern Germany, 43–44
  volatility during the 2002 campaign, 1–2
  See also specific party

Walser, Martin, 125
weapons of mass destruction (WMD), 189
Werner, Harald, 145
Westerwelle, Guido
  as FDP candidate, 119–122, 123–125, 128–129
  leadership and agenda in FDP, 13, 63, 76, 77, 95, 108–109, 111, 113, 116, 176, 177

on party goals and 2002 election outcome, 130–131
Wilensky, Harold L., 206
women voters
  blocs and trends of, 153–166
  campaign issues regarding, 73, 160–165
  East/West dichotomy in, 156
  on German troops in Iraq, 165–166, 193, 203n25
  as Green supporters, 99
  history of voting behaviors by, 154–155, 155f, 156
  as majority in Germany, 160
  media campaigns for, 154, 158–160
  quota systems for, 162–164
  role of women in eastern Germany, 156
  in SPD party, 32, 154–155, 155f, 193
  supporters of CDU/CSU, 78
  women in German politics, 156–158, 167n16
  on women in the work place, 162–164
Workers Struggle, 178
World Economic Outlook, 244
World Values survey, 196
Wulff, Christian, 67, 68

Young Communists, 137
Young Liberals, 120

Zimmer, Gabrielle, 145, 149, 151
Zum Goldenen Hirschen, 94, 95, 98